POLITICAL

INVERSIONS

POLITICAL
INVERSIONS

Homosexuality, Fascism, &
the Modernist Imaginary

ANDREW HEWITT

Stanford University Press   Stanford, California 1996

Stanford University Press
Stanford, California
© 1996 by the Board of Trustees of the
Leland Stanford Junior University

Printed in the United States of America

CIP data appear at the end of the book

Stanford University Press publications are distributed
exclusively by Stanford University Press within the United
States, Canada, Mexico, and Central America; they are
distributed exclusively by Cambridge University Press
throughout the rest of the world.

For Our Friend,
Tony Grimaglia

Acknowledgments

Parts of this work have appeared in somewhat altered form elsewhere, and I wish to acknowledge those prior publications here. Chapter 5, "Fables of Modernity," appeared fundamentally unchanged as "Wyndham Lewis: Fascism, Modernism, and the Politics of Homosexuality," in *ELH* 60, no. 2 (Summer 1993). The reading of Moravia in Chapter 7, "Murder and Melancholy," has previously formed the basis for reflections on the nature of apocalyptic thought. This earlier version—which incorporates some of the material on Adorno and Lyotard covered here in Chapter 1— can be found as "Coitus Interruptus: Moravia and the Deaths of History," in *Postmodern Apocalypse: Theory and Cultural Practice at the End*, ed. Richard Dellamora (Philadelphia: University of Pennsylvania Press, 1995).

Contents

POLITICAL
INVERSIONS

The Construction of Homo-Fascism

> We are not very far from identifying homosexuality with
> fascism. . . . How can it be that the antifascist press places
> the words "murder and paederasts" alongside each
> other almost as often as the Nazi press does the words
> "Jews and traitors"?
>
> Klaus Mann, "Homosexuality and Fascism"

This is not a history book. That is to say, for all its interest in the question of history, this book will not attempt to detail the (mis-)treatment of homosexuals under Italian Fascism and National Socialism, nor to reconstruct in coherent form the ideological position of the various fascisms with respect to sexual "deviance." Much important and useful work has recently been done on these questions, and I will draw to a great extent on that historical work.[1] This book concerns itself with another fascism, however: an imaginary construct that has emerged in theoretical and literary representations since World War II and is motivated not by a fixed historical phenomenon but rather by an anxiety about the possibility of fixing historical phenomena at all. It is the "unrepresentable" fascism that we find represented over and over and over again. This fascism does not defer to historical distinctions of Italian and German, but tends, if anything, to read the former through the latter. It is the fascism that, according to Susan Sontag, still fascinates today; a store of representational fragments that are constantly recycled in popular culture, where they acquire an erotic charge they never really exerted the first time around. Consequently, where I seek historical precedent—in the chapters on Hans Blüher, Otto Weininger, Benedict Friedlaender, and John Henry Mackay, for example—I seek it not in the spirit of intellectual history, but as a context whose erotic charge might prefigure the sexualization—that is to say, the homosexualization—of fascism in the present.

Political Inversions takes its cue, then, from the observation—both anecdotal and theoretical—of a recurrent conflation and/or association of homosexuality and fascism. Why do history books still invoke homosexuality as a cover for the clearly class-political realpolitik of Hitler's "purging" of the SA (Sturmabteilung)? Why is Helmut Berger staring down at me in full Dietrich-drag from the box of *The Damned* at my local video store? What is Wyndham Lewis doing frequenting Berlin transvestite bars while ostensibly reporting as a journalist on the rise of Hitler in 1930? Why do the communists seek to pin the 1933 Reichstag fire on the Nazis by uncovering a homosexual plot? Why do art historians and critical theorists consistently point to the "homoerotic" forms of Nazi sculpture, when such works seem intent on the effacement of *all* desire? Why was homosexuality felt—in the Cold War era of political persecutions—to be intrinsically and politically subversive, the mark of an un-American, antidemocratic—"pinko"—totalitarian libido? At the level of theory and its academic appropriation, what is the function of "the currently respectable homophobic feminist-theory fantasy" that Eve Sedgwick identifies in *Tendencies,* and that culminates in "the identification (in the work of, for example, Irigaray) as flatly, transhistorically 'homosexual' of the male homosocial bonds that largely structure patriarchal culture" (49)? Why do thinkers like Theodor Adorno—a theorist I grew up with, whose thought helped shape my own—lend critical and intellectual credence to such charges of totalitarianism?[2]

I should stress that the use of the word "homosexual" in this book refers exclusively to homosexual men. I use the term in this problematic fashion both because the term retains something clinical that resists application to specific identities and subject positions, and because it is primarily around figures of masculine homosexuality that what Eve Sedgwick has called "homosexual panic" infuses the political and aesthetic questions I deal with here. But if terminology poses problems of a theoretical and political nature, I must also confront what I can only assume to be a perfectly sincere liberal skepticism I have encountered at a more mundane level. Addressing a conflation of fascism and homosexuality that I had taken to be operative at the level both of critical theory and of the popular imagination, I was repeatedly struck by the surprised response of casual inquirers into my project: "Oh, really?" they would reply, awaiting enlightenment. "There's a link between homosexuality and fascism?" Basing my work on a conflation that seemed all too evident, I was confronted by a persistent denial of any such ideological operation. Convinced that the conflation of homosexuality and fascism was not the product of my own paranoia, however, I began to question the reaction implicit in such responses to this book. I was struck by how much easier it was for those who expressed surprise at my project to find a "way in" through homosexuality, rather than through fascism: "Oh, now I get it! You mean leather and S&M, and all that stuff! Oh, I see now. That's very interesting!"

A word to the wise: I do not "mean" leather and S&M. Implicit in such doubtless well-meaning responses is a willingness to examine how homosexuals manipulate (the iconography of) fascism, rather than to address the question of how fascism has— ideologically and physically—manipulated homosexuals. Once again, the homosexual is more readily imagined as the subject of some imagined fascism, than as its object or victim. A continuing heterosexual fascination with fascism conceals itself as a fascination with the imagined sexual activities of homosexuals. Although it would be disingenuous on my part to deny the appropriation by gay men and lesbians (or, I might add, of persons of any sexual persuasion) of "fascistic" iconography in the context of sexual play, it is not my concern at this point. This is no more a book of social anthropology than it is a book of historical data.

Now that I have established what I do not mean—positivist historiography or popular anthropology—I might move to what I do propose in this work. First, as I hope to show in this chapter, the conflation of homosexuality and fascism is neither a historical curio nor a product of unreflective prejudice: it is still in operation at both the theoretical and what I have called the anecdotal level. Thus, for example, in a "Homosexuality" edition of *Salmagundi*, in a piece on Jean Genet, we read that "Genet's attraction to the Nazis goes deeper than Sartre thinks. The Nazis built their movement by attracting men just like Genet. He would have been at home in the SA which was, among other things, a cult of decadent homosexual toughs and aesthetes."[3] The outrage that such an assertion must cause in any homosexual reader is, frankly, perhaps the least offensive thing about the argument. So, the SA was—"among other things"—a decadent homosexual clique: but among what other things? Things such as murder, torture, and intimidation, perhaps? And of people such as Jews, socialists, and, of course, homosexuals? To read fascism through the psychologizing prism of homosexuality is, I contend, to trivialize its historical reality: that which is invoked to explain the crime (i.e., homosexuality) itself becomes the crime.[4] The SA somehow becomes "aesthetes." It is Klaus Mann who—in an essay on "Homosexuality and Fascism" from the very earliest period of anti-fascist writing—is clearest on this point:

> In the end they always dredge up the "*Führer*": supposedly the quasi-religious adoration of his person necessarily demonstrates conscious or unconscious homosexual tendencies. . . . But the deciding factor must remain: Who is revering which *Führer* and how? Have Marxists forgotten that the dogma and typology of the *Führer* that we oppose is itself determined by economic factors? And that Hitler—who, incidentally, is more fervently and hysterically adored by *petite bourgeoise* housewives than by soldier males or effeminate men—did not come to power because "German youth had been infected with homosexuality," but because Thyssen financed him and because the lies that money bought confused a hungry populace? (11)

Mann's point is well taken, and I should note in all honesty that the type of material political analysis he calls for is not one that will be pursued here. The aim is not to demonstrate somehow that homosexuality is not at the root of fascism, but to inquire as to how —in our readings of fascism as a mythology—it managed to find itself there.

I will go on in this introductory chapter to parallel two debates—one from the 1930's, one from the 1980's—that turn on the linkage of homosexuality and fascism. But it is perhaps Mann's articulate critique that most clearly demonstrates how little movement has been made in the terms of such debates. Mann focuses on the phenomenon of the *Führerprinzip*—a charismatic investment in the great leader—as the traditional linchpin in the Left's homosexualization of fascism, and it is to just this principle that several influential schools of postwar theory will return in their linkage of homosexuality and fascism through the terminology of psychohistory. Thus, the Mitscherlichs—whose model of mourning we will invoke and oppose in the final chapter—argue in *The Inability to Mourn* that the narcissistic nature of the Germans' cathexis of Hitler has led to an inability to mourn their loss and a state of melancholy avoided only by a massive denial of the past:

> There is, however, yet another difference between mourning and melancholia.
>
> Mourning arises when the lost object was loved for its own sake. Or, to put it somewhat differently, mourning can occur only when one individual is capable of empathy with another. This other person enriched me through his otherness, as man and woman can enrich each other by experiencing their difference. Loss that gives rise to melancholia reveals, as Otto Rank recognized, a narcissistic object choice. I chose the now vanished object after my own image and because it was willing to adapt itself to my fantasy. This applied perfectly to the Führer, he fulfilled the ideal of greatness for his subjects who had long been crippled by absolutism and, in turn, projected *his* ideas of greatness onto the "race" which supposedly gave distinction to the German people. (27–28)

That this narcissistic inability to mourn is intrinsically homosexual should be clear from the passage. Clearly, for example, the Mitscherlichs' desire for a return to the work of mourning is a desire for a return to heterosexuality. They quite explicitly—if not at any length—identify mourning with a heterosexual loss—the loss, indeed, *of* heterosexuality. Mourning is the remembrance paid a man by a woman, whereas the present political state (a state the Mitscherlichs characterize not as melancholy, but as the resistance to mass melancholia) results from the narcissistic, homosexual attachment to the *Führer*. Without the diacritical differential of gender, it seems that the representation of loss becomes impossible and the historical condition of (homosexual) melancholy inevitable (though *The Inability to Mourn* is, of course, about precisely those mechanisms through which melancholy is avoided). Germany cannot mourn the victims of fascism, in other words, because its attachment to fascism is still homosexually narcissistic. The Mitscherlichs' analysis of the repressions through which Germany guards itself against mass melancholy might, then, be read as an analysis of the suppression of homosexuality as a political force.[5]

This work is historically specific in its application to the postwar German situation—as specific, in this sense, as Walter Benjamin's "Theories of German Fascism," a text that will be important later for its reconstruction of fascism as a system of representation—but the structural gestures of the study replicate those to be found elsewhere in psychosocial studies of fascism and might be said to aspire to a more general methodological application. I do not wish to enter into a discussion, at this point, of political epistemes and historical ruptures, but it is important to note the specifically sexualized and gendered context in which such psychopolitical analyses are developed. In postwar theoretical discussion of homosexuality and fascism, psychoanalysis has permitted a return to ideological distortions that Klaus Mann already discredited in the earliest years of Nazism.

Since it is almost impossible to reduce fascism—no matter how narrowly defined—to theoretical and ideological coherence on any social question, I contend that it is necessary to deconstruct the theoretical work of homosexuality rather than to reconstruct an ideological position. What work does the identification of homosexuality with fascism—already glimpsed on the Left by Klaus Mann, in the 1930's—perform in the order of our political imagination? To this extent, I will be dealing with fascism at at least one remove, as itself a function within the political imaginary of the present. Of course, such an approach leaves the theorist open to the charge that history has thereby been reduced to text and the historical specificity of fascism obfuscated; and, indeed, this charge has traditionally carried particular weight with respect to historical fascism. Already in my first book—*Fascist Modernism*—I began to feel uneasy at dealing with something as concrete and horrifying as fascism in terms of its representational stratagems, and in this book I seek not to ease my conscience, but to examine the persistence of those stratagems in the political thought of the present. This is not to say that I believe that certain strains of political thought dealt with in this book are intrinsically "fascist"—but only that I challenge the right of such discourses to speak about fascism in terms already employed by the fascists themselves. Nazis were not fascist solely because they deployed certain ideological commonplaces—it has been argued well, I think, that there was little at the level of ideology in fascism that could not have been found earlier elsewhere—and to redeploy such ideologemes does not therefore necessarily make one a fascist. Adorno, to take one pressing example from the present work, is by no means a "fascist" because of his dependence on a heterosexist political order entirely acceptable to Nazi and fascist ideologues alike. But it is important, I think, to question the analysis of fascism that Adorno derives by employing that order.[6]

If fascism somehow defies representation, it has nevertheless been represented with obsessive frequency at any number of discursive levels—not least of all as a marker (if not a representation) of the historical dilemma of unrepresentability. Fascism links itself at one and the same time to questions about the nature of historical experience ("Is history a 'text'?") and to questions about the nature of mimetic representation ("Can there be such a thing as a text?"). It is this fact, then—fascism as a historical and political representation that somehow defines for us today the limits of political and historical representation—that provides the basis for the current work. And it is a certain conception of homosexuality—

or so I hope to contend throughout this book—that has facilitated the reappropriation of the unimaginable to the terms of the political imaginary, that has served, in other words, to represent the unrepresentable.

This assertion is not one I seek to pursue at this point—and it will be examined most fully only in the final chapter of the book, where I examine the way in which the topos of homosexuality is utilized by Alberto Moravia in his novel *The Conformist* to resuscitate the novel itself as a viable form of historical mimesis. At this point, the assertion simply marks a methodology: homosexuality and fascism will emerge as imaginary constructs in this work rather than as empirical entities (although—as is apparent in the chapters on Blüher and Mackay, for example—the imaginary in question will always necessarily be "historically" specific). I contend that it is a certain instrumentalization of homosexuality and fascism that makes possible the imagination of—among other things—empirical phenomena such as the Nazis' persecution of homosexuals. Methodologically, it is ideological deformation that provides access to empirical historical formations, rather than the reverse.

Ernst Bloch, one of the few prominent, exiled anti-fascists to show any sensitivity to questions of rhetoric and representation in political movements, was acutely aware of the difficulty of addressing fascism in existing political vocabularies. His essay "Der Nazi und das Unsägliche," from 1938, highlights the problem of fascism and language in a way that is helpful to us in the current study. Bloch's essay points out that there always was something *unsäglich*—unspeakable—about fascism, something that confounded conventional political terminology. Fascism—and not just "Auschwitz," as Jean-François Lyotard tends to argue—resists phrasing, and the task of this study is, above all, to examine some of the consequences of our attempt to phrase this *Unsägliches*.

The second thing that Bloch's essay alerts us to—through a perhaps fortuitous title—is the very structure of *das Unsägliche*, for has not homosexuality too—that "love that dare not speak its name"—been historically unspeakable? A constant theme of this work will be precisely this conflation of two unspeakable phenomena—the negation of a negation, the silencing of a silence—through which fascism has been brought to speech. If homosexuality dare not speak its own name, it will nevertheless serve as the "name" of something else that cannot be spoken—fascism. In other words, I am suggesting that the conflation of homosexuality and fascism—while not grounded in historical fact—is by no means accidental. The allegorical press-ganging of homosexuality as a vehicle for articulating a historically resistant fascism relies on the fact that neither homosexuality nor fascism speaks in its own name.[7] The liberal fear of becoming fascist and the heterosexual, homosocial fear of becoming homosexual will prove themselves to be something more than parallel: homosexuality will be consistently figured as the desire that the fascist emerge from within the liberal. Through the dialectical negation of a negation, theory seeks to reinstate itself and reconstruct the possibility of historical narrative. Indeed—as I demonstrate in greater depth in the concluding chapter—it is the very structure of dialectical thought that has contributed to the identification of sexual and political deviance as homologous threats to narratives of historical progress.

Perhaps, however, there is another reason for the failure to acknowledge a pervasive conflation of homosexuality and fascism: perhaps, far from being a popular prejudice absent from critical political and literary theory, it is, in fact, a purely theoretical conflation. Perhaps, for those not versed in Freud—or in the reworkings of Freud at the hands of Wilhelm Reich and members of the Frankfurt School—the nexus of homosexuality and fascism is no more than an academic fancy. This line of defense is not really tenable: as we shall see, there has always been in "progressive" political thought a dichotomy between party leadership and the rank and file on the question of homosexuality. Far from being a theoretical abstraction in leftist ideology, the conflation of homosexuality and fascism seems to have marked an opportunistic capitulation of theory in the face of popular sentiment. The identification of proletarian revolution with values of virility and sexual potency leads all too easily to an attribution of homosexuality or effeminacy to the enemy: this observation holds for the communists' homosexualization of the fascist as much as it does for the fascists' effeminization of the Jew. The movement toward an identification of fascist, petit bourgeois, and homosexual can be noted in some of the political infighting on the Left during the 1930's, but once again we must stress that it is by no means moribund as a line of argument. Thus, for example, Hans-Georg Stümke—the leading historian on questions of fascism and the homosexual emancipation movement—offers in his study *Homosexuelle in Deutschland* the following excerpt from the *Berliner Tageszeitung* of November 24, 1987: "There can be no doubt that the National Socialist movement—particularly in its formative years in the 1920's—was decisively influenced and propagated by the peculiar dynamic of male-bonded homosexuality" (100–101).

It would certainly be a mistake to dismiss out of hand any affinities between the homosocial structures of early "masculinist" and/or "homosexual" movements and the male cadres of fascism, and I examine precisely these connections in the chapter that focuses on Blüher and Friedlaender. What interests me at this point is the question of why—even in the popular press—the well-known fact of the homosexuality of Ernst Röhm (the leader of the SA, ultimately purged in 1934 for reasons of political expediency masked as moral outrage) should be seized on so readily as a way of explaining fascism as a psychological and libidinal structure.

In an interview with Lawrence Mass, Richard Plant has formulated the most obvious answer: "This notion that the Nazi leadership was riddled with homosexuals is wishful thinking on the part of those who are looking for easy scapegoats and simple explanations. Unfortunately, even some of our most authoritative observers, writing at a time when ignorance and prejudice about homosexuality were still pervasive, reflect this problem" (194). Of course, the conflation of homosexuality and fascism reflects the (il)logic of all scapegoating—a logic all too familiar from the fascists' own ideology. But this response does not really answer the specific question regarding homosexuals: why them rather than some other group? To this second stage of questioning there is an equally obvious—and doubtless not incorrect—answer: homophobia. Once again this response answers little and covers much. Unless we are to understand homophobia as a clinical condition, it seems merely tautologous to characterize the acts that define homophobia as homophobic. At the very least, we might wish to use this theoretical and anecdotal summary as the ground for questioning our understanding of homophobia. Let me, at the outset, express some skepticism as to the usefulness of the diagnosis. If we are to understand a phobia as a fear of the other, then we risk hypostatizing homosexuality as absolutely external to the subject of homophobic social and political discourse. It is precisely this externalization that I seek to resist, by arguing that the linkage of homosexuality and fascism results from the parallel fears that all social order might result in fascism, and that all homosocial structures are potentially homosexual. The cathexis of a particular object as the representative of the "other"—as the object of the phobia—clearly indicates a differentiation made within the realm of that dedifferentiated other that threatens us, in turn, with effacement.

But in this direction lies a second problem with the analysis of homophobia. The selection of a specific representation of the nonspecific other (the representation, one might say—using a terminology that will become familiar—of the unrepresentable) has historically been interpreted as a (resisted) identification. I fear what I might become: the social democrat fears fascism, the homosocial order fears homosexuality. Again, this position is not altogether incompatible with the argument that will follow in this book, but there is a formulation of this position that must, I think, be strenuously resisted: namely, that the fascist fears homosexuality because he somehow "is"—or fears he will become, or reveal himself to have always already been—homosexual. Thus, for example, when confronted with the inconvenient fact of the Röhm purge and fascism's clear self-distantiation from all suspicion of homosexuality, the author of that article in the *Berliner Tageszeitung* quoted by Stümke has the following to say: "This bloody episode . . . is, in fact, a typical example of a persecution of homosexuals of which only other homosexuals (fearful for their own respectability) would be capable" (100–101). Clearly, the assertion is politically objectionable, explaining, as it does, persecution on the grounds of a more radical identification with the persecuted. The perpetrators are once again modeled psychically on the persecuted. The consideration of fascism in its psychosexual aspects is, in fact, hampered by the concept of homophobia as a projection of self-loathing, for all too often the sequence is inverted and the self-loathing taken as the cause of the projection, rather than the other way round.

Thus, homophobia becomes a characteristically homosexual phenomenon and victimization the very modality of homosexual identity. The differentiation of subject and object of oppression is lost. As such, this formulation serves both to sustain the homophobia it sought to analyze ("the fascists were, then, homosexual—and their persecution of homosexuals 'proves' it") and to reassert specific stereotypes ("Oh, you mean S&M!") of homosexuality. If homophobia is simply the expression of a repressed homosexual impulse, then persecution becomes a homosexual phenomenon, sadomasochism becomes the normative homosexual libidinal structure, and the homosexual self-loathing ("I hate myself in the other") that has traditionally legitimated heterosexual loathing of homosexuals is reaffirmed.

Of course, defenders of this formulation would argue that we are talking here only of repressed homosexual desire; that uninhibited homosexuality is not necessarily fascistic. As I will point out in this study, however, the differentiation—from the perspective of a normative, heterosexist political theory—between repressed and nonrepressed homosexuality will prove itself again and again to be disingenuous. Over and over again, homosexual desire will emerge in both its anecdotal and theoretical formulations as having been always already repressed, as a desire, indeed, *for* repression.

There is clearly something disturbing about dealing with regimes of political oppression, murder, and genocide within the sanitized confines of a "system of representation," or even—to use Benjamin's famous definition from "The Work of Art in the Age of Mechanical Reproduction"—as the "aestheticization of politics."

But if the accusation has by now become customary, so has the defense; fascism, we are to believe, defies representation. Indeed, to think it is possible to reconstruct a historical narrative in the face of untold human suffering is itself to do violence to that suffering—to reduce, in Lyotard's terms, a differend to the level of a litigation. For Lyotard, postwar invocations of fascism have tended to undertake just such a reduction, making sense out of fascism, if only as the marker of historical senselessness. In *The Differend* Lyotard sees this move—which we will trace in his critique of Adorno—as a fall out of the historical structure of the dialectic into the realm of the rhetorical. Whereas in the Greek State it is "the dialectical and rhetorical genre or genres" that cocreate legitimation according to Lyotard, in the wake of Nazism "the only way you can make a 'beautiful death' out of 'Auschwitz' death (nos. 156, 160) is by means of a rhetoric" (109). The debate over "Auschwitz" brings to a head a division of dialectic and rhetoric implicit in enlightened modernity, a division that clearly has an impact on the writing of history. At the conclusion of this book, I show how it is precisely the withering away of the dialectic as a historical metanarrative—a dialectic, that is, that has always been coded heterosexually—that unleashes a "homosexual panic" in theory.[8] The identification of homosexuality with "rhetoric"—and, implicitly, with the interruption of the dialectic—serves, as we shall see, to identify homosexuality with the purely "rhetorical" politics of fascism. Homosexuality, in short, serves as allegory for a new rhetorical regimen.

It is not Lyotard's intention—and it is certainly not mine—to legitimize the dialectic at the expense of rhetoric, for the persistence of dialectical historical analysis would, in fact, be one of the prime examples of the rhetoric he has in mind. I seek in this book to specify the rhetorical gestures that have, indeed, sought to make sense of fascism by linking it to homosexuality, and I hope by the conclusion to have shown how a certain allegorical understanding of homosexual desire has facilitated its allegorical implementation in representations of fascism. Lyotard's reading of fascism is, one might argue, itself rhetorically synecdochic in that it focuses on the question of "Auschwitz."[9] This book will argue for the allegorical and allegorizing function of fascism within the contemporary political and cultural imagination, but I would like at this point to develop briefly Lyotard's position, as he takes exception to Adorno's deployment of fascism in works such as *Negative Dialectics*. Although I, too, criticize Adorno for the specifics of his political analysis, I will nevertheless return to his deployment of the nonidentical in *Negative Dialectics* in order to reorient myself throughout this book, and it is therefore important to sketch out the parameters of what might be termed the "Lyotard-Adorno" debate with respect to the historical representability of fascism.

At issue, in my presentation of this debate, is the following: to what extent does the historical phenomenon of fascism usher in a change in our historical sensibility, and to what extent is any such change attributable to a reconfiguration of the categories of sexuality? Taking issue with Adorno, one of the first philosophers to reflect (in *Negative Dialectics*) on the ethical significance of genocide for speculative discourse, Lyotard resists a modal reading of "Auschwitz"—its reduction, that is, to the level of a philosophical model. Reading "Auschwitz" modally, Adorno reacts to his fear that any thought seeking to represent "Auschwitz" to itself will necessarily trivialize genocide, reducing it, in turn, to the level of mere representation. Clearly, Lyotard is sensitive to such fears, which also animate his own insistence on the nonlitigational nature of the differend, but in *The Differend* he explains his critique of Adorno in the following terms:

> For [Adorno], "Auschwitz" is a model, not an example. From Plato through Hegelian dialectics, the example has the function in philosophy of illustrating an idea; it does not enter into a necessary relation with what it illustrates, but remains "indifferent" to it. The model, on the other hand, "brings negative dialectics into the real." . . . The idea of the model corresponds to this reversal in the destiny of dialectics: the model is the name for a kind of para-experience, where dialectics would encounter a non-negatable negative [*un négatif non niable*], and would abide in the impossibility of redoubling that negative into a "result." . . . The "Auschwitz" model would designate an "experience" of language that brings speculative discourse to a halt. (88)

A modal (rather than exemplary) reading of "Auschwitz" is a reading that will inevitably reinstate—albeit in negative form—the dialectical mode of analysis that "Auschwitz" has supposedly discredited. Understanding "Auschwitz" as the sublation of a historical dialectic—albeit negative—involves making sense of something that must resist sense: the historical phenomenon that belies the historical validity of the dialectic is itself nevertheless accounted for in terms of that dialectic. Such a reading is, one might say, properly apocalyptic, in that it understands fascism as an "end"— both as a completion (telos) and as a destruction. Such apocalyptic thinking rhetoricizes the dialectic.[10]

Lyotard objects that Adorno's presentation of "Auschwitz," while refusing mere reparation, nevertheless makes sense of senselessness, retaining the essentials of a historical dialectic (albeit in negated form) and thereby projecting beyond its own death the historical consciousness that has supposedly come to an end. This projection of the dialectical method beyond its own death ignores—from Lyotard's perspective—the ethical disfiguration enacted by fascism and relies on a model of sublation and "beautiful death" that "Auschwitz" has rendered anachronistic. As a model, "Auschwitz" brings about its end from within the terms of the thing it supposedly ends—in this case, the dialectic. By asserting that "Auschwitz" "brings negative dialectics into the real" Adorno rejoins the idealist historical dialectic. Consequently, Lyotard argues that the end Adorno envisages is an end in both senses of the word: a rupture, but also a teleological completion. If "Auschwitz" cannot be made sense of, it would seem that it itself nevertheless makes sense—in Adorno's presentation—of the historical determinants that bring it about: it is not indifferent, as the example would be, and therefore it assumes a historical essence that is modally (though negatively) articulated.

Curiously, however, though fascism seems to mark the limits of historical representation—in different ways for both Lyotard and Adorno—it has itself nevertheless continued to exert a fascination that has led to a proliferation of representations of fascism. This peculiarity of fascism is one that I will seek to explain in this book—and most consistently in the final chapter—through what I call the allegorical function of fascism. This allegorical function I derive from Benjamin as a way of explaining how—as Lyotard points out in regard to Adorno—meaning is constantly resurrected in the face of historical meaninglessness. As Benjamin argues in *The Origin of German Tragic Drama*, allegory is the proper modality of the melancholic, who inhabits a historical landscape in which events have ceased to emanate their own meaning. It is this very meaninglessness of historical phenomena that renders them susceptible to multiple and arbitrary—allegorical—deployments: "If the object becomes allegorical under the gaze of melancholy, if melancholy causes life to flow out of it and it remains behind dead, but eternally secure, then it is exposed to the allegorist; it is unconditionally in his power. That is to say it is now quite incapable of emanating any meaning or significance of its own; such significance as it has it acquires from the allegorist" (183–84). The very ambiguity of fascism as ideologeme results from its reification at the hands of a melancholic historical sensibility, a sensibility that is beyond mourning, beyond the amends that may be made by a litigation. Just as Lyotard writes of "Auschwitz" becoming a name, so Benjamin allows us to see how fascism as allegory is at the mercy of its current theorists: it can be made to mean anything at all precisely because it seems to have no meaning proper to it, because to adduce any such essential meaning would be to make sense of it, to justify it by reconstructing its logic. In other words, Benjamin's notion of allegory—as the evacuation of what is "proper" in meaning—allows us to understand how the polemics around the supposedly unrepresentable fascism actually proliferate and disseminate ceaseless representations. I will argue that the unrepresentable—unspeakable—crime of homosexuality has been subject to a parallel proliferation.

I hope that this allegorical deployment of fascism will become apparent throughout the work, particularly with regard to the utilizing of homosexuality as an allegory of allegorical ("rhetoricized") politics, an allegory of fascism. Whereas this conjunction of Lyotard and Benjamin allows us to understand how fascism—at the very time it supposedly marks the limits of historical represen-

tation—has become an obsessive and privileged representational
vehicle, I will seek to demonstrate in this book the forms in which
homosexuality, too, has been allegorized. Meaningless from the
perspective of a historical sensibility organized around tropes of
heterosexual reproduction and regeneration, homosexuality becomes a vehicle for representing the otherwise unrepresentable—
fascism. (I should point out that my invocation of a melancholic
historical sensibility denotes a mode of representation—and is derived from Benjamin—rather than a psychological state derived
from, say, the Mitscherlichs' study *The Inability to Mourn*. To psychologize historical phenomena as the Mitscherlichs do in their
work is to assume a subject of history—which is precisely what fascism questions, at the level of both a collective and a coherent individual subject. To this extent, the homo-fascist—pre-Oedipal,
failed Oedipus—will serve as the subject of this postsubjective melancholic history.)

If, as I will be arguing, homosexuality serves as an allegory of
allegory—as a Lyotardian "rhetoric"—this representational structure is itself one familiar from studies of fascist ideology. I am
thinking, of course, of Lacoue-Labarthe and Nancy's characterization of Nazism as the myth of myth, a myth whose power derives not from its content but from its structure. Indeed, I might
invoke their essay "The Nazi Myth" as a methodological introduction to the work being undertaken here on both homosexuality and fascism: "That is why we will not speak here of Nazism's
myths, in the plural. But only of the myth of Nazism, or of the
National-Socialist myth *as such*. We will speak, in other words, of
the fashion by which National Socialism constitutes itself, with or
without the use of myths, in a dimension, for a function, and with
a self-assurance that all three can be properly termed mythic"
(292). For Lacoue-Labarthe and Nancy, *the* myth of Nazism concerns not the content of mythology, but the very performative
function of myth. The specificity of Nazism lies not in its ideological material, but in its belief in the efficacy of mythic narrative in
the construction of national identity. It is not what is believed that
is specifically fascist, but the belief in belief itself as the generator

of historical subjectivity, as the foundation of the *Volk*. Insofar as it is possible to disengage the myths of Nazism from the myth of Nazism, we might argue that it is this myth—*the* myth—that will concern us in this study. For no amount of debunking of the mythological underpinnings of Nazi ideology will serve to deconstruct the myth that is Nazism, the myth that Nazism has become. As the myth of myth—or what I will be referring to, in the context of a rhetoricized politics outlined by Lyotard, as the allegory of allegory—fascism still represents a mode of political thought, a mode of thought that cannot be reduced to specific ideological material. It is possible to believe fascistically without believing in fascism. As Lacoue-Labarthe and Nancy will argue, "The characteristic of Nazism (and in many respects that of Italian fascism) is to have proposed its own movement, and its own State, as the effective realization of a myth, or as a living myth. As Alfred Rosenberg says: Odin is dead, but in another way, as essence of the German soul, Odin is resuscitating before our very eyes" (304).

I wish to deploy the rhetoric of allegory in this study to show just how that resuscitation can also take place within theories of fascism, how this resuscitation of Odin and the Christological resurrection analyzed by Benjamin in and through allegory persist in our conflation of homosexuality and fascism. Homosexuality will serve homophobic theoretical and cultural logic as the allegorical resuscitation of fascism, the resurrection of fascism as allegory. In opposing such a reading, I might invoke a passage from Max Horkheimer and Adorno's *Dialectic of Enlightenment* where the figure of Odin again occurs. Horkheimer and Adorno cite "the famous Norse myth according to which Odin hung for his own sake as a sacrifice on the tree" as an example of the mythic origins of "the identically persistent self which arises in the abrogation of sacrifice" (54). In other words, to read against the grain of Odin—this figure central to fascism and to theoretical rereadings of fascism—is necessarily to read against the structures of identity that fascism failed definitively to dislodge. This theme of nonidentity is one that will recur throughout the book in my recasting of a potential homosexual episteme.

In what follows, I wish to demonstrate the ways in which contemporary debates about the libidinal coding of fascism have moved but a short distance from similar debates in the 1930's. The Mitscherlichs' desire for a return to mourning as the modality of a historical "working through" presupposes the existence of a historical subject (in this case, the nation—Germany) who has traditionally provided the focus for both the Left and the Right in their models of progress. If, in what follows, it is primarily the discourse of the Left that comes under attack, I should stress that my aim is to demonstrate the ways in which those historical subjects have always depended on a heterosexist model that figures the homosexual as an abomination to historical generation—or to the generation of history. In essence, fascism demonstrated in its emergence the ideological indifference of notions of collective subjectivity—proletariat or *Volk?*—and in its demise the crisis of a subject-centered history.

In turning now to parallel debates from the 1930's and the 1980's, I wish to show how the historical conflation of homosexuality and fascism serves as a rearguard action against the demise of a subject-centered, "heterosexual" history. By choosing two examples that reflect, respectively, a political and an aesthetic confrontation with homo-fascism, I wish also to show how the conflation of homosexuality and fascism itself rests on a certain aestheticization and eroticization of politics. In what remains of this introduction, I wish to examine two exemplary cases of the linkage of homosexuality and fascism, one from the 1930's and one from the recent present: the communist analysis of the Reichstag fire and the recent debate in Germany over Nazi statuary in the museums. By tracing a continuum of sorts from the one polemic to the other, I hope to demonstrate the ways in which the conflation of certain sexual and political structures has been intrinsic to the construction of our political imaginary.

While it should be pointed out that throughout the history of homosexual reform attempts in Wilhelmine and Weimar Germany, the only consistent support for reform of the infamous paragraph 175 came from the Left, and that by the end of the Weimar Re-

public the most consistent parliamentary support for reform came
from the KPD (Kommunistische Partei Deutschlands), there seems
to have been a discrepancy between party line and popular leftist
sentiment. Campaigns for homosexual liberation always sat un-
easily with a popular iconography of proletarian virility. In this respect we can note something that will recur consistently in discourses on homo-fascism, namely, a vacillation as to whether homosexuality is intrinsically fascistic, or whether it is the repression
of desire that finds its form in fascism. Though the Left's campaign
for reform rests on a notion of human rights and sees in the liberation of homosexual desire a political liberation, at the same time
there is an opportunistic linkage of homosexuality per se with a
desire for repression that is intrinsically totalitarian. This ambiguity on the Left—one might call it opportunism—came to light in
the series of scandals involving high-ranking personalities in the
Wilhelmine establishment in the first decade of the century. Thus,
for example, it was the socialist publication *Vorwärts* that first revealed the names and details of the Krupps scandal in 1902—in
an article that called for the repeal of paragraph 175 while invoking antihomosexual sentiment in the ideological struggle against
the ruling class. By 1932—that is, before Hitler's ascendancy to
the position of chancellor—the KPD's *Berlin am Morgen* argued
that "the Hitler racket is based on homosexual tendencies and
hypocrisy." Again, the statement is clearly ambiguous: is it the homosexual tendencies or hypocrisy that is at the root of the problem? Clearly, at this point the Left was riding two horses at once.[11]

   With the final ascent to power of the Nazis, the KPD's party
line—while still remaining committed to human rights reform—
began to reflect an equation of fascism and homosexuality. I wish
now to demonstrate this shift by looking in more detail at the
KPD's position as elaborated in the famous *Braunbuch* that pur-
ported to reveal the truth behind a Nazi plot to raze the Reichstag. In the KPD's attempts to place the responsibility for the
Reichstag fire at the feet of the National Socialists, the languages of
political and sexual deviance are almost inextricably intertwined.
At the core of the argument is the assertion that Marinus van der

Lubbe, the Dutch *Rätekommunist* arrested and sentenced for the crime, was, in fact, a stool pigeon for the Nazis, to whom he had been drawn by a net of homosexual affiliation: "Enquiries into his life in Leyden," we are told, "have definitely established the fact that he was homosexual. This is of great importance for his later history" (55). Logistically, this (apparently spurious) homosexual pedigree for van der Lubbe provides a connection to the SA, by whom he is said to have been recruited for the deed. More than this, however, homosexuality itself—as a character structure—further befits him for the role he is to play.

The characterological importance of van der Lubbe's homosexuality lies in the assumption on the part of the authors that homosexuals are vain and self-aggrandizing, a quality that also ill suits them to any collective class action. Again and again we read of the failure of the young homosexual, Marinus, to develop the necessary class consciousness: he is considered a "foreign element" by his comrades, and his exit from the Dutch Communist Party is attributed to a desire for personal glory as well as to his return to his petit bourgeois roots. The inability to stick to gender binarisms expresses itself politically in the inability to respect fundamental class distinctions. It would not be too fanciful, I think, to see in this assumption that homosexuality reflects a failure of class allegiance an application to the political field of the notion of sexual *Zwischenstufen*, or intermediates. This theory, adopted and developed by Magnus Hirschfeld from the nineteenth-century sexologists, sought to understand homosexuality in terms of gender disturbances and placed the homosexual as a gender apart between male and female.[12] The inability to occupy a clear class position is reflected in such theories by an inability to embrace a definitive gender role: the intermediary petite bourgeoisie is at the same time the natural home of the sexual intermediate. Furthermore, the explanation of van der Lubbe's difficulties within the party is extremely interesting in itself, for it raises two important issues in the homosexualization of fascism: first, the status of sexual analyses in relation to class, and second, the relationship of homosexuality to anarchism.

With regard to the first of these questions, Stümke and Finkler—in their assessment of the KPD line—conclude: "Psycho-Pro-
file: the proletarianized young homo becomes a worker, but remains a *petit bourgeois*" (157). Once again, the position articulated
on the Left is ambiguous: on the surface, the inference is that homosexuality is a petit bourgeois vice, alien to the virile proletariat,
and this position was certainly reflected at the time in the crimi-
nalization of homosexuality in the Soviet Union. At the same time,
it seems also that it is the very *déclassement* of van der Lubbe that
is coded homosexually, as if homosexuality were itself the name
given to the insufficiency of class consciousness. Psychosexual
analyses take up where strict class allegiances no longer function,
and the animus of the KPD's assessment seems to be driven largely
by its recognition of this supplementary relationship, denoting an
insufficiency in its own analytic framework. Indeed, from the very
outset, fascism frustrated traditional economic and class-based
modes of analysis, lending itself more easily to alternative interpretive paradigms. Reich's analysis, *The Mass Psychology of Fascism*,
was among the first of such studies, interpreting fascism in the light
of an underlying crisis at the patriarchal ideological core of capitalism. From the party-political perspective of the Left this interference in political orthodoxy is figured as a deviance from a heterosexual norm. Heterosexuality functions not only as a norm encoded within the framing normative discourse of class analysis, but
as a fundamental norm on which that analysis depends. The disruption of categories of class is represented as a disruption of sexual norms. In other words, we cannot simply draw the parallel of
sexual and class deviation, because the supplementary nature of
the relation of political and sexual necessarily displaces class analysis from its interpretive privilege at the "base."

In terms of the political—rather than class—coding of sexual
deviance, van der Lubbe—the young "foreign element"—finds
political expression in anarchism. This linkage of anarchism, homosexuality, and fascism is nothing new: it manifests itself in various forms of analysis. Thus, for example, when we pursue in more
specific terms Benjamin's analysis of fascism as the aestheticization

of politics—when we seek, in other words, to specify exactly which aesthetic he has in mind—it is clear that he bases his argument on an aesthetic lineage running from the late-nineteenth-century decadents to the avant-garde of Futurism. Benjamin's dependence on the genealogy of decadence—an aesthetic movement traditionally identified with both anarchists and homosexuals—serves as just one example of the way in which political analysis, in the face of fascism, consistently seeks to legitimate itself in terms of aesthetic genealogies, thereby replicating the very gesture of aestheticization it seeks to repudiate.[13]

At this point I wish only to point to the consideration of Mackay—the anarchist and editor of the works of Max Stirner—in Chapter 4. A reading of Mackay—who wrote as a homosexual emancipationist and *littérateur* under the pseudonym "Sagitta"—through the prism of anarchic politics serves, I think, to undermine some of the assumptions that prompted me to examine his work in the first place. Essentially a "masculinist" thinker—an opponent, that is of the "third-sex" theory of Magnus Hirschfeld—Mackay might be expected to exemplify a patriarchal and misogynistic homosexual ideology sympathetic to fascist doctrine. One literary historian, James W. Jones, refers—in a study entitled *"We of the Third Sex"*—to Mackay's "negative attitude toward his fellow homosexuals (with whom Mackay adamantly refused to be classed)," which supposedly "expresses not only his affinity with the *Gemeinschaft der Eigenen* but also his philosophy of 'individual anarchism'" (263). Indeed, in the dissertation on which his book was based, Jones goes so far as to assert "the spiritual affinity of . . . one entire wing of the homosexual emancipation movement to fascism. That group began with Friedlaender, Blüher, and others who believed in the superiority of homoerotic relationships and developed a bond of varying degrees of closeness to the National Socialist philosophy" (577). Although it is important to examine any such "spiritual affinity" seriously, we must beware of simply conflating fascism once again with a certain strain—the "masculinist" strain—of fascism. For if van der Lubbe is devirilized by his essentially hysterical anarchism, the anarchism of Mackay, on the contrary, is considered protofascistic in the exaggerated phal-locentrism of its masculinism. Indeed, although it is through the invocation of anarchy that an ideological continuum from homo-sexuality to fascism has been established, this charge could still, nevertheless, be leveled from within the homosexual camp. Thus, Kurt Hiller, for example, politically active on the Left and the suc-cessor to Hirschfeld's position at the institute, was also to refer to van der Lubbe as a "confused social-anarchist" and "the semi-crazed anarchist pyromaniac from Holland."[14]

If I can only gesture at this point to a debate pursued elsewhere in the book, I might at least avail myself of this charge of anar-chism to demonstrate the ways in which many of the common-places of the analysis of the *Braunbuch* still inform the Left's think-ing about fascism today. The charge of anarchism was based on the idea that van der Lubbe, like all homosexuals, was eager for notoriety, an inveterate petit bourgeois individualist incapable of collective action based on class consciousness. But more than this, anarchism—in its "homosexual" formation—figures as a dissem-bling politics, as a desire to pass for something else—something "better"—than it really is. If the homosexual is an anarchist, he is nevertheless more than pleased to represent something else, for the desire of the homosexual is a self-aggrandizing desire, a desire, indeed, *to* represent. In *Rosa Winkel, Rosa Listen*, Stümke and Finkler thus correctly offer the following synopsis of the findings of the *Braunbuch*: "Van der Lubbe was selected for the task by the homosexual SA leaders, who marched with him in the ranks of the arsonists. He was to represent and personify communism at the setting of the fire. It was not difficult to convince this vain, half-blind dupe, eager for notoriety, that he had been selected to play 'a great role'" (153). The vanity of the homosexual is such that he wishes to play a great role, and that role is the role of representa-tion, the mere representation of political affiliation. I contend that it is this putative desire to represent that even today befits the ho-mosexual to the theoretical representation of an unrepresentable ideological position. The homosexual is, in the highest degree, *repräsentativ*—and what he represents is the merely *repräsentativ* politics of fascism.[15]

If the passage beyond established boundaries of gender reflects a passage beyond the parameters of class analysis, it is not surprising that fascism should have lent itself so early and so consistently to a libidinal analysis, since it instigates a passage beyond established binarisms of gender and class into the realms of sexual ideology. This passage marks contemporary debates around fascism no less than it did the debate in the 1930's. The question of Nazi aesthetics, for example, gave rise in the 1980's to a reevaluation—in Germany—of the relationship of homosexuality and fascism, and sparked a debate on the Left in which the usefulness of the conflation again asserted itself. An exhibition of works from what the Nazis' de facto state sculptor, Arno Breker, chose to call his "neoclassical" period sparked a debate in *Die Sammlung*, the self-proclaimed "Yearbook for Anti-fascist Literature and Art." This debate was reopened at the end of the decade when a leading German art collector commissioned a sculpted portrait by Breker, calling for an end to the moratorium on exhibitions of Nazi art. The protocols of this second stage of the debate were subsequently collected in a volume entitled *Nazi-Kunst ins Museum?*

Of course, the fevered debate about Nazi aesthetics reflects the predominance of an interpretive model that sees fascism in terms of the aestheticization of politics. If Nazi art becomes acceptable, then this may be but the thin end of the wedge, the reintroduction of a politics of aestheticization through the medium of art itself. Of interest, however, is the way in which the argument regarding aestheticization has now been inflected libidinally—more specifically, through a consideration of a political homoerotics. We should note that the analysis of aestheticization was from the very beginning genealogically tied to a homosexualized literary tradition. In essays on André Gide and on Stefan George, Benjamin had already made it clear that *l'art pour l'art*—the aesthetic in whose name fascism aestheticizes—derives from a specifically homosexual aesthetic and cultural project. As a theoretical construct, then, the aestheticization of politics derives from a cultural and political tradition coded homosexually.

The shift toward a libidinal understanding of fascist aestheticization involves a form of structural reading, in which it is economies and structures of political desire rather than its specific embodiments that are considered fascist. This shift becomes clear in the debate concerning so-called homoerotic fascist statuary. Thus, in a somewhat schematic contribution to the debate, entitled "The Body and Power in Fascism: Analysis of a Fascination Through the Example of Breker," the influential leftist critic Wolfgang Fritz Haug asserts that "there is no predicate 'fascist' attached to the various elements. It is the social ordering that is fascist, rather than that which is ordered" (203). Haug's article is written to explain a reversal of his previous call for the banning of the Breker exhibition. The structural turn allows him to make the argument that what has been constructed can, in turn, be deconstructed; but this also means that fascism as a structural phenomenon remains an ongoing threat, a threat that will be bodied forth as homosexuality—perhaps as what Eve Sedgwick has referred to as "homosexual panic." With the clinical and juridical codification of homosexuality by the turn of the century, the affects previously operative within the terms of Sedgwick's homosexual panic are unbound and enter the political realm. The dichotomy between a definition of homosexuality tied to the category of object choice (a definition that seemed to contain homosexuality, since one could—by avoiding the wrong object choices—avoid homosexuality) and a definition based on a modality of desire (i.e., specular narcissism) dramatizes the way in which even clinical discourse provided an escape route whereby homosexuality might escape and inhabit the socius. Notably, the phobia that equates homosexuality and fascism consistently stresses the category of narcissism, whereby homosexuality releases itself into the very structure of all desire. Just as Haug insists that there is no "predicate 'fascist'," so one might argue that there is no "predicate 'homosexual'"—and therein lies the problem.

Summarily, it might be said that those who identify Nazi statuary with the homoerotic tend to stress the question of the *homo-*, while those who resist the identification stress the *erotic*—or its lack. Thus, one might resist the conflation by arguing that the dehumanizing monumentalism of the works of Breker and Josef Thorak withdraws them from the realm of the erotic. This line of defense, however, merely reaffirms the claims made for the prosecution: for while the charge that fascist statuary is homoerotic at first seems to rest on the assumption that any reduction of the male form to the level of an object of desire is potentially homosexualizing (for both subject and object), in fact the assertion also involves a certain understanding of the modality of homosexual desire. Precisely because it is dehumanizing and de-eroticizing this statuary will be portrayed as homoerotic: homosexual desire dehumanizes (or so the argument goes) by dislodging the male speculative subject and reifying him as an object of consumption. Homosexual desire—or, at least, its cultural representation and instantiation—seems to involve an abrogation of the responsibilities of subjectivity. De-eroticization will itself also serve in this model as the virtual point of all homosexual desire, which is the desire for the relinquishing of desire, the desire to submit. The masculine statuary that forbids and demands our erotic investment is the very prototype of homosexual libido for those who would conflate homosexual and protofascist libido.

Haug's problematic of "social ordering" aims to address the question of the museum as institution and the possibilities of critical exhibition within such institutions, but his structural analysis also extends to the very structure of the works in question and their specular consumption. Homoeroticism inheres not only in the selection of a masculine object of the gaze, but in the very act of gazing. For Haug, the potentially fascistic moment of "ordering" occurs in the gaze itself, in perspective—which unavoidably creates relations of power.[16] However, he does not argue that the fascism of Breker's work is purely in the eye of the beholder (even if he does insist that the museum can effect a necessary shift in perspective, and—therefore—a defascisticization). Breker's works— he will argue—are themselves about perspective, about the act of gazing and of subduing through the gaze. The process of social ordering, then, is internal to the works themselves, rather than the necessary effect of our own historical distancing from the works in question.

The fascism of Breker's work lies in its attempt to structure the gaze. To quote Haug's conclusion, "Breker works primarily for the homosexual voyeurs of our ruling class" (203). Suddenly, the question of the gaze has been diverted into the question of homosexual desire at the same time that the problematic of "ordering" has been displaced from the level of the gaze of the viewer to the level of a representation. Homosexuality—in other words—enters the picture at the moment we seek to represent: it is the structural analogy that arises when the possibility of an enactment of fascism is recontained within the representation of such a possibility, when—in short—our own voyeurism takes cover in the thematization of voyeurism. Clearly, Haug's argument makes massive assumptions that can scarcely be grounded, and in a response —also in *Die Sammlung*—to Haug's argument, Rainer Bohn, Hans-Jörg Schimmel, and Eckhard Seidel have commented:

> Starting from the merely asserted homosexual voyeurism of the ruling class, Haug goes on to posit "a ruling homosexual voyeurism" and, finally, to assert with no further ado the "implication of homosexual desire" in the concept of "domination" in general. Haug suggests quite explicitly that the homosexuality—or "homosexual voyeurism"—of the ruling classes is a necessary element in the unfolding of fascist power. Furthermore, he claims to have glimpsed in these "ruling voyeurs the basis of all domination and war," thereby reducing both fascism and war to socio-psychological determinants. (146–47)

This response raises objections at two levels: for if we are to note the rejection of the identification of homosexuality and power, we should note also that the respondents first reject a prior slippage from "the homosexual voyeurism of the ruling class" to "the ruling homosexual voyeurism." That is to say, they reject the leakage of homosexual desire from the simplified structures of class analysis into the paradigmatic analysis of a social imaginary. The protest against identifying homosexual desire with protofascist political structures results only from a more rigorous rejection of the paradigmatic nature of homosexual desire for the construction of the social order itself. Haug is rejected not primarily because he calls homosexuals fascists, but because he calls us all homosexual: even the line of defense is panicked.

We should also note what has happened to homosexual desire in this process: it has been specularized. Homosexuality is identified with voyeurism precisely because our relation to it as a phenomenon is intrinsically voyeuristic. Rather than acknowledge the inherence of lack in the structure of desire, we call "homosexual" only that desire that foregrounds this lack. We identify homosexuality and voyeurism because it is only through the prism of homosexual desire that we are able to represent to ourselves the phenomenon of fascism at all: we look on homosexuality as the desire to look—in order that it might enable us to look on fascism. So, while the response to Haug documents well his ungrounded assumption of the homosexuality of the ruling classes, and the subsequent identification of homosexuality as the constitutive factor in all systems of control and war, it nevertheless leaves untouched the identification of homosexuality and voyeurism. Why is voyeurism homosexual—and why, by extension, is homosexuality voyeuristic?

With all the lasciviousness of the political prude, Haug argues that Breker's sculptures respond to the desire of the ruling class for "young, naked bodies," which take on two forms in his work: "Essentially he sculpts two types of body: the object of the voyeur and the face of the voyeur. These faces too are a form of body" (203). The body is both the object of desire and the objectification of the desiring subject. The voyeur craves not only the young, naked bodies—but also the representation of his own body. In fact, Haug breaks with the Benjaminian tradition of analysis here—for Benjamin insists that one of the fundamental rights and demands of the workers is the right to be represented and reproduced, but in Haug's argument that desire is homosexualized and stigmatized. Of the gaze, he writes, "Hardly ever (with one exception, Cosima Wagner) does Breker represent the female gaze; women and their bodies feature in Breker's work only as the objects of the gaze. Men, on the other hand, appear in two forms: as heads [*Kopfkör-per*] and torsos [*Leibkörper*]. Clearly Breker panders to the desires of those whose heads he represents. Who are they?" (205).

This rather dubious mode of visual analysis is, nevertheless, extremely important for what it tells us about the introduction of homosexual desire into the analysis of fascism. Consider: Breker's art is being cited as homosexual—because it objectifies and leers at women's bodies. Clearly, the charge of homosexuality is actually introduced through the structure of narcissism: I desire to see my seeing. The desire to objectify not only the object of the gaze but the gaze itself is a desire to reduce desire—and political phenomena—to the level of representation. But in Haug's presentation this desire is substantively heterosexual. Curiously, the homosexuality Haug now invokes is homosexual by virtue of its contemplation of women's young bodies: it is homosexual not in its object choice but by virtue of its investment in the narcissistic contemplation of its own contemplation. In the analysis of the relationship of homosexuality and fascism, we leave behind the question of object choice—primarily for the analysis of narcissism.

Haug's analysis is caught within a rhetoric of (re-)production—derived from a privileging of productive labor as the key interpretive term in Marxist theory—that links the productive force of the heterosexual proletariat with sexual reproduction. Thus, the fact that fascist sculpture takes "a voyeuristic pleasure in young bodies, and in particular in their genitals" (203) is cited as evidence that such works mark a homosexual and capitalist reification of the labor of the proletarian body. Under the gaze of the homosexual, the embodied subject of history is reduced to the bodily object of desire. Homosexuality short-circuits the subject-centered logic of Marxist (re-)production and therefore operates in the service of capitalist exploitation, which likewise denies the productive body its historical subjectivity by alienating its labor. In its focus on limbs—*Glieder*—and specifically, on the genitals—*das Glied*—the homo-fascist aesthetic dismantles the organic proletarian body into seriality no less than does the division of labor in capitalism.

This dismemberment of the body—posited by Haug—will return in our final chapter as a precondition of the allegorical functioning of homosexual desire. The desire that dismembers the body as an organic totality frees up that body for ideological—allegorical—purposes.[17]

What, then, is the status of the object in such an analysis? Does this structural analysis empty out all content of the gaze? No: for despite his stress on the narcissistic, Haug still seems to be operating ideologically in terms of a model of object choice. I think we must figure the relationship of these two forms of analysis—object choice and narcissism—as follows: the object of desire is only ever the representation and trace of the functioning of desire as a structuring principle. I think we need to be clear about what exactly Nazi art is representing, according to Haug. There is the body—masculine or feminine—that is distorted and pummeled into an armorlike *Bereitschaft* in Breker's work.[18] The charge of homosexuality does not lie in this representation. It lies, instead, in the representation of the *Kopfkörper*, in the narcissistic self-representation of the ordering gaze—not, then, in that which has been ordered, but in the act of ordering itself. Haug's argument, though, is potentially more complex, for the aesthetic failure of Nazi art is taken to be its reduction of the principle of "ordering" to the level of "that which has been ordered"—a representation. Not content to control through representation, Nazi voyeurism must gaze on itself, that is, reduce itself to the level of object. The structure (ordering) becomes object (that which has been ordered) in the *Kopfkörper*. What I think we see in operation here is an implicit invocation of kitsch as both a homosexual and a fascist aesthetic: though inherent in the performance of the work—in the voyeuristic gaze—both homosexual libido and fascist power seek to represent themselves; seek, that is, to reinscribe their post-representational aesthetic in representational terms. Thus, if fascism is the unrepresentable—a principle of ordering that is the ground of representation—it nevertheless seeks to figure itself.

Again, I do not wish to pursue this line of argument fully at this point, since it necessarily involves the question of kitsch and mimeticism and links both homosexuality and fascism to the broader trajectory of aesthetic modernism. I will elaborate on the points I have just been making in the chapters on Alfred Jarry and Mackay, where I engage the analysis of kitsch and homosexual desire offered by Eve Sedgwick in her *Epistemology of the Closet*. For now, I will avail myself of Haug's foregrounding of these questions to explain the way this book is itself structured. Originally intended as a study of the linkage of homosexuality and fascism as imaginary structures, the work developed—through a confrontation with the problems of representability posed by fascism—into a reflection on the rhetorical structures allowing homosexuality to stand in for fascism. To the extent that the book still reflects these two agendas, its predominant discourses will be psychoanalytic and rhetorical, its central figures narcissism and allegory. These figures meet, I will contend, in the discourse of melancholy, which should be understood less in the sense proposed by the Mitscherlichs— as the psychohistorical state of a collective subject whose existence fascism calls into question—than as the representational logic of allegory. Melancholy, one might say, is postapocalyptic, resurrecting through allegory that which it sought to characterize as unrepresentable: fascism and homosexuality.

Consequently, the book developed—influenced, no doubt, by the perspective on fascism elaborated in my earlier book, *Fascist Modernism*—into a broader consideration of the representational strategies characteristically coded homosexually in conflations of fascism and homosexuality. It is for this reason that the chapter on Mackay (an early homosexual emancipationist, anarchist, and "masculinist," whose position—as we have seen—some critics have characterized as protofascist) needed to be complemented by a chapter on Jarry. It was necessary to work out the terms of a debate between the twin possibilities of homosexual literary realism and a homosexual avant-garde. If the chapter on Mackay was motivated on the grounds of intellectual history (as a literary counterpiece to the philosophical chapter on Friedlaender, Blüher, and Weininger), it nevertheless raised aesthetic questions that opened up the terms of my study. Moreover, I felt that the work on Jarry

—a homosexual author never acknowledged as such in critical treatments—helped define the position of this work in relation to the current state of queer theory. It is through the confrontation with Sedgwick in the Jarry chapter that I hope not only to deconstruct the dichotomy of representationalism and antirepresentationalism with regard to early homosexual literary practice, but also to develop a counteraesthetic to the monumental realism of a supposedly homoerotic totalitarian art. For this the question of kitsch proved central.

The dilemma, then, was whether to organize this work around the broad problematic of representation—which would demand one logical progression—or around generic or intellectual-historical distinctions, which would demand another. I also felt it was important that the book flag the fact that the fascism with which it deals is an imaginary rather than empirical or historical phenomenon. For this reason, I begin with perhaps the most purely theoretical chapter—on the Frankfurt School, in whose work many homophobic commonplaces receive their most elaborate and rigorous articulation. Rather than demonstrating the casual homophobia of the Frankfurt School thinkers (whose analyses are otherwise so central to my own approach), I show how homophobia is systematic and necessary to their analyses. As will become apparent, many structures of argument developed at the theoretical level in this chapter will be encountered time and time again before the book's close. The most important of these is the characteristically disingenuous distinction drawn between repressed homosexuality and homosexuality per se. In the course of this book, this grounding second chapter will help explain the centrality of homosexuality to the political sensitivities of a certain strain of fascist modernism (in the chapter on Lewis) and the aesthetic project of the postwar novel as it deals with fascism (in the concluding chapter on Moravia).

I follow this chapter with perhaps the most concretely historical pieces in the book, in which I turn to the philosophical writings of a tradition whose work—if any—might be said to lend some credence to the historical alignment of homosexuality and fascism. Weininger, Friedlaender, and Blüher help set the scene for an understanding of homo-fascism by articulating a theory of masculinism not altogether antipathetic to the homosocial structures of National Socialism. In this elaboration of a theory of hypermasculine homosexuality they serve a second purpose in this book: challenging the predominance of Hirschfeld's third-sex theory in historical reconstructions of the homosexual emancipation movement. Finally, these figures allow me to inaugurate a debate that will be pursued in the chapters on both Mackay and Jarry regarding the political and epistemological status of paederasty in the development of the modern homosexual. It is in this chapter, we might say, that I come closest to a presentation of the case for the conflation of homosexuality and fascism in the guise of masculinism, but I seek also to demonstrate the decisive points on which that conflation becomes untenable.

I seek to demonstrate how it is quite specifically a heterosexual and homophobic fantasy of homosexuality (as developed by Weininger, a philosopher whose relation both to his own Jewish heritage and to homosexual proclivities were, to say the least, troubled) that can develop a model of masculinism accessible to fascism. To quote Sedgwick from *Tendencies*, "Fascism is distinctive in this century not for the intensity of its homoerotic charge, but rather for the virulence of the homophobic prohibition by which that charge, once crystallized as an object of knowledge, is then denied *to* knowledge and hence most manipulably mobilized. In a knowledge regime that pushes toward the homosexual heightening of homosocial bonds, it is the twinning with that push of an equally powerful homophobia, and most of all the enforcement of cognitive impermeability between the two, that will represent the access of fascism" (50–51). At the same time, as I seek to flesh out the perhaps overly stark historical framework sketched in by Sedgwick here, and to examine in more depth the processes by which her assessment is corrected, I hope by the end of the chapter to have provided ammunition for Sedgwick's position. What I seek to demonstrate, however, is how a variation of Sedgwick's thesis also provides grounds for a whole tradition of homophobic the-

ory. In this tradition, the peculiarly fascist coupling of homophobia and the "homoerotic charge" will be taken as characteristic of
all homosexual desire: fascism will be homosexual desire in the (ineluctable) condition of self-hatred.

Similar concerns about the political valence of a hypermasculine
countertradition, indeed, form the focus of the work of Mackay,
whom I read in the next chapter as a literary complement to the
philosophy of masculinism just developed. Mackay is of interest
precisely because he challenges the glib assumptions about the political coding of hypermasculine—and tendentially misogynistic—
male-male desire. An anarchist—and the editor of the influential
writings of Max Stirner—Mackay shows how paederastic desire
not only persisted as a viable alternative to the newly hegemonic
models of homosexuality that sought to stigmatize it, but also provided a lifeline to an earlier, anti-fascist political tradition.

I follow the work on Mackay with a chapter on Lewis, in which
I seek to set the scene both for the theoretical conflation of homosexuality and fascism in the literary modernism of the 1920's
and 1930's and for a critique of a certain hegemonizing concern
with modernism within Anglo-American queer theory. This tendency has led to the suppression of an alternative avant-garde tradition. Taking up a suggestion from Lewis—who characterizes his
diversion to the transvestite bars of Berlin as an "Introduction for
the Anglo-Saxon reader"—I use this chapter as an introduction to
a neglected continental tradition for critics writing within the Anglo-American theoretical canon. I feel that it is important to demonstrate how the linkage of homosexuality and fascism is not lo-
calized in continental traditions nor limited in its importance to
an appreciation of those literary and intellectual traditions alone.

In her most recent collection of essays, *Tendencies*, Eve Sedgwick has pointed out perhaps more explicitly than anywhere else
in the corpus of an emergent queer theory the importance of queer
theory to the political history of the twentieth century, when she
writes that "it is a chief motive for the study of the epistemology of
the closet, as indeed it is part of its implicit axiomatic grounding,
that a defining feature of twentieth-century fascisms—fascisms past

and fascism perhaps to recur—will prove to have been a double ideological thrust along the axis of same-sex bonding or desire." Making explicit a claim that had only been hinted at and sketchily developed in her chapter on Nietzsche and Wilde in *Epistemology of the Closet*, Sedgwick frames, I think, the task I set myself in this work. For if the study of masculinist sexualities helps us to understand the construction—if not the "reality"—of fascism, a study of fascism will also elucidate the construction of male-male sexuality on which much of queer theory bases itself. Consequently, if Sedgwick at least hints at the importance of queer theory to an understanding of fascism, I seek in this book to follow the opposite trajectory: to demonstrate the importance of a study of fascism to the historical work of queer theory.

I most openly challenge what is rapidly becoming an established modernist critical tradition in queer theory in the chapter on Jarry, which is of importance for reasons already outlined above. This chapter provides a counterpart to the work on Mackay insofar as it emerges from an entirely different aesthetic tradition (although we should note that the French symbolist milieu was particularly receptive to the philosophy of anarchism) and yet complements Mackay in focusing on a paederastic model of homosexuality. If Mackay relativizes the tradition of Blüher by demonstrating how desire does not carry within it a necessary political valence, Jarry relativizes Mackay by demonstrating that desire cannot dictate a particular aesthetic position either. Developing in the chapter on Jarry a notion of the homosexual avant-garde, I engage most directly the mainstream of Anglo-American work on homosexuality and modernism.

Finally, I return in the concluding chapter to many of the concerns I have flagged in this chapter. Specifically, I examine the function of the trope of homosexuality in reestablishing national literary traditions after fascism's defeat in Europe. I will develop then in its fullest form the argument I have sought to outline briefly here and that informs the book in its entirety, namely, the function of homosexuality as an allegorical displacement, a representation—and, supposedly, resurrection—of fascism. Finally, I seek to understand the challenge that the homosexual seems to pose to the self-understanding of a political and historical theory invested in notions of a dialectic whose workings have always reflected an un–self-critical heterosexism.

Embarking, then, on this study of *Political Inversions*, let me say—if only to acknowledge a remarkable body of work with which I occasionally take issue only because it is consistently articulated in the most provocative and suggestive terms—that my starting point could be sketched in by Sedgwick's observation in *Tendencies* that "it should be unnecessary to say that the fantasy of Nazi homosexuality is flatly false; according to any definition of homosexuality current in our culture, only one Nazi leader, Ernst Röhm, was homosexual, and he was murdered by the SS on Hitler's direct orders in 1934. What seems more precisely to be true is that at any rate German fascism (like, in less exacerbated form, twentieth-century Western culture at large) emerged on a social ground in which 'the homosexual question' had been made highly salient" (49). By the conclusion of the second section of the book, I hope to have shown how the emergence of both cultural modernism and the political forms of fascism against the background of this heightening of "the homosexual question" allows us to trace—through a discourse on and about masculinist homosexuality—a direct ideological relation between fascism and modernism. This, indeed, was the project of my first book—*Fascist Modernism*—and here I seek to demonstrate how homosexuality has been instrumentalized to deny that troubling relation.

CHAPTER 2

The Frankfurt School
and the Political Pathology
of Homosexuality

> "Homosexuality" is not a problem for doctors; it is a political problem that touches every one of us. Any theoretical attempt to divorce homosexuality either from masculinity or from the fate of sexuality in general has to be seen as contributing to the *status quo* in which *specific* forms of homosexual practice are denounced and pathologized.
>
> Klaus Theweleit, *Male Fantasies*

The theoretical construction of fascism has been profoundly influenced by the writings of the Frankfurt School. Even when these writings are based on empirical sociological observation—as in the collective study of *The Authoritarian Personality*—they bear the imprint of the broader theoretical and philosophical interests that this School inevitably brought to bear on sociological questions. More specifically, it is in the writings on fascism—and on totalitarianism in general—that we can best observe the Frankfurt School's incorporation of Freudian theory into its overall analysis of the processes of reification and rationalization. In this chapter I wish to take a closer look at some of these writings in order to understand the way in which theoretical models of fascism derived from Frankfurt School categories presume a heterosexual normalcy. I will argue that in the psychopolitical writings of Adorno and Horkheimer homosexuality is pathologized as a potentially fascistic fascination with the erotics of power, and that fascism, in turn, is presented as a psychosexual manifestation of homosexual narcissism.

I aim neither to reconstruct a coherent "Frankfurt School theory" of homosexuality, nor to rehearse debates around the Freudian models on which any such tentative theory would be based. Nevertheless, it will be necessary in the course of the presentation to elaborate on Freud's treatment of narcissism, in order to contextualize the work of those such as Adorno on the libidinal attractions of fascism. While this all-too-brief detour through Freud on narcissism will further frame questions of mimesis to be treated subsequently in the chapter on Mackay, I shall return here to Freudian texts only in two instances: either where members of the Frankfurt School (and I mean Adorno, primarily) seek to account for both fascism and homosexuality from within the ambiguities of the Freudian models, or where Freud offers some clarification of the ideological moves being made in Frankfurt School political analysis. As to the possibility of concocting a "Frankfurt School theory" of homosexual desire, it requires only the most superficial knowledge of the contrasting work of, say, Adorno and Marcuse to demonstrate the futility of any such attempt. At the very least, one must acknowledge that there is as much disagreement among the intellectuals of the Frankfurt School on the etiology and ideological function of homosexuality as there is on the question of fascism itself.[1]

To confront the problem head-on, however, we can do no better than cite the barest statement of Adorno's position—to be found in *Minima Moralia*—namely, that "totalitarianism and homosexuality belong together" (46). I am interested in examining the involutions that this assertion will bring about in Adorno's mode of arguing, in his appropriation of Freud, and in the broader development of his political project. But I am further interested in the fact that homosexuality should ever be accorded so central—and dismissive—a role in the political thought of this otherwise rigorous critical theorist. Is there a particular historical urgency to the question of homosexuality? Is that urgency in any way related to the historical challenge that fascism poses to traditional models of political analysis? In broad terms, it will become clear that Adorno operates with two models of homosexuality, which, though often intertwined, can at least be contrasted heuristically. These two models will be exemplified on the one hand by *The Authoritarian Personality*—in which Adorno elaborates a theory of homo-fascism as effeminization—and on the other by the theories of homo-fascist narcissism pursued in many of Adorno's essays and in *Minima Moralia*. Of course, the traditional coding of narcissism as feminine makes it difficult to isolate the two models: the homosexual will be effeminized by his very narcissism. Nevertheless, I will seek to argue that it is the model of narcissism that is at once more nuanced and more insidious. Not only does it accord with the tradition of "masculinist" homosexual thought to be presented throughout this book; it also exercises a lasting influence on the political iconography of fascism.

In "The Tasks of a Critical Theory of Society," Habermas surveys the psychopolitical work of the first generation of the Frankfurt School and begins to offer a framework for understanding what I will call the pathological function of homosexuality in their thought. Observing trends in both psychology and the cultural environment in general, Habermas notes that "classical hysterias have almost died out; the number of compulsion neuroses is drastically reduced; on the other hand, narcissistic disturbances are on the increase. Christopher Lasch has taken this symptomatic change as the occasion for a diagnosis of the times that goes beyond the clinical domain" (88).[2] Without kowtowing to popular theories of a "culture of narcissism," it does seem that Habermas is responding to a sense of political crisis linked to the phenomenon of narcissism. In this somewhat revisionist analysis of the first generation of the Frankfurt School, Habermas further distinguishes between a "crisis" and a "pathology" in the analysis of social structures. He writes:

These *systemic disequilibria* become *crises* only when the performances of economy and state remain manifestly below an established level of aspiration and harm the symbolic reproduction of the lifeworld by calling forth conflicts and reactions of resistance there. . . . But when steering crises—that is, perceived disturbances of material reproduction—are successfully intercepted by having recourse to lifeworld resources, pathologies arise in the lifeworld. . . . Culture and personality come under attack for the sake of warding off crises and stabilizing society. Instead of manifestations of anomie (and instead of the withdrawal of legitimation and motivation in place of anomie), phenomena of alienation and the unsettling of collective identity emerge. (86–87)

In other words, a pathology is to be understood as a compensatory structure, that is, as a compensation at the cultural and psychological level for crises arising at the level of material reproduction. The question, of course, is whether homosexuality—understood as a manifestation of narcissism—can be understood as a pathology, or whether it is not, in fact, its demonization that is pathological and indicative of a legitimation crisis in theory. This is the issue I wish to keep in mind in turning now to Adorno, and to which I shall return by way of conclusion. I mean to suggest that the symptomatic (the masculinist Blüher will, in reference to Freud, call it "pathographic") reading of homosexuality in the Frankfurt School's classic analyses of fascism and late capitalism itself constitutes a pathological compensation for the steering crisis in their own overarching theory.[3]

Before entering, unprepared and tentative, into a thematics of homosexuality in Adorno's work, it is necessary, first of all, to reacquaint ourselves with the context of Frankfurt School thinking on fascism. In those writings that have since become canonical, such as *The Dialectic of Enlightenment*, the concern is to draw parallels between the totalitarian (rather than authoritarian) aspects of fascism and late capitalism, but the thinkers grouped under the umbrella of the Frankfurt School were, in fact, rather fractiously divided on the question of fascism: Pollock and Horkheimer tended to stress its similarities to the Soviet regime, while Neumann and

Kirchheimer emphasized the continuity between fascism and monopoly capitalism. This ambiguity, however, turns largely around questions of economic and political analysis. From a psychological perspective—the perspective that has been handed down in works such as *The Authoritarian Personality* and *Dialectic of Enlightenment*, as well as in Adorno's writings on the possibilities of aesthetic response—totalitarianism is understood as a structure that subtends both fascism and advanced capitalism in its "post-patriarchal" phase (that is, in the phase in which the mediating and authoritative function of the nuclear family has been discarded).[4]

As Habermas notes in the essay cited above, the reliance of the first generation of the Frankfurt School on models derived primarily from Freud's metapsychological writings presupposes the acceptance of an essentially Oedipal ontogenesis. Placing Frankfurt School psychoanalysis in the broader context of Marxist theory, Habermas points out how "for a psychoanalysis viewed from a Marxist standpoint, the theory of the Oedipus complex interpreted sociologically, was pivotal for explaining how the functional imperatives of the economic system could establish themselves in the superego structures of the dominant social character" (87). Although the sociology Habermas outlines here buys into the tenets of the Oedipal configuration and transmission of power, its contribution to Freudian theory consists in observing the effects of the *collapse* of the Oedipal personality in totalitarian and late capitalist societies. It is because their view of the individual is, essentially, Oedipal that thinkers such as Horkheimer and Adorno can perceive political crises as psychological pathologies. They start from Oedipal assumptions to reach what are, essentially, post-Oedipal conclusions. Paradoxically, such analyses chart the demise of the (Oedipal) social model that nevertheless underpins their own critical assumptions. It is not surprising, then, that the problematic of narcissism should be so central to the elaboration of a theory of homo-fascism, for even within the framework of Freud's own oeuvre narcissism constantly threatens the Oedipal narrative.[5]

The investment of a thinker such as Adorno in the bourgeois, heterosexual familial order is directly linked to his inability to think of political liberation in anything other than Oedipalized terms. In *Minima Moralia*, for example, he makes explicit his own ambiguous relation to the demise of the family which facilitates the passage from authoritarian bourgeois hegemony to totalitarian power, arguing that "with the family there passes away, while the system lasts, not only the most effective agency of the bourgeoisie, but also the resistances that, though repressing the individual, also strengthened, perhaps even produced him" (23). The result for society, he will contend, is that "today it is beginning to regress to a state versed, not in the Oedipus complex, but in parricide." Adorno's investment in the family is an investment in the Oedipal subject. Clearly, he observes a post-Oedipal cast to modern society's direct socialization: one might say that fascism is ushered in by the acting out of the Oedipal impulse, by the murder, that is, of the symbolic father.

In a tradition of German political thought that finds perhaps its most cogent and explicit elaboration in Hegel's *Philosophy of Right*, the family has represented an immediate unity that must be superseded by the synthetic, mediated unity of the State: but if the family is to be transcended in the State, it nevertheless prefigures that State. For Adorno, however, the totalitarian impetus behind the Hegelian State can at the same time be deferred by the model of nontotalitarian unity offered by the family—by what Hegel, indeed, calls "love." Psychologically, moreover, it is only within the family—for Adorno—that an autonomous subject capable of resisting the forces of totalitarian integration can be formed. In other words, the Oedipal family preforms authoritarian subjects, but *as* subjects, at least. The only resistance to a totalitarian Oedipus is Oedipal. Only when the mediating function of the supposedly immediate familial unity is bypassed—through a direct cathexis of social forces—is the structure of totalitarianism complete. Homosexuality—as a structure that short-circuits Oedipal subject formation—therefore necessarily poses the threat of totalitarian (non-)subjectivity for Adorno. Thus, he would read the attacks on the social and political function of the family to be encountered in the writings of masculinist philosophers and social theorists (in the next chapter) as clearly totalitarian in their anti-Oedipal intent. Only the mediation of the relation to the State through the family holds back the erotic from an immediate and fascisticized celebration of power itself.

For Adorno, then, the internalization of authority necessary both to the observance of the paternal interdiction and to the establishment of the autonomous subject has been replaced by a parricidal impulse that threatens the murderous individual no less than it does the social collective. The immediacy of desire's investment of existing power structures is figured as a parricide, as the rejection of the symbolic function of the father in the mediation of power. Without imposing on Adorno an anachronistically Lacanian frame, we might say that the historical murder of the father (a murder achieved in the proletarianization of labor and the displacement of the paterfamilias) represents the descent into a homosexually fascisticized politics of the imaginary. To this extent, then, fascist society figures as postpatriarchal: in fascist societies the socializing guilt for a crime never committed—the Oedipal parricide—is replaced by the guiltless act itself. Rather than acquiesce completely, however, to the patriarchal structures of bourgeois society as the sole guarantors of liberational potential, Adorno will resort—as we shall see—to the figure of an "archaic" pre-Oedipal, narcissistically cathected father figure. What I will argue is that the establishing of this figure obliges Adorno to invoke illegitimately— through an entirely anaclitic or "heterosexual" logic—the specter of homosexual narcissism as the origin of fascism. Homosexuality functions as a supplement to heterosexuality in Adorno's analysis of the political libido.

If Habermas notes that the Oedipal construct is crucial to the synthesis of Freudian and Marxist models in the work of the Frankfurt School, he is right only within certain strict limits: Adorno's analysis of narcissism threatens yet reinvokes the primacy of the Oedipal subject. At this point, however, I would like to present that line of thought in Adorno's work that does, in fact, rest on a clearly Oedipal foundation: his association of homo-fascism with emasculation and effeminization. With this aim, I will begin with perhaps the least satisfactory of Adorno's works on fascist psychology, a work completed in collaboration with others during his period of work in the United States. Based on a detailed program of empirical research, *The Authoritarian Personality* is in many ways less nuanced and more simplistic than the theoretical works on fascist narcissism to be examined later in the chapter.

Even the reference in the title to the structure of authoritarianism serves to de-differentiate the categories of authoritarian and totalitarian contrasted elsewhere in the Frankfurt School's psychopolitical studies. This potential blurring of focus is reflected in the Oedipal premise of the study, as outlined by Adorno's collaborator Else Frenkel-Brunswik:

> In the case of a man, it was important to learn whether there was at any time an explicit rebellion against the father and against what sort of father, or whether there was only passive submission. The assumption behind this question, later proved correct, was that the pattern developed in the relationship to the father tends to be transferred to other authorities and thus becomes crucial in forming social and political beliefs in man.   (315)

The Oedipal framework for the research could not be clearer, but the undialectical opposition of "rebellion" and "passive submission" obviously flies in the face of Adorno's recognition that resistance becomes possible only through submission to the paternal order of Oedipus. Submission—as we shall see in Adorno's presentation of the Oedipal configuration—itself harbors rebellious and aggressive traits (this much, at least, the study acknowledges); and, likewise, rebellion is itself the structural prerequisite of acquiescence to the patriarchal structure. The ontogenetic reenactment of phylogenetic collective guilt depends on the rebellious impulse. More than this, however, the assumption formulated above operates purely within the parameters of the Oedipal family: the question of rebellion and submission has been rendered familial, whereas Adorno's other writings deal precisely with the breakdown of the family as a machine for the construction of social identity. In other words, the Oedipalization—and homosexualization—of protofascism in *The Authoritarian Personality* depends on the mediational structure of the family even when it is the very absence of such mediation that will elsewhere be taken as the key to fascism.

Frenkel-Brunswik's stress on passive submission indicates the direction in which the analysis is to be pushed: any nuanced consideration of narcissistic structures is to be pushed aside by the discourse of passivity. In other words, fascism will be homosexualized by way of an effeminized passivity, rather than through an analysis of a putatively homosexual narcissism. In fact, this simplification of the narcissistic model outlined later in this chapter leads to a serious terminological difficulty in *The Authoritarian Personality*. Whereas Adorno and Horkheimer insist—in works such as *Dialectic of Enlightenment*—on the qualitative difference between a system of domination (authoritarianism), in which authority is exercised from outside the individual, and a system of power (totalitarianism), in which the principle of authority has been internalized, *The Authoritarian Personality* simply overlooks this distinction by analyzing protofascism in terms of domination rather than power. The slippage into passive submission is the nearest the analysis comes to explaining the movement from an authoritarianism—in which submission is necessary—to a totalitarianism—in which it has become superfluous. The analysis of totalitarianism fits more closely the structure of a narcissistic direct socialization, while the analysis of authoritarianism can more readily be reduced to questions of simple submission. Fascism figured as effeminization thus tends to push the Frankfurt School away from considerations of (narcissistic) totalitarianism toward a consideration of authoritarianism, thereby vitiating key political distinctions in their analysis.

Consonant with the re-Oedipalization of homosexuality (and fascism) in *The Authoritarian Personality* is the avoidance of questions of pre-Oedipal development suggested elsewhere in Adorno's work. For example, though the study first mentions homosexuality in the context of the pre-Oedipal structures of orality and anality, it is made clear that "the terms 'anality' and 'orality' do not refer here to the earlier psychogenetic stages but rather to special character syndromes found in the adult personality" (445). Consequently, it will be assumed that "the problem of homosexuality is related to the different ways of failure in resolving the Oedipal conflict and the resultant regression to earlier phases" (316) and that orality and anality are therefore merely retroconstructions of a failed Oedipal conflict. Clearly, in the retroactive (*nachträglich*) figuration of the pre-Oedipal here, the researchers vitiate one of their key tenets: since the homosexual fails to construct a fully coherent symbolic structure through which he might be fully socialized, it must necessarily be wrong to deal with orality and anality as symbolic terms. The orality or anality of the homosexual would result from a failure in ego formation that precluded the merely symbolic function of the term—unless, that is, anality or orality might themselves ground an alternative symbolic order.[6] Homosexuality is in every sense "reactionary": it is itself a reaction to Oedipus (a failure to resolve), and as a reaction it takes the form of a "reactionary" regression to pre-Oedipal stages of orality and anality. We always already begin from the position of an assumed Oedipal subjectivity.

Rather than accounting for political reaction from within the terms of a socioeconomic analysis (in which Adorno has, anyway, lost faith), this purely symbolic invocation of orality and anality displaces the rhetoric of progress onto the level of an ontogenetic development. I am arguing that *The Authoritarian Personality* reconstructs as ontogenesis a discredited political discourse of historical progress. In opposition to Adorno's directly political analyses, *The Authoritarian Personality* seeks to reinstate at the level of the individual psyche a historical trajectory of (heterosexual) progress threatened by both homosexuality and fascism. Having lost faith in the metanarrative of political perfectability, the researchers nevertheless seek to reinstate it at the level of the individual psyche as the narrative of the Oedipal subject's emergence. The frailty of this project, however, is indicated by the central yet supplementary role played by homosexual "failure." The homosexual failure negatively invokes a possibility of success that Adorno will consistently reject at the level of metanarrative: homosexual "failure" is the negative image of an impossible "success" in the historical formation of a political ego.

For all that the analysis of *The Authoritarian Personality* simplifies the question of narcissism in the direction of effeminization, however, some of the structural implications of Freud's analysis of narcissism remain in this work. The most troubling of these is the identification of homosexuality not with a wrong or misplaced object choice, but with a failure to cathect at all. Thus it is argued that "a lack of adequate heterosexual adjustment on the physical level is usually found together with inadequate object-relationships on the psychological level; it is manifested in a lack of fusion of sex and love, or in promiscuity, or in inhibition, or in a dependent and exploitative attitude toward the other sex" (318). The homophobia of the assertion is plain: homosexuality is a nonchoice rather than an alternative choice. Clearly, though, the work does not seek merely to denigrate homosexuality, but also to normalize heterosexuality. Sexual exploitation and promiscuity are presented as abnormal rather than as possibilities encoded in our cultural construction of "normal" heterosexual desire. Thus, the study will ultimately conclude that the "high-scorers" (i.e., those who score highly on the indicators of authoritarian tendencies) demonstrate "a lack of individuation and of real object relationship" (404) typical of the homosexual in Freud's analysis. The homosexual is derealized: he is not a subject because he lacks a real object.

The "lack of fusion of sex and love" detailed here recalls both Adorno's assertion (in *Negative Dialectics*) that in the religion of fascism "the mitigating impact of the religious doctrine of love vanished" and Hegel's linkage of the family to the unmediated affect of love. In his *Philosophy of Right*, Hegel sees in marriage the dialectical resolution of the pure immediacy of "love" and the merely formal, contractual relations between members of civil society. Thus, one marries not for love (for this is mere immediacy), but one must learn to love in order to affirm the "contractual" social relation as something whose reality transcends that contract. Marriage makes a contractual relation socially and politically real, while at the same time providing an affective and intellectual reality to a social abstraction. With respect to Adorno, I am arguing, in effect, that the lack of "love" in his presentation of homosexuality short-circuits any such dialectic. The subjectivity of the homosexual is purely contractual, and the type of contract he makes is, ultimately, sadomasochistic in a way that a whole tradition of enlightened contract theory would abhor. The subjectivity of the Other becomes a mere device for the purely formal, abstract postulation of my own subjectivity; but in acting on this recognition—by sadistically crushing the subjectivity of the Other in erotic enslavement—I necessarily derealize myself. To this extent, homosexual desire is always—yet never—actualized. Promiscuity—which serves in Adorno's presentation as an ambiguous alternative to and/or synonym for homosexuality—uncouples sex and love in the same way that fascism uncouples libido and love in its channeling of social urges. It sunders the ethical progression from familial to constitutional bonds. At this point Adorno nevertheless seems to revert to the very Hegelianism he would seek to resist.

Homosexuality—in its authoritarian guise—seems to consist less in a wrong object choice, then, than in a failure to cathect. To students of Freud there will be nothing new in this. Insofar as *The Authoritarian Personality* organizes its analysis around the Oedipal conflict, it will do so with reference primarily to questions of (non-)identification rather than object choice since, as we have seen, no actual object is chosen. Homosexuality and fascism both threaten the logic of (desiring) identity on which the bourgeois political subject is based. Thus for example, Frenkel-Brunswik will analyze homo-fascism as an "underlying ego-alien identification with the opposite sex parent's role" (444). But if the process of identification designates the modality of the ego's formation, how can any identification be classified as "ego-alien"? The assumption is that masculinity and femininity confer characteristics of ego identity prior to the process of identification—for only in this sense could a "mistaken" identification be "ego-alien."

The Oedipal configuration—in which object choice and identification facilitate each other through a play of gender—has been reduced, with the falling away of the object, to a frantic struggle for alternative strategies of identification. Indeed, the undialectical understanding of object choice in its relations to identification (and vice versa) fundamentally prejudices the analyst's reading of respondents. At crucial points the analysis presented is guilty of arguing for its own hypotheses even where those hypotheses are proven false. Thus, for example, it is assumed that a "low-scorer" (i.e., one who scores low on all the indicators of authoritarian personality structure) "will reveal evidence of the normal trend of having more cathexis on the parent of the opposite sex. This would be in line with his more clear-cut heterosexual attitude" (452–53). The assumption from the outset is that the nonauthoritarian personality will be heterosexual. This may be objectionable, but it is nevertheless a perfectly acceptable and falsifiable hypothesis. However, when the hypothesis is, indeed, empirically falsified, Frenkel-Brunswik immediately seeks to recontain the simplistic homo-/ hetero-, fascist/antifascist dichotomy, by explaining that "due perhaps to the insufficient material on this score, or to the fact that the crucial difference has to be sought in the way of handling— rather than in the mere presence or absence—of the normal resolution of the Oedipal situation, this anticipated difference did not turn out to be statistically significant" (453). In other words, one of the key assertions of the study is statistically insignificant! Although it is possible that Frenkel-Brunswik's excuses are valid, at no point does she acknowledge that the hypothesis might just be wrong. It is in passages such as these that *The Authoritarian Personality* begins to read as a sustained attempt to pathologize homosexuality and homosexualize fascism.

Since we are dealing with an empirical analysis we might further examine the role played by the questionnaire in shaping the ultimate typology of the authoritarian personality, for *The Authoritarian Personality* attempts even in the questions it poses to reassert a heterosexual normalcy over and against the psychosexual perversions of homosexualized fascism. It is clear from the presentation of methodology that the authoritarian personality is consistently assumed to be masculine, despite the inclusion of women in the analysis. Thus, for example, Frenkel-Brunswik outlines the key familial questions to be posed to the respondents and adds that "considerations analogous to those made in the preceding paragraphs were also applied to women" (316). Although this aside clearly indicates the androcentrism of the analysis, it is also important to note that the movement toward an analysis of effeminization in male respondents necessarily leads to a marginalization of actual female respondents, for whom the model of effeminization clearly cannot hold (unless the feminine psyche is assumed to be fascistic from the outset). In the retroactive construction of a sex-political stereotype, it would seem that the effeminate male proves more useful than the masculine female. Fascisticization lies not in gender—masculine or feminine—but in the transgression of gender supposedly enacted in male homosexuality.

It is most important to insist that these problems in the questionnaire reflect more than my concern with a certain empirical methodology in its concrete form: in many instances the questions demonstrate the ways in which the openness of the researchers is, in fact, a mere pretense, covering assumptions that have already been made. This becomes particularly clear with regard to Frenkel-Brunswik's—shall we say "generous"?—contention that it is not homosexuality per se that is the problem, but rather "the way of handling" homosexuality as a possible resolution of the Oedipal conflict. Thus, she will demonstrate more explicitly elsewhere how

> again and again it became evident that the difference between the ethnocentric and the non-ethnocentric extremes hinges more on the rejection vs. the acceptance of such depth factors as homosexuality, or aggression, or passivity, or anality than it does on the mere presence or absence of one or another of these tendencies. In other words, it was not primarily the relative strength of such tendencies that seemed to matter, but rather the way in which these tendencies were handled in the motivational dynamics of the subject in question. (442)

I wish to spend some time on what might otherwise seem to be a simple question of methodology because we encounter here for the first time a rhetorical structure to be repeated time and again in materials covered in this book: namely, the contention that it is

not homosexuality itself but *repressed* homosexuality that is indicative of authoritarian and protofascist sympathies.

This move is important not for the way in which it apparently
shies away from a blanket identification of homosexuality with fascism, but rather for the way it further consolidates that identification by a series of moves that will become all too familiar by the
end of this book. As the basis for an argument against what Marcuse would call "surplus repression," against the fascistic and fascis-
ticizing structures of homophobia, the modification envisaged here
might be of value. The contention, however, seems to provide no
such basis. There are two reasons for this, I would contend. First,
the essentially positivist structure of the empirical research blinds
the analysis to its own complicity in the structures it seeks to uncover. Rather than merely pointing out the existence of repressive
structures, the analysis tends to replicate them in its own methodology. A clear example of this complicity can be found in the "Suggested Direct Questions" provided for interviewers probing the
crucial area of sex. They read as follows:

> Where did you get your sex instruction?
> What is the earliest sex experience you can remember?
> How important is sex in marriage?
> What main difficulties have you found in married life?
> Have you met many homosexuals in your travels?   (319)

The studied indirection of this final "direct question" is startling
and should be taken as indicative of something more than a
methodological weakness of the study. Homosexuality is figured
as something one encounters rather than something one experiences: no homosexual subject is envisaged. If the researchers are
interested primarily in questions of how homosexual tendencies
are handled, they can envisage in their questions only one way of
handling them: repression and/or projection. Moreover, if this direct question is intended merely as a lead into a questioning of the
interviewee's own homosexual experiences, then it already places
those experiences under a sign of negation. Homosexuality will
never be direct, but always indirect, something one must be tricked
into. In other words, the questioning both reinforces a system of

repression it holds responsible for the fascistic distortion of homosexual desire and assumes that such desire is always already distorted and indirect—always, in other words, potentially fascistic. If only repressed homosexuality is fascistic, all homosexuality is repressed.

This problem at the level of methodology (a problem we must assume to be fundamental to the assumptions of the analysis, rather than a mere glitch in the wording of a questionnaire) is replicated structurally at the level of argument. A further collaborator, R. Nevitt Sanford, builds on Frenkel-Brunswik's hypothesis regarding repressed or "mis-handled" homosexuality to explain the structure of authoritarian submission. He writes of one protofascist "high-scorer" that "one might say that his only recourse in the face of what he conceived to be the father's irresistible power was to submit—and then to gain a sense of adequacy by participating psychologically in the father's power. This, in the last analysis, is the homosexual solution of the Oedipus problem. It is not surprising, therefore, to find in Mack's T.A.T. productions clear indications of his fear of homosexual attack" (798). What Nevitt Sanford claims here of homosexuality describes instead, I would contend, the structure of homosocial patriarchy. The submission that empowers is precisely the socializing submission that Oedipus makes possible: it is not intrinsically homosexual, and can be understood as such only on the basis of an undialectical reading of the relationship of rebellion to submission. Thus, the fear of homosexual attack experienced by the protofascistic respondent, Mack, might best be understood in terms of what Eve Sedgwick has aptly termed a "homosexual panic" on the part of the heterosexual who must acknowledge his own passage through a ritual of "passivity" (and implicit effeminization) in the introjection of the paternal law.

There is more to the assertion than this, however. Clearly, the allusion is to the effeminization model of homosexuality: passive submission to authority is effeminate and therefore homosexual. The argument will continue as follows: "In so far as authoritarian submission is a means for overcoming weakness it stands as a kind of defense against the underlying homosexual submission and passivity: it remains to be pointed out that this surface trend offers at the same time gratification for these very same needs" (804). I wish to concentrate on this passage, for it, too, displays in a particularly clear form a structure of argumentation that we will see repeated again and again with regard to homo-fascism. If the structure of questioning in *The Authoritarian Personality* sets forth and reinforces the repression of homosexuality that supposedly grounds fascism, this passage takes the argument a step further by arguing that the homosexual never submits: that the homosexual desire *for* submission, in other words, ensures that the homosexual will live out his erotic fantasies even when (and precisely because) he renounces them.

The argument is insidious. Authoritarian submission is at first an escape from homosexual submission: I submit to authority in order that it regulate in me the submissive homosexual impulses I can no longer regulate myself. But as a submission, this acceptance of authority is itself intrinsically homosexual in its passivity: in order to repress my homosexual urges, I must become a homosexual. In other words, the very structures the homosexual inhabits in his denial of homosexuality are themselves homosexual. Thus, while authoritarian submission supposedly sublimates homosexual desires, it in fact offers an immediate gratification of those very desires. Homosexuality (in its specifically "fascist" form) thus figures as a direct—rather than merely sublimated—investment in the structures of power. Moreover, it is always already repressed and self-repressing: or, more accurately, it is capable of drawing pleasure from a structure of repression experienced as submission. Consequently, the argument that it is not homosexuality per se but merely repressed homosexuality that is authoritarian no longer holds: homosexuality is at home in its repression. Structured as it is around a fundamental submission, homosexuality experiences the renunciation of its desire as desirable; and homosexuality—as a potential identity structure—is based on an authoritarian repression of the desires it supposedly denotes.

Clearly, this play of repression and the satisfaction it paradoxically provides will tie homosexuality to the paradigm of sado-masochism in Adorno's model; and it is in a consideration of sado-masochism in *Minima Moralia* that the infamous identification of homosexuality and fascism occurs. Whereas Marcuse is able to distinguish between an SS officer and two consenting adults playing at power, the difference between such scenarios dwindles into insignificance within Adorno's model of homosexuality as the eroticization—one might say, aestheticization—of power.[7] It is through this paradigm of the sadomasochistic relationship—a paradigm that becomes unavoidable once the criterion of submission has been invoked as the mark of homosexual desire—that Adorno opens up his analysis of effeminization into a more nuanced reflection on narcissism. The assertion that "totalitarianism and homosexuality belong together" is framed in *Minima Moralia* by a consideration of the dialectics of effeminacy—the phenomenon of what Adorno calls the "Tough Baby"—in which hypermasculinity (a phenomenon Adorno does not really confront elsewhere in his passing considerations of homosexuality) is presented as effeminate, and gender, in turn, is arranged around the axiom of sexual power. This passage is of particular interest for the way in which it confronts precisely the form of "masculinist" homosexual tradition being dealt with here, by reducing it to a form of effeminacy. Adorno makes this move in the following terms: "He-men are thus, in their own constitution, what film-plots usually present them to be, masochists. At the root of their sadism is a lie, and only as liars do they truly become sadists, agents of repression. This lie, however, is nothing other than repressed homosexuality presenting itself as the only approved form of heterosexuality" (46).

As I think this quote makes clear, Adorno's strictly dichotomous—heterosexual—presentation of gender relations is necessarily replicated in the field of sexuality by an inescapable sadomasochism: if sexuality is the realm in which gender relations are definitively established along a subject-object axis, then Adorno will be predisposed to view sexuality in terms of submission and domination. In other words, I am not accusing Adorno of homophobia in any casual sense—although I would!—but rather I am arguing that he instrumentalizes homosexuality to lay bare what in fact lies at the basis of his strictly heterosexual view of sexuality. Since the domination-submission dyad can no longer be mapped onto the male-female opposition, it is—so to speak—denaturalized, estranged. Adorno is homophobic not—or not only—in his evaluation of the homosexual, but in his very formulation of the homosexual as category.

If homosexuality acts as estrangement here—a mirror in which heterosexual relations confront and displace themselves—Adorno goes further by mapping the sadomasochistic dichotomy onto the opposition hetero-/homo- rather than masculine/feminine. Submission is no longer just feminine, it is homosexual—as masochism—and domination is not just masculine, but rather—as sadism—heterosexual. Or so it seems. For in a remarkable move Adorno situates *homo*sexuality at the origin and presents heterosexuality—in its necessarily sadomasochistic form—as a displacement and elaboration of homosexual libido. The logic seems to run as follows: heterosexual sadism is grounded in a homosexual masochism, a desire that desires to renounce itself, but that—in renunciation—acts out the anger of renunciation as sadism. This is a doubled sadism, fueled by the (homosexual) pleasure in renunciation and the (equally homosexual) frustration at that renunciation. In its very fulfillment (which is to say, in its self-renunciation) homosexual desire will always be frustrated desire. It is precisely because he is not a sadist (but rather a masochist) that the homosexual will be particularly sadistic: on the one hand because he vents his frustration at renouncing his own masochistic desire, but on the other because he in fact desires that renunciation, taking pleasure in the sadistic role he masochistically allows to have forced on him in his guise as a "Tough Baby." The homosexual is a sadist because he must merely act the sadism of heterosexuality: his sadism is fueled by a frustration at the renunciation of primary masochistic desires.[8] The logic of *Minima Moralia* is—quite literally—inescapable: even protofascist heterosexual he-men are, ultimately, homosexual.

Adorno's use—in the passage quoted above—of the film actor as an example of the homosexual hypermasculine is important, for it would seem to be the very act of mimesis that effeminizes: the hyperbole of the actor marks his difference from actual masculinity. For Adorno homosexuality is intrinsically performative, acting itself out in the performance of something else: heterosexuality. Identified with false mimesis—or with the troubling suspicion that *all* mimesis is false—homosexual desire acquires its specificity in its ability—and, indeed, its eagerness—to masquerade as something else. In effect, Adorno is ontologizing the condition of repression: the desire that is repressed is at the same time a (mimetic) desire *for* repression, a desire for representation as repression. For all the differences dividing their positions on the question of modernity and de-auraticized art, one can almost sense in Adorno's implicit line of argument here the resurgence of a commonplace from Benjamin's "Work of Art" essay, namely, the assertion that "fascism sees its salvation in giving these masses not their right, but instead a chance to express themselves" (241). Homosexuality—in its desire for normalization—seeks to become heterosexuality; it seeks expression—through submission to the symbolic structure of heterosexuality—rather than its "rights" in the form of pleasure.

Naturally, homosexuality will lend itself handily to any form of political expression once this basic tenet of Adorno's analysis has been grasped: it lies in the very nature of homosexuality to lie, to present itself as heterosexuality. Of course, Adorno hereby identifies homosexuality with a specifically philosophical as well as a political problem. The homosexual is a liar (specifically, in masquerading as a protofascistic, sadistic heterosexual), which is to say that he "is" not at all. For the truth of the homosexual cannot be reduced to the ontology of his desire, which is irreducibly other in its submissiveness. There is no desire grounding the homosexual, and thus the entire structure of this psychopolitics begins to crumble. The homosexual reveals that desire is not identity, he celebrates in mimesis not the adequation and channeling of desire, but its displacement. "In the end," Adorno will conclude in *Minima Moralia*,

> the tough guys are the truly effeminate ones, who need the weaklings as their victims in order not to admit that they are like them. Totali-

tarianism and homosexuality belong together. In its downfall the subject negates everything which is not of its own kind. The opposites of
the strong man and the compliant youth merge in an order which asserts unalloyed the male principle of domination. In making all without exception, even supposed subjects, its objects, this principle becomes totally passive, virtually feminine.   (46)

This passage is of interest for more than its straightforward homophobic logic; in it homosexuality is figured as a threat to an entire philosophy of consciousness thought through the prism of desire. Homosexuality is totalitarian by "making all without exception, even supposed subjects, its objects." Effeminization, in other
words, means the effacement of the subject position traditionally
figured as masculine. Thus, homosexual desire is not only sadistic
in its antipathy to any object cathexis and in its destructive impulses toward those objects forced on it: it is equally destructive
of the (male) subject position. Adorno has effectively deconstructed—in a characteristically homophobic manner—the primacy
of heterosexuality to present homosexuality as the definitive historical mode of social libido under late capitalism and fascism. The
result of this, however, is the downfall of the very category of the
subject. The homosexual is therefore not the subject of desire or
the subject of a political ideology (fascism), but the negation of
political subjectivity. In other words, Adorno is forced to hypostatize the homo-fascist subject only as a way of invoking the collapse of political subjectivity in general. There are fascists because
there "are" no homosexuals: or alternatively, there are fascists because there are *only* homosexuals, *only* "mimetic" rather than ontological subjects.

At the same time, however, we begin to note Adorno's move in
this passage toward the second—narcissistic—paradigm of homosexuality. Philosophical and libidinal narcissism—already implicit
in the collapse of the subject-object relation, and the homosexual
failure to cathect—is figured in a quite specific and seemingly in-
appropriate form of homosexual relation: narcissism emerges here
not from an ideal of effeminized androgyny, but from within the
very heart of masculinist paederasty. If I began this chapter by as-

serting that Adorno finds himself caught between two (not unrelated) models of homosexuality—one defined in terms of narcissism, and the other in terms of effeminization—in the passage just cited we can begin to see the ways in which these two models are intertwined. Adorno's analysis of "the strong man and the compliant youth" articulates a differentiated understanding of homosexuality, in which differences of age and power replace differences of gender. In short, the paederastic model is reformulated in terms of its homology to gender roles, to active and passive defined in terms of masculine and feminine (or effeminate). However, Adorno's observation that "the opposites of the strong man and the compliant youth *merge* in an order that asserts unalloyed the male principle of domination" (my emphasis) marks a historical mutation in his presentation of homosexuality, a mutation he links retrospectively to fascism's assertion of the "unalloyed . . . male principle of domination." The paederastic differential of young and old, strong and compliant has been replaced by a narcissistic self-contemplation in which such differences remain, but are glossed over. In other words, the de-differentiation described by Sedgwick—specifically, the disappearance of paederasty into narcissistic models of homosexuality based on similarity—is only completed, for Adorno, in fascism.[9]

Taken in the context of Adorno's writing on the similarities and differences of capitalism and fascism, we might say that the movement from paederasty to narcissism parallels a movement from a hierarchical system of social domination (erotically coded as sadomasochism) to the totalitarian indifference of the political subject (coded as narcissism). I would like to use this pivotal passage from *Minima Moralia*—a text from which one so often gleans anecdotal indications of the broader structure of Adorno's thought —as a segue into the consideration of Adorno's refiguring of a Freudian narcissistic paradigm of homosexuality. Having deferred any direct consideration of Freud's various writings on narcissism thus far, however, I feel it is only possible to effect this transition by way of Freud; for Adorno's hidden agenda in the passages just cited—his rearguard action on behalf of the embattled (male) sub-

ject of both desire and consciousness—can be traced back directly
to Freud.

In his seminal essay "On Narcissism: An Introduction" (*Standard Edition* 14: 69–102) Freud presents narcissism as a modality of desire opposed to the anaclitic desire that proceeds from relations of need and dependence to bonds of affection. "According to the narcissistic type," Freud argues, a person may love

(a) what he himself is (i.e., himself),
(b) what he himself was,
(c) what he himself would like to be,
(d) someone who was once part of himself.   (90)

Even at this early stage in the development of the concept Freud takes time out to observe that "the significance of narcissistic object choice for homosexuality in men" deserves particular attention—attention he devotes to it in his study of Leonardo and elsewhere. I wish to focus at this point, however, on a rhetorical and logical figure that will become crucial in Adorno's subsequent conflation of homosexuality and fascism. I mean, of course, the fundamental distinction between anaclisis and narcissism, which Adorno will necessarily confuse in his construction of homofascism.

Anaclitic object choice arises from the fact that "the sexual instincts are at the outset attached to the satisfaction of the ego instincts" (87): simplified somewhat, it is a sexualization of ego instincts, whereby the life-sustaining importance of figures such as the mother provides a basis for sexual object choice. Narcissistic object choice, meanwhile is typical of "people whose libidinal development has suffered some disturbance, such as perverts and homosexuals" and those who "have taken as a model not their mother but their own selves" (88). Freud will subsequently code these forms of attachment in terms of gender, arguing that "complete object-love of the attachment type is, properly speaking, characteristic of the male" (88). Already explicit in Freud's presentation of narcissism as the origin of homosexuality, then, is a gendered narrative, in which the homosexual engages in a feminine mode of object choice.

Freud insists, however, that he is not proposing a strict di-chotomy: "We may say that a human being has originally two sex-ual objects—himself and the woman who nurses him—and in do-ing so we are postulating a primary narcissism in everyone, which may in some cases manifest itself in a dominating fashion in his object-choice" (88). This controversial introduction of the con-cept of primary narcissism obviously has an impact on any desire to stigmatize either a gender or a sexual preference as narcissistic (and for Freud—though the terms are primarily descriptive—nar-cissism clearly is a stigma, the sign of a disturbance or an immatu-rity).[10] Heterosexual, male object love of the attachment type is it-self a derivative of "the child's original narcissism" (88). Freud, then, will be obliged to go beyond any simple dichotomy of nar-cissism and anaclisis to examine how an original narcissism is dif-ferently developed in homo- and heterosexual subjects.

Throughout the essay "On Narcissism," the dyad narcissism-anaclisis will run parallel to two others: feminine-masculine, and homosexual-heterosexual. These binary oppositions consistently break down, however, as Freud is led to assert homosexual un-derpinnings to heterosexuality and heterosexual origins for ho-mosexuality. In fact, prior to the narcissism paper, Freud's first ref-erence to this concept is to be found in the context of any early developmental explanation of inversion. In a note made in 1910 to the original text of 1905, Freud observes how

> in all the cases we have examined we have established the fact that the future inverts, in the earliest years of their childhood, pass through a phase of very intense but short-lived fixation to a woman (usually their mother), and that, after leaving this behind, they identify themselves with a woman and take themselves as their sexual object. That is to say, they proceed from a narcissistic basis, and look for a young man who resembles themselves, whom they may love as their mother loved them. (*Standard Edition* 7: 145)

This curious passage articulates the parallel operation of homo-phobia and misogyny in Freud's texts through the synthetic dis-course of heterosexism. Most striking in the passage is the way in which the immediacy of homosexual desire is necessarily denied:

homosexuality, here, is the product of a heterosexual phantasm—
at no point in this etiology does a person love a person of the same
sex. At the moment of the homosexual's love for a younger boy,
he is himself already a woman (his own phantasmatic mother). Homosexuality, then, is but a parody (indeed, an inversion, since the
boy becomes his own mother) of an Oedipalized heterosexual love
relationship. Moreover, the impetus to narcissism was a heterosexual overvaluation of the mother. In Freud's presentation, the
homosexual actually emerges from an overly intense heterosexual
bond. This intensity, it would seem, is what precipitates his narcissistic identification—as if the child could not envisage offering
himself so completely to a (m)other and must therefore become
the one to whom he entrusts himself. Narcissism, then, would not
be in its origin homosexual, but—quite the reverse—rabidly heterosexual. Male homosexuality emerges, we might say, from the
child's fear of engulfment, and as a stabilizing gesture in which the
boy regains the subject position in desire.[11]

Woman's narcissism, meanwhile, is treated as a gender characteristic.[12] The passages where Freud insists on—or simply takes for
granted as a cultural commonplace—the narcissism of women are
numerous; but I would like to show how that line of thinking enters into Freud's presentation of male sexuality in the passage I
have just cited. Thus, for example, there is a moment of ambiguity in this passage, when Freud writes of the homosexuals that
"they identify themselves with a woman and take themselves as
their sexual object." On the surface, Freud seems to be saying that
the child identifies with the mother and takes his former self as a
love-object, and that the identification with the mother would be
no more than an expedient toward self-love—one identifies with
the mother in order to love the self. At the same time, however,
it is clear that for Freud the very desire to love oneself is itself already a symptom of the boy's identification with the mother; such
narcissism is already feminine. When "they identify themselves with
a woman and take themselves as their sexual object," the act of
identification is not simply an expedient that enables the process
of self-love: the process of self-love is the very modality of identi-

fication. They love themselves—in the same way that women love themselves—in order to love themselves. It becomes almost undecidable whether the homosexual effeminizes in order to realize his narcissism, or becomes narcissistic in order to become a woman. To this extent, then, we can see how models we have set up as potentially dichotomous in Adorno's presentation of homofascism—narcissism and effeminization—can, in fact, be reconciled through Freud's identification of femininity and narcissism.

If women are intrinsically narcissistic, the effects of this feminine narcissism on heterosexual masculine desire are no less interesting. In the essay "On Narcissism" Freud asserts that "such women have the greatest fascination for men, not only for aesthetic reasons, since as a rule they are the most beautiful, but also because of a combination of interesting psychological factors. (For it seems very evident that another person's narcissism has a great attraction for those who have renounced part of their own narcissism and are in search of object-love)" (89). For reasons that should become clear throughout this book, this passage describing the heterosexual male's desire for the narcissistic female is extremely important, and we should take some time to unravel what is a rather complicated relationship. Women, we are to assume, are narcissistic; men alone are capable of object love. However, the motivation for the masculine, anaclitic object love specified here is itself a narcissistic attraction. Man desires—to cite one of Freud's defining categories—"what he himself was," or even, one might say, "what he himself would like to be," namely, a self-sufficient, narcissistic desiring machine. Man's desire for the narcissistic woman is fired by the desire to regain his own lost (primary) narcissism. Rather than narcissism causing a love of the self, here it causes a love of that other that embodies a lost part of the self (as, indeed, it did in the homosexual paederastic model). The homosexual loves the self that his mother once loved; the heterosexual loves the self that he himself once loved. Only by suppressing this specifically heterosexual narcissistic desire for one's own lost narcissism can Freud allow his gender structure to stand. If the homosexual desires as a woman would (both in terms of object choice

—a man/boy—and in terms of modality—i.e., narcissistically), the heterosexual desires as only a man can (true object choice), and his love object is a woman.

Homosexual desire, in Freud's model, would be a desire in which the subject—*as subject*—identifies with a woman (his mother). This is what seems too radical for Freud to countenance—the homosexual's introduction of the feminine into the position of subject of desire. Heterosexual desire, meanwhile, would be a desire in which the subject identifies himself with a woman only as object. In both cases, a man experiences desire for himself: in both cases, that narcissistic desire is heterosexualized—the difference lies in the casting of this particular drama, and in the play of temporality it involves. Homosexually, I—as desiring subject in the present—identify with a woman in order to love my past self as a boy (homosexuality is essentially differentiated as paederasty even at the heart of those passages where Freud is describing the narcissistic "de-differentiation" of which Sedgwick writes). Heterosexually, I—as a desiring subject in the present—identify with a man in order to love a woman, who is the representative of my past (narcissistic) self. In homosexuality, it is the male subject—in the present—who is a woman: in heterosexuality, it is the male object—in the past—who is a woman. Heterosexuality, therefore, is a structure of desire that not only affirms the unassailability of the male gender in the here and now, but that also denies to women access to the position of desiring subject.

To conclude this diversionary return to Freud: within the narcissistic paradigm the homosexual is homosexual not in terms of his object choice itself (as gender) but in terms of the subject position he takes up in that choice (i.e., the male homosexual is homosexual not simply because he desires men, but because he desires narcissistically, and because—in order to do so—he must occupy a feminine—or maternal—subject position). But the heterosexual also desires narcissistically—and, indeed, homosexual desire is itself but a response to an originally overcathected heterosexual attachment to the mother. In narcissistically desiring the lost narcissistic self (embodied by the woman) the heterosexual merely fails in what the homosexual phantasmatically succeeds at— a closure of the narcissistic wound. Both the heterosexual and the homosexual partake of a narcissistic desire, and in both the male is identified at some stage of the desiring displacement with a woman. The ultimate difference, it would seem, is that the homosexual identifies with the woman as a subject, whereas the heterosexual identifies with her as an object. One might say that the homosexual becomes a woman in order to desire (to be) a man. The heterosexual desires a woman in order to become (whole through) her, to find his narcissistic image in her.

In other words, narcissism is the very structure that deconstructs the complementary relationship of object choice to subject position. The homosexual posits himself as entire but other—the heterosexual experiences himself split, yet immanent (in his own desire). I desire—as a homosexual—to identify with my object choice: I choose—as a heterosexual—to dramatize the narcissistic split in my identity through the act of object choice. The heterosexual desire for the narcissistic female introduces the mechanisms of narcissism into the otherwise anaclitic desire of heterosexuality: the heterosexual male desires such a woman not as a result of an Oedipal displacement of desire for the mother, but as a reflection of his own earlier (renounced) narcissistic desire for himself. What differentiates the homosexual from the heterosexual, then, would be the passage of desire through the subject position of the mother.

We should keep in mind the convolutions of this structure— in which heterosexual desire for the narcissistic self-desire of the woman is itself understood as narcissism on the male's part—as we turn now to Adorno's analysis of the putatively homosexual mass cathexis of the narcissistic *Führer*. Our diversion through Freud will prove important because we will encounter the same slippage of homo- and hetero-, anaclisis and narcissism, in the Frankfurt School analysis of narcissistic homo-fascism. In the passages we have been dealing with, Freud demonstrates how structures

Adorno will insist on as homosexual are, in fact, heterosexual. Adorno's avoidance of this fact is typical of his willful and systematic identification of homosexuality and fascism.

In the essay "Freudian Theory and the Pattern of Fascist Propaganda," for example, Adorno is quite explicit about the direction in which he wishes to advance Freud's theory of mass political behavior. Seeking to explain the urge to conformity within mass political movements, he refers to Freud, who in turn refers to Mac-Dougall for the recognition that in mass political movements "it is a pleasurable experience for those who are concerned to surrender themselves so unreservedly to their passions and thus to become merged in the group and to lose the sense of the limits of their individuality" (122). In terms of Adorno's binary construction of homo-fascism—narcissism and effeminization—the rhetoric of surrender forwarded here will have become familiar from the earlier equation of submission and effeminization. It is in this essay, however, that we can perhaps best observe the way in which the effeminization hypothesis feeds into the more nuanced and far-reaching analysis of the homosexual narcissism supposedly at the root of fascism. We will recall that for Adorno, even as the homosexual surrenders his desire, he in fact acts it out—as a desire *to* surrender. What is surrendered is no longer simply desire alone, however, but the cognitive identity of the desiring male subject: by becoming a woman, the fascist *Massenmensch* becomes nobody—becomes a homosexual. Homosexual effeminization therefore involves a loss of identity.

What, now, is the nature of this homosexual surrender? If, according to MacDougall, the members of mass-political movements "surrender themselves so unreservedly to their passions," is it the passion itself that is—substantively—a homosexual passion, or the act of surrender to that passion that enacts—structurally—homosexual desire? Is homosexuality, in other words, being invoked as an object-specific desire, or as a modality of desire? What I seek to argue is that Adorno systematically operates between these two possibilities to set up a double bind wherein homosexual desire is always already necessarily protofascistic. In essence, at those mo-

ments where he denies that homosexuality (surrendering to another man) is fascistic, he falls back on the notion that passion itself (or surrendering to one's passions) is homo-fascistic. Surrender
and submission undergo a crucial mutation here: on the one hand
they signify the surrender *of* desire to the immediate demands of
the socius, while on the other they signify the surrender *to* desire, despite the interests of the socius. Homosexuality seems to
reveal something dangerous—and, again, something culturally
identified with the feminine—in the very nature of all passion.
Thus, while Adorno seems to argue that it is the repression and
false sublation of homosexual desire that is dangerous, he inevitably
argues at other points that it is *un*repressed desire (homosexual
desire for surrender) that is dangerous. The homosexual is a fascist because he is repressed—and a fascist because he is not repressed enough!

Clearly, the conflation of homosexuality and femininity does
not provide the sole ground on which Adorno bases his homosexualization of fascism in this essay. According to Adorno it is in
his analysis of the narcissistic structure of mass identification that
Freud truly moves beyond previous theorists of psychopolitics.
Notwithstanding the cultural identification of narcissism with the
feminine psyche (an identification to which Freud's work stands
witness), it should be pointed out that the effeminization model
and the narcissism model are not seamlessly compatible in the
analysis Adorno provides here. In fact he invokes each model to
find a way out of the aporias and contradictions of the other in an
attempt to homosexualize fascism. There can be no return to political normalcy postfascism, but we might at least—it would
seem—return to sexual normalcy.

Although narcissism is invoked as a mode of identity formation as well as of desire, Adorno will argue that homo-fascist narcissism in fact inaugurates a *post* identitarian politics; to this extent
we might concur with Habermas's comments on the centrality of
Oedipus to Freudo-Marxism. In the presentation of Adorno's
"Propaganda" essay, narcissism—confronted with the absence that
was the self—short-circuits the process of identity formation.

Adorno will again paraphrase Freud, to assert that "identification is 'the earliest expression of an emotional tie with another person,' playing 'a part in the early history of the Oedipus complex'" (125), but will then go on to reconstrue Freud: "It may well be that this pre-oedipal component of identification helps to bring about the separation of the leader image as that of an all-powerful primal father, from the actual father image. Since the child's identification with his father as an answer to the Oedipus complex is only a secondary phenomenon, infantile regression may go beyond this father image and through an 'anaclitic' process reach an archaic one" (125). The "early history of the Oedipus complex" has been subtly reshaped here as a "pre-oedipal component," and this shift to the pre-Oedipal has—as we have seen—enjoyed a certain popularity in more recent analyses of fascism.

The tortuousness of Adorno's reworking of Freud, however, is evident in his description of the mechanism of this shift to the pre-Oedipal. The metonymic displacement onto the archaic father is a symbolic anaclisis, but by invoking this logic of anaclisis as the basis of a narcissistic cathexis, Adorno actually invokes that mode of cathexis that opposes narcissism. In Freud's analysis it is precisely the failure of a fully anaclitic mode of affective displacement that leaves the way clear for narcissistic cathexis; here, however, narcissism is the result of an anaclisis that—in Freud's model—should have precluded it. Furthermore, there is something anachronistic in this description of narcissistic identification; the leader image can scarcely be recognized—as Adorno will subsequently argue—as an enlargement of the subject's own personality, when the process being described is the process of personality formation. As a category of political analysis, it would seem, the pre-Oedipal—as the field of both fascism and homosexuality—is constantly prey to the projections of a purely imaginary Oedipus.

The reasons for Adorno's obfuscations and conflations are not difficult to discern, since he wishes to argue that the fundamental problem of authoritarian personality formation (be it fascist or late capitalist) is the bypassing of the familial Oedipal structure. Consequently, he is constrained in the "Propaganda" essay to posit

pre-Oedipal narcissism as an alternative model of (non-)identifi-
cation, arguing that

> the primitively narcissistic aspect of identification as an act of *devour-*
> *ing*, of making the beloved object part of oneself, may provide us with
> a clue to the fact that the modern leader image sometimes seems to
> be the enlargement of the subject's own personality, a collective pro-
> jection of himself rather than the image of the father whose role dur-
> ing the later phases of the subject's infancy may well have decreased in
> present-day society. (125)

The pre-Oedipal mode of identification—identification with the
archaic father—provides the basis for Adorno's structuring of a
new, negative, postidentitarian narcissism. He will build on this
notion of "devouring" as a way of theorizing potential differences
between the political forms of late capitalist mass society and fascist
social organization. If both exemplify the post-Oedipal phenomenon of direct socialization, fascism differs through its mobilization
of a postidentitarian, totalitarian structure of idealization.[13]

In simplified terms, Freud distinguishes between identification
and idealization on the basis of the latter structure's essential narcissism. Idealization does not sublimate but "devours"—to use
Adorno's term—creating its object in itself. One might see in this
structure of idealization the resolution of Adorno's ambiguity regarding the nature of homosexual "surrender." Idealization figures an early narcissistic identification "as an act of *devouring*, of
making the beloved object part of oneself," in which it is "a collective projection of himself, rather than the image of the father,"
that is cathected. We might reconstruct Adorno's assumption as
follows: identification involves the positing of the father as the
self—involves, in other words, the surrender of the self to an other
who will in turn guarantee the integrity of the self. Idealization,
meanwhile—that act of devouring—is a form of introjection in
which the self is posited as the father. This idealization, then, is intrinsically aggressive toward the father as an autonomous, external principle. Rather than sacrifice the self to the forces of socialization that pass through the father, we subjugate the father to our
own presocial, narcissistic demands for gratification. It is no longer

a question of homosexual, passive surrender: the problem with the fascist homosexual is now his *inability* to surrender. The homosexual surrenders to his own passions—albeit in the absence of an identity that would ground a notion of property or ownership—rather than to the passions of the father.

In this sense, then, the fascist scenario is not one of authoritarian surrender—an Oedipal structure—but rather an abrogation on the part of society of its Oedipalizing and civilizing functions. It is a problem of too little rather than too much control, it would seem. Of course, what Adorno relies on here is the distinction between authoritarian control—which is external—and totalitarian control—which is necessarily internalized to the extent that "one's own passions" are always already collectivized. If—as Freud argues—hate can be grounded in self-love, Adorno's analysis seeks to show how the reverse is also the case: some of the aggression directed toward the object of our narcissistic identification necessarily rebounds on the self. Thus, for the *Führer* "the people he has to reckon with generally undergo the characteristic modern conflict between a strongly developed rational, self-preserving ego-agency and the continuous failure to satisfy their own ego demands" (127). Adorno builds here a groundwork for a structure of self-loathing that will ultimately serve his homophobic conflation of homosexual self-perception and fascist politics.

However, it is important to note the extent to which Adorno's elaboration of Freud's idealization model reiterates structures that Freud himself identifies—in his writings on narcissism—with *heterosexual* desire. Thus, for example, Adorno sees the basis for the narcissistic identification with the *Führer* in the putative narcissism of the object itself: "In order to allow the narcissistic identification, the leader has to appear himself as absolutely narcissistic. . . . The leader can be loved only if he himself does not love" (126–27). Narcissistic desire, then, breaks out of a merely dyadic, reflective structure, in that it identifies with the mode of desire of the other. Narcissism consists less in a desire for the self than in a desire for the representation of one's lost desire through the desire of another. As such, narcissism can never become entirely hermetic. While the inference is that homosexual desire is fascistic in its nonreciprocity (I desire the *Führer*, but he does not desire me), in fact Adorno is doing little more than rephrasing Freud's classic analysis—cited earlier—of the heterosexual male's desire for the narcissistic woman as recompense for his own surrendered narcissism. Whereas Oedipalized desire enacts a surrender of sorts—to the object of the desire of the father, and, subsequently, to the impossibility of that object—narcissistic desire of the type outlined here seems to involve a surrender to one's "own" passions (as we noted earlier), but a surrender that reenacts the modality (rather than the object) of the desire of the other.

Of course, a narcissism so construed necessarily negates itself. In Adorno's reading, any narcissism that seeks to mediate itself in this way through a third figure is necessarily fascistic. The homo-fascist moment in narcissism lies in the desire to bypass the subject-object relations within which representation is thinkable, yet nevertheless to represent one's own narcissism (one's ontological subjectivity) in an object, the *Führer*. In Adorno's presentation, the fascist subject's narcissistic desire cathects—and represents itself in—the narcissistic desire of the *Führer* (just as the heterosexual male seeks his own narcissism in the narcissistic woman), but by that very desire (for his desire) I introduce into the narcissistic structure of my own desire an other. My narcissistic desire, then, is not truly narcissistic in any immanent sense; and in this failure or lack of narcissism lies the basis for my idealization of the *Führer*. My self-loathing is a function of my self-love, which will never be as complete as the self-love of him who does not love me in return. Thus "the leader image gratifies the follower's twofold wish to submit to authority and to be the authority himself" (127). The narcissistic subject comes into being—as a self-loathing, self-idealizing monster—by being subjected. For Adorno, then, fascism would be the necessary fate of narcissism in a post-Oedipal age—and homo-fascist narcissism is the sole inheritance of a post-Oedipal politics.

For other Frankfurt School thinkers such as Marcuse, of course, Narcissus would provide a model of how societies might organize themselves after the liberation from bourgeois notions of identity. Thus Marcuse—in an altogether more positive, and even utopian, valorization of homosexuality—provides in his model of narcissism one of the cornerstones of New Left thought in the 1950's and 1960's, arguing, in his influential *Eros and Civilization*, that

> if Prometheus is the culture-hero of toil, productivity and progress through repression, then the symbols of another reality principle must be sought at the opposite pole. Orpheus and Narcissus (like Diony-sus to whom they are akin: the antagonist of the god who sanctions the logic of domination, the realm of reason) stand for a very differ-ent reality. They have not become the culture-heroes of the Western world; theirs is the image of joy and fulfillment; the voice which does not command but sings; the gesture which offers and receives; the deed which is peace and ends the labor of conquest; the liberation from time which unites man with god, man with nature.   (161–62)

Marcuse's invocation of Orpheus and Narcissus offers a mythopo-etic and utopian alternative to a prevalent, "Promethean," and ex-ploitative lifeworld.[14] "The hypothesis all but revolutionizes the idea of sublimation," he argues; "it hints at a non-repressive model of sublimation which results from an extension rather than from a constraining deflection of the ego" (169–70).

Marcuse could hardly be more explicit in his coupling of ho-mosexuality and nonrepressive sublimation. Rather than simply use Adorno and Marcuse as illustrations of the breadth of posi-tions articulated by various members of the Frankfurt School, how-ever, I wish to argue that for Adorno, too, homosexuality presents itself with the force of a historical necessity. In so doing, I hope to have shown that his consistent denigration of homosexuality and narcissism results from a dependence on models of subjectivity he himself shows to be outdated. Adorno offers an essentially con-servative response to a political and historical crisis by recontain-ing historical rupture within an ontogenetic narrative of hetero-sexual normalcy.

I leave Marcuse only as a passing reference for a second rea-son: it is from within the very heart of Adorno's own homophobia that I seek to elaborate a way out of the homophobic structures of the political discourse he inaugurates. We began this examination of two models of homosexuality in Adorno's thought on the basis of an apparent confluence in *Minima Moralia*, where "totalitarianism and homosexuality belong together" precisely because in them "the opposites of the strong man and the compliant youth merge in an order which asserts unalloyed the male principle of domination." Narcissism is for Adorno both that structure in which hierarchical (and, therefore, resistible) relations of domination pass over into a self-enclosed totality of power, and the structure in which homosexuality de-differentiates itself, eschewing the differential of subject and object that alone makes possible an autonomous political and psychological agency. *Minima Moralia* is the text in which Adorno most resolutely confronts the political implications of a postidentitarian erotics of narcissism. In another passage from this book entitled "Always speak of it, never think of it"—itself an inversion, this time verbal, of a commonplace of the conservative revolution—Adorno notes how "narcissism, deprived of its libidinal object by the decay of the self is replaced by the masochistic satisfaction of no longer being a self, and the rising generation guards few of its goods as jealously as its selflessness, its communal and lasting possession" (65). The loss of the self is glorified as a sacrifice of the self to the collective: homosociality grounds itself in a frustrated homosexual narcissism. Adorno here effectively postulates nothing less than an ethical break in which the broader structure of German fascism—including, I would contend, genocide—becomes thinkable. Fascism—in this curiously evacuated narcissism, this negative image of the liberal ideal—consists of a community of nonentities. Communitarian selflessness is, perversely, realized in fascism. Fascism, then, takes as its social principle the lack of identity already figured as homosexual; but in this collective absence of self, the homosexual failure to cathect—the absence of cathexis—is reworked as a cathexis of absence. In other words, the totalitarian reworking of homosexual, narcissistic libido consists in the repositivization of an essential lack.

By arguing—in the essay on fascist propaganda—that for the totalitarian masses "their coherence is a reaction formation against their primary jealousy of each other, pressed into the service of group coherence" (131), Adorno asserts the ultimately destructive impetus of this homosexual libidinal tie. In order that the Other be like me, it, too, must sacrifice the self; and indeed, this sacrifice is the very act of its becoming like me. I do not desire to be the object; I desire that the object cease to be—like me.[15] This selflessness projected onto the Other can take two forms; on the one hand it might consist in the reciprocal selflessness of the racial comrade, but on the other it might also—in the case of anti-Semitism—take the form of a destruction of the "self" of the Other. Jewish "selfishness"—thus would run our extrapolation from Adorno's analysis—serves as a fateful, untimely, mocking reminder of the persistence of the Self: and as such it is to be eradicated. In other words, while it has become a commonplace in analyses of collective movements to stress the importance of the "Other" in opposition to which the national/racial/religious/etc. collective can define itself, Adorno's model of postidentitarian narcissism serves to question this assumption.[16]

Implicit in any model that insists on the subject-object split and the need for the Other as an instance of self-definition, is a belief in the interdependence of subject and object and a recognition of the interest of the subject in the continued existence of its object-other. The urge to destruction of which Adorno writes here necessarily reconfigures the logic of Self and Other. What does it mean when the relation to the Other is a relation oriented toward destruction—a destruction that, in terms of its own logic, necessarily entails the destruction of the Self? Adorno's analysis allows us, I think, to disengage fascism from a glib tradition of Otherness that would seek precedents in earlier racial, sexual, or medical discourses. In the shift traced by Adorno from the hetero-logy of collective identity to the homo-logy of postidentitarian narcissism, the desire for the end of the existence of the Other is also an assimilative desire. "I" do not exist and I desire that the Other cease to exist in order that I might catch a narcissistic reflection of my own (non-)existence in its demise. In Benjaminian terms, the "right" to existence has been replaced by the narcissistic "expression" of *non*existence.

We observe in this passage Adorno's historical departure from a Freudian analysis of Otherness as a response to the demise of bourgeois subjectivity in a directly socialized, totalitarian society. Adorno cites Freud's analysis of the hatred of the outsider group as a desire to deny—or even exterminate—all that is incommensurate with the narcissistic Self. This leads Freud to argue that "in the undisguised antipathies and aversions which people feel towards strangers with whom they have to do, we may recognize the expression of self-love—of narcissism. This self-love works for the self-assertion of the individual, and behaves as though the occurrence of any divergence from his own particular lines of development involved a criticism of them and a demand for their alteration" (quoted in Adorno, "Propaganda," 130). Freud writes here of "alteration," as if it were a question of the need to fashion the Other in the image of the Self. But where—as in Adorno's analysis—there is no image of the Self, this demand for alteration easily transmutes into a desire to annihilate: if I do not exist, I can at least "express" that nonexistence in the destruction of the existence of others. Adorno will go on to argue that the structure of idealization—which recasts all Other as Self—is necessarily aggressive to all alterity and forms the basis of a genocidal mentality. Narcissistic homogenization now serves not the existence of the narcissistic subject—who no longer exists for Adorno in this analysis of fascism—but merely the representation of its nonexistence. Thus, destructive urges (at the extreme point, genocide) derive, for Adorno, not from the fear that the Other is too like me (a variation of Sedgwick's homosexual panic) but rather from the recognition that the other cannot "be" like me, insofar as "I" have ceased to "be" at all.

In a postidentitarian, post-Oedipal age, narcissism emerges not simply as an alternative to Oedipal character formation, but as itself marked by the failure of Oedipus; there is no longer (or not yet) a Self to love. My critical prevarication here on the question of the "no longer / not yet" is justified, I feel, by the compensatory relationship in which phylo- and ontogenetic so often stand in Adorno. Historically—as a phylogenetic inheritance—the Oedipal subject is no longer possible under the conditions of fascism and late capitalism; but this impossibility is figured—or "seeks its expression"—ontogenetically in the temporality of a "not yet," in the form of the pre-Oedipal. Homosexuality is at one and the same time a historically validated mode of (non-)subjectivity (if Oedipal subjects are no longer possible, it is fruitless to pursue a bourgeois politics in such a subject's name), and quintessentially regressive and reactionary (or even anachronistic)—an infantile "not yet" of subjectivity. In other words, the figuring of the historical "no longer" as the ontogenetic "not yet" serves to reaffirm a narrative of progress (political and psychical) that is purely ideological: the progress of a nonexistent subject.

Recalling Habermas's analysis of crisis in terms of a "deformation of the lifeworld," are we to conclude, then, that homosexuality—as a historical pathology of sorts—corresponds to the lifeworld distortions necessitated by the "underachievement of the economic and political spheres"? We should beware, I think—warier than Adorno himself generally is—of invoking any such notion of a historically legitimated mode of sexuality. In a more sober moment of the "Propaganda" essay, Adorno himself will even remind us that "psychological dispositions do not actually cause fascism; rather, fascism defines a psychological area which can be successfully exploited by the forces which promote it for entirely nonpsychological reasons of self-interest" (135). Such unwonted caution on Adorno's part clearly problematizes any attempt to think the "necessary" historical relationship of homosexuality to fascism, but in moving now toward a conclusion we should be quite clear as to the nature of the problems Adorno raises here. First, he is simply urging caution in moving from any observation of structural parallels in psychological and political phenomena to the assertion of a causality. He problematizes, in short, the very idea of historical neurosis. But it is precisely homosexuality—or his formulation of it—that makes such leaps from homology to causality impossible; for the only thing homosexuality does render necessary is a break with the language of historical necessity. In other words—and another terminology, Habermas's—homosexuality poses a legitimation crisis not only in the political structures of advanced capitalist democracies, but in the very structure of Freudo-Marxist critical theory as exemplified by the Frankfurt School. The disequilibria to which homo-fascism responds are essentially theoretical.

We have seen how Adorno surmounts the death of that Oedipal subject assumed by Habermas to be so essential to any synthesis of Marx and Freud. This death in fact provides a new analytic paradigm of narcissism that Adorno exploits to the full. More problematic, though, is the antagonistic—even anachronistic—structure of the "no longer / not yet." If it is through the metapsychological writings that Adorno harnesses Freud to social critique, then he encounters in both homosexuality and fascism the uncoupling of any historical phylogenesis from the ontogenesis of the preidentitarian subject. By way of paradox, homosexuality and fascism—one a psychoanalytic category, the other political—enact a break—a historically necessary break—with the notion of historical necessity. Adorno identifies homosexuality and fascism in such a cavalier way—and the rhetorical bravado of the phrase "totalitarianism and homosexuality belong together" is unmistakable—because what he confronts is a loss of faith in any structure of identification that would make the equation possible. The confrontation with homosexuality is the definitive and destructive crisis in the Frankfurt School's whole Freudo-Marxist project.

It would certainly go beyond the purview of this chapter to extrapolate as to what lies beyond this legitimation crisis for the political evaluation of homosexuality, but it is perhaps Adorno himself who offers us—in *Negative Dialectics*—a constellation in which we might begin to rethink homosexuality. The problem with speaking of any historical necessity in Adorno's work is that we thereby reinscribe him into a logic of historical self-identity against which *Negative Dialectics* is written; hence we might—through the prism of the *nonidentical* invoked here only as the incommensurability of psychoanalysis and history—reconfigure the politics of homosexual narcissism not as a contingent failure in the formation of identity, but as the very condition of *all* political identity. Is it a specifically negative narcissism—the narcissism of the nonidentical—that grounds political categories? Rather than isolating homosexuality within the taxonomy of narcissism, might it not be through the medium of narcissism that "homosexuality" in fact informs the political discourse? The narcissism, that is, of a fictive subject for its reflection in a fictive object—the Self, the State, the *Volk*? What follows in this book—beginning with the writings of philosophers and social theorists specifically concerned with the role of the homosexual in the politics of the State—is the presentation of a series of texts elaborating on this possibility.

CHAPTER 3

The Philosophy of Masculinism

T hanks to some excellent historical work, the makeup of early homosexual emancipation movements in Wilhelmine Germany (for which the term "movement" perhaps implies too great a degree of cohesion) has recently been revealed to us, and it is certainly not my aim here to re-present that historical material.[1] Nevertheless, it is fair to say that our current understanding of homosexual emancipation suffers from a lack of historical imagination. While the more organized movements of the Weimar Republic emerged as part of a modernist social, aesthetic, and political sensibility and are therefore still culturally accessible to us today, the writings of earlier emancipationists seem, in comparison, steeped in an alien, classical, and classicizing culture, imbued with a suspiciously elitist or even authoritarian view of social order. It is precisely for this reason that these writers must interest us here: for our objective is to understand the extent to which a classical culture provided both political and erotic models for a "masculinist" tradition that in fact continued into Weimar society, where it was overshadowed by the more widely publicized—and historically promulgated—work of activists and thinkers such as Hirschfeld.

Although I do not seek to write empirical history, I do, nevertheless, wish to redress a certain imbalance in our understanding of the history of homosexual emancipation—a history that has been disproportionately dominated by Hirschfeld and his notions of a "third sex." Polemically—and, therefore, somewhat schematically—I am drawing a distinction between the "third-sexers" (exemplified by Hirschfeld, but with historical roots in the very earliest self-consciously homosexual writings) and a group I call the "masculinists." The latter group is represented in this chapter by Hans Blüher and Benedict Friedlaender and later in the book by John Henry Mackay, but it encompasses figures not treated here: figures such as Adolf Brand, the moving force behind the *Gemeinschaft der Eigenen*, and Friedrich Radszuweit of the *Bund für Menschenrechte*. The contribution of these latter individuals to an emergent homosexual subculture—while intellectually and philosophically meager in comparison to either Blüher or Mackay—was nonetheless vital. The masculinists will be examined with two objectives in mind: first, to demonstrate the ways in which a queer theory dominated by a Foucauldian historical paradigm has tended to downplay the importance of philosophical and literary texts in reconstructing the emerging concept of homosexuality; and second, to provide a historical and philosophical framework for the assertion made by Eve Sedgwick in *Tendencies* that "while most of the early gay rights discourse was strongly antifascist, it appeared for some time that the homosexual heightening involved in early fascism might offer potent affordances to at least some forms of homosexual advocacy" (50).

Rather than rework the debate concerning homosociality and its relation to homosexuality—a debate certainly crucial to this book, but one that has been played out exhaustively already—we might begin more modestly by outlining what is meant here by a "masculinist" tradition in homosexual emancipatory thought. By "masculinist" I wish to indicate a strain of thought within the homosexual emancipation movement (but not limited to that movement) that perceives male-male Eros as a distillation of a fundamentally masculine social instinct, and that therefore resists any attempt to explain homosexuality as a form of effeminization. More specifically, I wish to indicate the development of this line of thought as a specifically cultural—that is, classicizing—response to the biologizing tendencies of third-sex theory. The masculinist tradition has rarely been taken into account in Anglo-American queer theory and historiography, and its reception in German historical and academic writings has been somewhat uncomfortable and trivializing. In fact, as I hope to show, these masculinists engage debates currently central to queer theory and oblige us to rethink what threaten to become unquestioned critical commonplaces in that theory.

By reading historical texts in some sense teleologically—as progressive textual constructions of homosexual identity—queer historiography has overlooked the broader debates in which those texts were engaged, further isolating the interests of queer theory from their broader political and philosophical context. Those same texts that we now read as constructions of homosexual identity were at one and the same time interventions in the "mainstream" political and philosophical crises of their day. We must therefore be sensitive to the strategic *function* of an emerging homosexuality. Rather than asking What was homosexuality? (or, in Foucauldian terms, When and how was homosexuality?), we need to understand what homosexuality was (and is) *for*. What political options did it provide, what ways out of an aporetic heterosexism in politics and philosophy? What function did it serve within its contemporary political and philosophical framework?

In returning to the masculinists, I pose two fundamental questions, important both to a specifically gay male theory and to our understanding of the modernist episteme in general. First, are male homosexuals to be understood through the prism of gender as fundamentally effeminized, and legitimated on the juridico-medical basis of their existence as a third sex? Second—and more crucial to the broader political concerns within which early homosexual emancipation must be read—what are the social implications of locating within this third sex certain socializing functions formerly linked to the family? Is Blüher the first theorist—and a reactionary one at that—of the Queer Nation?

Since Lesbian and Gay Studies emerged historically out of an institutional and critical framework fashioned by a preceding generation of feminists, it is perhaps not surprising that it should have found little place for the essentially misogynistic tradition of masculinism. The virtual omission of masculinism from even more recent queer historiography has led, however, to certain critical assumptions that need now to be questioned: assumptions about the relation of the political and the libidinal. In short, politically reactionary masculinism has been linked to a supposed sexophobia with the result that any erotic reading of politically reactionary movements has been foreclosed. Just as the authors of the *Braun-buch* avoided examining the political appeal of fascism to the proletariat by insisting on van der Lubbe's homosexual lack of class consciousness, so queer theory has tended to extricate itself from embarrassing political self-examination by stressing the supposedly sexophobic cultural ambitions of masculinism rather than its (usually paederastic) presentation of sexuality.[2]

Thus, in their invaluable study *Rosa Winkel, Rosa Listen*, for example, Stümke and Finkler quote from a remarkable article, "Nationalsozialismus und Inversion," first published in Hirschfeld's *Mitteilungen des Wissenschaftlich-Humanitären Komittees* (o. 32, Jan.–Mar. 1932), in which a homosexual SA member argues his somewhat astonishing case. The SA man distinguishes between the merely sexual and the suprasexual: "We cherish the creative Eros: we fight no battle for the Eros of coitus, though we do not despise it. Since we feel that the sexual instinct is fundamental, we believe that a part of its energies can be sublimated without harm. This does not mean that we seek to repress. On the contrary" (Stümke and Finkler, 101). In this article the SA man goes on to oppose the specifics of Hirschfeld's emancipatory program by asserting that "his major political agitation—the petition to the German Reichstag—consists simply of the attempt to liberate the mouth, thighs, and backside of the invert. In the battle for these erogenous zones the mind and the soul—the human body in its entirety—has been forgotten" (104). Rather than engaging in any sort of close reading of the text produced by this homosexual Nazi, Stümke and Finkler dismiss these writings by pointing out how "such theories are possible only on the basis of a massive sexophobia" (101).[3] In a sense, their own reading is itself caught within the political tradition of liberalism that the Nazi himself critiques. The Nazi author's opposition to a partial, erogenous liberation is not necessarily an opposition to sexual liberation per se. It proposes instead another model of liberation—a totalitarian model—that we need not approve but must at least recognize. For the homosexual Nazi author, the sexual liberation of the body (politic) will be one in which the partial independence of limbs and organs ("mouth, thighs, and backside") is no more relevant than the anachronistic political autonomy of the bourgeois liberal subject. We need to use Stümke and Finkler's research to reverse the charges they lay at the door of masculinism. Is the SA man sexophobic in his attacks on Hirschfeld and in his evocation of alternative, antidemocratic models of power? Or is it merely a sexophobic reading—a reading that fears the radical and unsettling plurality of queer sexualities—that is deaf to his rhetoric?

Stümke and Finkler willfully overlook the rhetoric of the body that runs through the SA man's article, and yet they are somehow subliminally aware of the political and erotic charge of that discourse. They recoil at his invocation of "a hand . . . that knows how to strike, but also how to caress" and quote the author's assertion that "the *Führer* knows better than anyone that the battalions of Brown Shirts *embody* today the power of the party, and tomorrow the power of the State" (109, my emphasis). The SA man invokes the hand of the *Führer* as a hand of discipline but also of caress. Clearly, the so-called sexophobia of the fascist homosexual does not involve any avoidance of the body: the State is an embodiment, and the aim is to free the total body, not just "mouth, thighs, and backside." One conception of liberation—the liberal—essentially argues for the freedom of the parts of the body—politically speaking, that is, for the freedom of the individ-

ual political subject. The SA man, meanwhile, argues not for a liberation of the parts of the body from the organization of the
whole, but for the liberation of the whole from the purely contingent demands of the parts.

The parallel of political and libidinal agendas—the totalitarian
and the liberal—could scarcely be more striking. Striking also is
the double bind that "liberal sexuality" imposes on transgressive
homosexual desire. If—as Stümke and Finkler imply—an emancipatory sexuality expresses itself by resisting any totalitarian sublation of the body, then we are left with the possibility of a reading
such as that proposed by Haug in the article cited in Chapter 1,
in which the homosexual insistence on body parts—or, specifically,
on "the" *Glied*—is taken as an attack on the coherent, integrated
political subject. This cathexis of mere parts will, of course, itself
be fixated—in Haug's reading—on the *Glied* par excellence, the
penis. Phallic homosexuality—or so an extrapolation of Haug's argument would lead us to conclude—represents its own attack on
political representation through the penis/phallus, which is at once
something more and something less than a person: just a body
part, and a part that sublates the body. We find ourselves caught,
as it were, between the penis and the phallus: for Stümke and Finkler the attack on genitality is an attack on homosexuality in the
name of an idealized totalitarian body, but any "partial" celebration of genitality might also be read (in the tradition of Haug) as
a celebration of a rigid (totalitarian) phallic order! Masculinism
stands accused both of dismemberment and of an obsessive over-
valorization of the member, the *Glied*, the phallus.

To what extent is sexophobia rooted, then, in an idealist sublation of the body and to what extent in a bourgeois disgust at the
body—a disgust that might lead, in its most virulent form, to a desire to destroy bodies? To cite Blüher as an example of masculinist
thought, it seems clear that such sexophobia is by no means a necessary element of masculinism. Blüher—no less than the SA man,
who disclaims sexophobia—is clear in stating that "it is not our
opinion that Eros consists only of something *spiritual* and ethe-
real. The body and its drives are always present" (183). The ex-

plicit eroticism of Blüher's argument will suggest that Stümke and Finkler's analysis of the SA man's antigenital sexuality in fact reflects merely their own inability to appreciate the erotic possibilities of the totalitarian body. Where does this leave us in terms of the contemporary debate, and what are the implications of that early debate for the present day? Stümke and Finkler argue for an erotics of tenderness and stigmatize as potentially fascist any homosexuality that might not immediately fit that model: their own sexophobia manifests itself as antimasculinism rather than as antifeminism.

Curiously, the SA man confronts us with the possibility that the practical political efforts of those such as Hirschfeld—the liberation of acts, linked to the liberation of body parts—is itself phallic with regard to existing power structures. The SA man argues not for the suppression of the body, but for its liberation and, ultimately, sublation in the State. What is not endorsed is "the Eros of coitus"; and this opposition to coitus must itself be philosophically examined (see the concluding chapter). Hirschfeld's liberation of body parts is linked here to a merely partial social democratic political agenda, whereas the erotics of fascism promise (if they will not deliver) a total and totalitarian liberation of the entire body and spirit. This is not sexophobia; it is schizosex. As a working hypothesis for the consideration of masculinism in this chapter, then (but also as a framework for the broader concerns of this book), we might proffer the following: homoerotic protofascism cannot be identified with masculinism insofar as we identify the masculine with either patriarchy or the phallic symbolic order. On the contrary, it is precisely that model of sexuality orienting itself around the (inversion of the) dyad of gender that is most rigidly caught within phallocentrism. We must confront the reality that both fascism and homosexual masculinism were real and radical attacks on that order—even though their historical and empirical instantiations were anything but liberatory in any accepted sense.

It should be further noted at the very outset that the masculinist tradition can think liberation only through the prism of gender. Masculinism views emancipation as man's emancipation *as* man, and woman's emancipation *as* woman. Clearly, man's liberation *as* man and woman's liberation *as* woman imply an essentialist understanding of the terms "man" and "woman." In fact, this is not—or not entirely—the case. The essence of man lies for the masculinists in his cultural self-fashioning: the essentialism-constructivism opposition is overcome by an essentially cultural view of masculinity, in which the essence of the homosexual male is precisely his function as the bearer of culture. Women, on the other hand, are accorded a limited cultural role in masculinist thought, and that role is usually linked to maternity, understood as both a biological and a cultural concept. Herein lies the indubitably misogynist element of masculinism: the homology of nature and culture in man is the product of a willed cultural self-construction; in women it is the result of a natural, biological propensity. In other words, the biologizing tendencies in masculinist constructions of femininity should not be understood as a simple inconsistency in an otherwise culturalist ideology: women can be biologized because they are not yet cultured. This distinction— clearly a cultural distinction that at the same time seeks to define the very threshold of culture—has direct political implications in the work of the masculinists, and will, indeed, replicate itself in Blüher's attitude toward the Jews. Blüher will understand the effeminizing family as antipathetic to the cultural task of the male (and the Jew's investment in the family is, in turn, incompatible with the duty of State building), while for Friedlaender the countercultural strivings of femininity have paradoxically taken on the cultural form of religion and sexual asceticism.

The other major obstacle to a reading of Wilhelmine masculinists today is the classical tradition within which they write and which questions essentially heterosexualized contemporary constructions of homosexuality. So long as we think of homosexuality as an alternative, a challenge, or—homophobically—an abomination to heterosexual hegemony we will have missed the point of the classical masculinists. If the "Uranian" third-sex tradition poses problems for us in its conflation of cultural and biological phenomena—specifically, of homosexuality and androgyny—the masculinists pose no less of a problem in their reversal of this trend. Where biologism reduces cultural phenomena to biological reflexes, the masculinists tend to ontologize social conditions as natural forces. Masculinism reappropriates Hellenic cultural models—specifically, the paederastic model of male development—through the medium of the German idealist tradition in philosophy. Cultural constructions of masculinity and femininity are ontologized in the service of a countercultural critique. Citing figures such as Gustav Jäger and Arthur Schopenhauer from a misogynistic social, philosophical, and eugenic tradition, the masculinists attempt to think the political consequences of that tradition for a theory of the State. In subsequent critical analyses of a putative "homosexual fascination" operative in fascism, the working assumption has traditionally been that the masculinist strain of thought contributed to a homosexual intellectual tradition potentially sympathetic to authoritarian and totalitarian political models. In fact, as I hope to demonstrate, there is no real unity on specifically political questions among the masculinists, and the deciding factor in the shaping of political thought will, in fact, prove to be the encounter with Freud rather than with a political theory.

The battle between masculinists and third-sexers was played out as a struggle for the legitimational force of a Hellenic precedent that the third-sexers had already earmarked as "Uranian." But this cultural antipathy is simultaneously a struggle between two diverging views of society. Hans Blüher—whose work on *The Role of Eroticism in Masculine Society* provides the primary focus of this chapter—will observe dismissively of his third-sex opponents in the analysis of male-male eros: "the fact that a pitiful bunch chooses to call itself 'Uranian' just because they have the hots for young boys and feel they have to take a little 'soul' into the bargain says nothing about this sublime Greek notion. It speaks volumes about the present" (1: 66). Clearly, the battle for control of homosexual self-definition is a battle for control of the Hellenic cultural and pedagogical tradition, a tradition that promised to locate homosexualized homosocial structures at the very core of the social order.

Certainly, I am not the first to distinguish between masculinists and third-sexers. In their dealings with one another the various theorists and activists were already sharply and polemically aware of the issues dividing them. Critically, however, the division has since been noted only in an overtly partisan matter, such as in Jones's assertion (cited earlier) in "The 'Third Sex' in German Literature" of "the spiritual affinity of . . . one entire wing of the homosexual emancipation movement to fascism" (577). Writing in *"We of the Third Sex,"* Jones will chastise Mackay, for example, for "a negative attitude toward his fellow homosexuals," an attitude that supposedly "expresses not only his affinity with the *Gemeinschaft der Eigenen* but also his personal philosophy of 'individual anarchism'" (268). We should take seriously the possibility of an ideological continuum linking homosexual masculinism to protofascism, but we should be wary of the political conflations on which such arguments are built. The anarchist Mackay—whose elitism and individualism supposedly divert him from collective action and mass politics—is somehow yoked to a protofascist political tradition. Just as the writers of the *Braunbuch* saw in the homosexual an anarchic petit bourgeois individual inevitably alienated from class interests and aligned him with the interests of reaction, so queer historiography has tended to stigmatize masculinist individualism as alien to the interests of one's "fellow homosexuals."

In response to the masculinist tradition, Stümke and Finkler point out its characteristic intolerance toward effeminacy and lay the charge of *Tuntenhaß* (the hatred of effeminate homosexuals), building on the basic charge of sexophobia to claim that "this widespread form of racism among 'normal' inverts was the result of a persistent pressure to conform to a heterosexually constructed society. They sought to avoid being confused in the public imagination with 'such creatures'" (26). Of course, Stümke and Finkler here plug masculinism into the ongoing dilemma over separatism and assimilation, but in the context of the early debate—

and of our concern with fascism in this book—the almost casual charge of racism acquires a new and literal urgency.[4] To what extent does a eugenic discourse responsible for modern forms of racism also provide a discourse within which homosexual/heterosexual difference can first be conceptualized? From the other side of this question, to what extent does a specifically scientific eugenics feed off classical cultural traditions central to an emerging masculinist homosexual identity?

With respect to the charge that masculinism depends on a latent racism in its opposition to effeminized homosexuals, it should of course be noted that there is certainly a consistent strain of anti-Semitism in masculinist thought. Stümke and Finkler have even gone so far as to argue that *Tuntenhaß* necessarily proves itself amenable to other forms of fascism and racism. We need to be more careful, however, in our reconstruction of racism—or, more specifically, anti-Semitism—as a political practice: for in many ways, the third-sexers' own obsession with biological and physiological argument partakes of a potentially racist logic just as much as the cultural anti-Semitism of the masculinists. Thus, I confront in this chapter an assertion and a charge that I hope, ultimately, to unsettle—namely, that fascism fascinates through a certain (masculinist) form of homosexual desire, to which a racialized taxonomy is essential. I propose to inaugurate, at least, an examination of the relationship between the politics of an erotic relation and the Eros of the political itself.

I will conclude the chapter with a consideration of how the masculinist tradition of thinking about homosexuality lent itself both to a certain ideology of race (ideology, that is, in the strictest terms: biologistic racialism is not the stuff of the masculinists) and to the development of a theory of the State. To put my thesis bluntly: the movement from a physiological to a psychological understanding of homosexuality—roughly, the movement to be traced here from Friedlaender and Weininger to Blüher—parallels the movement from an understanding of the State legitimated in terms of a *Naturgesetz* (law of nature) to a recognition of the essentially cultural (and I link the terms quite consciously) function of the State. The move away from a biologically deterministic view of politics—centered on the idea of a *Naturgesetz*—opens up the possibility of radical political action (for figures such as Mackay) at the same time as it unhinges politics from the redemptive ideal of a natural order.

If I begin with Weininger in my presentation of the masculinist tradition, I do so primarily because the structure of his thought sets into relief the work of the masculinists per se. For his work can easily be situated within a tradition of idealized biologistic thinking about sexuality in terms of existing gender dyads, and yet it paves the way, paradoxically, for radical theories of homosexual desire. His attempt to create a generalizable theory of desire that could account for both homo- and heterosexual attraction is important in the current critical context, because he both exemplifies and undercuts the newly paradigmatic status Sedgwick has claimed for homosexual desire in the twentieth century. In *Epistemology of the Closet* and elsewhere Sedgwick has argued—most convincingly—that the development of homosexuality as a model of desire served to threaten existing models of desire based on difference; that while attempts were made to pathologize homosexuality in terms of its de-differentiation, it nevertheless began to usurp the assumed primacy of heterosexuality in the construction of generalizable models of desire. That is to say, whereas existing models of desire depended on a gender difference that reinforced a tradition of subject-object thinking in philosophy, homosexuality necessarily questioned that tradition. It posed, in other words, an epistemological threat. We have already seen, in the previous chapter, how for Adorno the rise of narcissism as a social and sexual pathology parallels the rise of fascism as a political force and the end of a philosophy of the subject. These are the paradigmatic shifts that Sedgwick points to and that, as we shall see, are explicitly proposed in the work of the masculinists.

Weininger—like Friedlaender after him—raises in explicit form what Sedgwick argues in her *Epistemology of the Closet*; namely, the possibility of grounding philosophically a general theory of desire. As Sedgwick has pointed out, theories of desire serve a paradigmatic function within the philosophy of consciousness, establishing the relationship of subject to object as a relation of self-constituting alterity: I am who I am (a man) by desiring what I am not (a woman). It is this alterity that homosexuality seems to repudiate and, thus, this tradition of thought that it seems to call into question. Utilizing a psychoanalytic vocabulary that only becomes pertinent for Blüher, the last of our three theorists, Sedgwick argues that

> the *homo* in the emerging concept of the homosexual seems to have the potential to perform a definitive de-differentiation—setting up a permanent avenue of potential slippage—between two sets of relations that had previously been seen as relatively distinct: identification and desire. . . . For the first time since the Renaissance, there existed the potential for a discourse in which a man's desire for a woman could not guarantee his difference from her—in which it might even, rather, suggest his likeness to her. (159–60)

The point she makes, however, is exactly one that Friedlaender will have already made with respect to heterosexuality; namely, that those men who love women might themselves be unmanly and practically effeminate. The homosexual slippage of identification and desire contaminates the very discourse of desire itself to the extent that a male's heterosexual desire for an object can be confused with a desire for her subject position of femininity: birds of a feather flock together.

In concordance with Sedgwick's argument, Weininger does, indeed, implicitly take an essentially *homo*sexual attraction as the basis of his theory of desire. To this extent the formulation of homosexual desire does, as Sedgwick argues, necessitate a rethinking of desire as such; but he does not—as Sedgwick hypothesizes—effect a shift away from a subject-object desiring dichotomy into a theory of fundamental narcissism. Instead, his project is to reconcile theories of homosexual desire to the tradition of a philosophy of consciousness. Weininger demonstrates the ways in which Sedgwick's "narcissistic turn" can, in fact, be accounted for from within a traditional, differentiated model of subject-object desire. His strategy is to uncover the latent homosexual logic to the structure of subject-object affinities, rather than to refute—in the name of narcissism—the diacritical difference encoded in traditional models of desire.

We might use Sedgwick as a way into considering the masculinist tradition by examining the challenge she would pose to Weininger's project of a general theory. What Weininger demonstrates is the limitation imposed on models of desire by a restrictive insistence on gender as the sole defining moment of difference. He argues that desire originates in incompletion and that we all seek our supplement (rather than our opposite) through sexual attraction. How, then, are we to account for the gender identity of subject and object in the homosexual desiring relation? How can a theory that demands difference as the basis of desire account for this relation of desiring identification? Weininger is quite clear on this point and takes up Sedgwick's challenge to prove rather than problematize his general theory of desire. *Sex and Character*—Weininger's major work—seeks to elaborate an algebra of sexual attraction that he finally distills into the following formula: "For true sexual union it is necessary that there come together a complete male (M) and a complete female (F), even though in different cases the M and F are distributed between the two individuals in different proportions" (29). Sexual union is the completion of incomplete ideals (or "ideoplasms") of masculine and feminine: thus, a 75 percent masculine man will seek a woman with 25 percent masculinity to complement and complete his own, just as he will complete her own incomplete femininity. This formula for heterosexual attraction can scarcely be understood in terms of a heterosexual logic, however, since Weininger is arguing that sexual union is motivated by the affinity of a gendered "ideoplasm" for its own completion: the 75 percent of male desires not the feminine in the other, but rather the supplementary masculine 25 percent. To this extent, Sedgwick's point is well taken: the homosexual longing of the male ideoplasm for its masculine supplement does, indeed, take identity rather than difference as the basis of desire—even to the extent of an apparently narcissistic striving for self-completion.

The theory of differential desire elaborated within the idealist tradition depends, however, not so much on Sedgwick's ultimately dialectical binarisms—dichotomous in structure, and supposedly threatened by homosexual de-differentiation in the form of narcissistic desire—as it does on a logic of affinities or supplementarity. The desire of the 75 percent for the 25 percent can be understood as narcissistic only if the logic of supplementarity is reduced to a *com*plementary logic of narcissism predicated on a (sundered) identity. The logic of narcissism—ultimately a form of identity thinking—implies a desire for the self in which identity is an origin. The logic of supplementarity—which I posit elsewhere in this book as a more satisfactory way to think narcissism—takes identity only as its virtual telos, and rupture as origin. Rebutting Sedgwick's assertion that a de-differentiated homosexual desire undermines the feasibility of an entire metaphysics of desire, Weininger argues that "sexual inverts of both sexes are to be defined as individuals in whom the factor a . . . is very nearly 0.5 and so is practically equal to a'; in other words, individuals in whom there is as much maleness as femaleness" (47). Weininger is arguing, in effect, that homosexuality arises in instances where the masculine ideoplasm constitutes around 50 percent of the psychical makeup. Since this person will seek an approximate 50 percent of masculinity in another, it is possible that he will find it in a particularly masculine woman, in whom femininity and masculinity are evenly balanced at around 50 percent. If we accept this, then "this explains the fact that sexual inverts usually associate only with persons of similar character. . . . The sexual attraction is mutual and this explains why sexual inverts so readily recognise each other" (50). The homosexual—like the heterosexual—seeks his supplement, but in this case his own share of masculinity is only about 50 percent and can therefore be met by either a masculine female or an effeminate male. To this extent, of course, we have to differentiate Weininger from the theorists of masculinism, to whom the assumption that the homosexual is in some sense only 50 percent masculine would be anathema.

The apparently narcissistic homosexual in fact serves as classic "proof" of Weininger's theory: the androgynous male homosexual seeks an androgynous partner, who might also be male (i.e., in whom $a = 0.5$). The logic of homosexuality is the logic of the supplement. In other words, whereas Sedgwick quite rightly asserts that, with the conceptualization of homosexual desire, differentiated heterosexual desire begins to appear only as a special case of the fundamentally narcissistic structure of *all* desire, Weininger demonstrates that her model is by no means universally applicable. A forerunner of the masculinists—for whom "de-differentiated" homosexual desire remains within the logic of difference, as paederasty—Weininger demonstrates how an apparent narcissism might, in fact, be but the limit case of a logic of supplementarity rather than vice versa. In other words, rather than grounding differentiated desire in narcissism, Weininger grounds narcissism in difference. Whereas Sedgwick assumes an antipathy between narcissistic (or de-differentiating) models of homosexuality and traditional models of inversion or paederasty, it is clear that narcissism and inversion are entirely compatible here.

Far from offering a threat to traditional models of desire (based not, as Sedgwick assumes, on binarisms, but on supplementarity) homo-style helps ground a generalizable theory. Sedgwick argues that the aesthetics and politics of homosexuality depend on a process of de-differentiation (that questions, for example, the project of a mimesis based on signifying differentials), and that "it is with *homo*-style homosexuality, and *not* with inversion, paederasty, or sodomy (least of all, of course, with cross-gender sexuality) that an erotic language, an erotic discourse comes into existence that makes available a continuing possibility for symbolizing slippages between identification and desire" (159). It is important to question some of the suppositions of her argument with respect to the masculinist theorists treated here, however. Intrinsic to her argument is the assumption that paederasty represents a discourse of differentiation (in terms of age, class, experience, etc.) while homo-style (predicated primarily on a model of narcissistic de-differentiation and identification) facilitates that slippage from object choice to identification. Certain objections or modifications need to be raised to this formulation as it stands. First, the paederastic discourse—though based on difference—*is* understood as a discourse of identification, at least in the sense of an identity *formation*: I love in the other that which I would be (or, in Weininger's case, that which completes me, my supplement rather than my mere complement). Of course, this formulation does not really threaten Sedgwick's narcissistic hypothesis, since the desire for an ideal image of oneself provides one of the basic categories of narcissism as analyzed by Freud.[5]

More important, however, is the way that in the texts of the masculinists it is paederasty and not narcissism that poses the greatest threat to a general theory of desire (and to a generalizable philosophical system). Sedgwick's privileging of the epistemological threat of homosexual de-differentiation will lead her to celebrate the emergence of what she calls a "homo-style" at the cost of paederastic models of desire. Although there is certainly much truth to her hypothesis concerning the gradual eclipse of paederasty, her implicit valorizations need to be questioned. In Weininger's case, for example, it is certainly paederastic—that is, supposedly "differentiated"—desire that poses the greatest threat to a generalizable theory of desire. The emergence of "homo-style"—far from threatening a tradition of philosophical thinking on desire—actually reflected a new introspection on the part of that tradition: an examination of the homosexual logic of elective affinities. It is masculinism, in the form of paederastic desire—apparently so anachronistic—that poses the real threat to a generalizable discourse on desire. For Weininger's totalizing model of desire does, indeed, acknowledge a threat: not from a de-differentiated desire (for which, as we have seen, it can account effortlessly) but from precisely that differentiated model of desire whose "eclipse" Sedgwick suggests.

It is precisely the paederast who (pace Sedgwick) undermines traditional and generalizable theories of desire, and in Weininger's work we see developed in its clearest form a distinction between two modes of homosexual identity: one identified with a classical, paederastic ideal and the other with the newly defined homosexual.

To this extent, Weininger's work can be read as a fulcral point in the movement from biologistic, gendered understandings of homosexuality to a philosophy of desire focused on object choice. In confronting the reality of a masculine desire for masculinity, however, Weininger will be obliged to confess the limits of his model. Starting from a physiological assumption entirely alien to Blüher's subsequent strict division of psychological and physiological data, Weininger argues

> that in all cases of sexual inversion, there will be found indications of the anatomical characters of the opposite sex. There is no such thing as genuine "psycho-sexual hermaphroditism"; the men who are sexually attracted by men have outward marks of effeminacy, just as women of a similar disposition to those of their own sex exhibit male characters. That this should be so is quite intelligible if we admit the close parallelism between body and mind.   (45)

The linking of sexual inversion to physiological effeminization—clearly distinguishing Weininger from the masculinists—derives from a mimetological philosophical tradition that in turn assumes "the close parallelism between mind and body." A decisive difference between Weininger and Blüher, then, will be not merely the move from biologism to culturalism, but the movement away from mimetology, away from the conceptualization of the mind-body relation in terms of a *representation*.

Weininger confronts an objection to his own totalizing theory, however, by admitting "that there are men with very little taint or femaleness about them who yet exert a very strong influence on members of their own sex" (51–52). In other words, the threat to a generalizable theory of desire derives in this case not from the new "homo-style" delineated from Sedgwick, but from an older masculinist tradition. Of course, Weininger is not the first to note distinctions within the species homosexual, and he himself refers to the work of Albert Moll. What is interesting, however, is the way in which he chooses to code the distinction in terms of homosexuality and paederasty:

> The distinction may be expressed as follows: The homosexualist is that type of sexual invert who prefers very female men or very male

women, in accordance with the general law of sexual attraction. The pederast, on the other hand, may be attracted either by very male men or by very female women, but in the latter case only in so far as he is not pederastic. . . . The origin of pederasty is a problem in itself and remains unsolved by this investigation. (52)

The homosexual—in Weininger's definition—is not necessarily "homosexual" in the contemporary sense: he might, in fact, desire "very male women." It is only the confrontation with masculinist homosexuality—figured as paederasty—that first obliges Weininger to confront homosexuality as a "psychosexual" phenomenon, a "problem" left "unsolved" by his own attempt at a general theory of desire.

If Weininger defines the problematic of masculinism, he can be linked to the masculinist tradition only tenuously and against his own wishes: the confrontation with masculinist homosexuality (or "pederasty") serves to refute rather than prove his hypotheses, thereby making possible and necessary the work of those such as Blüher. In other words, while it is Blüher's acquaintance with the work of Freud that will allow him to posit a specifically homosexual psyche, for Weininger the reverse is the case: it is only the scandalous existence of a specifically homosexual psyche (a man's desire for a man) that necessitates a break—an unthinkable break—with prevailing biologistic discourses on homosexuality. In fact, it is paederasty that gives the lie to Weininger's theory, and he is obliged to acknowledge that the desire of a masculine man for another masculine man poses the most serious threat to his model, which constructs an ethics of supplementarity on the basis of a physiological attraction. Consequently, though Weininger will argue that "there is no ethical difference" (51) between homo- and heterosexual union once they are understood in terms of his formula of complementarity, it is clear that paederasty—unlike Sedgwick's "homo-style"—unsettles the ethical relation of alterity central to existing theories of sexual attraction.

From the perspective of Weininger's theory it becomes virtually impossible to speak of a masculinist tradition at all: for the very thing that defines the modern understanding of homosexuality—

the desire of a man for another man or of a woman for another
woman—is excluded from his study as an unsolvable problem,
even though it grounds the very structure of supplementarity central to the theory. Although he claims simply to ignore the problem of paederasty in his work, one senses that it comes back to
haunt him when—at the book's conclusion—he argues for sexual
abstinence, arguing that "sexual union has no place in the idea of
mankind" (347). Having formulated sexual attraction on the basis of an ethical (and mathematical) reciprocity, Weininger nevertheless concludes by renouncing such union and the ethic it
grounds. From the perspective of an ethics grounded in natural
and generalizable laws, the paederastic homosexual is necessarily
a scandal. Homosexual desire must always be explained in terms
of its ultimately theatrical (mimetological) reenactment of a heterosexual biological attraction. It is this desire to figure homosexuality as (mis-)representation that Blüher will subsequently term
pathography and criticize in the work of Freud.

I will return to Weininger at the end of the chapter to examine the importance of the Freudian, Oedipal problematic to the
understanding of racism both in his own writings and in the work
of Blüher. I hope to demonstrate that there is a resistance in each
of these different thinkers to the ideological, psychological, and
political implications of Oedipus; an attempt to ground the State
in something other than a familial structure explicitly identified—
in both cases—as "Jewish." For now, however, I wish to consider
the work of Friedlaender, in which anti-Semitism emerges only in
the context of a broader attack on religious (effeminized) attitudes
to male sexuality. It is important to note that this attack will be
launched not in the name of one religion against another, not in
the name of one race against another—but in the name of one culture against another: Hellenic ideals provide a nurturing ground
both for an emerging homosexual identity and for an ultimately
racist cultural discourse.

The masculinist tradition drew its decisive intellectual and
moral impetus from a return to a Greek (paederastic) idealism,
whose binarisms it sees elaborated in the Western philosophical

tradition, but it is not enough to see in the emergence of a masculinist homosexual ideology the reassertion of a lost Hellenism. The years intervening between the publication of the works of Friedlaender, Weininger, and then Blüher were years in which the discourse of psychoanalysis had begun to establish its authority and—potentially—to pose a threat to the Hellenic clarity of the masculinist tradition. Even in the writings of Friedlaender, however—untouched by the psychoanalytic method and terminology so central to Blüher—masculinism is already self-consciously revisionist in its appropriation of classical homoerotic material.

Historically, Friedlaender's work is of interest for the position it occupies between the physiological approach to psychiatry developed by Lombroso (and subsequently popularized by Nordau) and the Freudian psychoanalytic method first integrated into the masculinist tradition through Blüher.[6] According to Friedlaender's historical narrative, the Hellenic paederastic ideal was eclipsed in the Middle Ages and resurfaced only fitfully in the Renaissance. Christianity is but one manifestation of an ascetic tradition that Friedlaender holds responsible for the demise of same-sex love, a tradition effected—he claims—by *das Liebesmonopol der Weiber und der Priester* (the erotic monopoly of women and the priesthood) (20). Despite his opposition to the model of effeminization, Friedlaender offers an account of effeminate homosexuality in the following terms: "If it then proves true that a substantial number of extreme homosexuals demonstrate specifically feminine attributes, this should not be traced back to the admixture of positively feminine elements, but rather to a lesser development in their masculine sexuality" (230). Femininity in the male is figured as absence or lack, rather than as a positive trait: the homosexual is not more feminine, just less masculine. The question, of course, would be *why* masculine sexual instincts would be less pronounced in the homosexual. Friedlaender argues that it is sexuality in general that is sublimated as part of a division of social labor in which the homosexual plays a disproportionately important role.[7]

Despite this assumption of a sexual sublimation, we should note Friedlaender's essential eroticism and his appeal to an en-

lightened sexuality that casts off the asceticism of the Christian tradition, placing him—as we shall see—in opposition to the ascetic
Weininger. However, he is quick to point out that the Hellenic
ideal was itself far from undifferentiated, and—surprisingly—it is
precisely Plato who comes under attack: "In general it was taken as
a trivial truism that the masculine instinct for love might develop
in *both* directions. Only Plato seems to have assumed that some
were predisposed by nature for one and others for the opposite direction. We shall have reason to speak of this later, for this particular opinion of Plato has acquired a special importance in the present day" (6). Friedlaender is arguing from the position of a nuanced primal bisexuality and sees Plato as an exception to the
Hellenic ethos in his positing of two potential forms of desire:
homo- and heterosexual. Thus, while Stümke and Finkler might
attack masculinists such as Friedlaender for a lack of solidarity with
their "fellow homosexuals," it is important to remember that by
refusing the Platonic tradition as presented here, Friedlaender quite
consciously problematizes all sexual identity and negates the possibility of any homosexual identity politics. At the same time he is
entering a polemic for control of the Hellenic ideal.

As will become apparent, Friedlaender shares with Weininger
a theory of desire that accounts for both homo- and heterosexuality along a continuum, while not positing identity on the basis
of either form of desire. This continuum is politically crucial—as
we shall see—because it allows for the unification of the disparate
social functions performed by homo- and heterosocial structures.
Friedlaender is unwilling—for political reasons we will examine below—to dissociate these functions from each other and laments an
unfortunate tradition derived from Plato and exemplified in modern sexology by such theorists as Hössli, Ulrichs, and Hirschfeld:
"The modern division of 'heterosexuals' and 'homosexuals'—or
'Dionings' and 'Urnings'—clearly derives from that famous moment in Plato's *Symposium*. . . . As I have already pointed out, it
was on the basis of this passage that Ulrichs divided people into
the two classes of 'Dionings' and 'Urnings,' artificial categories
that distorted even further a classification that was already far from

satisfactory" (71–72). Of course, the opposition to the Ulrichs formulation forms the very backbone of the masculinist position, but what is remarkable here is Friedlaender's recognition that such a tradition of thought is itself also grounded in classical, Platonic precedent.

What Friedlaender specifically rejects is the reduction of the question of same-sex desire to the question of effeminization; but this rejection extends to the category of homosexuality *tout court*. He posits a bisexual continuum with gradations of same-sex or other-sex desire (though he is not consistently averse to the notion that at a certain point of preference it becomes possible to speak—albeit dismissively—of a homosexual identity). Through this sexual continuum Friedlaender seeks to rescue a political model in which the demands of the family and the demands of the State on the male can be reconciled through bisexuality. His is not a revolutionary project. The argument for a primary bisexuality—though apparently radical—is, in fact, politically invested in the status quo: homosexuality can thereby be integrated into existing familial structures as a necessary political supplement. Friedlaender implicitly recognizes that the emergence of a homosexual identity necessarily places masculinity in opposition to the social order, for it withdraws male subjects from the orbit of the family. While he welcomes this as an attack on the "erotic monopoly of women and the priesthood," it nevertheless poses questions of social structure—of the relation of familial to State authority.

Within the masculinist tradition of thought represented here by Friedlaender the homosexual obtains a specific function in the maintenance of the State or of the human community. As we shall see, the central arguments of Blüher's sophisticated analysis are already foreshadowed in Friedlaender's conclusion that "we encounter here a sort of division of labor between the demands of reproduction and the new demands of socialization, which—taken together—would be too much for one individual" (231). With this division of labor, though, Friedlaender is undermining the work of social cohesion he sought to reinforce through the image of "the Athenians, who were at one and the same time heads of the family and the lovers of young men" (72). His concessionary acceptance of a *Zwischenstufentheorie* (or theory of sexual inter-mediates)—in spite of his rejection of an effeminizing third-sex ar-gument—is motivated by a desire to offer a point of contact for family and State. If the Athenian can be at once a father and a paederastic lover, the two functions of social order—family and State—can be reconciled, and Friedlaender himself inserted into a Hegelian tradition of State theory. Third-sex theory would sun-der this continuum by uncoupling the paederastic responsibilities of State from the role of father and husband. By the very end of his analysis—when he castigates "an artificial hypertrophy of the familial instincts and an equally artificial depletion of the physio-logical fundaments of further socialization" (249)—Friedlaender will open up an oppositional field that Blüher will subsequently inhabit. This specifically Christianized hypertrophy will, in Blüher, be identified with the Jew.

It is important to see Friedlaender as a threshold figure in this respect also: he marks a final (failed) attempt to reconcile the com-munity-oriented goals of masculinism with the bourgeois ideal of the family. The failure of this reconciliation might be seen as a fail-ure of the Hellenic tradition of those *Familienväter* in whom the (homo-)sociality of same-sex desire is reconciled with the het-erosocial duties of the paterfamilias. The specialization—Fried-laender's division of labor—of family and community responsibil-ities partakes of the logic of rationalization and is coextensive with the emergence of modern homosexual identity. This specializa-tion, moreover, constitutes a political crisis—a crisis of a certain Greek ideal, a crisis of democracy: for the ideal of the integrated *demos* depends on a bisexuality sundered by the emergence of the self-conscious homosexual. In the work of both Friedlaender and Blüher we encounter, then, not the chance superimposition of ho-mosexuality and antidemocratic politics, but the necessary con-struction of homosexuality from the perspective of a disillusioned, postdemocratic modernity. It is possible for homosexuality to emerge (specifically, in Blüher's work) as a distinct form of iden-tity only at a certain point of crisis in the self-legitimation of bourgeois political structures. The homosexual emerges from the ruins of the Hegelian dialectic of a State grounded in the self-dissolving family.

Friedlaender's primary bisexuality therefore reconciles homosexual acts to a heterosocial order. It is precisely this accommodation that becomes problematic in the work of Blüher, for whom homosexual identity necessarily questions the dialectical sublation of the heterosexual family in a homosocial State. I am arguing, then, that masculinism begins by resisting homosexual identification, but necessarily posits a model of identity deriving from the crisis of the bourgeois family's relation to social and political structures. Friedlaender continues to hold more resolutely than will Blüher to the notion of bisexuality, scorning as atrophied *Kümmerlinge* all who are incapable of loving partners of either gender. Blüher, with his quasi-Nietzschean notion of the *Männerheld,* will be prepared to move toward a more one-sided celebration of homosexual bonds. Both, however, seek to valorize what Friedlaender refers to as those "feelings of sympathy that find individual expression in friendship, and that we know in their broader forms as (true) patriotism and a (sincere) love of one's fellow man" (x). This concern for the nation (if not necessarily for the State) is certainly a characteristic of masculinist political thought. Both Blüher and Friedlaender are concerned with establishing a continuum from homosexual desire through to patriotism, a concern that will lead Blüher to foreground in his work the theory of the State. This is what is under threat in the development of a homosexual identity from within masculinism: the harmonious relation of bourgeois family and State (personified in the bisexual Athenian father).

It was historically necessary—for a homosexual subject position to emerge from within masculinism—to reject the bourgeois social accommodation of family and State; necessary, in other words, to confront the extremes of anarchism (as exemplified in the next chapter by Mackay) or homosocial totalitarianism. Eve Sedgwick—drawing on the wealth of material becoming available to historians of homosexual emancipation in Germany—comments in *Tendencies* on how

the newly crystallizing German state was itself more densely inner-
vated than any other site with the newly insistent, internally incoher-
ent but increasingly foregrounded discourses of homosexual identity,
recognition, prohibition, advocacy, demographic specification and political controversy. Virtually all of the competing, conflicting figures
for understanding same-sex desire—archaic ones and modern ones,
medicalized and politicizing, those emphasizing pederastic relations,
gender inversion, or "homo-" homosexuality—were coined and cir-
culated in this period in the first place in Germany and through German culture, medicine and politics.   (66)

What I hope to have demonstrated—with reference to the philo-
sophico-political tradition treated only tangentially in Sedgwick's
trinity of "culture, medicine and politics"—is how the intersection
of an emergent homosexual identity and potentially totalitarian
theories of the State depended ultimately on the collapse of a tradition best exemplified in Hegel's *Philosophy of Right*. This tradition will seek—as a final defense, in the work of Friedlaender—to
ground the movement from family to State along the trajectory of
an original bisexuality, allowing the paterfamilias to ensure both
public and private reproduction. Homosexual identity emerges in
Blüher precisely as a *crisis*—rather than apotheosis—of the tradition of thought toward which Sedgwick gestures.

Moving from the pre-Freudian Friedlaender to the work of
Blüher—who in fact corresponded briefly with Freud—one need
only glance at the different tables of contents to appreciate the impact that psychoanalysis exerted on the essentially culturalist tradition of masculinism.[8] Friedlaender's *Renaissance of Eros Uranios*
begins with an "Introduction to Physiology and Morality," and—
before drawing some practical conclusions on what is to be done—
consistently interweaves considerations of moral and philosophical questions with disquisitions on physiology and biology. All of
this would be anathema to Blüher, whose work *The Role of Eroticism in Masculine Society* depends on a rigid opposition of nature
and culture (even if culture will, in fact, acquire all the force of legitimation once ascribed to the natural order). One can most easily note this transition from Friedlaender to Blüher in their re-

spective theories of repression and sublimation, theories that, in turn, reflect their views of society and the State.

Friedlaender is rather straightforward in his explanation for the preponderance of homosexuals among the great men of history, and his explanation bears no trace of a Freudian mechanism of repression and sublimation. He argues:

> Any repression of deep-seated physiological or psychical tendencies *harms* the body and spirit. . . . Consequently, we can understand why the great men of post-classical and recent times have so often sinned against both custom and the law on this particular point [homosexuality]: had they accommodated themselves to law and custom and sinned against their own nature, they might not have accomplished the achievements that have made their names immortal. (63)

Homosexuals are apparently to be encountered among the ranks of great men precisely because only a great man is capable of shrugging off the claustrophobic demands of an effeminate culture. A commitment to culture is necessarily a commitment to an erotic homosociality. The greatness of homosexuals can be accounted for precisely by their lack of sublimation, by their refusal to ignore the instincts ignored by so many other average men. Clearly, Friedlaender's model of sexual adjustment is closely tied to an ideal of personal self-actualization, and to a Hellenic notion of harmony that is prepared to see the model of social order in the natural order of human instinct.

For Blüher, meanwhile, the possibility for any untrammeled self-actualization is always already lost—his axiom is "to be human and to have culture are identical." Blüher's homosexual is always already socialized. His definitive methodological breakthrough is an insistence on the separation of physical androgyny and erotic inversion as the fundamental starting point of any attempt to understand the political importance of the homosexual as *Typus inversus*. It is in this insistence that he is led to what one might read as *the* classical statement of the most developed masculinist position: "Bisexuality and androgyny were simply conflated, the former being mistaken for the latter, the latter for the former, and—

if necessary—either one for both. . . . The writings and comments on homosexuality have failed to note that we fundamentally deny it when we see it as the product or psychical complement of a man's material femininity" (1: 27). The move toward a strictly cultural understanding of sexuality is clearly conditioned by an exposure to the work of Freud, but Blüher is concerned—while rejecting the biologism of those such as Friedlaender and Weininger on the one hand—to reject, on the other, what he calls the "pathographic" aspects of Freud. This pathography—whose contours we might divine from the similarly pathographic elements within Frankfurt School theory outlined in the previous chapter—consists in the persistent displacement of homosexual desire; in a concern for its etiology, or in its interpretation as symptom or (mis-)representation. Homosexual desire will continually be explained (away), argues Blüher, in such a way that its material and social existence is lost. Thus, just as prepsychological theories of homosexuality had sought to harness questions of sexuality to an already existing discourse of gender by seeing in homosexual desire only the mental modality of physiological hermaphroditism, so Freud's pathography will continue to read this desire as something other, as a reflection.

Blüher concerns himself not with ideology—not with meaning as a system of displacement and interpretation—but rather with meaning as immanence, as the social instantiation of the fact of homosexual desire. Rejecting the assertion "that every invert is psychically incomplete or malformed," he asserts that "sexuality creates (indeed, must create) *two* fully developed, originary and indestructible types of man; one desires men, the other women" (167). Homosexuality, then, is not to be understood from the perspective of heterosexuality—as a failure of full development—but rather in terms of its own logic. It is not something that has to be explained, but rather something that—as Eros—makes explanation and meaning possible. Thus, Blüher refuses any explanation that reduces homosexuality to the level of symptom or even to the level of displaced desire or erotic substitution. More specifically, he rejects a theory—somewhat vaguely attributed to "the Freudian

School"—of homosexuality as the fear of incest: "It is said that that inversion in the male results from an overwhelmingly strong desire for the mother during childhood; as soon as this desire reaches a certain threshold of irritation and must therefore be repressed, a simple avoidance of the female type of the mother is no longer enough: rather, the patient *avoids the entire feminine sex* in order to safeguard against any possible incest" (1: 162).

Blüher argues that this model quite unnecessarily sees homosexuality as unfulfilled and unfulfillable. According to the argument outlined above, the homosexual would be fated (even more than the heterosexual, whose desire is also displaced, if not so dramatically *mis*placed) never to experience real erotic pleasure. The reality of homosexual desire, however, is—for Blüher—itself enough of a rebuttal to this position: "The true paederast *achieves* this happiness, however, and for this very reason such theories are mistaken. It takes account of singular cases of illness and ignores the *Typus inversus*. A sincere, complete and satisfying dedication to one's own sex is *never* a mere avoidance of incest" (1: 163). This move is extremely important, for it seeks to legitimate homosexuality not as a natural aberration that should at the very least be pitied, but as a cultural phenomenon that is at the same time entirely sexually satisfying. By arguing in this manner Blüher is one of the first theorists to actually posit the sufficiency of a homosexual pleasure, to accord homosexuality a place rather than a *dis*placement.

In his appropriation of Freud, Blüher prefers the metapsychological writings and the theory of culture they suggest. He pursues a Freudian dialectic, but gives it a somewhat different intonation, by arguing that "the repression of sexuality does not result from culture, but the reverse: culture results from the repression of sexuality. This does not mean that retro-actions are impossible; specific cultural values resulting from repression might in turn reinforce the pressures that are brought to bear on sexuality. To be human and to have culture are identical" (1: 70). Blüher is concerned with a specifically cultural impulse rather than with the creation of impulses through the constraints of society.[9] The starting point of his analysis—as opposed to the symptomatic pathography he opposes—is the assertion that Eros is a meaningful and meaning-constitutive phenomenon that can be reduced neither to mere symptom nor to biology. His primary concern is to differentiate the biological from the behavioral—as for example, in his insistence on the difference between androgyny (a physiological state) and bisexuality (a form of behavior). He inverts the traditional biologism of sexology by insisting "wherever sexuality makes itself noticed in man it has already been taken up into the workings of Eros and acquired thereby a *meaning*" (1: 38). With this assertion, Blüher wishes to demonstrate the purely heuristic value of the category of "sexuality." One can hypothesize that sexuality is a raw material subsequently worked into Eros, but this assumption offers no real explanation of the problem, since sexuality is always already erotically inscribed. In other words, the nature-culture division that might be constructed on the basis of sexuality and Eros is deconstructed, and Nature loses any legitimational force. The key term in Blüher's analysis, of course, is Eros itself, which he defines as "not a merely quantitative phenomenon. Indeed, it is not a sexological concept strictly speaking, for it always bears within itself a cultural aspect" (1: 37).

Erotik, then, is presented as sexuality with a qualitative distinction.[10] Although the concepts of sexuality and libido are potentially biological terms for Blüher, it is with the advent of Eros that we enter the cultural—and political—realm; that admixture to sexuality that makes of it Eros is an admixture of meaning. Nevertheless, it is an admixture that cannot, in the first place, be recognized as such, since the thing to which it is appended (sexuality) never appears in pure form, and is therefore something of a fiction. Moreover, it is an admixture that totally changes the nature of the investigation, vitiating science precisely where it sought to grasp sexuality. For Blüher, it is sexuality—the putative biological origin—that is an abstraction, and Eros—the cultural fact of desire—that provides the sole concrete ground for analysis. In the context of an analysis of homosexuality, of course, this move serves to disarm the objection that homosexuality is "against nature," but more than this Blüher disarms the very category of nature as origin.

Whereas Friedlaender was forced to confront the collapse of his own anti-Platonic Hellenic political ideals in the collapse of bisexuality into the specialized sexualities homo- and hetero-, Blüher denies the existence of the sexual outside of the meaning-constitutive erotic and seeks to reintegrate sexuality (as Eros) into a new and meaningful political framework. Eros, we might provisionally conjecture, is sexuality in the realm of meaning. Blüher is also particularly concerned to differentiate his own notion of *Sexualität* (sexuality) from a variety of alternative Germanicized terms for sexuality deriving from the root *Geschlecht-*, or gender (such as *Geschlechtlichkeit*, *Geschlechtigkeit*, or even *Geschlechthaftigkeit*): the question of sexuality and the question of gender are to be dissociated. These Germanicized terms are purely biological and designate what Blüher calls a merely spatial discourse on the body, whereas the notion of sexuality is intrinsically temporal, reflecting not the organization of matter, but the dynamics of an instinct.[11] (It is this desire to dissociate sex from sexuality that makes the transition from the first to the second volume of Blüher's work so abrupt and dissatisfying—since the second volume will concentrate specifically on those questions of gender bracketed out of the first volume.)

Whereas biologistic notions of a *Naturgesetz* sought to resolve the nature-culture dichotomy in the name of an originary natural order (for example, bisexuality), Blüher's insistence on the inextricability of sexuality and Eros reprivileges the supposedly derivative term of culture.[12] With the failure of Friedlaender's attempt to fuse familial and societal functions through the category of bisexuality, the question of homosexuality becomes inextricably linked—in Blüher's work—to the question of the *männliche Gesellschaft* (masculine society) and the State. In his prologue to the first volume, Blüher elaborates on what he takes to be the fundamental contribution of his work: "Before this book, the idea of basing man's existence in the State on *Eros* has never been coherently pursued" (4). If the claim is somewhat exaggerated, Blüher's real advance is to *begin* with the question of the State, and—on the basis of this question—to reject both the idealist and the materialist analysis of its emergence. "Man's existence in a State," he argues, "depends neither upon spirit [*Geist*] nor upon economy" (1: 3).[13]

Responding to this analysis based on a linkage of Eros and the State, one might seek to reject its implicitly totalitarian and charismatic theory of a State, in which the erotic replaces rational calculation as the basis of political action. Such thinking is typical of radical right-wing ideologies at the early part of this century. We should beware, however, of consigning Blüher to such a camp without taking note of some of the arguments that differentiate his thought from the mainstream of reactionary or conservative thought (he would reject both nomenclatures).[14] First, we should note that Blüher—for all that his work is imbued with anti-Semitism, as we shall see—offers his analysis of the political Eros as an antidote to simplistic but increasingly popular racial theories of the State. Indeed, for Blüher, Eros—and politics—commences precisely where race leaves off:

> The State differs in its very essence from the herd. If I randomly throw a dozen each of various species of bird into a cage and let them come to rest, by the evening I will find the birds huddled together according to their species. This form of socialization we call the herd. . . . Necessary for the existence of a State is the illusion of an objective will; the State presupposes the potential insignificance of the individual, service to the whole, sacrifice to the transcendent collective. Man is not a herd animal, but by his very essence constitutes a State.   (1: 4–5)

In other words, the State is not—as in the liberal understanding—a pragmatic or contractual accommodation of individual wills and desires. It is itself an expression of an "objective will." What defines man is his *Staathaftigkeit* prior to the grounding of any historical State.[15]

While the invocation of objective will, the insistence on sacrifice, on the relative unimportance of the individual can all be seen as precursors of a strain of totalitarian political thought, Blüher quite specifically offers this antilibertarian model in opposition to those biologizing racial theories of the State typically identified with Nazism. Whereas Friedlaender's theory of nonsublimation—according to which homosexual heroes are great not because they sublimate, but because they refuse to sublimate their desires, and thereby keep their nature intact—depends on a notion of individuality, for Blüher the human being—qua human being—is defined by his embeddedness in the collective, by his *Staathaftigkeit.* For Blüher, the question of the State takes precedence over the questions of individual or race, which are, in fact, strictly prepolitical questions for him.

Blüher insists that the level of race is the level of the herd, and that what differentiates man—*as* race, one might say—is his movement beyond the simple herd existence. The collecting of animals about each other for warmth or mutual physical support is merely racial, merely the habit of the herd. Man is different: "The State differs in its very essence from the herd." The movement from nature to culture is radical and definitive: the State is not simply the social construction placed on nature, but rather the political phenomenon which itself defines a specifically *human* nature. In answer to the charge of masculinist racism made by Stümke and Finkler, we must respond that it would be logically impossible for Blüher to ground a political opinion on questions of race, since race is a question of the herd, whereas the political cannot—by very definition—partake of any such biologics. Although Blüher seems to close down the possibility of racist politics here, he in fact suggests that the liberal understanding of the State (as a pragmatic arrangement that accommodates the warring needs of otherwise asocial creatures) differs not politically from the conservative, but biologically: it is the (non-)politics of the herd. In other words, Blüher's masculinism takes race not as political ideologeme but as a structuring principle of political discourse in general.

Having demonstrated the play of totalitarian categories of race in Blüher's work, we need now to establish the role played by the homoerotic impulse in his social and political order, and to examine the extent to which this homosocial construct is compatible with familial and patriarchal social organization. Blüher starts from the hypothesis that "beyond the socializing principle of the family that feeds off the Eros of male and female, a second principle is at work in mankind, 'masculine society' [*die männliche Gesellschaft*], which owes its existence to male-male Eros, and finds its expression in male-bonding [*Männerbünden*]" (1: 7). His central thesis is that homosexuality provides the homosocial fundament for the establishing of a State structure above and beyond the microcosm of the familial unit:

> In all species where the familial urge is the sole determinant—where sexuality, in other words, expresses itself solely in this type of socialization—the construction of a collective is impossible. The family can function as a constitutive element of the State, but not more. And *wherever nature has produced species capable of developing a viable State, this has been made possible only by smashing the role of the family and male-female sexual urges as sole social determinants.* (1: 6)

Blüher dissociates the structure of the State from the structure of the family and resituates homosocial relations within the field of an Eros constitutive of the State. In this presentation, the erotic structure of the family not only differs from, but potentially constrains, the erotic fundaments of the State. Although the heterosexual family is referred to as the "first constitutive principle of the State" (1: 8), the State itself is fundamentally a homoerotic construct. Thus "the doctor," for example, "overlooks a fundamental fact: that which he calls 'the social order' in fact consists of two diametrically opposed forms of sociality, the family and masculine society" (1: 175).

The question remains, however, whether these two poles—the heterosexual/familial and the homosexual/State—are necessarily opposed, or whether they can, in fact, be reconciled. Certainly, the political function of the *männliche Gesellschaft* is the conscious political subversion of the family, and in making this point clear Blüher recurs to a strain of natural imagery otherwise alien to his strict division of natural and cultural phenomena. He writes, "Masculine society is supported by a type of human being that plays a role equivalent to that played by the worker in the state structure of bees and ants. At least these groups have the same sociological function: challenging the primacy of the family. Unlike their equivalents in the insect States, however, these men are not marked by a physiological atrophy of crucial organs; they differ only in their spiritual constitution from those men who head families" (1: 8–9). Here we have a full-fledged sociological paradigm in which the function of socialization is divided into the socialization through the family—which creates *Gesellschaft*—and socialization through the *männliche Gesellschaft*—which creates the State. The parallelisms fundamental to the analysis of patriarchy are sundered, the continuum from family to State apparently denied.

It is not only the patriarchal analysis that Blüher is opposing, however, but also the analysis offered by economism: subtly—or not so subtly—he undermines a class analysis. Thus in the passage above we note the identification of the *Typus inversus* with the *Arbeitergeschlecht*—or worker bees—of the insect world. Indeed, characterizing the structure of insect States, Blüher goes so far as to claim that "their males are cretinized and possess only a minuscule brain; the females—who have a somewhat larger brain—fulfill a purely reproductive function; the workers, meanwhile—who constitute a kind of third sex incapable of sexual relations—are the masters" (1: 6–7). By referring to the workers as "a kind of third sex," Blüher deftly links the argument of the third-sexers to the political and social models of the left. By rejecting the notion of a third sex as intrinsically biologistic, meanwhile, he implies the same fundamental misunderstanding in any social theory in which class—and the function of the worker—is modeled along the lines of a natural division of labor. In turn, both of these lines of argumentation—third-sexism and socialism—are linked to the unacceptable methodological conflation of natural and cultural phenomena.

Blüher is quite clearly not characterizing the *Typus inversus* in terms of a third sex, then: the very invocation of the natural parallel serves to accentuate the difference between the herd organizations of the animal world and social order. In terms of human society it is precisely this form of third-sex theory that Blüher wishes to attack. In humans the homosocial task of creating the State is not delegated to a third sex, but rather superimposed on all male members of society, because human beings are fundamentally bisexual and therefore capable of fulfilling both roles, without any specific third sex being necessary: "Nature, in creating the *Typus inversus* in man, did not create any corresponding 'third sex'" (1: 130).

At the same time as he denies third-sex theory, however, Blüher is concerned with developing the *Typus inversus* as the bearer of State power and transfamilial allegiance. In other words, there *is* a class of men who perform the function of the worker ants, but that function is not preordained by biology: this third sex cannot be measured in terms of the binarism set up between the other two sexes. We will recall that Friedlaender accounted for homosexual effeminacy by arguing not that the homosexual suffers from an admixture of feminine attributes but rather that his social—rather than directly sexual—function leads to a withering of specifically masculine sexual attributes, with the result that a form of atrophied androgyny asserts itself. For Weininger, the very act of succumbing to sexual desire—even of the most rampantly heterosexual sort—was itself a form of effeminization. Clearly, Blüher's consistent move away from the confusion of bisexuality and androgyny—part of his methodological move away from Friedlaender's physiologism—must lead him to reject the notion of effeminization through sexual atrophy.

If "inversion" cannot be understood merely as a functional condition latent within an already existing gender binarism—the inversion of masculine into feminine or vice versa—then the key to understanding inversion in Blüher's usage lies in dissociating heterosexuality from masculinity. Rejecting the parallel of heterosexuality and masculinity and the explanation of homosexuality in terms of effeminization, Blüher points out how the physiological effects of such a parallel cannot be noted empirically:

> The difficulty is that precisely those things that ought to progress in tandem—for example the depletion of masculinity (effeminization) and the depletion of heterosexuality (homosexual tendencies)—unfortunately do *not* do us this favor. In this regard, we encounter in-

stead—as we shall see subsequently in our rejection of the *Zwischen-stufen* theory of homosexuality—the wildest variations. The coexistence of effeminization and homosexualization must therefore be examined in terms of a relationship that is not causal. (1: 29)

At the same time, Blüher notes the possible parallelism of homosexuality and effeminization, while refusing to see that parallel as in any way a causal relationship. The devaluation of gendered binarisms and the attempt to cast inversion outside of questions of masculinity lead to the privileging of alternative binarisms.

To understand the role of the erotic in Blüher's construction of the State, it is necessary to examine the fundamental distinction he draws between the allo- and the autoerotic.[16] That any political collective should be alloerotically grounded seems a truism: as a libidinal bond, every political structure must depend on a reaching out toward others. For Blüher, however, the alloerotic and the autoerotic are determined on the basis of an internal affective orientation, rather than being constituted around a series of acts, so that "autoerotism, as the simplest form of sexual satisfaction, is defined by the fact that the subject of the excitation establishes no relation to any object outside of himself. It is completely self-contained and autarchic" (1: 22). The allo-/auto- distinction does not differentiate modes of physical gratification, but is a specifically imaginary or, indeed, social distinction: it is a relation to (or an absence of relation to) a real or imaginary object. In other words, the alloerotic would define itself not necessarily as a relation to an actual object, but as the internalized relation to any imagined object. Thus, for example, the act of masturbation is not intrinsically autoerotic, for every sexual act can be divided into its auto- and its alloerotic form. In truly autoerotic masturbation "a purely self-contained irritation is produced entering into no relation with the corporeal world and thus marking the personality accordingly" (1: 113). The problem with autoerotic masturbation is that it is retarded at the level of the physical—of bodies, of the irritant *Juck-reiz*—that it is, in other words, sexual rather than erotic: it lacks the meaning-giving force of Eros. What is lacking is not the real, but rather the introjected object. Blüher further links this form of sexuality to the infantile stage of development, and it will retain, throughout his analysis, an overtone of infantilism.

Nevertheless, Blüher insists that masturbation cannot be reduced to a simple manipulation of the sexual or erogenous organs. In alloerotic masturbation, meanwhile, "an object desired by the consciousness remains unattainable. The subject therefore presents that object to itself in its imagination and gratifies itself as if the object were present in reality. This form of masturbation is unproblematic. Such a character is never perverse" (1: 112). Of note here is the indifference of the alloerotic to the reality of its object. Alloerotic masturbation is an act in which the cathected object has been internalized. Whereas autoerotic sexuality is a merely physical *Juckreiz*, the role of the imagination within the alloerotic clearly opens it up to the play of the social.[17] Indeed, one might take alloerotic masturbation as *the* paradigmatic form of the socioerotic insofar as it involves the introjection of the Other into the imaginary structures whereby the self constitutes itself and derives pleasure. In other words, it is not simply a question of the subject relating to an object in one form of sexuality (the alloerotic), and withdrawing from the world in another (the autoerotic), but rather of a difference in internal structure in the two forms. Blüher is concerned—in the presentation of an erotic socialization—less with the actuality of the object of desire than with the inculcation of desire—that is, alloerotic desire—within the imaginary subject.

The subject is constituted, it would seem, through its introjected—imagined and imaginary—alloerotic attachments, as a political subject, as the subject of a social imagination. It is in this context, then—the context of the allo- and the autoerotic, the context of the social imaginary—rather than in terms of another binarism of male and female, that Blüher's homosexual must be understood. It is not simply a question of binding the individual to the alterity of the collective or State, but rather of creating a certain type of subject—a subject at once open to the play of the imaginary, but indifferent also to the reality of the thing to which he is bound, an ideological subject. A desire fixated at the level of the real, unable to move beyond the confines set by the mother, the first object of desire, meanwhile, would be infantile. In Blüher's presentation, this infantilism is itself further differentiated into alloerotic and autoerotic forms: there is a form of autoerotic infantilism—which Blüher calls "playful"—and an alloerotic form. Paradoxically—given the intrinsically socializing function of the alloerotic—it is this latter form that can result in a parental fixation. In other words, the functions of the auto- and alloerotic seem to have switched: it is now the autoerotic that is responsible for a play (of signifiers)—a play that Blüher characterizes as a mistake, a *Verkennung*. Social order, we might say, is grounded in a *méconnaissance* of desire. Infantile autoerotism establishes the play of mis-cognition (*Verkennung*), on the basis of which the onticological cognitive function of Eros will subsequently be established. The alloerotic, however, is reduced to the psychic equivalent of the autoerotic *Juckreiz*, when the child is unable to replace the mother as the merely prototypical symbol of the affective object.

This second—alloerotic—form of infantilism begins to sound extremely Oedipal with the crucial difference, of course, that in it the play of displacement is not possible. Whereas, for Blüher, the Oedipal functions in such a way that "the *image* [my emphasis] of the mother wordlessly helps the boy simply by fulfilling the love life of his childhood and determining the *type* that will most facilitate his most lasting love in marriage" (1: 103), an infantile parental fixation remains blocked in the real, a fixation on the actual parents rather than the *Bild*, the imaginary parents: "For the infantile individual the process is quite different. His development is facilitated not by the *type* of the mother—a specific feminine *typology*—but by *the actual mother herself*: he remains fixated upon *her*, not upon her type" (1: 104). In infantilism, there is a failure to symbolize and thereby transcend the real mother. There is, in other words, that same problem of the literal—of the real—that we previously encountered as a problem of the *auto*erotic. Thus, one crucial distinction between the two seems to crumble: failure to accede to the imaginary is possible in the mode of both auto- and alloerotism. Rather than seeing the Oedipal configuration as that which inaugurates the development of a sociosymbolic order,

Blüher sees it as an arrestation of the powers of a social imaginary. The fixation on the family forecloses rather than prefigures the political and erotic (or homosexual) cathexis of the homosocial State. To this extent, Blüher is, indeed, "anti-Oedipal." Further, it is to the extent that he is anti-Oedipal that he will be anti-Semitic, for this hypertrophy of the family will be identified with a caricature of what Lyotard has, in another context, referred to as the "Jewish Oedipus."[18]

Blüher's insistence on the imaginary as the socializing introjection of the alloerotic object returns us immediately to Weininger, for whom the reality of the sexual object and of sexual practices was likewise subjugated to the imaginary—this time to the imaginary self-constitution of the subject. One need only examine the terms in which Weininger rejects coitus, for example—when he argues that "during coitus a man forgets all about everything, he forgets the woman; she no longer has a psychic but only a physical existence for him" (337). Here, Weininger complains that coitus fixes man in the realm of the real and the material (the realm of woman, in other words) and thereby forecloses the possibility of any imaginary community such as Blüher would construct. Coitus stands for the meaningless conjunction of two physical entities and is dissociated from any social interaction. Contrasted to this coital "forgetting" is a masculine indifference to materiality that recalls Blüher's privileging of the imaginary relation. Weininger writes, "that the human race should persist is of no interest whatever to reason; he who would perpetuate humanity would perpetuate the problem and the guilt, the only problem and the only guilt" (346). I would like now to follow up what I see as the potentially chilling consequences of this insistence on an imaginary social structure—an insistence that, in its extreme case, desires the *destruction* of the "real" objects of desire. For what matters—I have sought to argue—in this privileging of the alloerotic is not at all the "otherness" of the object of desire, but its very introjection as an imaginary construct.

For all the similarities, we must first insist on the radical differences separating Blüher and Weininger on this question.

Blüher's typological insistence on the ideality of the object in the process of the subject's socialization has been pushed much further in Weininger's *Sex and Character*. For Weininger, man's "forgetting" of the woman in coitus means reducing her to the level of physicality. Even in the sexual act the emphasis must be on the ideality of the sexual object, whereas for Blüher—quite contrary to the charge of sexophobia leveled by Stümke and Finkler—the physical enactment of homosexual Eros is crucial as the ontico-logical component of his philosophy of the State. In Weininger's work, it is in its homophobic—rather than homosexual—form that masculinist philosophy becomes at once sexophobic and, I would argue, potentially genocidal in its sublation of all physical existence in ideality. For where biologism places procreation, Weininger places reason. His indifference to life—an indifference that is not unrelated, I think, to the ideological structure of a certain form of genocidal racism touched on in the previous chapter—is the result of a rebellion against mere biology and takes its rationale from philosophy. Thus, though we are used to explaining racism from within the vocabulary of a biologistic eugenics—the propagation of the race, the extermination of racial aberrations, etc.—in Weininger it emerges from something quite different, from an ideal eugenics that must reject *all* materiality (or raciality) as a failure of the self-sublating reason. The substantive and structural elements of masculinism that potentially link a discourse on same-sex desire and a racist, life-destroying discourse are here established only in the context of an explicitly homophobic masculinism. It is precisely a theorist who resists envisaging an erotics of masculinism—a theorist who asserts his heterosexuality through a stigmatization of the homosexual—who forges the homo-fascist link.

From Blüher's perspective, on the contrary, Weininger's problem lies precisely in the subjugation of all phenomena to the structure of reason. Masculinist logic becomes totalitarian—and potentially genocidal in its indifference to the materiality of human bodies—not in the context of a pseudoscientific biologism, but in the attempt to ground itself in an idealist philosophy. An examination of the problematic relation of Eros to Logos is at the very core of Blüher's work, which clearly opposes Weininger's subjugation of the erotic to the rational by claiming that "Eros and Logos—pursued to their respective ends—stand in deadly opposition to one another" (1: 236). Weininger's mistake is the desire to fuse the two, to sublate all physicality in a reason that is indifferent to physical existence.[19] His reduction of matter to the ideoplasm is no less invalid than the sexologists' reduction of cultural to biological phenomena. Instead, Blüher sees in the force of Eros the onticological counterpart to the cognitive process of *Erkenntnis*:

> Cognition [*Erkenntnis*] places its emphasis on the general (in pathetic terms, the "eternal") as opposed to the specific (pathetically, the "ephemeral"). Even where it seeks to grasp something that is by its very nature unique (a specific individual, for example) the act of cognition always can do so only from the position of general concepts. Eros proceeds in quite the opposite direction. It takes as its central position the love of one individual for another: it affirms with an equal fanaticism—an equally urgent determinacy—the absolutely unique. *Only* because it is singular and unique can it be affirmed. Eros is the philosophy of the particular. (1: 236)

Eros is the philosophy of the particular—and it is for this reason that Blüher insists on the physicality of the homosocial eros. What Blüher potentially presents as an alternative to the structure of *Erkenntnis* is, in fact, a component of it—the onticological. Weininger's mistake lies in the failure to recognize the onticological—sexual—component of Truth contained in the specificity of the homoerotic relation. Thus, the very possibility of developing any general theory of erotic attraction will itself inevitably lead—in Weininger—to precisely the form of sexophobia Stümke and Finkler criticize (wrongly) in all masculinism. The erotic is never generalizable for Blüher, and draws its specificity from the creation of an instantiated social and sexual meaning.

In concluding this overview of the philosophy of masculinism, however, we still need to explain the persistence of an anti-Semitic rhetoric—the rhetoric of racism—in Weininger and Blüher, whose theories are otherwise so divergent. I believe that the psychoanalytic discourse within which Blüher frames his Hellenized *männliche Gesellschaft* also helps explain the anti-Semitism of those such as Weininger. In Weininger's case, racism is clearly related to the representation of gender difference as a racial difference—a commonplace of misogynistic philosophy found in exemplary fashion in Schopenhauer, to whom all these thinkers are indebted. Thus, for Weininger, "paternity cannot satisfy the deepest longings of a man, and the idea that he is to be lost in the race is repellent to him" (223). Women, meanwhile—who fall for both Blüher and Weininger into the categories of mother/wife or whore —define themselves (as mothers) in the continuance of the race: "It is the permanence of the race that gives the mother her courage and fearlessness in contrast with the cowardliness and fear of the prostitute" (223). In other words, women are not just one example of a race; their very self-awareness (or, indeed, lack of it) is the consciousness of race. Women—like the Jews in Blüher—are identified with race *tout court*. Consequently, all race consciousness will be taken as a form of effeminization, or—more specifically—of matriarchalization.

Weininger's racism, then, is grounded in a critique of the familial, "feminine" unit. "The family in this biological sense," he will argue, "is feminine and maternal in its origin, and has no relation to the State or to society" (310). This opposition to the matriarchal foreclosure of the State must, however, confront the reality of feminine desire in the figure of the prostitute, and indeed Weininger at least credits the prostitute with an acknowledgment of the irreducible specificity of the male: "The dissimilarity in the relations of mother and prostitute to their child is rich in important conclusions. A woman in whom the prostitute element is strong will perceive her son's manhood and always stand in a sexual relation to him. But as no woman is the perfect type of mother, there is something sexual in the relation of every mother and son" (222). What I wish to stress in this passage is the imaginary figure of the prostitute/mother, the conjunction of feminine polarities. For it is this conjunction, I will argue, that constructs the classical Oedipal relation; and it is an opposition to Oedipalization that we confront in Weininger. The Oedipal comes to mean the foreclosure of the exogamous (and, in its purest form, homosexual) desire for the idea of the State. The mother-turned-prostitute—the Oedipal mother—recognizes the insufficiency of the familial structure to masculine desire and seeks to rebind that desire through her own "imaginary" promiscuity.

Clearly, Weininger is tracing out Freud's analysis of the Oedipal, but from within an intellectual tradition that will identify this Oedipal configuration specifically with the Jew.[20] Consistent with Weininger's indifference to material physical procreation is a form of racism we will also recognize in Blüher, a racism that does not oppose one race to another, but that opposes the very category of race per se. Whereas Blüher's insistence on the *Staathaftigkeit* of mankind will go hand in hand with a refusal to dissociate raw sexuality from its embeddedness in a meaning-constitutive discourse of Eros, Weininger's view of social order is, in a sense, more traditionally liberal, insisting on the transcendental quality of individual subjects. Thus, for example, his "radical" anti-Semitism sounds curiously bourgeois when articulated in the following terms:

> It is notable that the Jews, even now when at least a relative security of tenure is possible, prefer moveable property, and, in spite of their acquisitiveness, have little real sense of personal property, especially in its most characteristic form, landed property. Property is indissolubly connected with the self, with individuality. It is in harmony with the foregoing that the Jew is so readily disposed to communism. Communism must be distinguished clearly from socialism, the former being based on a community of goods, an absence of individual property, the latter meaning, in the first place a co-operation of individual with individual, of worker with worker, and a recognition of human individuality in every one. (306–7)

It is easy to see how the ground is laid here for a National Socialist rhetoric of Aryanism, of Judaism as moveable *Finanzkapital*, of a Jewish lack of selfhood, but we can also see in Weininger how such a discourse itself emerges from essentially bourgeois concerns with the establishment of political subjectivity through the medium of property—a tradition we can trace back to Kant and beyond.[21] The political sympathies expressed in *Sex and Character* for so-

cialism over communism derive from his essentially liberal understanding of citizenship.

It is through the metapsychological writings of Freud, meanwhile, that Blüher most consistently addresses questions of race,
and of the Jew in particular. In the second volume of *The Role of
Eroticism in Masculine Society*—in a footnote—Blüher will write:

> With the Jews it is as follows: they suffer at one and the same time
> from a *weakness in male-bonding* [*Männerbundschwäche*] and a *hy-
> pertrophy of the family*. They are submerged in the family and familial
> relations, but as to the relations among men, the old saying holds
> true: Judaeus Judaeo lupus. Loyalty, unity, and bonding are no con-
> cern of the Jew. Consequently, where other peoples profit from a fruit-
> ful interaction of the two forms of socialization, with the Jews there is
> a sterile division. Nature has visited this fate upon them and thus they
> wander through history, cursed never to be a people [*Volk*], always to
> remain a mere race. They have lost their State.   (2: 170)

The Jew has failed to develop a political consciousness adequate
to the formation of a State precisely because his erotic energies
have been focused on the family. The family, moreover, provides
the basis not for the *Volk*, but for the race. In other words, the Jew
is not an inferior race because the Teuton is a superior race: the
Jew is inferior because he is nothing *but* race. This may seem like
an ideological quibble, but it marks, I think, an important dividing
line in right-wing thought between the simple racism of a mis-
construed Lombrosian social Darwinism (exemplified by the
Nazis) and the kind of dismissive infantilization (in Freudian terms,
Oedipalization) of the Jew in right-wing masculinist thought.

I would like to take the opportunity offered by this passage to
elaborate on a point I raised in the previous chapter regarding the
specificity of Nazi racism. In considering the specifically genocidal
project of Nazism, I argued there that such a project necessarily
breaks with the tradition of nineteenth-century medical thought
that has been invoked as its ideological precedent. This becomes
clear again here. It is not within a biological discourse that Blüher
establishes the category of race, but rather against it. If nineteenth-
century biologistic racism is a relativist and comparative science,

genocidal anti-Semitism becomes thinkable only once such rela-
tivism has been left behind. It is perhaps Claude Lefort who has
best characterized the shift in ideological function with the emergence of totalitarian societies and who allows us to think such shifts
in terms of racism, writing that

> in a society which does not tolerate the image of an internal social di-
> vision, which claims that it is homogeneous despite all the differences
> which exist in fact, it is the other as such who acquires the fantastic
> features of the destroyer; the other, however he is defined, to what-
> ever group he belongs, is the representative of the *outside*. Whereas
> in bourgeois ideology, the essence of man is affirmed with regard to a
> sub-humanity (even though the latter is relegated to the lower regions
> of society and is never plunged so far down into "nature" that it does
> not pose the problem of how to manage it, for it is perceived as *in*
> society). (223)

To explain totalitarian racism in terms of bourgeois precedents
is to misunderstand it entirely. If the bureaucratic language of
Nazism presents a "solution" to "the Jewish question"—and
thereby invokes the technocratic language of "management"—an-
nihilation and genocide, as a "final solution," no longer depend
on notions of management. The nineteenth-century subhuman
must be "managed" precisely in order that it continue to exist as
the trace of the external. This is no longer the case in Nazism. In
other words, Nazi racism—within such a model—functions not to
assert the superiority of one race over another (Nazi rhetoric notwithstanding) but rather to present the Jew as an inferior historical condition: the prepolitical condition of raciality. Even where
Volk is to be established on the grounds of *Rasse*, it immediately
vitiates race once it enters the political scene.

I would argue that the term for anti-Semitism such as Blüher's
must be something other than "racist" because it exists precisely
in the obliteration of the question of race, and in the indignation
at the Jewish incarnation of that question. The Jew is problematic
because he seeks to articulate specifically familial and racial questions within a political discourse that is constituted precisely by the
exclusion of such questions. Racism functions not as an intrapo-

litical ideology, but rather as that discourse which defines the very parameters of the political. It is the very racialism—the stateless-ness—of the Jew that makes him inferior, since *Staatlichkeit* is what differentiates the animal from the human being. Anti-Semitism in this form can never function as an ideological appendage to the political—as an element which may be accepted or discarded at will. So long as the Jew is defined politically by his very exemption from the polity—by his statelessness—he necessarily marks the very limits of political discourse. The Jew is the negative ground of the political.[22]

In terms of Blüher's political logic, then, the Jew does not exist—or rather, should not (and in this *should* lies the legitimation, I think, of a genocidal project). And yet he does exist—and shall continue to do so. Just as Weininger confronted a crucial refutation of his general theory in the figure of the masculine homosexual attractive to and attracted by other masculine men, so Blüher senses a similar scandal in the figure of the Jew. The Jew challenges Blüher's masculinist theory just as the masculinist homosexual challenged Weininger's heterosexist theory. Anti-Semitism replicates within masculinist thought the gestures of exclusion that a panicked heterosexist discourse sought to enact on homosexuality.

Since the Jew is incapable of grounding a State—due to his embroilment in the family—he should, by historical right, have ceased to exist as a political entity. What is scandalous about anti-Semitism, from this perspective, is that there should still be Jews to make it necessary. Blüher attempts to account for this anomaly: "There are peoples [*Völker*] who are simply exterminated *as* peoples and who therefore disappear. But this cannot be the case with the Jews, for a secret process internal to their being as a people constantly displaces the energies typically directed toward male bonding onto the family, in such a way that the *father's* profit is the *friend's* loss. Consequently the Jews maintain themselves as *race* through this overemphasis on the family" (2: 171). The Jews constitute a political scandal—a scandal of the political. They should not exist—but they do. They exist as race rather than as

State, thereby hampering human progress toward meaningful self-realization (self-realization in erotic meaningfulness, that is) in the State.

We must note here the process of self-preservation by which the Jews reconstitute themselves. It is by a displacement of communal impulses onto the family that they continue to flourish. The regression to the level of the herd, the persistence at the level of race, the falling away from the structure of the State—all are synonymous with the fixation of socializing impulses on the family. What, then—for Blüher—is the basis of the Jewish family? Although he is not primarily concerned with this question and offers no closely detailed argumentation, the question reemerges in his study with some consistency. Thus, in the second volume—where he deals with the question of the woman-as-wife (Penelope) and the woman-as-whore (Calypso)—Blüher notes a specifically "Jewish" mutation of his Odyssean binarisms:

> There are men so burdened by the incestuous drives of the Penelope type that they are driven to marry into a foreign race. This is particularly characteristic of the Jews and, notably, even among Zionist Jews, who consciously promote their own racial type for both sexes while being unconsciously driven toward foreign races. Odysseus marries Calypso: and his longing for Penelope—whom he may not touch—leads him to dedicate all his energies of masculine creativity to the adoration of the race of his mother. (2: 21)

Of course, the passage reiterates an anti-Semitic commonplace, with its assertion that Jews have an inordinate desire for non-Jewish women. Beyond this, however, there is, I think, a more nuanced argument; one that draws on Freudian Oedipal models to explain societal phenomena. The family—which the Jew seeks to make the basis of society—transgresses the order of the feminine outlined by Blüher. The Jewish family is not the private family excluded from politics by Blüher, but rather a directly politicized embodiment of the un- or antipolitical impulse. The Jew marries not the wife, but the whore, not the Jewess, but the Gentile, and this miscegenation is linked to the construction of the Oedipal whore/mother we have already seen imagined in Weininger. In other words, the Jewish family that grounds the State is incommensurable with the familial construct abstracted from the Odyssey: in this case "Odysseus marries Calypso." The experience of the diaspora—the Jewish statelessness—is at the same time an exile from the familial order that the Jew only apparently overvalues. Jewish overvaluation of the family is the result of the introjection of erotic energy into the familial unit through the marriage with the Calypso-figure—the prostitute, the Gentile. Thus, the Jew threatens not only the State, but also the family—as the State's antithesis. The Jewish family is, in this sense, dysfunctional, in that the Jewish insistence on the centrality of the family to the State essentially misperceives the relationship of family to society. The marriage to Calypso is, indeed, a prostitution of the very idea of family.

Blüher's attack on the Jew is at the same time an attack on the Oedipal family. Whereas Weininger had to develop for himself the typology of the whore/mother who acknowledges the masculinity of her sons, Blüher has at hand a Freudian terminology. Nevertheless, he is loathe to generalize the Freudian Oedipal model precisely because it threatens to *verjuden* the social project and the establishment of a State. This threat will be presented as a potential failure of the social imaginary. Once the mother becomes the horizon of alloerotic desire she necessarily threatens the State. Indeed—as we have seen (note 19)—rather than accept Oedipus as a generalizable structure, Blüher assigns it only a limited—and rather lowly, infantilized—place within his broader erotic typology.

The Oedipal framework is therefore crucial to any examination of what Blüher has to say about the Jew. The Jew marries the whore (Calypso) in an attempt to escape the overcathexis of the actual mother in childhood. This *mésalliance* is at the origin of the Jew's inability to ground a State, since it binds the erotic forces that constitute the masculine State to the feminine family. In Blüher's terms, the obsessive incest taboo of the Jew functions as an inverse reflection on his libido; he must marry outside his race, because he cannot trust himself anywhere (racially) near his mother. The strength of the prohibition is proportional to the strength of the desire. Paradoxically, however, the proscription of representation at the same time necessitates representation, in that the image of the mother must be obliterated beneath the displacements that will "represent" her. In other words, representation functions not as the revelation of the truth of desire, but rather—as Lyotard has argued in his presentation of a "Jewish Oedipus"—as its necessary veiling. Blüher's reading of the Jew's desire is quite explicitly pathographic, in distinct opposition to his own methodological premises. Masculinist anti-Semitism is therefore a form of anti-Oedipalism opposing any fixation of the social imaginary to the familial "real." This fixation on the real—the same fixation, we will recall, that supposedly directs Jewish erotic energies toward other races—provides the basis for a symbolic social organization that is always neurotic.[23] In Oedipalizing the Jew, Blüher renders his desire a mere deflection of actual desire: the lascivious desire for the Gentile woman is but a hyperdisplacement of the desire for the mother. The Jew becomes an Oedipal sacrifice, so to speak, taking the position normally accorded the homosexual in a pathographic discourse. One displaced desire is displaced by another—the Homosexual by the Jew. Masculinist anti-Semitism—followed in its trajectory from Weininger to Blüher—marks a methodological capitulation in the face of Oedipus.

Notably, Blüher is concerned with developing an opposition of Greek and Jew—not Jew and Christian, nor Jew and German. His anti-Semitism derives from a classicizing discourse invoked both to ground a theory of the State and to legitimate a specific, paederastic form of male-male Eros. The shortfalls of Judaism are measured against the norm of a Hellenic myth: the force impelling the Jewish exogamy is the force of the incest taboo, the force of a radically interiorized Oedipal construct. The eroticized homosociality of Blüher's *männliche Gesellschaft* and the assertion of the impossibility of Jewish statehood thus stem from the same Hellenizing tendencies. If early homosexual thinkers sought to legitimize their desire by recourse to a self-aestheticizing model of Hellenic paederasty, it would seem that this same Hellenizing discourse also provided ideological shelter to an anti-Semitic political impulse. The Greek State offers itself to right-wing ideologues as an alternative to "Jewish," "liberal" democracy. In other words, though the relationship is far from a necessary one, it is possible to see how a celebration of Hellenic culture—re-Oedipalized, despite protestations to the contrary—potentially lends itself to forms of anti-Semitism, just as it lends itself to a revalorization of homosexuality. Hellas figures not only as the cultural legitimation of male-male desire, but also as a cultural counterdiscourse to the depredations of Judaeo-Christian civilization. As the culmination of a long and varied sociophilosophical tradition, Blüher's masculinism is the desire to think Hellenism without Oedipus. Anti-Semitism is the apotheosis of that attempt.

CHAPTER 4

Paederasty and the Dialectic
of Emancipation:
Mackay's 'Books of Nameless Love'

In a study of *Paris Gay 1925*, Gilles Barbedette and
Michel Carassou seek to profile the emergence of a
French homosexual emancipation movement by contrasting it with
the German model that has—by and large—tended to dominate
historical reconstructions of early homosexual emancipation. Observing that "unlike the German homosexual movement created
by 'men of science,' it is undeniable that homosexuals in France
felt their first hours of freedom when men and women of letters
set out to write on the subject, thereby partly thwarting the psychiatric trap which sought to contain homosexuality" (102), they
elaborate national differences in terms of the oppositional discourses of art and science. In the light of this opposition of French
literature and German science, there is a historical necessity in
reevaluating the literary production of the early homosexual emancipation movement in Germany. It is not, however, in response to
a historical lacuna that I wish to examine here the writings of John
Henry Mackay (1864–1933). Mackay, a homosexual poet-anarchist, who published—under the name of Sagitta—a collection of
works entitled *The Books of Nameless Love* (*Die Bücher der namen-*

losen Liebe), poses questions resonant both for contemporary queer theory and for any consideration of the emancipatory possibilities of the literary and aesthetic sphere. Second, I wish to revisit the problematic areas of narcissism and nonidentity first raised in our consideration of the Frankfurt School in order to show how Mackay's specifically paederastic desire serves to deconstruct precisely those models of narcissism that have long served to identify masculinism with homo-fascism.

In their schematic presentation of a French-German split, Barbedette and Carassou clearly favor the literary over the scientific, opposing the "first hours of freedom" of the French literati to the "psychiatric trap" of the German emancipation movement. It should be said that the terms of this opposition—literary emancipation versus scientific pathologization—correspond rather accurately to the terms in which those German men of letters opposed to the scientific and biologizing model of emancipation—Mackay included—chose to view the matter. Indeed, one sympathetic review of Mackay's work by the avant-garde Expressionist journal *Die Aktion* (included in the second volume of the reprinted *Books of Nameless Love*) chose to foreground precisely this question of science versus literature: "One might wish this book in the possession of all those who have thus far examined this issue only from the scientific perspective. Art is more than mere science: where science sees life through dead systems, art sees it in its unity and makes of it an experience—the only form in which we can really grasp, really feel life."

The reviewer's rhetoric of life and death—or experience and dead systems—seems hyperbolic, but it is not without reason that one strain of gay emancipatory theory has tended to resist the claims of science in the project of liberation. At the same time, however, it must be noted that some of Freud's more consequence-laden pronouncements on the pathology of homosexuality stem as much from his reading of literature (one need think only of the category of narcissism itself) as from his research as a man of science. The distinction of science and literature with respect to theories of homosexuality is, therefore, by no means rigorous. In this chapter, I wish to examine this opposition of art and science—or, more broadly, art and other such dead systems as the juridical discourse—as a battle (played out through the question of homosexual emancipation) over the nature of the bourgeois public sphere. I wish to examine the way in which the emergence of homosexual emancipation movements led to a recoding of traditionally gendered categories of public and private and to suggest that the stress laid by Foucault on legal and medical discourses has led us both to underestimate the role of literature in homosexual emancipation, and to misunderstand the functioning of the public sphere.

Carassou and Barbedette present an image of homosexuality as "trap," thereby necessarily problematizing the very notion of emancipation. To what extent—and this, perhaps, is the unvoiced question around which turns the opposition of literature and science—is the liberation *of* the homosexual (as political subject) necessarily also a liberation *from* the homosexual (as categorical object)? To what extent, in other words, is the (pathological) identification of the homosexual a necessary moment in his or her liberation, and to what extent a taxonomy that serves merely to reinforce the normative claims of a classificatory, heterosexist positivism? By way of a familiar dialectical logic, the categories around which emancipation organizes itself—the category, in this case, of the homosexual—function simultaneously as the categories of oppression. It is the desire to separate out the ambiguities of the category (of homosexuality) that leads, I would argue, to the opposition of literature and science as, respectively, the emancipatory and the oppressive modalities of (self-)identification. I will further argue that the anarchic masculinist Mackay avoids this reified opposition by elaborating a specifically homosexual identity only while deconstructing the category of identity itself.

My aim at this juncture is to examine in modest literary-historical terms the possibilities opened up—or, even, closed down—by the binary opposition of literary and scientific models of emancipation. More specifically, I wish to examine—through an exemplary reading of Mackay—the perspective of a German literary class active in the homosexual emancipation movement, in order to understand the stakes of their opposition to prevailing scientific interpretations of homosexuality. Thus, it will be necessary not simply to understand the various ways in which homosexual identity has been constructed within literature, but rather to examine a structural and discursive opposition and interaction of literature and other "public" discourses, such as science and politics. It is not, then, a question of examining the homosexual *in* literature, but of understanding the ways in which homosexuality might be constructed in the public sphere by way *of* literature. Beyond this, it will be necessary to examine the ways in which the very construction of homosexuality will be affected by the aesthetic demands placed on it within literature: not only, then, homosexuality in the aesthetic, but rather, homosexuality as aesthetic. I shall contend that the value of aesthetic discourse—in this case, specifically, literature—was felt to lie precisely in its permeability, in its supposed nonclosure, and in its ultimate resistance to the entrapments (or seductions) of alternative models of liberational politics.

One might begin to flesh out this contention through a historical study of the structure of the bourgeois public sphere and the dialectics of aesthetic autonomy, whereby autonomy is guaranteed only on the grounds of the political disqualification and disempowerment of literary and aesthetic discourse. Rather than trace this process sociologically, however, I wish to enter directly into a debate from within the homosexual emancipation movement of the early years of this century. Specifically, I wish to examine the writings of Sagitta (Mackay) in their engagement with and opposition to the predominant strain of an emancipation movement represented by Hirschfeld and the Wissenschaftlich-Humanitäres Komitee he founded in 1897. Already sketched in the previous chapter as a countermodel to masculinism, Hirschfeld's position differs both substantively and structurally from the masculinists, reflecting a disagreement not only as to the nature of homosexuality itself, but also with respect to strategies of liberation and the process of self-identification. *In nuce,* the differences can be understood as differences dictated by a confrontation of Hirschfeld's "science" with Mackay's "literature."

Although Magnus Hirschfeld was undoubtedly the most influential, respected—and despised—advocate of the homosexual liberation movement in the first half of this century, he was, nevertheless, not altogether representative of advocates of homosexual rights in late Wilhelmine Germany and during the Weimar Republic. The synecdochic deployment of his name in the historicizing of homosexual emancipation has been responsible for the impoverishment of our understanding of a multifarious and internally disunited movement. Moreover, one is tempted to question why it should be that the public imagination—and, subsequently, the wrath of the Nazis—alighted on Hirschfeld as *the* representative of the campaign to abolish the infamous paragraph 175 criminalizing homosexuality. It might be argued that Hirschfeld himself operated within a model that would subsequently provide a spurious eugenic legitimacy and rationale to the excesses of the Nazi regime. The notion of a "third sex"—a notion Hirschfeld was himself subsequently to modify, moving away from the terminology of "sexual intermediaries" (*Zwischenstufen*) to a more nuanced "general taxonomy" (*Einteilungsprinzip*)—potentially legitimated the differentiation of homosexuality along eugenic lines. More fundamentally, however—and such will be the structural thrust of Mackay's critique—the very reliance on a scientific terminology potentially disempowered homosexuals by placing their pathology within the hands of experts—benign like Hirschfeld, or, potentially, less benign. Attacking the retention of paragraph 175, which drew its sole legitimacy from an ideological appeal to *das gesunde Volksempfinden*—or healthy popular sensibilities—Hirschfeld nevertheless moves within a field of health and sickness defined by scientific discourse.[1] If he himself subsequently fell prey to "healthy popular opinion"—which as Stümke and Finkler point out is "no accidental, natural product, but rather the result and consequence of a politics that reflects many different levels of domination" (12)—one might argue that he had never gone far enough in questioning a simple imperative of psychosexual health that would subsequently find virulent political form.

I have already gone some way—in the previous chapter—to suggest the parameters of the masculinist critique of "third-sexers" and the implications of that (largely forgotten) critique for contemporary theory, but it should be stressed that the laudable desire for an inclusive model of emancipation voiced by such as Stümke and Finkler has led to a misreading of some of the "anti-effeminate" political elements of the homosexual emancipation movement. Thus, while Brand's insistence on the "productive capacities of male-male Eros," for example, certainly reflects a desire to assimilate both to a capitalist ideology of production and to a bourgeois ideology of *re*production, it also articulates a mistrust of a more fundamental ideological and methodological assimilationism in Hirschfeld's own approach. Thus, when he argues in a promotional piece for his journal *Der Eigene* that "our own energies and our sense of our own value to society will help man more than any science," Brand is not simply manifesting an assimilationist form of internalized homophobia. The insistence on "our own energies" and "our sense of our own value" asserts a strategic autonomy undreamed of in Hirschfeld's model of redemption through science. The fate of homosexuals can and must be decided by homosexuals themselves, he argues, not by experts.

Consequently, though gender construction is certainly the substantive issue around which the disagreements are articulated, there are also underlying strategic differences at play. Brand stresses self-liberation, yet assimilates to a prevailing masculinist ideology: Hirschfeld, meanwhile, undermines this ideology, but at the cost of an assimilationist appeal to the prevailing political, juridical, and scientific structures. The question of assimilationism versus nonassimilationism, therefore, cannot be mapped in any straightforward manner onto the question of gender construction. More than this, the charge of racism leveled against the masculinists—who do, indeed, tend to accord gender differences the value of racial differences—has failed to address an alternative form of scapegoating that has traditionally taken place in gay communities. Presenting

Mackay here as a literary representative of masculinism, I present him as a specifically paederastic representative, one whose exploration of the limits of sexual freedom is in many ways more challenging, radical, and unsettling than a simple transgression of gender binarisms.

From the perspective of masculinists such as Brand and Mackay (whose positions I do not otherwise seek to conflate) Hirschfeld's utilization of scientific systems of legitimation results in an objectification and reification of the homosexual as the object rather than the subject of emancipation. Although articulating the possibility of a subject *position*, Hirschfeld's notion of a third sex nevertheless potentially negates the subject itself. If this is most apparent in the adoption of scientistic terminology, it is also reflected in Hirschfeld's political methods, which are either pragmatic or assimilationist, according to one's point of view. Seeking the support of eminent public figures and members of parliament, Hirschfeld sought to effect change largely through recourse to existing political structures. It is less a question of homosexuals speaking for themselves—either sexually or politically—than of scientists discoursing on them and of politicians choosing (or, in fact, not choosing) to emancipate them. Hirschfeld's attempt to create an autonomous space—the space of the third sex—seems to fail when an attempt is made to integrate this space into the broader public sphere, as if the introduction of a third term—a third sex—were impossible within the ideological binarism of public and private. In other words, the binarism of masculine and feminine seems to find an ideological underpinning in the binarism public-private. I will seek later in this chapter to show how Mackay works through these binarisms to invert the traditional identifications masculine-public, feminine-private.

What I seek to illuminate, in short, is the function of the literary sphere in the construction and articulation of the category of homosexuality. Within this problematic, gender cannot be inscribed as a simple "scientific" given in any positivist sense—it, too, assumes literary shape. If we accept—as recent historiographical work in queer theory has indicated—that homosexuality is in and of itself a discursive production, created in large part by those discourses that claim merely to reflect on it, then the reading of "queer literature"—or any "literary" reading of the "queer"—must reexamine its operative paradigms. It is necessary to examine the most fundamental presuppositions; why, for example, does anybody write about homosexuality, anyway? Traditionally, one might answer: Because it is there; because homosexuality exists in the everyday and creative thinkers and writers respond to the challenge of the everyday. But this, of course, implies precisely a representational episteme we have since left behind. Homosexuality is not simply "there" if it is itself produced and constructed as discourse—among other things, in the act of writing. Writing itself becomes a form of positing, a reification, a location of a "there" where homosexuality might subsequently "be." Homosexuality is, in fact, not quite "there" at all: methodologically, the dilemma is not to elucidate "homosexuality," then, but rather to question the seemingly least problematic of terms. Only in locating the "there" of writing and in elucidating the "Being" of homosexuality itself does one fundamentally question the paradigm of aesthetic reflection and begin to understand writing as a process of construction.

Why, then, would literary figures write (about) homosexuality? An answer, I think, has been indicated by the discussion above. Literary writers may write (about) homosexuality because the literary represents a "there"—as opposed to the space of law and medicine—where homosexuality might profitably "be." In other words, the introduction—the systematic introduction—of homosexuality into the literary sphere does not simply mark the response of the fictional to the real. Homosexuality does not simply appear in literature because it is "there" in life. The aesthetic—for the homosexual, perhaps more than for any other—is itself a mode of "being there," a mode of being in the public sphere, rather than a mere reflection of some preexisting reality. What this means, effectively, is that the literary representation—or, I would argue, the literary *enactment*—of homosexuality should not simply be taken as the reflection of a given phenomenon, a phenomenon on which Hirschfeld, within different parameters, was also discoursing.

I am not simply reiterating the vulgarized Foucauldian commonplace—that discourse invents and fashions its putative object. What I am contending—with regard to the segmentation of the public sphere into competing and often antagonistic discourses— is that the literary representation and construction of homosexuality is not only substantively, but also structurally, differentiated from its invocation within other discourses. It is not simply the what of the saying of homosexuality that is to be examined, but the where of its enunciation. One might begin to examine the modalities of homosexual self-fashioning in this light. Thus, for example, the strategies of self-aestheticization that stretch from Wilde to Foucault can no longer be reduced to an interpretation on the basis of a psycholiterary narcissism—as they so often are— precisely because the aesthetic in operation here is no longer one of (self-)reflection. Self-fashioning and self-reflection do not partake of the same narcissistic logic. I will expand on this contention later with specific reference to Mackay, but for now I would simply like to preface my readings with the assertion that the construction of a homosexual identity within the literary sphere—once that sphere is understood as something more than merely representational—does not constitute a narcissistic retreat. "Aestheticization"—if such be the term we choose for the phenomenon of literary self-construction—is not synonymous with narcissism (primary or otherwise), for the movement beyond a representational understanding of the literary potentially implies a concomitant move beyond vulgar psychoanalytic paradigms of homosexuality. Literature does not simply present and give expression to homosexual realities, but offers a space of potential fabulation that counters the ideological "passivity" and representationalism of other discourses on homosexuality.

All of this might seem to be pushing homosexual writing inexorably to the brink of the antirepresentational avant-garde (and I do, indeed, examine this possibility in considering Jarry in Chapter 6). Clearly, though, an important function of early homosexual writing *was* the fairly straightforward depiction of a homosexual milieu: such literature does not create identities out of thin air, but builds them on the basis of a representational project. Thus, John Henry Mackay, to return to the example at hand, could not seriously be said to question "traditional" literary models in his writing: he is, essentially, a naturalist. Nevertheless, as we shall see, it is precisely his naturalism that leads him to question the viability for a homosexual writing of traditional gender and genre distinctions. It is precisely by working within existing literary conventions—such as the *Bildungsroman*, for example—and by insisting on a "naturalistic" portrayal of homosexual life in his novels, that Mackay serves to uncover the ideological implications of representational literary forms oriented toward the construction of a heterosexual subject.

I will approach Mackay's work by stages, tackling—at first— the institutional and strategic questions that he himself sees as crucial to his efforts, before addressing the texts themselves. In fact, Mackay prefaces *The Books of Nameless Love* with a text entitled "A History of the Struggle for the Nameless Love," a chronology of the work's publication that foregrounds the very question of the literary institution and its function within the bourgeois public sphere. Here we learn that the first attempt to launch Sagitta's writings consisted of an invitation to subscribe to a volume containing the first two "books" (*Nameless Love: A Confession* and *Who Are We? A Poem of Nameless Love*). Subscription was opened in August 1905, but there was very little response, for reasons that I will go into later. In July of 1906, Sagitta launched a second subscription drive, this time for the third and fourth "books," *Fenny Skaller: The Life of a Nameless Love* and *On the Marble Steps: A Scene of Nameless Love*. The response was again disappointing.

According to Sagitta's own history of events, historical circumstance took over at this point and prevented him from simply abandoning the project. In the winter of 1907–8, the homosexual scandals surrounding leading politicians, aristocrats, and industrialists (and, it was mooted, the Kaiser himself) had put the otherwise "nameless love" on everyone's lips. Changing tack at this point, Sagitta decides to write a *Flugschrift* for popular dissemination. In his introduction to the collection, he summarizes his project thus far:

> After defining the concept of "nameless love" and offering a poetic answer to the question; "Who are we?" in the first two books, I wished in the third ("Fenny Skaller") to lend the concept some psychological depth and in the fourth ("On the Marble Steps") and fifth books to celebrate this love in song, before finally coming to grips with the specific issues in the sixth and last book ("The Book of Letters"). (1: 32)

This flyer was dispatched to Protestant youth groups, members of the Reichstag, newspapers (which ignored it), and state and local libraries. As a result of complaints from various Protestant ministers, legal proceedings were inaugurated against the publication, and on March 12, 1908, the flyer and both of the first volumes were seized. At this point, Mackay became involved in an expensive and protracted trial, in the course of which he nevertheless sent out (in May 1909) an invitation to subscribe to the sixth "book," *At Life's Margins.* The trial was lost and response to the call for subscription was—not surprisingly—minimal. Sagitta's reaction was to insist—in the face of both apathy from potential subscribers and persecution at the hands of the authorities—on the importance of individual efforts. Consequently, the first collected volume of *The Books of Nameless Love* was published in 1912.

So much for the history—but what does it tell us? Certainly it seems to tell Sagitta something, as he concludes that his endeavor has failed as a result of several fundamental mistakes. The first mistake, he claims, lies in the attempt to present this nameless love as a special form of love, better and more noble than heterosexual love: "It is not. This is a love like any other, no better but also no worse; and—if it is true love—blissful in its consequences like any other love. The struggle *for* this form of love should never degenerate into a struggle *against* any other, for love is equally legitimate in all its forms, each of which draws sustenance from the same source" (1: 62). In other words, homosexual liberation must partake of a broader erotic liberation. It would be easy, I think, to misconstrue Sagitta here. No one is clearer than he, throughout the pieces in this volume, as to the social and moral conditions that make of this particular form of love a special problem: it is not a question, here, of assimilation to a heterosexual model of liberation. Sagitta is trying to achieve two things: a general consensus among homosexuals, first, not to split on those issues of effeminacy and masculinity that we addressed earlier (though he, himself, is clearly a masculinist); and, second, not to eradicate the paederastic form of love that interests him. Thus, the question of homosexual liberation intersects directly with questions of gender and sexual majority—questions, in other words, of the limits of sexual freedom.

In fact, in his presentation of the second mistake, Sagitta directly addresses the gender issue:

> Similar, all too understandable sentiments have often sought to obtain man's freedom in questions of love at the expense of women. This too is a mistake. However false the position of the opposite sex may still be today (in all social classes), to limit and deny their potential development will only serve to make today's enemies into irreconcilable enemies tomorrow and in perpetuity, instead of making friends of our foes. Such a strategy completely misunderstands the law of the future, the law of freedom. And freedom embraces all, rejecting none. (1: 62)

The ambiguity is clear here: Sagitta's misogyny is reflected in the assertion that the position of the opposite sex is "completely false," and yet he insists on the erotic liberation of women also. In fact, there is a direct relation between Mackay's "separate but equal" policy on the sexual liberation of women and his obvious dislike of effeminization in homosexual men. Gender—as is so often the case with those who chose not to follow Hirschfeld in his reexamination of gender distinctions—serves as origin rather than telos. The liberation *of* the masculine is not the liberation *from* the masculine—any more than the liberation of the feminine should, for Mackay, be a liberation from the feminine. In other words, the homosexual male does not necessarily question gender constructions, but serves, in fact, to rearticulate them. In the same way, the liberation *of* women is understood as their liberation *as* women—that is (for want of any model that would allow women to articulate their self-understanding), liberation understood as the freedom to be whatever society has constructed women to be anyway.

According to Sagitta, the final—fatal—mistake lies in the scientific approach to homosexuality:

> This love, persecuted by the judges and cursed by the priests has taken refuge among the doctors, as if it were a sickness that they might cure. It is not a sickness, however. Doctors have no more place here with their investigations than the judges, and those who have turned to the doctors—like sick men—are mistaken if they believe they can free themselves from the snares of power by signing a pact with that same power.   (1: 62–63)

The argument is somewhat ambiguous. Mackay opines that since positivistic science persecutes and pathologizes homosexuals, it is therefore impossible that such a science should liberate them. Examined more closely, however, Sagitta's argument actually moves in the opposite direction. It is the *doctors* who are mistaken in thinking that they can cooperate with this "sick" form of love and thereby "cure" it. The argument runs in two directions, then: homosexuality is not an illness and cannot (and need not), therefore, be cured; but at the same time homosexuality potentially undermines the powers of positivistic science by demonstrating its limitations and scorning its efforts. This love is made sick by a discursive *Gewalt* from which doctors cannot liberate it; for it is they themselves who are entrapped within the terms of that system of power and domination.

Before passing on to the literary counterdiscourse that Sagitta opposes to this scientific *Gewalt*, it is important to identify a fourth "problem" of homosexual liberation that Sagitta does not place directly alongside the other three, but that is intrinsic to his entire project. This problem turns on the question of paederasty both as a form of desire and as a literary trope. Sagitta's struggle is based not only on the recognition that the oppressive languages of science and jurisprudence cannot be implemented in order to liberate homosexuals, but also on the contention that liberation must be the work of homosexuals themselves. Implicit in this argument, however, is the recognition that the failure of self-liberation thus far is a failure *of* homosexuals. Thus, Sagitta concludes "that we must finally acknowledge that we are our own worst enemies" (1: 52). This recognition should not be mistaken for a form of internalized homophobia, or as a straightforward internecine jab at other campaigners; Sagitta is clear as to the sociological reasons for the problem: "The unique position our love occupies in life has—it must be said—led to a destitution of character, a confusion of judgment that has turned us—sad though it is to admit—against our own cause" (1: 34). In other words, the oppression of homosexuals has led to a homosexual self-fashioning entirely within the terms of the oppressive discourse. Heterosexist societies necessarily create the conditions in which homosexuals become that which heterosexist ideology has always understood them to be.

This question of the self-fulfillment of heterosexist ideology, however, is but one side of Sagitta's argument here. He is quite clearly taking aim also at the divisive political strategies employed by leading homosexual rights advocates—such as Hirschfeld—to gain general and legal acceptance. More specifically, he is arguing against the stigmatization of paederasty from within the ranks of homosexual emancipation movements. Clearly, Sagitta's attacks on other "*Führer*" (a term he himself almost always uses in quotation marks, as if to mark the impossibility—for an anarchist such as himself—of a liberation based on leadership) of the homosexual liberation movement is motivated by their marginalization of the paederastic tradition. If, as Stümke and Finkler argue, the masculinist or antieffeminate homosexuals were potentially guilty—unlike Hirschfeld—of a form of *Tuntenhaß* that sacrificed the rights of effeminate homosexuals in order to assert the respectability of the male-identified homosexual, leaders such as Hirschfeld were no less guilty—in their desire to decriminalize homosexuality in its more acceptable forms—of a sacrifice of the paederast to criminal legislation.

The paederastic question is so fundamental to Sagitta's consideration of emancipation that it undercuts the very category of homosexuality itself. Is the paederast primarily a male lover of males, or an adult lover of children? Sagitta's polemic is such that it is difficult to determine whether he attributes his marginalization to the specificity of male-male desire or to the particular construction of paederasty. One could argue—on the one hand—that the sexual freedom of the paederast is unthinkable without a prior liberation of the homosexual—but such an argument assumes the overarching and prior concerns of the homosexual movement. Sagitta—on the other hand—can quite easily envisage (though not approve of) such a liberation without a concomitant liberation of all forms of homosexuality. Thus, for example, to liberate paederasty might be to reinstitute a certain pedagogical mechanism for the construction of masculinity within society. Such a liberation envisages no role for the effeminate homosexual. Although Sagitta's priorities may at times seem confused—split, that is, between homosexual and paederastic liberation—and though he makes particular claims for paederasty, he at no point allows his distaste for effeminization to lead him to condemn a homosexual emancipation that would embrace the effeminate homosexual also. What does occur, though—as a result of Sagitta's specifically paederastic polemic—is a rethinking of the mechanisms of liberation, a rethinking of strategy in the light of the erotics of paederasty. In other words, paederasty is central to Sagitta's project not only as the subject and the object of emancipation, but in the very modality of that emancipation. Paederasty dictates a certain political sensibility that—for all its masculinism—opposes the central ideological function of the protofascist *Führer*.

By 1924, Sagitta's disappointment is such that he is able to articulate it in a direct political attack on other elements of the homosexual emancipation movement. First of all, he attacks those who simply refuse to acknowledge the political work to be done and the extent of the discrimination exercised against them. He goes on, however, to critique those who *do* engage in political action in the following terms: "As for the others, the politicians in the struggle, the effeminate, the sly, lukewarm half-men; we can expect nothing of them. They are malign bigots who know, but cannot or will not see" (1: 68). The prejudices of the political activists are—presumably—prejudices against the paederasts within the homosexual movement, but it is interesting that Sagitta should refer to the activists themselves as "the effeminates." Two elements of Sagitta's position leap out at us here: first, as we have observed elsewhere, the comment implies a lack of affinity for all but the most masculine models of homosexuality; and second—and more interesting, perhaps—the association of women with ineffectual political machinations questions the suitability of the political sphere as an arena for homosexual emancipation.

The identification of politicians with *die Weibischen* is somewhat puzzling, given the traditional gender coding of the bourgeois public and private spheres. Mackay's public lobbying for the case of the invert seems itself to invert traditional gender codings of public and private. Ostensibly, Mackay is opposing politics as a separate, rationalized sphere of action, but beyond this I think we need to take into account the way in which the emergence of a "homosexual problem" necessarily led to a reconfiguration of public and private. The public, in Mackay's masculinist presentation, is identified with show, with ornament—with femininity. The politicians are mere "representatives" caught within a system of representation, robbed of immanent (masculine) subjectivity. The private, meanwhile, becomes the sole arena for untrammeled masculine self-actualization. The problem, then, will be how to instrument a public appeal for private sexual freedoms.

How do women—or, rather, effeminized men—come to be identified with the sphere of politics from which they have traditionally been excluded? To answer this question one must, I think, insist on Sagitta's own anarchic political ideology. It is, quite specifically, something in the *bourgeois* political sphere that effeminizes. More precisely, it is the bureaucracy of the State that emasculates all self-emancipatory movements. Returning to his critique of the enemy within—the homosexual enemies of homosexual liberation—Sagitta pursues that critique in the following terms: "In recent years it has once again become clear that this love encoun-

ters its greatest enemies not from outside but in its own camp.
Once again, those who call themselves 'Führer' in this struggle
and sign themselves in public as such in a pathetic and demeaning
petition to the powers that be, declare themselves in favor of an
age of consent [*Schützalter*] to protect not children but mature
boys and youths!" (1: 69).

The anarchic distrust of all claims at *Führung* is clear, but—
more than this—Sagitta seems to be projecting a certain aporia of
the reformist position in its political efforts. First, the leaders themselves replicate the paederastic power relationship (at least, the relationship as they themselves see it) vis-à-vis homosexuals by placing themselves in the position of guardians of the homosexual
cause. What they injure—according to Sagitta—is not the sexual
freedom of the lover, who will always be free to seduce (*Verführen*)
but the rights of the beloved to love. In other words, those who
fight in the name of the homosexuals do not lead, but seduce and
traduce. They name the nameless love and thereby betray it. They
fight—as adults—for the infantilized homosexual, and include in
that fight a denial of the sexual liberation of the child. While mar-
ginalizing paederasty as a form of homosexual desire, such political reformers actually replicate the structures of authority they seek
to repress.

Tropologically, then, by potentially infantilizing the homosexual within a model of (political) representation—by speaking *for*
the homosexual—leaders such as Hirschfeld deny to those whose
freedom they seek the freedom to speak for themselves. By leading, the leader seduces—and seduction is precisely that which one
fears from women. The identification of seduction with femininity is implicit, then, in Sagitta's characterization of the political
sphere as effeminate. But there is more: the relationship of the pe-
titioners themselves to the law replicates a position of disempowerment. These "leaders" are not leaders at all, but have themselves
been seduced by the rhetoric of democratic reformism: they are
but the children of a democracy who have themselves not yet
reached their majority, who cannot themselves assert their freedom but have to request it—like children—from a paternalistic ju-

diciary. In other words, while developing a model of paederasty that is not dependent on monodirectional models of power, and that insists on autonomy, Sagitta demonstrates how precisely those who oppose the rights of the paederastic man and boy themselves replicate a caricature of paederastic seduction (*Verführung*) both in their paternalistic relations to homosexuals in general and in their infantilized relationship to a paternalistic State. Politics is seduction.

Sagitta himself seeks to develop a paederastic model in which the conflation of seduction and leadership—*Verführung* and *Führung*—is avoided. In essence, his model of paederastic love marks an attempt to overcome the insistent superimposition of models of power on a specific configuration of desire. Indeed, Sagitta sees in paederasty an inevitable logic that will necessarily carry the day for the homosexual cause. At the close of his introduction to the collected volume in 1912, he writes, "The task of those of us who love the young is to win them over to our cause: not by persuasion and seduction, but through love and friendship. . . . Then that bright future we seek is ours even in this gloomy present. For the future belongs to youth" (1: 66). What is particularly important here is Sagitta's insistence on love as opposed to seduction (*Verführung*) as an insistence on the autonomy of the beloved and on the absence of models of leadership (*Führung*). There is a notion of historical continuity built into the paederastic model—a passage from generation to generation—but Sagitta insists on the impossibility of dictating the nature of the future through a seduction of the beloved. The autonomy of the beloved and the alterity of the future are intertwined.

That paederasty should claim for itself a privileged relation to future liberation is not altogether surprising. What is of interest, however, is the way in which paederasty affects Sagitta's understanding of political strategy itself. The consistency of his position is apparent, paradoxically, at precisely the point where he ceases to be consistent. Notably, it is in the pamphlet "LISTEN . . . Just One Moment . . . A Cry" that the valorization of *Führung* shifts. The fact is noteworthy precisely because Sagitta himself indicates—in his preface—that this pamphlet marked a very real change in strategy away from an attempt to rally support among a closed body of individuals pledged to limit their interests in the texts to the private sphere, to an open, political cry for public support. In other words, the concept of *Führung*—otherwise apparently anathema to Sagitta's model of paederasty—suddenly acquires a new positive value once he shifts his strategy away from the literary and into the directly political sphere. The following might serve as an example of Sagitta's new logic in this pamphlet:

> Just one more word regarding seduction.
>
> No law can protect the young from seduction. Only enlightenment can do that. . . . But let us not only see seducers [*Verführer*] everywhere. For there are leaders [*Führer*] too. A seducer is someone who raises questions and offers answers before those questions have posed themselves. . . . I have no truck with these seducers. . . . A leader, on the other hand, is one who patiently waits until he sees the questions pushing for an answer—one who cherishes the bud, but does not deny the blossom the soil that feeds it. (1: 463)

Or the following: "The awakening boy, the young man who has already awoken, seek with dogged persistence for answers to their questions—for a *Führer* in the midst of their confusion" (1: 464). The potential affinity to a right-wing political project is clear, but the point is not simply to equate certain literary—and erotic—tropes with certain political eventualities, but rather to identify the ways in which certain models of homosexuality change in valence once displaced from the literary to the political sphere. Sagitta's Hellenizing literary model resists subsumption into the political and yet—once subsumed, through direct appeal to the public sphere—reveals its affiliations with forms of political reaction. If it is impossible for Sagitta to introduce his paederastic model into the political sphere without disfiguring it, one is left with an unsettling assumption: there is apparently something fasciticizing in the politicization of (this) desire. Such is the seduction of the political.

If political reformers address themselves publicly to the ruling powers, Sagitta forces us, in our consideration of his "deviant" strain of a liberation movement, to rethink the relationship of the public to the private sphere, and the role of the literary within this opposition. It is impossible to understand the politics of Sagitta's project without understanding first the role to be played within that politics by the public sphere. In turn, it is impossible to understand Sagitta's conception of the public sphere without first locating the respective roles of the aesthetic and the political within it. Sagitta describes as follows the first attempt—in August of 1905—to develop a list of subscribers: "The criteria for subscribers were most carefully formulated: the public was to be entirely excluded. The subscriber could obtain each of the books only by stating explicitly in his own handwriting that he 'in principle took no offense at literary and artistic creations liable to offend the modesty of so-called "normal" people' and, finally, that he was acquiring the book solely for private use" (1: 21).

Ostensibly, what Sagitta is marshaling here is a traditional argument about the autonomy of the private sphere. The public sphere is being excluded or bypassed and the works are themselves to be consumed only in private. However, we should beware of simply reifying the distinction between public and private by such a reading, for Sagitta himself envisages a much more mediated relation in which the retreat from the public sphere is merely tactical, intended only "so long as it is possible for one group of people to control through force not only the actions but also the thoughts of another and so to influence arbitrarily the course of culture" (1: 21). What ought to be noted immediately here is a Foucauldian distinction between the control of actions (*Handeln*) and the control of thought (*Denken*). In polemicizing for a cause—the term, *Sache*, occurs again and again—Sagitta implicitly raises the question of paederasty from the realm of mere actions to the realm of discourse, identity, or thought. Again, of course, there is an implied distinction between public and private in this distinction between thought and action—but what is being highlighted is not simply the intrusion of the State into the rights of the individual, but the new political problems presented by the recognition of paederasty as a disposition or way of thinking. Thus, Sagitta is quite clear with regard to what he takes to be the intended object of the mechanisms of control: "The point was to attack not the book and its dissemination, but the will that stood behind it" (1: 46). In the same way that it is thought, not action, that is to be controlled, it is a will, rather than a book, that is to be suppressed. A paederastic identity becomes possible—as thought and self-conscious identity rather than as mere actions—and yet at the same time control and repression of that identity are made possible. This is a classic Foucauldian dialectic of incitement and control.

Sagitta, however, complicates the Foucauldian model of the construction of homosexual identity by focusing on the ways in which that identity is established precisely by virtue of a concentration on *acts* rather than on identity itself. Thus, for example, in the novel *Fenny Skaller*, Sagitta asks, "What could these people know of this love, of which they chose to know nothing? . . . All these people can imagine here only 'actions,' though they would never think of such things with regard to their own form of love" (1: 282). In other words, the construction of a homosexual identity is organized around precisely that notion of a singular sodomitic *Handlung* that the notion of homosexual identity itself traditionally displaces in neo-Foucauldian queer historiography. The epistemic rupture from acts to identities does not so much create as instrumentalize the homosexual. Heterosexual identity—Sagitta seems to argue—is established to the extent where it need no longer organize itself around the sexual acts that supposedly define it.

Homosexual identity, however—and this is where some modification of Foucault would be necessary—has never broken entirely free of this dependence on acts. The construction of homosexuality cannot be understood in straightforward terms as a pathologization creating identities from previously disparate acts: for the identity created is an identity fixated—in the popular imagination—around the specificity of the act itself. It is not, as Foucault would suggest, a paradigm shift, but rather a dialectic sublation of sorts—a sublation in which the earlier model of acts (the "sodomitic" model) is retained within the contours of a new homosexual identity. The "new" identity is fixated on acts and therefore unstable and illegitimate as a (self-)identity. One might argue, in fact, that what is pathological about homosexual identity as constructed within medical and juridical discourses is precisely the failure of the subject identity to assert itself over and above its instantiation in any specific homosexual act. This would constitute the epistemological promiscuity of homosexuality: if homosexuality asserts itself through a fixation on acts, the homosexual is compelled—paradoxically, in order to assert his transcendent identity—to engage incessantly in homosexual acts. Homosexuality becomes, as it were, compulsive in the fixation—which Mackay protests—on the act.

By displacing the question of homosexuality into the literary sphere, Mackay attempts to develop—on the basis, originally, of Hellenistic paederasty—a homosexual culture, a homosexual style that would be irreducible to the act. It should be made clear from the outset that he at no point argues that sexuality is a purely private affair, to be left to the discretion of the individuals involved: indeed, he polemicizes against precisely this position. Thus, at the end of the introduction he insists that "this love is at the very deepest level a social issue: the struggle of the individual for his freedom from any form of repression" (61). He is not advocating a politics based on the division of public and private, even if—in the hostile environment in which he writes—the private clearly offers a refuge of sorts. What is at stake is less the privatization of desire than the literary reconstruction of the public sphere on "Hellenistic" lines. That is to say, what Sagitta envisages is a public sphere constituted not on the cognitive claims of politics and positivist science, but on the cultural interaction of desiring individuals. Paederasty would be but one example of Sagitta's intention. The problem will lie in his attempt to graft a Hellenistic model of desire—a model, one ought to point out, that has been cleansed of its own historically specific political power structures—onto a bourgeois public sphere in which the aesthetic has already been assigned specific—largely residual and affirmative—functions.[2] In short, from the perspective of the aesthetic Sagitta polemicizes—

in the name of an Hellenic ideal—against the rationalization of human activity and discourse; but his polemic is itself possible only within the framework of a rationalized lifeworld that has differentiated out a space of the aesthetic. Thus, Sagitta is obliged to work from a basis of social rationalization in order to posit a public arena in which such rationalization might be displaced. The aesthetic will serve him—therefore—as the temporary locus of social desire. In terms of the dialectic traced by Habermas in his study of *The Structural Transformation of the Public Sphere*, Mackay wishes to utilize the ideological autonomy of the aesthetic—an autonomy guaranteed by the rationalization and specialization of discourses— to propose a Hellenic ideal in which such rationalization and specialization are abolished.

None of this, however, exhausts the claims Sagitta makes on art and literature as tools in his struggle. We have already had reason to comment—in the context of Sagitta's disagreements with "*Führer*" such as Hirschfeld—on the strong resistance to any pseudo-scientific liberational strategy. But Sagitta offers a quite specific alternative. The initial invitation to subscribe was oriented to those interested in "artistic and literary creations," and it is clearly under the auspices of the aesthetic—more specifically, of the literary—that Sagitta is to make his appeal. He will present the attack on his cause as an attack on the traditional autonomy of the aesthetic sphere, rather than as simply an attack on the rights to privacy of the individual: "This love is misunderstood and despised, persecuted and misrepresented like nothing else in the world! . . . Here life ceases to be life; and art is no longer art!" (1: 54). In other words, the attack on the sexual freedom of the paederast is figured as an attack on the autonomy of the aesthetic: having failed to evoke a moral outrage at the attack on individual freedom, Sagitta invokes the autonomy claims of the aesthetic. In a sense, then, sexual freedom is displaced onto the freedom to read: what is threatened is not just the right of the reader to act in a certain way, but the freedom to even read what he is at this very moment reading. Rather than constructing identity around the sexual persona, Sagitta constructs it around readership itself, so that the address is necessarily directed, necessarily an address to the reader, who cannot claim impartiality or disinterest. In other words, the attack on aesthetic autonomy is presented not as an attack on the sexual rights of the paederast, but rather as an attack on that ideal of a literate culture that underpins the bourgeois public sphere. The rights of the individual and the privileges of the aesthetic are, in this sense, conflated. What is being invoked is an aesthetic of rights—a right, one might say, *to* the aesthetic.

This conflation of a discourse of desire with a conventional understanding of the autonomy of the aesthetic necessarily leads to a very specific understanding of the nature of paederastic homosexuality in *The Books of Nameless Love*. In the discourse of the aesthetic is encrypted not only the possibility of political action and paederastic liberation—but also the very construction of paederastic identity. I would like to turn now from Sagitta's polemical to his more traditionally literary writings—primarily, to the short novel *Fenny Skaller*—in order to understand how paederasty is constructed within the literary sphere. We have already commented on a potential tension in Sagitta's writing between a Hellenistic understanding of paederastic desire as a broad, socializing force and the invocation of the aesthetic—itself already a rationalized social sub-discourse—as an autonomous realm for the realization of that vision. In *Fenny Skaller*, neo-Hellenism is invoked both to specify the eponymous hero's own particular brand of paederastic idealism and to suggest a specific political vision. In both cases, the question of the aesthetic is central. Sagitta's own precarious position between a pseudo-classical and an Enlightenment understanding of the public sphere is reflected in Fenny's status as a professional translator—as a literary, but not a creative individual. For it is precisely a task of translation that both Sagitta and Fenny must undertake, the translation of a transliterary phenomenon into the limited terms of the autonomous literary sphere. Rather than concentrate exclusively on questions of the literary institution, however, I prefer to use *Fenny Skaller* as a way into the construction of a desire, a desire that necessarily articulates and questions the institutional parameters defining it.

The model of paederasty invoked in the novel takes as its starting point that opposition of masculine and effeminate desire elaborated earlier. In this case, however, Sagitta superimposes a historical narrative that suggests specific political possibilities. First,
he contrasts his own Hellenism—and his own masculinist ideals—
to the politicized effeminacy of Rome:

> On reflection he saw that within the circle of this love for one's own
> sex there was a huge, unbridgeable chasm as wide as that between
> Man and Woman; it is the chasm separating the masculine man whose
> masculine desire tends toward masculine youths—the ancient love of
> the Hellenes—from the effeminate man, or rather from the woman
> who has taken on the external form of masculinity and gives herself
> to men—the late Roman empire offers numerous unmistakable ex-
> amples of this, even though they had nothing to do with its eventual
> fall.   (1: 262–63)

What is interesting in the case of Rome is not that the admixture
of paederasty to political intrigue harms the State—whose demise
paederasty does not affect—but rather that the admixture of the
political to the paederastic should somehow render it effeminate.
Paederasty does not corrupt politics, politics corrupts paederasty.
This suspicion is reinforced by that passage quoted earlier in which
Sagitta rejected "effeminized" politicians, thereby inverting traditional gender codings of the public and the private sphere. Politics is somehow intrinsically effeminate and effeminizing specifically because it involves compromise and accepts the partiality of all
actions in the public sphere. Where art totalizes and synthesizes
(and is masculine), politics operates purely within the fragmented,
rationalized public sphere (and is feminine).

Of particular interest, however, is the way in which Sagitta reconstructs the paederastic model of the Greeks. Toward the end
of *Fenny Skaller*, commenting on the difficulties of embarking on
a relationship with an inexperienced and changeable adolescent,
Sagitta writes, "This age as yet knows no judgment of its own.
How, indeed, should it possess its own judgment! It was confused
and vacillating, this age, instinctual and lacking in insight. They
say one must educate it. But he was no educator. He could only

befriend it, nothing more, nothing less" (1: 321). Clearly, Hellenistic ideals are not being invoked as the guarantors of the sexual freedom of all individuals (including children): it is not a question of a radicalized democracy in which individual political freedom will be extended to all and the sexual disenfranchisement of children made good. At the same time, however, Sagitta quite specifically rejects the pedagogical model—the model of the educator—that one might otherwise associate with Hellenistic paederasty. We might begin by asking why this should be the case and why—if it is the case—he would take Hellenism as a model in the first place? Clearly, what is being rejected is a liberation based on notions of leadership—that is, on that notion of *Führung* that, for the anarchist Mackay, is necessarily a *Verführung*. For Sagitta, Hellenistic love is clearly reciprocal. However, it is more than the simple power relationship that is problematic: the specifically paederastic cast of Sagitta's desire necessarily foregrounds questions of temporality—not just age—in the construction of homosexuality in these works.

Fenny Skaller both can and cannot be read as a *Bildungsroman*. Ostensibly, it deals with the sexual and erotic development of the eponymous hero from the age of about fourteen to the age of 41. This development is mapped against the background of a series of photographs of the various boys whom he has loved or who have had an impact on his life. Within the framework of the *Bildungsroman*, this paederastic fixation on an object of desire that changes faces but does not itself age (all the boys, bar the first, are aged fourteen to seventeen) necessarily reflects on the developmental construction of the subject. Essentialistic notions of self—ascribing to the subject a permanence, a core, whose development might subsequently be traced—become problematic. For what is permanent here? The unswerving attraction to boys of a certain age? Or the boys themselves, the age itself? And if the concept of immutability is projected outside the subject, can we speak of a coherent subject at all? The fixation of desire seems to derive from the inability to fix the position of the desiring subject. Moreover,

if desire is itself fixated—if it does not "progress"—can we speak
in terms of the developmental *Bildung* of that subject?

It is this concern with temporality—thought and experienced
through the prism of paederastic desire—that both positions and
displaces *Fenny Skaller* as a *Bildungsroman*. Fenny's progressive
development—or lack of it—throughout the narrative is countered
by two other temporal schema that alternately set off or undercut
the developmental structure of the *Bildungsroman* form. First, as
we have commented, there is the atemporality of representation—
the photographs themselves—which do not age.[3] If Fenny has developed, then he has done so despite retaining a taste for a specific
age. Thus, at the very outset, he is himself described as someone
"who was so thoroughly a man, but who could still be a complete
child—who had matured before his time, but who could never
mature—who was still youthful in his desire, but who had never
been young" (1: 166). The temporal disparity between lover and
beloved is not contingent on the ageing of the hero. Fenny was
never young. Or, indeed, he is never old (in his desire). The traditional trajectory of the *Bildungsroman*, then, is of questionable
value in tracing the life of the paederastic hero, who does not age.
What is at stake, in fact, is an atemporal desire that negates the ed-
ucative passion of the bourgeois hero of a *Bildungsroman*. We shall
return to this topos later in an examination of Sagitta's etiology of
paederastic desire.

There is, however, a second temporal arrangement superimposed on the narrative of *Bildung*. This is the temporal framework
of the narration itself, that begins after (yet another) broken rendezvous, from which Fenny returns home to console himself with
the photographs of past loves. As he sifts through the photographs,
he observes the changing scene outside his window—from early
afternoon through to early morning and the dawn of the new day.
The act of narrating itself is, then, temporally situated, a recollection and retelling, played out in the course of one night. Within
the broader context of *The Books of Nameless Love*, however, the
trajectory of the act of narrating acquires great significance: for in
the political writings it is in terms of the dawning of a new day that

Sagitta habitually figures his own historical mission of emancipation. In *Fenny Skaller*, the dawning is contemporaneous with—one might even say, dependent on—the act of narration. In other words, I would contend that *Fenny Skaller* functions as a *Bildungsroman* not because of the narrative it retells, but because of the time of telling itself. Enlightenment takes place not in the narrative, but through it, or alongside it.

Where do such narratological niceties get us? First, I think we must recognize that the focusing of the developmental time scale on the moment of narration itself obliges us to question the status of Fenny—or the suitability of a homosexual protagonist—as a *Bildungsroman* subject. In a sense, the narrative—as a narrative of desire—does not present any development. At best, what we have is a recognition brought about at the moment of narration itself, by a recontemplation of the photographs. Fenny realizes that his own desire for boys of a certain age itself derives from the time he was himself that age:

> How strange it was!
> Then already!—Already at *that* age! . . .
> Even as his senses lay in deepest slumber they longed to follow the paths that nature had prescribed for them! (1: 178).

Sagitta is invoking a natural essence—Fenny's paederastic desire—in which the subject is grounded, but that essence is actualized only at the moment of recollection. The homosexual hero of the *Bildungsroman* constructs himself in the moment of fabulation. He is not a subject with a story to tell, but a story, with a subject to construct. Narrative is constructive rather than representational, to the extent that the diegetic and the extradiegetic cannot be unscrambled.

Fenny's recognition of his own "nature" is overshadowed by the resolution that the evening brings about in him—a resolution to fight for justice. What is actualized in the act of narration is not only the autonomous subject—Fenny—but the new dawn, the political recognition of Sagitta's cause, his *Sache*. The temporality of this novel of atemporal desire is nonsubjective: it is the temporality of a dawning *En-lightenment*: in other words, the construction of the homosexual subject is subjugated to the actualization of the homosexual cause. I think that we can frame this consideration of narrative and narration in terms of the revision to the Foucauldian model that I proposed earlier. If the *Bildungsroman* is about the representation of identity, then the identity of the homosexual hero is itself, as yet, too tentative to be presented as a novelistic subject. This subject identity will be *enacted*—at the level of narration, rather than of narrative—in the course of the novel's construction. In other words, narrative—not sexual acts—becomes the definitive *Handlung* constitutive of homosexual identity. Thus, as we observed earlier, if homosexual identity is the identity of the subject who has not yet disentangled himself from the pre-identitarian fixation on acts, at the novelistic level it will be the act of narration, rather than the subject of narrative, that will allow us to posit a homosexual identity. Sagitta's subjugation of subjective concerns to the concerns of political En-lightenment in this novel, moreover, also allows us to rework the charge of a homo-fascist, pre-identitarian pathology (which he opposes) into a positive post-identitarian politics.

The subject, then, is an absent center to this novel: the question is whether this absence should be interpreted as lack or—as we have begun to intimate—as the imperative impelling the "hero" beyond the limits of personal self-realization toward a political articulation of a cause. The novel is ambiguous in its simultaneous construction and deconstruction of identity. Mackay's model of paederastic desire—as I hope to show now—deconstructs at the private level of desire the structures of identity he seems to be erecting as political agency. The logic of renunciation, whereby Fenny resigns himself to personal frustration, while pledging himself to collective emancipation, is such that the ideological structure of the *Bildungsroman*—the movement toward an individualistic *self*-fulfillment—no longer applies. If the possibility of self-actualization has been foreclosed, the very conventionality of the genre demands a closure that will be displaced into the political.

In effect, Mackay will invert the aborted teleology of the novel and ontologize the lack of fulfillment as a structural principle of desire rather than as an accidental effect of social prejudice. The self will not be actualized because the self is itself the product of an originary diremption. Thus, as we shall see, it would in fact be wrong to hypostatize the act of narrating as the locus of homosexual self-fabulation and self-fulfillment—for that act itself projects a second level of narrative identity. The homosexual hero of the *Bildungsroman* exists neither at the level of narrative, nor in the act of narrating—but in the incommensurability of the two.

Let us return to those photographs. If, in the structure implied by the series of photographs, the hero's life is shown to have progressed by virtue of a series of repetitions, and thereby to lack a teleological orientation, it is no easier to construct an ontological origin to ground the hero's narrative. The repetitive nature of Fenny's desire serves to cloud the possibility of positing any origin. If desire is real and actual in each instantiation, what can it be a repetition *of*? The question arises, for example, at the very beginning of the narrative, when Fenny attempts to understand why the missed rendezvous with the boy should be of such importance to him: he seems to be about to break the chain of repetition by recognizing it *as* repetition, thereby transcending it. Why is the boy's face so important?

> Suddenly, he thought he knew: because it reminded him of another face.
> Another—but which?
> He thought and thought but could not place it. And yet it must lie somewhere on the very floor of his memory, cast aside by the years, cast aside and forgotten.   (1: 167)

The paradox of memory is the paradox of desire, which is always and never real and originary. At the moment of remembrance, we have not forgotten the thing we remember—we are not *re*minded, but rather *mindful* of it. Likewise, to trace desire back to an origin is to render all desire simulacral—which is precisely what desire is not: to think one desires something and to actually desire it cannot, at the moment of desire itself, be differentiated. What Sagitta is proposing is a radical forgetfulness, however, rather than a simple parapraxis: "No, what tortured him now was the memory of something long since forgotten, something that had once entered his life somewhere only to disappear in the next moment; something he had lost before he had even known it, and whose loss had nevertheless left him with a slight, stinging wound" (1: 168). In other words, the absence of origin—of the original that all other desire would merely copy—both radicalizes and derealizes desire. Either there is no original and so all desire—even the first— is unreal, or there is no original desire on whose authority other desire would be deemed simulacral and repetitious. Fenny does not return to the photographs to find the face of which he was reminded by the boy who failed to keep the rendezvous—"he would not find there what he sought" (1: 168). As a voyage of self-discovery, then, the confrontation with the photographs—with the past—is bound to fail precisely because that which has to be retrieved is already irretrievably lost.

In fact, Sagitta takes the irretrievable loss—this radical forgetfulness—to be the central paradox of paederastic love.[4] The question, however—which may be unanswerable—is: precisely what is lost in this loss? Of course, it is in the very nature of this loss that what has been lost should be irretrievable, in the very nature of this love that it be nameless. Nevertheless, if Sagitta renounces any reconstruction of an origin of desire, he is still concerned with understanding the nature of his desire in the present. Thus, we are faced with a paradox of sorts: a desire that denies explication with regard to its origin, but that moves, nevertheless, toward an immanent self-understanding. The attempt to understand desire first locates itself in an examination of the *object*: these boys at least share something in common that might explain desire with regard to its object. However, in reviewing the photographs Fenny realizes that no two are alike and that none of them corresponds to a classical ideal of beauty. This leads him to the conclusion—expressed in its most lapidary form in the better known work, *The Hustler*—that "it is the age itself that you love" (2: 361). The attempt to psychologize this desire for a certain age will lead to some of the most interesting insights of Sagitta's work.

Why should one fall in love with this age? Certainly, it does not present itself in a particularly attractive light in this novel and Fenny himself moves toward a recognition of its cruelty: "More and more he became acquainted with the age he loved so. It was a terrible age: only now could he see how cold and cruel this age was. Yes, it was cruel, cruel and pitiless" (1: 321). Is it this cruelty, this severity, that he loves, an ethos of discipline potentially compatible with a rightist political project or a sadomasochistic libido? We cannot draw such conclusions, for the ethos of cruelty and severity is not linked—in the case of these boys—to an insistence on self or identity. Indeed, we will recall that the reverse is the case: "This age as yet knows no judgment of its own. How, indeed, should it possess its own judgment! It was confused and vacillating, this age, instinctual and lacking in insight" (1: 321). It is not, then, the severity of the ego that is being invoked—but rather the cruelty of the unformed psyche.[5] These boys cannot be identical to each other (Fenny's desire is not simply a cycle of exchange) for they are not identical to themselves. Were we to name and identify the object of Fenny's desire, it would need be the state of nonidentity itself.

We speak, then, of the cruelty of the unformed psyche, but Sagitta is certainly not celebrating some protofascistic Dionysian reconstruction of the Hellenic ideal. What is cruel is the inability of the object itself to cohere *as* a cathected object. Why, then, should this instability be both attractive and threatening to paederastic desire? As Fenny considers the pictures—among them, pictures of himself, looking serious beyond his years—he reexperiences something of the past: "They returned to him, those years that should have been the strongest and happiest of his life, the most carefree, but which in reality had been nothing but one long, endless, hopeless struggle with himself" (1: 189). To say that he *re*experiences his past is, in fact, inaccurate; for the point is that Fenny now experiences—through his love for young boys, and through the simulacral evocation of that love—what he never experienced in the first place: his youth. In attempting to psychologize Fenny's desire, Sagitta reverses the logic of the object in order to explain the desiring subject. Fenny attempts to reconstruct a past self that—

according to the logic of radical forgetfulness—itself never was. This is a circular logic: Fenny himself was never an adolescent, and he therefore desires in adolescents the youth he himself missed; yet he missed this youth because—"already at that age!"—he always already desired those youths. It was through desire that he lost his youth and desire that he seeks to explicate through that loss. In other words, paederastic desire is being posited as its own origin, as both cause and effect. The subject loves in order to recapture the youth he never had, and he never had that youth because he was always already in love. Paederastic desire seems—for Sagitta—to legitimate and perpetuate itself in a perfect circularity: one loves what one lost by loving.

This circular logic can be looked at another way. These boys ostensibly represent everything that Fenny was not—they are playful where he was serious, thoughtless where he was ponderous. His own youth was nothing more than "one long, endless, hopeless struggle with himself." And yet is it not a very similar uncertainty—"confused and vacillating"—that he desires in the boys themselves? In fact, the desire for self-identity—a desire that in its very doubling as a performative, necessarily undoes the identity that is desired—is not simply contrasted with the naive self-identity of the other boys. These boys are attractive not because they are self-identical (he desires them precisely because their identity is as yet unformed) but because they do not desire such self-identity. Thus, when Mackay writes, "If only I were like you! . . . Thoughtless like you!" (*Wäre ich wie Du! . . . Ohne Gedanken gleich Dir!*) (1: 339), Fenny is actually a lot closer to the object of his own desire than he dare admit. This last quotation, with its desire to emulate the object of desire, clearly raises the question of narcissism as a paradigmatic understanding of homosexual—or, in this case, specifically paederastic—desire. It is on this question that I wish to close my consideration of Sagitta's writings.

In simple terms: do the writings of Sagitta propose an alternative to the narcissistic model of homosexual desire, or do they oblige a reconsideration of the terms of that model? To what extent would any rethinking of the narcissistic model be implicit in

Sagitta's *literary* approach to the question of homosexuality? To begin to answer these questions—without entering into the technicalities of the psychoanalytic method—we should recall that the narcissistic mechanism functions (according to Freud) by fixating the desire of the subject on

(a) what he himself is (i.e., himself)
(b) what he himself was
(c) what he himself would like to be
(d) someone who was once part of himself.   (*Standard Edition* 14: 90)

Of course, these four categories cover a multitude of sins, and we are on solid ground only when we compare Sagitta's work directly with them. Essentially, what the paederastic desire constructed by Sagitta demonstrates is the room for conflict and contradiction within these categories and the impossibility of tracing those contradictions back to a common origin. To take in isolation Fenny's desperate exclamation "Wäre ich wie Du!" it would not be difficult to take it as a direct expression of Fenny's desire for "what he himself would like to be." But as a performative, the statement is at the same time a reaffirmation of nonidentity: Fenny is not like the person he desires. It is, in essence, a melancholic narcissism reminiscent of that structure we have already derived from Adorno, wherein the narcissistic desire for the desire of the other necessarily places us in an inferior position to the object of our desire. The object's desire is immanent and self-enclosed, but the circle of our narcissism is broken by the need to reflect itself in and through the narcissism of the beloved object.[6]

Fenny desires to be—but is not—the object he desires. Under the category of "what he himself would like to be" Freud tends to range the subject's cathexis of its own process of development, the movement toward ego formation. This is a teleological desire in which the subject desires—to put it in banal terms—a "role model." In Sagitta's rewriting, however, it is precisely the powers that deconstruct rather than constitute the coherence of the ego—anarchic powers, one might say, drawing an erotic inference from Mackay's political agenda—that are attractive. It is not an ego ideal that Fenny desires, but rather a deconstruction of the ego. The desire expressed in the exclamation "Wäre ich wie Du!" ("If only I were like you!") must be examined at a grammatical level prior to the constitution of the entities hypostatized in *Ich* and *Du*: this is, after all, the nameless love, a love that potentially shuns even the nomenclature of the pronomial subject.

Let us dissect this lapidary expression of paederastic, "narcissistic" (though, I would say, melancholic) desire: *Wäre ich . . .* ; here there is a desire for a coming into being. The desire is a desire to be. This is not the assertion *of* an ego, but a desire *for* it; a recognition of its nonconstitution: ego as virtual object, rather than originary subject of desire. *Wie Du!* implies on the contrary the prior constitution of the desired boy. My being and my desire are in the subjunctive mode; his are indicative.[7] But we have the evidence of the child's nonformation ("confused and vacillating") and the narcissistic assimilation of subject and object further removes the object of desire from the condition of indicative subjectivity. If my subjunctive desire is to be fulfilled, then the *Du* must become subjunctive too. The implicitly indicative *Wie Du* becomes a *Wärest Du*. The process of this desire would be as follows then: "If only I could be like you" becomes "If only I could *be*—like you." This in turn becomes "If only you could *be*, that I might be (like you)." The object of desire itself *is* not—it "is" precisely that age of development where the subject has not been fully formed. Desire is the desire to constitute first the object and then the effect of a subject through the object. The logic, then would not be: "If only *I* (an already existing subject) could be more like *you* (my object, and a full subject in your own right)," but rather, "If only you could *be* in order that I might be also, by being like you." It is a logic we shall reencounter in Jarry, for whom the apparently narcissistic relation raises questions about the existence of the Other.[8]

If such is the logic, however, there is clearly something perverse in the choice of this object that "is" not, that is "confused and vacillating." In the desiring dialectic of self-constitution, the paederastic subject chooses an object who will hamper rather than facilitate his own self-constitution. In this presentation, then, paederastic desire holds at bay the condition of subjectivity potentially invoked in the act of desire itself. The narcissism involved here—if such be the correct term—is involuted indeed. Fenny wishes to be like someone who is not—by virtue of his age—even like himself. But is this not, then, a further elaboration on the logic of narcissism itself? I split myself by desiring another, who *is* (like) me: he *is* (like) me by virtue of being himself split, half man, half boy. By a logic of narcissistic identification, two nonidentical subjects are linked in desire: I am not like myself, you are not like yourself, therefore we are alike in not being alike. It is an identification based not on identity, but on the *non*identity of the desiring subject and his adolescent object.

Now, it would be tempting to claim that Sagitta's reworking and undermining of the narcissistic model is really a function of paederasty rather than of homosexuality and that he is not really accounting for the gender-specificity of the subject and object in this particular configuration of desire. However, it should be pointed out that Freud himself often invokes paederasty as an exemplary form of homosexuality and uses it precisely to ground his own model of narcissism, as, for example, in the following passage from "Some Neurotic Mechanisms in Jealousy, Paranoia and Homosexuality":

> The typical process, already established in innumerable cases, is that a few years after the termination of puberty a young man, who until this time has been strongly fixated to his mother, changes his attitude; he identifies himself with his mother, and looks about for love-objects in whom he can re-discover himself, and whom he might then love as his mother loved him. The characteristic mark of this process is that for several years one of the necessary conditions for his love is usually that the male object shall be of the same age as he himself was when the change took place. (*Standard Edition* 18: 230)

The paradigm is clearly paederastic here, for the love object is an adolescent, someone of the same age as the desiring subject when he made the break with the mother. What I am proposing is that the possibility opened up in our reading of Adorno—the possibility of a narcissistic logic oriented around a category of the non-identical—is precisely what Mackay is exploring in his reworking of a classical paederastic paradigm. Adorno's model allows us, I think, to see "negative narcissism" as the condition of a desire (the condition of *all* desire?) that seeks to construct (rather than work from) the position of a subjectivity. This construction, however, necessarily deconstructs the category of subject it seeks to construct for itself. I will return once again to this notion in the final chapter, when I consider the question of melancholy as a mode of both desire and representation.

Meanwhile, however, the passage just cited from Freud moves us along in its introduction of a term not discussed thus far with reference to Mackay—the mother. What would be her role in Sagitta's reconstruction of paederastic desire? Moreover, can we see in the figure of the mother an impulse toward the regendering of public and private in Mackay's political and aesthetic project? Freud seems to place paederasty squarely at the center of his model of homosexuality: the object choice occurs in the years directly following puberty, and the object itself will be of that age. The question as it poses itself to us in the immediate context of Mackay is whether or not the paederastic model of homosexuality that Mackay develops is narcissistic.

Mackay's antieffeminism is such that females play very little role in his narratives. At one point, he writes of Fenny: "He wanted nothing to do with women. Although he enjoyed talking occasionally with wise—and particularly with older—women, all those specifically feminine traits that other men clearly did not perceive offended his very soul" (1: 265). These qualities include "vanity, a love of gossip, and pettiness. Chatter and general fussiness." There is, however, a role for the mother, and—in *The Hustler*—it is to a woman that the hero returns for consolation. So what is the role of these mother figures in Mackay's problematization of the narcissistic paradigm?

We have already commented on the impossibility of naming the love of which Sagitta writes, of tracing it to any origin. Thus, it is impossible in Sagitta's case to introduce the mother as a unitary term that somehow explains paederastic desire in the manner outlined by Freud. Nevertheless, there is one photograph among those many in *Fenny Skaller* that we have not mentioned. One of only two photographs displayed in Fenny's home is of his mother, who died around the same time as the young boy Fenny loved most dearly. In fact, the boy died while Fenny was away attending his mother's funeral. Clearly, the death of the mother and the death of this boy are linked, but they are linked ambiguously—the love for mother both parallels and yet distracts and detracts from the love for the boy. In a sense, this death of the mother might be read in terms of Freud's account of the rupture with the mother as object, which leads to a narcissistic identification and in turn takes as its object a boy such as oneself, a boy such as one's mother might have loved. But the death of the mother and the death of the boy take place at one and the same time. The new object dies along with the old—in the same way as the age one loves is necessarily an age one leaves behind. To fixate desire on the age is to accept that the object of love is the rupture itself, or the loss—a moment of loss of identity prior to the (re-)identification with the mother. In other words, Mackay sketches a scenario in which the rupture with the mother does not result in a paederastic object choice to replace the mother, but rather in an object choice (still paederastic) that serves to represent and reenact the rupture. In being reminded again and again of the diacritical distance between myself and my object of desire, I do not replace one full entity (the mother) with another (the boy), but rather cathect the rupture itself, that break with an age I never was anyway.

Potentially, then—and it is this, above all, that Sagitta's writings seem to convey—the logic of narcissism reinforces an identity whose *loss* is at the heart of paederastic desire. The mother as origin—one might say—functions only at the level of narrative, as the story one tells oneself of one's desire; but the desire is in the telling, in the construction of a self through narration. It is thus, perhaps, that we might understand the ending of *The Hustler*, where the bourgeois lover of the fickle proletarian hustler—released from prison—recalls a note sent to him by a distant aunt, inviting him to visit her in any time of trouble. It is she who reveals to him his fate and his condition, and—in gratitude—he addresses her thus:

> "I cannot call you 'auntie' [*Tante*]," he said embarrassedly, "the word is disagreeable to me."
> "Then call me 'mother'!"
> She kissed his brow.   (2: 358)

Ostensibly, there is a return to the mother—and yet there is an insistence that the word is just a word, a word that replaces the name of *Tante*. After this "return" to the nonoriginary mother, there immediately begins a line of questioning: "Tell me about my mother," he demands (2: 358). The return to this imaginary mother is nevertheless enacted against the recognition that she is *not* the mother. The hero is liberated not by way of a return that would symbolically reaffirm the originality of the *Bildungsroman* hero, but by way of a narrative that recontains the form of the mother. The return is at the same time a displacement. Moreover, the homosexual terminology of this return is unmistakable in the light of the charge of *Tuntenhaß* leveled against masculinists such as Mackay. He finds the imaginary mother precisely because he cannot bear the term *Tante*—the word for both "aunt" and "fairy." Mackay's masculinism is ideological in its reconstruction of a self-consciously displaced semblance of the origin (of desire) impelled by a hatred of effeminized homosexuality. The *Tante* becomes the mother.

It would seem, then, that Sagitta is quite specifically presenting paederastic desire as a desire that is denied the luxury of narcissistic self-reflection. Instead, it partakes of a process of self-constitution that nevertheless defers the moment of closure around identity. The object of desire is not a model of identity, but is quite clearly lacking in that quality. Thus, the logic of Narcissus serves to undermine narcissistic self-identification: I identify with the nonidentical. The process of self-constitution is entirely consonant with the new model of writing outlined earlier, in which the aim is to construct rather than reflect. The homosexual narrative is not narcissistic in any simplistic sense, since it cannot confront the self with its simple reflection. At a more complex level of understanding Narcissus, however, one might take that writing as a narcissistic act, with all the paradoxes this implies. One constructs a self, but not an identity, since the originary split within identity is itself replicated by the division of narrative and narrating. In essence, I think one must argue that Sagitta is manipulating the paederastic model as a way of undermining a metaphysics of identity that heterosexual desire claims for itself.

This manipulation is perhaps best summed up in a parable from the pamphlet, "LISTEN . . . Just One Moment . . . A Cry!" where Sagitta evokes the narcissistic scenario in the following terms:

> Listen: can you not hear a rustling about us in the silence of this night, deep and sonorous like the rustling of a distant stream?—It is the stream of love that flows through the world. Out of the distant secrets of time it gushes forth. There its waters spring pure and clear— at the beginning of all worlds, the origin of all Being. The people bend over it to drink of life. All may come and drink strength, health, beauty and joy there. Only we stand to one side. We alone of all people. For our spring—originating here also—is poisoned: poisoned by prejudice and rendered impure by hatred. And as we bend over it to quench our thirst, we are assailed by the putrefaction of corpses, the corpses of those who drank, and who had to die because they drank. Shuddering, we step back, again and again—to drink anyway and die, like them, or to go thirsty. (1: 475)

All but the homosexual can lean across the water and see their own reflection, draw sustenance from it. The homosexual sees only into waters that not only muddy an image that would otherwise be there, but render impossible the projection of any such image. What we seem to be dealing with in this parable of the leaning over the waters is a negation of the narcissistic impulse in the context of self-narration. What is at stake is the impossibility of a narcissistic narrative thought purely in terms of reflection. The question that Sagitta's texts pose—or that the phenomenon of paederasty itself perhaps poses—is the following: is it the identity of the paederast that is lacking, or the reflective medium of identification itself? It is the water that is muddied: thus, is it a question of representation, of a move beyond mere reflection, or is it a more fundamental metaphysical question of rethinking the *Ursprung alles Seins*, the reflective, narcissistic construct of identity itself? In other words, are we to read Sagitta's project as the attempt—failed or self-deferring—to posit a paederastic identity, or as an attempt to problematize—by way of paederastic desire—the category of identity itself? Or, in terms of our project in this book: must we, like Adorno, identify masculinism with a kind of "poisoned" narcissism? Should we not, instead, note the reworking of the narcissistic scenario in early homosexual writers such as Mackay in the name of a specifically anarchic, anti-identitarian politics, that questions at the most fundamental level the ideology of identity and embodiment crucial to the self-representation of the fascist *Volk*?

CHAPTER 5

Fables of Modernity: Wyndham Lewis and the Homosexual as Fascist

I n this chapter I will concentrate on three texts by Wyndham Lewis (from 1926, 1930, and 1939) that trace not only the rise and wane of his interest in Nazism, but also his growing recognition of the importance of fascism to the self-consciousness of literary and aesthetic modernism. I wish, thereby, to move in this second section of the book toward a consideration of the way in which the political and sexual problematic of homo-fascism was manipulated within a modernist—and repudiated within an avant-garde—tradition in literature. The reading will take as its pivotal moment Lewis's journalistic reports of a visit to Germany in 1930, in which he inexplicably feels it necessary—before addressing directly the emergence of Nazism in Germany, the ostensible subject of the series of articles he was writing—to offer an "Introduction for the Anglo-Saxon reader." If, as Sedgwick has pointed out in *Tendencies*, Germany served as the imaginary repository of both fears and aspirations regarding emergent homosexual identities, I wish to examine here in more detail how the Germany of Mackay, the Germany of the Friedrichstraße and of the *Puppen-*

junge, entered into the modern—or, more specifically, modern*ist*—
Anglo-American cultural project.

I propose to follow Lewis's detour—a detour he makes in spite
(or because) of his avowed intent to reveal the political essence of
Nazism, stripped of all moralizing, as a purely political phenomenon. This detour—which takes the intrepid "modernist as re-
porter" through the transvestite bars, for which Berlin was so famous and which still color our historical imaginary of that city—is
important to the project of this book in its linking of questions of
sexual politics and representational strategies to the emergence of
fascism. Lewis articulates a sociosexual analysis of fascism as the
"inversion" of prevailing political and sexual paradigms. In examining one leading modernist's attempts to chart both his fascination—and subsequent disenchantment—with fascism through a
general theory of "inversion," I seek to work out the fundamental
ideological displacement that gives a name to this study of *Political Inversions.* I will argue that Lewis's analysis of modernity—his
critique of contemporary politics, and his original enthusiasm for
Nazism—is structured taxonomically in terms of an analysis of homosexuality. It is Lewis who makes explicit the importance of
"homo-fascism" to any queer deconstruction of Anglo-American
modernism.

Following, as it does, on our consideration of Mackay's naturalistic depiction of the late Wilhelmine homosexual subculture,
Lewis's preamble serves as an introduction not only to the politics of fascism, but also to the aesthetics of modernism. For all its
attempts at a bluff, "common-sensical" approach to the subject of
Nazism, Lewis's 1930 articles turn inevitably on the impossibility
of any straightforward portrayal of Nazism as a political phenomenon, and this impossibility is dramatized in his encounter with
the transvestites of the Berlin homosexual subculture. To this extent we might say that the works of Lewis to be examined here
form the fulcral point to this book; for between the reservedly celebratory articles of 1930 and Lewis's belated renunciation of
Nazism in 1939, homosexuality transforms itself from a figure for
the decadence and social instability that fascism will combat into

a figure for fascism itself. If—as Eve Sedgwick has, I think rightly, suggested, and as we shall examine in more detail in the next chapter—the modernist aesthetic of abstraction insistently invokes a kitsch, homosexual representationalism as its debased other, Lewis's texts allow us to observe the historical mutation within modernism itself, as it confronts fascism. In short, I am suggesting that the set of binary oppositions demonstrated by Sedgwick— in which homosexuality is linked to a retardataire representational aesthetic and progressive literary practice to relentless antirepresentationalism—is, in the course of the texts under consideration here, gradually replaced by a more fundamental binarism that displaces the very *episteme* of representationalism (to which literary modernism remains bound by way of negation) by a putatively "homo-fascist" aesthetics of performance. More radically, I am suggesting that the project of literary modernity is curtailed not by a reactionary return to representation, but rather by a more radical shift into the politics, the aesthetics, the sexual practices of performativity. Moreover, Lewis—whose own relationship to literary modernists of his own time was, at best, strained—provides a privileged insight into this shift precisely because his own counterdemocratic ideology—even where it most vigorously rails against effeminization—consistently reveals itself as dependent on a certain "homosexualized," or performative, notion of masculinity.

Fredric Jameson somewhat embarrassedly writes off the essays Lewis was subsequently to collect in his volume *Hitler* as a "slapdash series of newspaper articles," but it is clear that Lewis transforms the reportage form into a paradoxically modernist vehicle for reflection on the possibility of naturalistic representation. Surprisingly, in this reflection the transvestite figures not the passage beyond traditional ("natural") representational codes, but rather a "dull naturalism." In other words, sexual inversion will be figured as pre- rather than proto-postmodern. What I am proposing is that Lewis—albeit unintentionally—effectively figures the passage from premodern naturalism to a modernist reflection on reflection as the passage from a homosexuality understood through the prism of gender transgression (the transvestites) to a homosexuality understood as what he will call "supermasculinity." In other words, though literary historical chronology is not in our favor, I would argue that Lewis belatedly helps us understand the displacement of a brand of homosexual naturalism still found in Mackay (a naturalism, after all, that bases itself on an unproblematic understanding of what "nature" is) by a masculinism (exemplified by Jarry) that can only be termed postnaturalist.

I should stress that this movement within masculinism is one with which Lewis—who would himself rather cling to traditional gender binarisms—is not at all comfortable. Lewis figures the shift away from naturalism not in terms of a movement from representation to abstraction (or antirepresentation) but rather as a more fundamental paradigm shift from representation to performance. As I hope to show, his ostensible project is to demonstrate how a virile, masculinist political ideology (exemplified in Nazism, but also—unfortunately for Lewis—in such homosexual figures as Frederick the Great) can rescue the decadent Western democracies from their political effeminization. Despite this, his celebrations of masculinity finally fall prey to an essentially performative notion of gender most consistently elaborated in his visit with the transvestites of the Eldorado bar.

In *Hitler*, Lewis resigns himself to a curious methodological paradox: Berlin will be presented as "the *quartier-général* of dogmatic Perversity—the Perverts' Paradise, the Mecca of both Lesb. and So." (21). To realize the incommensurability of morality and politics, the Anglo-Saxon reader—the "sightseer"—must nevertheless take a diversion through the gilded halls of the transvestite bar, the "Eldorado." There he will encounter the following scene:

> Elegant and usually eyeglassed young women will receive him, with an expensive politeness, and he will buy one of these a drink, and thus become at home. Still, he will have to be a sightseer of some penetration not to think that his sight-seeing eyes may not this time be destined to gloat, upon what he had promised them they should find there. Then these bland Junos-gone-wrong, bare-shouldered and braceleted (as statuesque as feminine showgirl guardees), after a drink or two, will whisper to the outlandish sightseer that they are *men*. Oh dear!—so, after all, the sight-seeing eyes are going to be satisfied! And

they will goggle at the slightly smiling bland Edwardian "tart" at their side—still disposed to regard this as a hoax after all, for it is *too* like, it is too true to nature by far.   (24)

Before asking exactly what this scene is doing here, we should first look closely at its dramatization of deception and revelation with respect to transvestism. The expectation of the "sightseer" is itself disguised—travestied, perhaps—by a set of double negatives: "He will have to be a sightseer of some penetration *not* to think that his sight-seeing eyes may *not* this time be destined to gloat, upon what he had promised them they should find there" (my emphasis). Denuded of its negatives, the sentence indicates that the sightseer has, in fact, come in search not of women, but of the transvestite—and that, "after all, the sight-seeing eyes are going to be satisfied." In other words, the deception of the transvestite does not lie primarily in the convincing representation of a woman, but in the unconvincing representation of a transvestite. Deception and disappointment cannot be disentangled. The "original"— that which is sought—is the transvestite, the representation, not the woman. At the moment of revelation, it is no longer a question of the man impersonating the woman, but rather of an imaginary woman impersonating the man who impersonates her. The transvestite who simply looks like a woman is not enough, for what is required is a double deception: first, deception—in the sense of disappointment—that this woman is, after all, only a woman, followed by the recognition of the deception, of the fact that she is a man.

The paradoxical situation of the transvestite, then, results from the double bind of all representation: he is "*too* like, . . . too true to nature by far." Strangely, the transvestite is not rejected as something contrary to nature: quite the opposite, s/he is potentially too true—to the extent, even, of a "dull naturalism." The transvestite must be like enough to convince—but unlike enough for the sightseer to recognize the art of impersonation. As a result,

the "feminine" will never be quite the same for him again. Who can say if this will be for his good or no? The sex-absolute will to some extent have been disintegrated for him by this brief encounter—it will

have caused him to regard, with a certain sceptical squint, all specifically feminine personality. This may, after all (it is not too venture-
some to believe), be of great use to him, even, in the subsequent con-
duct of his life. Such radical *Enttäuschung* might even be of great economic value to the average sight-seer, in his struggle with nature and
her expensive traps and tricks.   (26)

The transvestite lifts femininity out of the realm of biology and
into the realm of politics in a way that woman—according to
Lewis—cannot. Such a position is, of course, clearly resonant of
the type of masculinism outlined in Chapter 3: gender (in this case,
femininity)—once estranged from the body (of the woman)—reveals itself as a categorical and political construction. The realm of
the political becomes synonymous with the realm of signs. The
transvestite denatures and politicizes not only the category of the
feminine, but the very modality of representation itself. Only
where the feminine is reduced to a system of signs opposed to the
dictates of biology does it reveal itself as an ideological social construct and material for political reconstruction. The naive faith in
appearance and the naive faith in woman are shed at one and the
same time.

   The questions foregrounded by Lewis here, however, are less
questions of gender than of modes of representation—aesthetic
questions. "Too true to nature by half," the transvestite enacts
"the dull naturalism of the male copycat," which—Lewis nevertheless asserts—"is not to be despised" (27). Far from offering
something "unnatural"—the usual moralistic response to homosexuality—the transvestite offers only a "dull naturalism." Lewis's
position is, after all, aesthetic rather than moral. But what is the
aesthetic value of his judgment? He does not despise such naturalism—but why not, if it is so "dull"? The answer would seem to
lie in the impossibility of the deception. In order that the transvestite be a transvestite, a certain game must be played with representation. The man apparently disappears into the woman—representation is complete. But in order to be complete as representation, a certain residue—exemplified in the Eldorado bar by "the
male token of the chin-stubble" (25)—is necessary to mark the

play of signifier and signified. This gendered residue represents
that element of the signifier that will not subsume itself in the signified. Thus, transvestism reveals the precise limitations of naturalism, subtly deconstructing its own aesthetic.

At the risk of getting ahead of ourselves, we should, perhaps,
pause at this encounter with the transvestite—this experience of
Enttäuschung—and trace its political implications for Lewis's own
subsequent disappointment with fascism. For, from the perspective of the encounter in the "Eldorado," this disappointment—
chronicled in 1939 in *The Hitler Cult*—will prove not to have been
a disappointment at all. Lewis—the "sightseer" in search of a specifically German phenomenon—will have found it not in fascism,
as he had thought, but in the transvestite whom he had sought to
depoliticize and marginalize. This realization emerges by 1939, as
Lewis reflects in *The Hitler Cult* that "Nietzsche, who was a philol-
ogist *de carrière*, believed that the word *Deutsche* was to be traced
to the same root as the verb *täuschen* (to deceive). The Germans,
he said, were the people who deceived: a *deceptive* people" (41).
If the transvestite might be said to be an embodiment at all, then
s/he is the embodiment of the Germanic *Täuschung*. Far from offering a mere diversion to the journalist in search of the new German essence, the transvestite—whose existence as representation
seems so contrary to all essence—*is* that essence. Like the transvestite—or so, at least, runs the narrative of Lewis's own disappointment—Germany does not offer the essence that was sought.
This deception and disappointment, indeed, is Germany's essence.
And if the sightseer is obliged to travel to Berlin to grasp the essence of the political, he will be disappointed: that is to say, he will
grasp that essence as deception.

If the transvestite shatters all faith in the signified—the feminine—he also shatters all faith in the infallible signifier. S/he cannot be resolved into either gender. The Germans themselves—the
Nazi "ascetics of politics" (*Hitler*, 28)—are no less irresolute.
When you feel that they reveal their essence, they deceive. But this
deception is their essence—and is, therefore, no deception at all.
This is the "radical *Enttäuschung*"—the recognition that the de-

ception is not a deception, that we are deceived in thinking it so. Lewis wishes to write the issue off as a simple *Enttäuschung* in the object—the feminine—but it should be remembered that the sightseer did not come in search of the feminine in the first place. He came in search of deception—or, rather, of *Enttäuschung* of de-deception—and this is what he finds; the sightseer in the transvestite, Lewis in fascism. In other words, a careful reading of the "Eldorado" episode will reveal as disingenuous Lewis's later narrative of his own political "disappointment."

From the perspective of an aesthetic focused on questions of representation and antirepresentation, the transvestites of the Eldorado bar can—entirely in accord with the binarism suggested by Sedgwick—be dismissed for their "dull naturalism," yet Lewis is strangely drawn to them, as they perform a Germanic essence he had thought to find in Nazism. These transvestites are of importance for Lewis not for the gendered naturalism of their representations (as he claims) but for their reduction of all natural categories of gender to performance. One might argue—contra Sedgwick—that the kitsch object of representation par excellence (the object that represents the very project of representationalism) is for Lewis not the male but rather the female body: it will be the transvestites' representation of femininity that Lewis characterizes as "dull naturalism." I am suggesting, then, that Sedgwick's analysis of the identification of the homoaesthetic with representationalism held only insofar as homosexuality was itself conceived in terms of gender binarisms or inversion.

What will trouble Lewis's essentially dismissive, aesthetic rejection of the politics of transvestism is the recognition that it is the transvestites who provide the most fundamental insight into the emergence of a new national, political order. In these articles we see a final "modernist" attempt to dismiss kitsch, "homosexual" representationalism give way to a recognition that transvestism questions the very notion of origin on which any notion of representation as secondary or derivative must depend. Gender and German national identity will both be performed rather than represented in the reports of Lewis's travels. For from Lewis's perspective, it is a performative aesthetic that also grounds what Benjamin was subsequently to characterize as fascism's aestheticization of politics. As we shall see, the homosexuals representing the process of effeminization from which fascism was to rescue the West insistently infiltrate Lewis's own model of protofascist masculinity. The transvestite teaches Lewis that all gender is performance—and that men generally perform the role of woman better than most women. That this homosexual denaturing of gender should be linked with the politics of totalitarianism might strike us as odd, since fascist ideology so often grounds itself in the invocation of a natural order. However, Lewis seems to exemplify the erasure of the category of nature—a masculinist commonplace, as we will recall from Blüher's rejection of the *Naturgesetz*—as the foreclosure of routes of political escape. The denaturing of gender becomes potentially totalitarian at the point where the ideology of nature no longer provides even the fictive force of an alternative to the status quo. If all gender is performative, from what position (certainly not fascist) is the transvestite to be condemned or the virile man of action celebrated?

Although it is not my aim at this point to speculate on fascist aesthetics, I think that Lewis further allows us to understand certain paradoxes that have consistently troubled theorists of Nazi art and produced reflections on homo-fascism such as those outlined in the first chapter. The stylized naturalism of Nazi art should be read not on the axis representation/antirepresentation, but in terms of a dichotomy of performance and essence. The very stylization of Nazi art marks its ideological distance from an aesthetic of naturalism: such art does not represent naturalistically, it *performs* naturalism as an act of faith. It represents representation—a stigmatic function Sedgwick has rightly identified with the male body in the demonology of modernism. This is the sense in which the Eldorado transvestites will become so inevitably paradigmatic for Lewis's understanding of Nazi aestheticization: the naïveté of a simplistic Nazi naturalism lies not in the inaccuracy of its representations, but in the subjugation of all representation to the redemptive, performative power of belief.[1]

I propose that we understand this move "beyond representation" as a move into "the mimetic." Before examining through
close reading Lewis's reflections on transvestism, I wish to outline
their relevance to questions of a performance and representation,
aesthetics and politics, that have informed subsequent theoretical
reconstructions of fascism as a political ideology in the strictest
sense. Jean-Luc Nancy and Philippe Lacoue-Labarthe have best
characterized what I mean by this formulation in their essay on
"The Nazi Myth," where they argue for their method in the following terms:

> In other words, the question posed by myth is that of *mimetism*, in-
> sofar as only mimetism is able to assure an identity. . . . The problem
> of myth is always indissociable from that of art, not so much because
> myth is a collective creation or work (the expression of the people,
> the constitution of their language and so on) as because myth, like
> the work of art that exploits it, is an instrument of *identification*. It
> is, in fact, *the* mimetic instrument par excellence.   (297–98)

The mimetic, then—a category embracing both art and politics—
serves to construct personal identities through the act of representation, claiming no ontological anteriority for the putative "subject" of representation. The mimetic performs as the mime performs, acting—and reenacting—a representation. The mimetic
does not truly oppose or negate representation, but stresses the
moment of presence inherent in the act of representation itself.
Paradoxically, one might say, this moment of presence is—quite
literally—bodied forth as the representation of representation, the
foregrounding of *différance*: in the case of the transvestites the
"mimetic" will retreat into the pores of the skin, in the chin stubble that for Lewis finally—and thankfully—marks the performance
of the transvestite *as* performance.

If we characterize Nazi ideology and aesthetics as "the performance of a representation," we thereby seek not to collapse the
two systems of representation and performance into one, but
rather to characterize fascism as "mimetic" in the most radical
sense. Methodologically, Lacoue-Labarthe and Nancy reflect not

on the specificity of Nazi mythic self-representation, but rather on the very structure of mythic identity, considering Nazism as the myth of mythic identification itself. However, this purely structural approach to fascism cannot sustain an absolute opposition of representation and performance, for—as I have claimed above—that which Nazism "performs" is the positively mythic power of representation itself. Lacoue-Labarthe and Nancy will therefore go on to claim that "the drama of Germany was also that it suffered an imitation *twice removed*, and saw itself obliged to imitate the imitation of antiquity that France did not cease to export for at least two centuries. Germany, in other words, was not only missing an identity, but also lacked the ownership of its means of identification" (299). Although I do not seek to support this argument on historical grounds, I think we can see how this historical elaboration of the question of mimesis fits the model Benjamin develops in his "Theories of German Fascism."

We will be considering the political and representational consequences of Benjamin's theory in some depth in the final chapter, but we would do well to recall it in outline here. Benjamin sees in fascism the final stage of Germany's attempt to come to terms with the loss of the war. Having passed through disingenuous denials of guilt and recriminations against those who supposedly betrayed them on the home front, the soldier males begin to embrace the very loss itself as the ground of a national identity. The war figures as the apotheosis of a historical martyrdom that can be redeemed only by the movement of history itself. In the soldier males' ontology, German identity will be hypostatized as the identity of those lacking a national identity. The absence at the core of identity will be rendered positive as an identity in abeyance. In representing my German identity, then, what matters is not the specific representation I produce, but the *performance* of the representation as an act of faith. This is what is German: the demeaning act of representation—in which I implicitly acknowledge the fictional status of my identity—is sublated in the act of mimesis. It is against this historical and political background that we

shall read Lewis's all-but-explicit assertion: that Nazism is a mode
of transvestism freed from all belief in gender as/or essence; that
Germany is a country in drag.

In the context of our work here, this question of mimesis posed
itself most acutely in Mackay's reworking of the narcissistic scenario, where the impossibility of homosexual self-representation
was itself represented in the figure of the homosexual, for whom
the very act of representation denies (through death) rather than
affirms self-identity. In Mackay's case, the trope through which
(non-)representation was itself represented became a performative
element of homosexual self-fashioning. The lack of identity—the
doubling—that Narcissus enacts is itself embraced as a condition of
homosexual consciousness. If we point out the similarities of
Mackay's formulation to Benjamin's assessment of German protofascism—which likewise ontologizes loss as a condition of (national) identity—it is not in order to suggest any necessary link,
however. (Such a linkage would be the move implicit in the
Mitscherlichs' invocation of narcissism as the cause of Germany's
post–World War II "inability to mourn".) Instead, I seek only to
suggest that the emergence of a homosexual identity and the emergence of a German national consciousness were both possible only
by virtue of a move beyond a strictly representational episteme, a
move necessitated by the recognition of the lack at the heart of
representation.

Such metaphysical niceties, however, are none of Lewis's bluff
concern. In *Hitler*, he sets out simply to present fascism as the essence of the political, as politics unencumbered by the moralizing
concerns of liberal Western democracies—concerns Lewis has already addressed in *The Art of Being Ruled*. What are opposed in
Hitler are "moralist *culs de sac*" (22–23)—with prohibition cited as
the prime example. Prohibition notwithstanding, however, the direct sexual coding of these *culs (de sac)* cannot be ignored: in his
most lapidary articulation of the relationship of morality to politics in *Hitler*—Lewis will observe that "the Bank is more important than the Backside" (22). It is "sex-moralism" that he is gun-

ning for in *Hitler* with his assessment that "the sex-moralist is not only a bore, but should, I think, always be suspect" (21). The sexual politics that concerns Lewis—or, rather, that does *not* concern him and that he shuns as a diversion—is predominantly a politics of anality. It is a politics that he has already identified—in *The Art of Being Ruled*—with the "homo," the "invert," the "joy-boy," the "*exoletos*," and the "shaman."

"Inversion"—as both phenomenon and structure—is a continuing obsession in Lewis's work, and it is only in terms of the later *Hitler* writings that the political machinations of *The Art of Being Ruled* can be understood. I will, therefore, begin with a consideration of the construction of homosexuality in *Hitler* in order to understand how—at one level—this text seems to complicate the one-sided presentation of homosexuality as effeminacy in the earlier work, but how, in fact, it serves to render explicit certain sexual and political tensions already operative in *The Art of Being Ruled*. Finally, it will be possible to trace the process of Lewis's disappointment with fascism through his reworking of the homosexual in the belated 1939 recantation text, *The Hitler Cult*.

Moving backwards in time, however, to *The Art of Being Ruled*, we can see that Lewis is not guilty of simply conflating the transvestite and the homosexual in his political taxonomies. In fact, the transvestite both radicalizes and negates Lewis's characterization of the "invert." Where the invert of *The Art of Being Ruled* will use signs—"a red tie, or its equivalent in the approved badges of sexual revolt" (237)—the transvestite *is* a sign; or, rather, s/he performs signification as a mode of (non-)identity. Above and beyond the figure of the transvestite, there is—in *Hitler*—a second paradigm of homosexuality that occurs in the context of Lewis's critique of "exoticism." The first indication of this substrain in the text comes as Lewis enumerates the sexual diversions offered by the Berlin nightlife, including the "sad wells of super-masculine loneliness" (13). In contrast to the effeminization both exemplified and deconstructed by the transvestite, these locales offer an exaggeration and perversion of an image of masculinity. If the trans-

vestite paradigm is itself already ambiguous enough, the thematization of homosexuality is now further complicated by this second
model of super-masculinity.

Clearly, the superimposition of a masculine-feminine dichotomy onto the question of homosexuality merely serves to reassert a gender order that homosexuality itself threatens to disrupt
within Lewis's argument. Nevertheless, it is important to note the
context in which homosexual super-masculinity is elaborated. Seeking an ideological pedigree for the "super-masculine," Lewis presents it as emerging from a tradition that also spawns the Nazi
Blutsgefühl:

> National socialism builds upon this blood-feeling! What Walt Whit-
> man termed "the talk of the turning eyeballs"—it is that that you are
> required to understand. But whereas Walt Whitman (with his cosmic
> enthusiasms, his bursting and blatant romanticism, his lyrical cult of a
> universal brotherhood) sought to enlist this sort of fleshly second-
> sight in the service of *diffusion*, the present-day *Blutsgefühl* doctri-
> naires invoke it on behalf of a greater *concentration*.   (*Hitler*, 106)

Lewis goes on to stress the differences between the two models—
represented by Whitman and by Nazism, respectively. The distinction between fascism and the super-masculine lies in that very
asceticism of fascism, in its *concentration*, as opposed to the *dif-
fusion* of the invert. However, the similarities (for Lewis) must not
be overlooked: the homosexual poet is being used both as an opponent and as a precursor of a certain Nazi racialism.

Whitman—though never explicitly acknowledged by Lewis as
a homosexual figure—is located within a tradition of "exoticism"
apparently stretching back even further to Blake. It is in describing
Blake that Lewis betrays the terms within which this second homosexual paradigm—the paradigm of super-masculinity—might
be thematized. He imagines "the naked figures of Mr. and Mrs.
Blake squatting in their suburban conservatory among the flower-
pots playing at being Adam and Eve before the Fall, taken straight
out of the puritan Bible," claiming that they "match very well the
rhetorical nudity of 'Walt', genitals well to the fore in true patriarchal fashion, in the Atlantic surf upon the distant shores of the

New World—the New Anglo-Saxony at that time" (*Hitler*, 107). Whitman and the Blakes mark the attempt to represent that edenic state prior to representation itself—and it is the phallus of Whitman ("well to the fore") that grounds this mode of representation. If we have spoken so far of a certain anality in the model of effeminization, it is clear that Whitman's super-masculinity is to be understood both genitally and patriarchally.

Lewis mocks Whitman as an example of Western exoticism—and therefore as a symptom of the decline he seeks to chart—but he nevertheless lets him stand as the emblem of a racial "New Anglo-Saxony." To leap ahead once more—preempting both my own argument and Lewis's political development—the implications of Whitman for Lewis's experience of fascism will subsequently be made explicit in the 1939 book on *The Hitler Cult*. Here—mocking Hitler's own "exoticism"—Lewis will note how "Adolf Hitler bathes in the music of Wagner much in the same way as Walt Whitman bathed in the surf of the Atlantic Ocean" (61). It is the similarity of Whitman's and Hitler's *Blutsgefühl*—rather than any differentiation—that proves more persistent in Lewis's political vision. If we note in passing that by 1939 Lewis is also referring to Hitler as a "dreamy-eyed hairdresser" (103), taking note of his "beautiful eyes" (vii) and the temperament of "a hysterical prima donna" (78), it will not be hard to imagine the type of ideological reconciliation that is going to take place in Lewis's characterizations of homosexuality and fascism: fascism itself will eventually be rejected as in some sense "homosexualized." What we should note, however, is that this assertion—legitimating Lewis's repudiation of National Socialism in 1939—is already quite clearly present in the text of *Hitler* that is so much more favorable to fascism.

In broadening his model of homosexuality to include the super-masculine, Lewis polarizes not only between the masculine and the feminine, but further between the rhetorical and the representational as aesthetic modalities. The transvestite was to be understood with reference to a certain system of representation that he merely seemed to transgress (as a man representing a woman) but that he in fact exemplified. This representation was figured as a form of clothing—a cross-dressing. What Whitman offers, meanwhile, in the ostentatious self-evidence of his genitals is a "rhetorical nudity." From the realm of clothing, the realm of the sign, we seem to have arrived at the possibility of a truth stripped of its dependence on signification. In terms of the naïveté Lewis is criticizing, one would be tempted to interpret this denuding as a false, ideological escape from rhetoric, as a stripping away of language in the immanence of ostentation—the presentation of the Whitmanesque phallus. But this nudity is itself merely "rhetorical." Lewis is rejecting the naïveté of any prelinguistic political utopia. What Whitman in fact offers—along with his doubtless most impressive penis—is naked rhetoric, pure presentation. Not, that is, the immanence *of* the true—but rather the immanence of the medium itself, of rhetoric. In other words, what we have is an asceticism—comparable to the political asceticism of the Nazi, though not necessarily to be conflated, politically, with it. This homosexualized asceticism is, however, at the same time an *aesthetic*, a "rhetorical nudity"—naked rhetoric, but a nakedness that is itself merely rhetorical, rather than real. It cannot be decided whether this ascetic aesthetic is "pure" precisely because it can only ever be the presentation of "impure" aesthetic representation in its "pure" ascetic form.

It is obvious, then, that Lewis seeks to ground his political thought within a tropology of homosexuality. The question is: How to theorize this fact? It is tempting—in the light of the obvious misogyny in *The Art of Being Ruled*, where Lewis insistently characterizes the "homo" as the "child of the suffragette" (244)—to subsume the treatment of homosexuality within the broader framework of a feminist critique of gender binarism. Any such temptation should be resisted for two reasons. First, the presentation of homosexuality—or "inversion" to use Lewis's ideologically loaded term—is by no means restricted to the terms of effeminization. By privileging and foregrounding this model—in the very use, for example, of the term "inversion" to suggest an axiomatic binarism of masculine and feminine—Lewis seeks to manipulate a scandal in order to confirm rather than question the gendered terms of his political critique. In fact, it is the figure of the noneffeminized homosexual that will cause Lewis much greater political embarrassment. Second, if the question of "sex-moralism" insists on raising its head in *Hitler*, it does so through the figure of a transvestite, who is not a necessarily homosexual figure, and who is troubling precisely because s/he resists the consignment of gender to the realm of biology. If politics exists in the public realm as the manipulation of signs of power—so too does transvestism. Moreover, the gender ambivalence of the transvestite provides a momentary and inevitable check to Lewis's critique of effeminization. As we shall see, s/he threatens not simply the straightforward social organization of gender, but also the critical gaze of the Anglo-Saxon political sightseer.

To summarize, then: *Hitler* seems to leave us with two crucial images. On the one hand, the transvestite, who is at once the apogee and the apocalypse both of effeminization and of a representational model of truth. On the other hand, the super-masculine, the homosocial exoticists of patriarchy. At a certain point in both of these paradigmatic presentations of inversion, the invert critiques precisely those ideological commonplaces of effeminization and universal brotherhood with which Lewis seeks to identify him. More than this, there are moments—most notably Whitman's "turning of the eye"—when the invert comes perilously close to embodying precisely those political options Lewis himself is seeking to put forward. The obsessive repression of sexuality—and the compulsive return of this repressed in the text of *Hitler*—would suggest that Lewis's "tolerance" of homosexuality (effected by virtue of its exclusion from the political sphere) is homophobic in the most radical sense of the word.[2] Not only is the depoliticization of sexuality always and necessarily a political disenfranchisement, but homosexuality itself fundamentally questions the analytic categories around which Lewis orients his political worldview. The question of homosexuality must necessarily occur obsessively in the texts precisely because it scrambles the political codes Lewis has earlier attempted to establish in *The Art of Being Ruled*.

Even in *The Art of Being Ruled*, however, the gendered binarisms around which Lewis seeks to thematize inversion are threatened by an instance of transvestism. In this case, however, Lewis
consciously manipulates a narrative of transvestism toward a critique of democracy. He traces the shortcomings of democracy back
to an exemplary act of cross-dressing: "It often occurs (and we
have to-day a unique picture of this in contemporary western society) that the ruler becomes a confirmed practitioner of one of
Haroun al Raschid's most objectionable habits, namely that of
spending his time disguised among his subjects as one of them.
This tendency in a ruler is very much indeed to be deplored" (96).
It is only when this notion of democracy as a fraternizing disguise
is placed alongside Lewis's gendered model of power—in which
"the contrast between the one class and the other is more like that
between the sexes than anything else. The ruled are the females
and the rulers the males" (*Being Ruled*, 95–96)—that Haroun al
Raschid's disguise reveals itself as drag. Disguised among his subjects, Haroun al Raschid must dress as a woman—for the subject is
always a woman, the ruler always a man. Thus, the transvestite is
the emblem of modern Western democratism—a ruler disguised
as the ruled, a man disguised as a woman.

The reappearance of the transvestite in Hitler, then, also functions as the disguised reappearance of the democratic. In refusing
simply to condemn the transvestite, the Nazi refuses a simple inversion or condemnation of liberal democracy. Thus, this "diversion" through the Eldorado is not a diversion at all; rather, it is
crucial to Lewis's understanding of fascism as something more radical than simple inversion. In *The Art of Being Ruled* Lewis has already confessed that "all the phrases of the sex-revolt—from the
suffragette to the joy-boy are equally *political* at the start—as they
certainly become at the finish. . . . Is it not the same old hag that
in a 'morality' would be labelled Power, and for whom pleasure in
the simplest sense, means very little, who has pupped this batch of
related passions?" (241). In other words, the "diversion" offered
by the Backside might not be altogether incommensurable with
an insistence on the "essence" of politics. In its essence, the polit-

ical distills itself into a form of sexual politics. The politics of feminism, and the politics of homosexuality, are both born of Power, and Power—the category central to Lewis's analysis of the political in *Hitler*—is presented as a character in a "morality." Morality—or *the* "morality"—provides both stage and scenario for the newly performative political.

It is not, then, a question of simply noting the veiled political importance of the invert, but rather of identifying the invert as that instance in which the moral inevitably becomes a political issue. The invert is paradigmatic rather than syntagmatic—and it is for this reason that Lewis must consistently refashion the radical revolutionary possibility of homosexuality into mere "inversion," into a purely determinate revolt against the intellect in which "each little sensation has to be decked out as though it were a 'big idea.' Again, simple sensation has become ashamed of itself. It is persuaded to complicate itself to *invert* itself with a movement of mechanical paradox. So, in reality, sensation pure and simple is disappearing, and a sort of spurious *idea* is everywhere taking its place" (*Being Ruled*, 244). The strategy of this analysis will have become familiar to us. The revolt of sensuality against the intellect—by presenting itself as "a big idea"—has already undone itself and capitulated before the conceptualism it ostensibly opposes. Inversion is not simply the reversal of a certain value system, it inverts each term into its other. But even in this "mechanical"—that is, "spurious, utilitarian" (14)—form of revolution, neither of the original binary terms remains intact. In this presentation, the sensation is clothed—"decked out"—as a big idea, as if transvestism were once again being taken as the model of inversion. However, the paradoxical reduction of the flesh to a "big idea" more accurately characterizes the ideology of that Whitmanesque, super-masculine homosexual, who—"genitals to the fore in true patriarchal fashion"—makes a "big idea" out of a small bodily organ. What Lewis seems to be suggesting is that phallocentric patriarchalism—as a "big idea"—is itself essentially effeminate. Subtly, the dichotomous model of *Hitler*—the division into effeminized and "super-masculine" models of inversion—is being undone. The

super-masculine is itself being grounded in a notion of travesty—
"decked out" as a big idea. What this entails is a reduction of the
questions of revolution and homosexuality—the questions of a
homosexual politics—to questions of representation and transvestism.

The very terminology—the language of "inversion"—already
suggests the position ascribed to homosexuality in Lewis's examination of revolution. Nothing could be more simple, more mechanical—more "spurious"—than this simple inversion of terms.
Yet, as we have seen in the case of the transvestite, the transcod-
ing of gender can never be reduced to a simple inversion of terms.
Although Lewis argues in *The Art of Being Ruled* that sexual inversion merely revolves around the organizational axes of the given
world, his analysis of this particular "vicious circle" nevertheless
produces—in the circle—a figure for the permanence of revolution celebrated elsewhere in the text.

Having located the phenomenon historically, it remains for
Lewis to pinpoint the sociological locus of inversion. There are
three fundamental factors in Lewis's account. First, as we have
seen, he is quite unambiguous in arguing that

> the sex-revolution of the invert is a *bourgeois* revolution, in other
> words. The *petit bourgeois* type predominates: a red tie, or its equiva-
> lent in the approved badges of sexual revolt, tells its theatrical tale.
> The puritan conscience, in Anglo-Saxon countries, provides the basis
> of the condiment and gives sex-inversion there its particular material
> physiognomy of *protest* and over-importance.   (*Being Ruled*, 237)

The invert must remain petit bourgeois in his dependence on the
value system he affronts. However, at the same time as he expresses
his distaste for the petit bourgeois invert Lewis goes on in this passage to state a preference for the "true-blue invert" for "certainly
he gives the impression of being much more male in the traditional
and doctrinaire sense than any other male" (238). The "super-
masculine" reasserts itself here—subsumed under the general category of inversion—but asserts itself as "true-blue." In other
words, Lewis is envisaging a genuine—perhaps "blue-blooded,"
or "aristocratic"?—revolutionary impulse emanating from the phe-

nomenon of inversion. The division derived from *Hitler*—the dual model of inversion as a caricature of the feminine (transvestism) and as a caricature of the masculine (the super-masculine)—explicates itself in socioeconomic terms, by suggesting a division into petit bourgeois and aristocratic models of revolt. This critique of bourgeois inversion is a sustained one. Elsewhere, the world of the petite bourgeoisie is referred to as "an unreal, small *middle-world* or no-man's land" (*Being Ruled*, 108)—and it is, perhaps, this formulation that best encapsulates the sociopolitical and historical significance of the invert for Lewis. The petite bourgeoisie is itself characterized as a "no-man's" land, and it is precisely the "no-man"—the invert—who has come to occupy it.

The second and third vectors for tracing the emergence of "inversion" as a pressing political question are both related to the war. Lewis argues that "it is in the experiences of wartime that we must seek not only the impulsion, but in some sense the justification of sex inversion, apart from its role in relation to the disintegration of the family unit" (*Being Ruled*, 279). Thus, inversion—as well as being a petit bourgeois phenomenon—results from the disintegration of the family unit. This observation, however, merely describes its impulsion: it will be in a third strain of analysis that Lewis will characterize its justification. Rather than seeing homosexuality as a reaction to the brutal masculinity of war, or as the frightened reaction of men seeking to avoid their role in that war, Lewis sees inversion as war by other means. Since the war to end all wars nevertheless left the violent structures of European expansionism intact, Lewis argues—in a chapter on "Different Solutions to the Problem of the Yahoo" (47–51)—that some other form of depopulation of the brutal white European must be found. Militarism was to have been its own cure—the militarists were to have killed each other off, but given the failure of World War I in this respect, Lewis offers homosexuality as an alternative: "Nature—let us give her credit for it—has come to the help of her children . . . by way of the glands, namely. I believe that (in one form or another) castration may be the solution. And the feminization of the white European and American is already far advanced, coming in the wake of war" (51). In other words, inversion is not so much a reaction to war as a continuation of it, aimed at the depopulation of Europe and North America.

Thus far, then, Lewis has isolated three factors in his genealogy of modern homosexuality: the disintegration of the family, the war experience, and the social emergence of the petite bourgeoisie. This particular configuration of determinant factors should itself raise a few eyebrows. For is it not precisely the same configuration that has long been held responsible for the emergence of fascism at a crucial moment of modernity?[3] Moreover, Lewis's own ambiguity with respect to each of these instances suggests that the invert might—by the very logic of self-inversion—surreptitiously represent the brand of fascism that so interests Lewis himself. Lewis, too, despises the family: and while despising brutality he nevertheless celebrates war as a decimation of the "brutal white European." Only with respect to the petit bourgeois origins of the inverts' revolution is he resolutely oppositional—and even here he holds out a possibility of reconciliation in his guarded celebration of the "true-blue invert."

The possibility arises, then—no more comforting to queer theory than it would be to Lewis—that the traditional political dichotomy of democracy and fascism, far from being supported by a certain caricature of homosexuality, is deconstructed by it. The collapse of the family, the war experience, and the emergence of the petite bourgeoisie—the historical preconditions of fascism and, for Lewis, of inversion—already indicate the possibility of this conjuncture. The key figure, it would seem, in the establishment of a continuum from inversion to fascism will be the "true-blue" invert, rather than the petit bourgeois effeminate or transvestite. This true-blue invert, however—"more male in the traditional and doctrinaire sense than any other male"—cannot automatically be identified with our second, Whitmanesque model of the super-masculine. Whitman's exoticism is intrinsically effeminate for Lewis, and—by making a "big idea" (a phallus) out of the penis—patriarchy itself is by no means exempted from the charge of effeminization. Presenting his genitals to the camera, Whitman seems not simply to be showing them off, but to be offering them for the castration that Lewis thinks might be the solution to European militarism.

Is there, then, a third figure in whom the militarism of the fascist and the revolutionary potential of the invert might transcend the limitations of petit bourgeois effeminacy? To find such a figure would be the challenge Lewis sets to any analysis seeking to elaborate a political conjunction of homosexuality and fascism in his work. In fact, such a figure does exist in Lewis's oeuvre, and he will become all the more important as Lewis revises his analysis of fascism in the 1930's. It is "Frederick the Great, living with his *heiduques* and grooms" who will finally complete the implicit homosexualization of Lewis's own political project. With Frederick, "living on familiar patriarchal terms with [one's] servants" (*Being Ruled*, 201) seems to have become an intramasculine affair, rather than the necessarily transvestite practice exemplified by Haroun al Raschid.

The ambiguity of Frederick—as a revolutionary and reactionary homosexual figure—lies in his "travesty of revolution" (*Being Ruled*, 201)—for now the Germanic travesty *of* revolution seems finally to have become travesty *as* revolution. It is as if Frederick were, so to speak, engaging in travesty not by dressing as a woman, but by refusing to do so. The fixation of transvestism to the feminine object has been completely overcome: the transvestite has dressed himself as a man, and thereby engages in the deception intrinsic to him. Revolution is no longer established within a simple paradigm of transgression—the signifier's masquerading as the signified—but rather in the transgression of that transgression. Revolution, in this instance, really is the "vicious circle" of undecidability—is it a man, a woman as man, a man as woman as man . . . ? Moreover, Frederick marks the point of convergence of the two models of inversion elucidated in *Hitler*, combining—in his particular form of authoritarian revolution—travesty and masculinity.

What is it then that Frederick—with his grooms and *heiduques*—tells us about those political configurations developed by Lewis through the 1920's that were subsequently to make fascism so appealing to him? More than anything, Frederick renders impossible any reduction of the homosexual question to a more simplistic opposition coded in terms of gender. To reduce the homosexual to a figure of effeminization is to accept at face value a dichotomy of gender the homosexual serves to question. The transgression effected by super-masculinity is more troubling to Lewis's politics not simply because the invert—who in *Hitler* questions the primacy of the feminine—now also questions the integrity of masculinity, but because he begins to appear as the double of Lewis's own political project. Sociologically, the collapse of the patriarchal family, the war experience, and the emergence of the petite bourgeoisie are as crucial to Lewis's analysis of inversion as they have been to analysts of fascism. The only constituent of this ideological trinity that Lewis himself—as a political thinker—would look on with distaste, is the centrality of the bourgeoisie. By recognizing in the fraternal and fraternizing tendencies of Frederick the Great a "true-blue" aristocratic model of inversion, he is—in effect—opening up fascism as a realm of homosexualized politics to which he would be sympathetic.

It would stretch the limits of this book to describe what that politics would look like. The aristocratic (homosexual) fascism suggested by Lewis should not be mistaken for fascism's empirical historical instantiation. We can only begin to outline the terms of the political sphere occupied by the true-blue invert, for Lewis's disappointment with Nazism forces us to respect a distinction between his intellectual and political project and the empirical, historical phenomenon of the Third Reich. At the same time, however, we have already observed the way in which the supposed *Enttäuschung* of 1939 was itself prefigured in the earlier works and cannot, in fact, be understood as a disappointment in the everyday sense of the word. *Enttäuschung*—in 1939—is the realization (rather than the disappointment) of the political project Lewis articulated through the 1920's and 1930's.

Taking up where *Hitler* and *The Art of Being Ruled* left off—with Frederick as a historical and homosexual precedent for Nazism—*The Hitler Cult* subtly reevaluates some of the topoi of the earlier works, making explicit connections we have reconstructed from those works (Whitman, for example). Frederick's role, too, is elucidated: "Frederick the Great was a National Socialist, as well as degenerate and what we should call to-day a crook" (131). Notable in this passage is the way in which a discourse of degeneracy is applied to homosexuality for the first time only when Lewis seeks to reverse the terms of his earlier critique and to present fascism—rather than liberalism—as effeminization. Previously, degeneration was itself implicitly valorized as the postbellum possibility of depopulating an incorrigibly aggressive Europe. Clearly, in order to distance himself from compromising political miscalculations, Lewis is obliged to reintroduce—paradoxically, in an inverted form—precisely that moralism that was previously to be excised. Apart from the superimposition of this arbitrary and extrinsic value system, however, little has changed in Lewis's structural presentation of the forces of fascism and inversion. As we have seen, fascism and inversion were never as antipathetic in Lewis's thought as he would have had us believe. As late as 1939—faced with the political and historical exigency of escaping the suspicion of fascist sympathies—Lewis seems more concerned with maintaining his modernist distance from the politics and aesthetics of homosexuality.

Having set up Frederick as a degenerate and a National Socialist, Lewis subsequently goes on in *The Hitler Cult* to distinguish him from Hitler in the following terms: "As to Frederick the Great, another of his models, to whom Hitler is sometimes compared, no two men could be less alike. That arrogant homosexual tyrant had about as much in common with Adolf Hitler as the Duke of Wellington would with Lord Nuffield" (78–79). Historically, and retrospectively, Lewis at last admits the embroilment of a certain homosexual strain in his presentation of Nazism, but argues that "the Röhm 'purge' may almost be regarded as a showdown between the homosexual and the non-homosexual end of the National Socialist movement" (95). Lewis settles his accounts with fascism and homosexuality long after Nazism itself has already confronted the question.

By the time of *The Hitler Cult*, the problem with Hitler—providing the ostensible grounds for Lewis's rejection of the regime—is, quite precisely, not homosexuality, for "the present German Chancellor is in the habit of threatening suicide: he weeps with considerable facility, his perorations are shaken with sobs; he storms and rages like a hysterical *prima donna*; he is very alive to flattery. Yet he is *not* homosexual, like many Germans. It is that that makes him a puzzle of a man" (78). In other words, while using homosexuality as a moral smoke screen for his political distancing from fascism, Lewis in fact rejects Hitler not because he is homosexual—but because he is not. The problem with Hitler, however, is something other than his simple heterosexuality (in fact, Lewis comments on his abstention from women and claims to find this the most unsettling characteristic of all). Does Hitler himself not replicate that *Enttäuschung* central to the political epiphany of the *Hitler* book? He acts like a homosexual—Lewis implies—but he is not one. In the same way, the transvestite acts like a woman, but is not one.

To restrict ourselves to this parallelism, however, is to fall prey to Lewis's revisionist reconstruction of his own political development. The sightseer of 1930 never came in search of women: he wanted the transvestite and—after a momentary and necessary disappointment—got exactly what he wanted. Likewise, Lewis sought fascism and got what he wanted. The political disappointment is, in fact, a realization—*Enttäuschung* is a liberation from one political *Täuschung* by means of another. In other words, in the *Hitler* book Lewis seeks to hold at bay the homosexual taxonomy implicitly underpinning his politics, whereas the 1939 repudiation seeks consciously to invoke that taxonomy to legitimate a retreat from fascism. The mea culpa implicit in this gesture seeks to exonerate the political project by invoking a moral (and homosexual) scapegoat. If Hitler is not homosexual, Lewis is implying, the pretense at being homosexual is itself "homosexual," typical of the homosexual's aestheticized play with appearance. This, if anything, is the lesson to be learned from the encounter in the Eldorado bar—the irreducibility of representation to either term in the dyad of representation. This is, indeed, the lesson Lewis *has* learned, and that allows him—in this entirely disingenuous self-distancing from fascism—to attribute both to inversion and to fascism that aestheticization of politics that so led him astray. Having enjoyed the spectacle of the Eldorado for what it was, Lewis would now have us believe that he was, in fact, seduced into fascism by one of those "bland Junos-gone-wrong."

If Lewis dramatizes a certain embarrassment—both political and sexual—at the heart of the modernist project, it is with a certain dismissive embarrassment that contemporary theory has itself touched on this conjuncture in the ideology of modernism. Thus Fredric Jameson—in his treatment of Lewis, a writer he otherwise admires—finally confronts *Hitler* as a "slapdash series of newspaper articles" (179) and divides narrative and ideology in a manner quite alien to his usual method of critical reading. Of the Eldorado scene Jameson writes:

> The political point made here is that Nazi street violence is essentially a reaction to Communist violence and provocation; yet the inevitable narrative point is rather different: "But elegant and usually eyeglassed young women will receive [the tourist], with an expensive politeness, and he will buy one of these a drink, and thus become at home. . . . Then these bland Junos-gone-wrong, bare-shouldered and braceleted (as statuesque as feminine show-girl guardees) after a drink or two, will whisper to the outlandish sightseer that they are *men*" (24). With this characteristic and obsessive motif out of the way, we come to the political analysis proper. (180)

Setting up a curious division between the two structures he is otherwise concerned to link—namely, "the political point" and "the inevitable narrative point"—Jameson presents homosexuality as something to be moved out of the way in order to clear the ground for "the political analysis proper." The "inevitable narrative point"—the encounter in the Eldorado bar—is evaded rather nicely, and the question of sexual undecidability introduced by the transvestite is rendered decidedly apolitical. I hope to have demonstrated here how the narrative of these "bland Junos-gone-wrong" is—on the contrary—itself an inevitably and crucially political moment in modernism's confrontation with the political reality of fascism. The "political point" and the "inevitable narrative point" that Jameson seeks to differentiate prove to have been one and the same all along.

The traditionally apolitical structure of the modernist text—apparent in Lewis even where he quite explicitly critiques the modernist tradition—maintains itself only through a sexualization. Rather—since Lewis is ultimately a thoroughly "political" writer—it is through homosexuality that the question of politics begins to infiltrate a narcissistically self-absorbed literary modernity. In the next chapter, I hope to show how the critical reticence of those such as Jameson has been challenged by contemporary queer theory and to indicate—beyond the limits of queer theory as currently practiced—the possibility of theorizing a homosexual avant-garde that moves beyond the ultimately representational episteme framing even the most resolutely antirepresentational analyses of modernism. What might a confrontation with the continental avant-garde portend for a queer theory that has elaborated many of its most exciting and important categories in the critical engagement with Anglo-American modernism?

CHAPTER 6

Adelphic Narcissism: Difference and Identity in the Homosexual Avant-Garde

> PYAST. It's not a fish, the Holy Ghost, so it swims in holy water. The Holy Ghost's a goldfish. Grace is an advance. From the back forward.
> HERREB. Grace is a pederast?
> NOSOCOME. In the front to backside sense.
>
> Alfred Jarry, *Days and Nights*

As I argued in my book *Fascist Modernism*, any discussion of cultural modernism must needs pass through a consideration of fascism and confront—even if only to reject, ultimately—Benjamin's characterization of fascism as an aestheticization of politics. If, as Benjamin suggests, the political sensibility that spawns fascism emerges as a mutation of the aestheticism of *l'art pour l'art*, and if—as Peter Bürger suggests in his *Theory of the Avant-Garde*—the avant-garde results from a parallel mutation, any cultural treatment of fascism must, at the very least, touch on the question of the avant-garde. In this chapter I will examine an important work by Alfred Jarry—the novel *Days and Nights*—both in the context of contemporary debates in queer literary theory and as a work that will help us further understand the putative homo-fascist nexus. By now, however, we have moved in the examination of this nexus beyond the realm of intellectual history, in which some causal relation might be posited, into purely theoretical considerations. As the confluence of Bürger and Benjamin indicates, late-nineteenth-century aestheticism currently enjoys a privileged position in theoretical discussions of both fascism and the avant-garde.[1] I intend to read Jarry as a paradigmatic expression of that moment in which the avant-garde stakes out a response to aestheticism—but to read him also as a homosexual author. How does the homosexual author allow us to theorize the conjunction—or is it opposition?—of fascism and the avant-garde?

If one might tentatively link Jarry, by means of his masculinism, to some of the other writers and thinkers treated here, it is nevertheless as an exemplar of the movement from aestheticism to avant-garde that he functions in this chapter.[2] If I have tried to take seriously, thus far, the theoretical and historical logic that posits homo-fascism, I might be forgiven for using this chapter to point out the variant directions taken by a specifically homosexual mutation of aestheticism. Thus far, we have taken a two-pronged approach to the question of homo-fascism. First, I have attempted to show how the tradition of homosexual masculinism most commonly used to justify the conflation of homosexuality and fascism in fact spanned a broader political spectrum, and to show that the more virulent forms of this intellectual tradition emerge only when it is used *against* emerging models of homosexuality (as in Weininger); second, I have attempted to demonstrate the way in which subsequent theoretical treatments of homo-fascism depended on analyses of narcissism and effeminization that ultimately undercut the legitimational basis of the theories themselves. In foregrounding Jarry at this point, I seek to reframe some of the issues raised thus far in terms of modernity and modernization as a historical and political process within the more limited terms of modernism as an aesthetically delimited concept. As I have shown elsewhere, there is a necessary though mediated relation between the two, but what I seek here is to show how my consideration of homo-fascism necessarily obliges us to rethink not only the theoretical construction of fascism, but also the relationship into which emerging homosexual identities enter with the cultural practices of modernism. In short, I wish to consider in this chapter a homosexual avant-garde as sibling and rival of a putative homofascism.

At this point we might venture the hypothesis: the conflation of homosexuality with fascism results from a perceived parallel in what we might call their "libidinal function." Lacoue-Labarthe has shown the way in which fascism responded to a legitimation crisis in democratic thought; the recognition of a lack at the very heart of the democratic polis. Likewise, the analyses of homosexuality that we have traced from Freud through the Frankfurt School have also insisted on a fundamental lack at the heart of homosexual desire, presenting it not as a simple confusion in object choice but as a (narcissistic) absence of cathexis that is repositivized as a destructive cathexis of absence. Fascism and homosexuality both point to the chasm on which political and desiring economies are built. But here the parallel ends. For fascism marks a response to that recognition, an attempt to conjure up a phantasmatic subject/object of desire. A textbook Lacanian *objet a*, fascist ideology conjures up its mythic objects of desire as fetishistic replacements for the absent political subject.[3] The messianic attendance of the *Volk*—or the geopolitical justification of *Lebensraum*—projects the condition of subjectivity into a thousand-year future. The object of national desire is the subject I am yet to become; the lack of the subject is projected as the plenitude of the object, and the original lack of desire thereby camouflaged. Even in the more homophobic caricatures, however, the same cannot be said of so-called homosexual desire as it has been invoked in the theories we have discussed. As we have seen, "homosexual" narcissism—constructed as a political category by Adorno—serves merely to demonstrate with unavoidable clarity the objectless state of *all* desire. In Freud it was the heterosexual who desired in the woman his own lost narcissism; for Adorno it was the homosexual who projected such desires onto the *Führer*. The homosexual is demonized not because he lacks an object, but because he obliges us to confront that lack—and he is feminized not because of the object of his desire, but because of our inability to accept his "subject-less" (feminine) state of desire. In other words, it is not homosexuality itself that responds—as fascism responds—to the lack at the heart of desire: it is the theoretical *figure* of the homosexual that performs the function of self-defense. The homosexual functions, in fact, as the fetishistic subject/object of a heterosexual political theory, because he serves as the projection of a feared loss of subjectivity. If fascism sought—through its ceremonial—to reenact and re-present the subject, it is heterosexist political theory that now performs the same function for our supposedly postfascist society.

This hypothesis does not necessarily help me in the transition from an analysis of fascism to the consideration of Jarry and the avant-garde in this chapter, however. Or does it? In the fascist ceremonial we can observe an ambiguity in the subject that we cannot find in revisionist theoretical constructions of the homo-fascist. If the fascist projects the condition of subjectivity into a mythic future as the representation of a racially purified *Volk*, he nevertheless performs subjectivity in the very act of that representation. The political collective is both the object of a mythic representation and the subject of that act of representation. The *Volk* is not merely that which will come, but the collective of those who await its coming. In other words, the desiring structure of fascism is specific not in its projection of the condition of subjectivity (all political structures engage in those metanarratives we have supposedly lost faith in, narratives of a transcendent subjectivity—the subject of knowledge, the subject of freedom, etc.) but in its performative reversal of the condition of lack, in its organization of those who lack Being into the collective subject on the *Zeppelinfeld*. What is specific to fascism is not, then, its mythification of political subjectivity or its inability to constitute a political subject, but quite the reverse—its *enactment* of subjectivity, its withdrawal of political subjectivity from the semiosis of a representation into the immanence of a performance. The semantic scandal of fascism lies in its performative contradiction—the creation of a subjectivity from a collective avowal of its lack. The political subject is the collective of those who—projecting their lack through a redemptive faith in the *Volk*—acknowledge the lack that conjoins them.

This reconstruction of subjectivity within a paradigm of performative rather than denotative speech acts (or, rather, the acknowledgment of the performative and contradictory speech act through which the subject is denoted in its lack) potentially provides a model, I think, for understanding the possibility of an avant-garde homosexual literary practice in the early years of this century and, indeed, in the fin de siècle. (This is not to say, of course, that the performance of subjectivity is in any sense *necessarily* fascistic.) As we observed with regard to Mackay, when confronted with a text that moves toward a subject position rather than from the position of an already constituted subjectivity, we cannot subsume even the most naturalistic of writing styles under the terms of a denotation. We cannot say that Mackay writes about homosexuals—or paederasts—because the historical object of that representation is itself constructed, in part, through his text. To paraphrase this observation in tendentially political terms: the literary text serves as *Lebensraum*—not, that is, as the space of a representation, but as the space of the performance of a Being. In the case of early "homosexual" writing, the text lacks its referent as desire lacks its subject/object.[4] Even where Mackay engaged in an apparently straightforward narrative of a series of loves, we observed how the diegetic function is, in fact, overshadowed by the extradiegetic. It is only in telling his story—to himself—that Fenny Skaller became the subject he is supposedly writing about. He recognizes recurrent structures in his behavior, and it is this recognition that provides the continuity of a subject. Denotation is subjugated to the performative function.

In this chapter, then, I add to Benjamin's mixture of aesthetics and politics a third vector—homosexuality—by arguing that Benjamin's formulation takes for granted the essentially and historically homosexual nature of aestheticization. When he argues that the introduction of aesthetics into political life represents "the consummation of *l'art pour l'art*," Benjamin goes at least some degree toward elucidating just what form fascist aestheticization might take. If he seeks a precedent in the aestheticism of the late nineteenth century, I seek here to flesh out this precedent, for— as Russell Berman has pointed out—"Benjamin avoids the specificity of Italy in the thirties, he avoids any discussion of National Socialism." Berman again points us in the right direction when he notes that "the characterization of art as incompatible with justice derives from Benjamin's early thought, before his political radicalization, where the symbolic work of art as an organic imitation of fallen nature is implicated in a disregard of divine justice. Only a melancholy insistence on the lack of redemption might anticipate a messianic intervention, the religious category which always lurks behind the later Benjamin's notion of revolution" (37–38). If it is from a religious terminology that the notion of a fallen nature is derived, it is in the aesthetic realm that this fall is reframed as a fall *away from* nature, implicitly as a sin *against* nature.

I shall return in the final chapter to Benjamin's notion of historical redemption, but I wish here merely to note the clearly homosexual coding of Benjamin's understanding of aestheticism. He examines it in greatest detail, for example, in an essay on Gide, of all people, whose work he links to a tradition of decadence, a tradition whose members read as a roll call of what might be called "the homosexual strain" in German literature. If I invoke Bürger in this context, it is because he allows us to theorize what remains thus far a purely thematic consideration on Benjamin's part. Bürger's argument in *Theory of the Avant-Garde*—that aestheticism takes the structural separation of art and life and makes it the content of art—moves us necessarily into a deliberation on the importance of mimesis in both the avant-garde and the homosexual literary tradition. That which distinguishes a (homosexual) aestheticism from a (heterosexual) avant-garde would seem to be the thematization or representation in the former of art's separation of life: the absence of content itself becomes the monotonous content or theme for the *poètes maudits.* Just as—might we hypothesize?—the absence of the (national) subject itself becomes the condition of subjectivity for the fascists? Or just as, perhaps, the homosexually absent cathexis becomes a cathexis of absence?

In Benjamin's essay "The Work of Art in the Age of Mechanical Reproduction," however, the question of decadence and modernism escapes the binary terms in which it is often phrased. It is not representation and antirepresentationalism that Benjamin invokes, but an aesthetic of *Ausdruck* that fascism opposes to the "rights" of the workers; "Fascism sees its salvation in giving these masses not their right, but instead a chance to express themselves" (241). What are we to make of this pathetic, expressive tradition? Does *Ausdruck* partake of the logic of representation by externalizing inner emotions, or is it *anti*representational in its tendential effacement of the object? For Benjamin, the question is moot. For even if *Ausdruck* is to be aligned with mimesis, it is mimesis only as *mis*representation. Representation is necessarily a reactionary misrepresentation since it is persists only in opposition to political enfranchisement.

On this point, however—as on so many—Benjamin's essay is ambiguous. Expressive mimesis—*Ausdruck*—is reactionary as an aestheticized politics, yet at the same time the entire essay is predicated on the emancipatory value of photographic representation. Thus, Benjamin will go on to argue that "in Western Europe the capitalistic exploitation of the film denies consideration to modern man's legitimate claim to being reproduced" (232). Recognizing a "legitimate claim to being reproduced," Benjamin revalorizes a representational aesthetic that capitalism has merely perverted. After all, he points out, the art of photography is developed at the same time as the politics of socialism. Mimesis is stigmatized as *Ausdruck* at the same time as it is valorized as an aesthetic and political emancipation. The ambiguities of Benjamin's arguments would subsequently be lost to future generations, as the equation of left and right totalitarianisms on the basis of their aesthetic representationalism (socialist realism and fascist monumentalism) became a commonplace of Cold War high modernist theory. Representation will come to be identified with a vaguely defined politics of totalitarianism—with Nazi art and Socialist Realism—from the perspective of liberal Western high modernism, as enshrined in aesthetic theory from the 1950's on. But if representation per se is both aesthetically and politically suspect from the perspective of modernism, in Benjamin's essay we face the possibilities of *two* representationalisms: a subjective and reactionary representationalism of *Ausdruck* and an objective representation of one's rights.

I have written elsewhere of the political function served by the aesthetics of modernism, and this question is not my focus here. Instead, I cite Benjamin primarily to demonstrate the centrality of the question of representationalism—epistemologically speaking, we might say *mimetology*—to the construction of a theory of fascism. And I stress representationalism because it plays so central a role in the development of a recognizably queer aesthetic in the twentieth century. Kitsch representationalism, I will argue, marks the aesthetic meeting point of homosexuality and fascism for the contemporary cultural imagination. The representation of cute boys in sharp black uniforms is (considered to be) homoerotically charged, not simply as a result of the specific object of representation, but by virtue of the frisson that representation—a dirty pleasure—itself invokes.

With this assertion I have perhaps reached that point in this book where I am most open to the idea of homo-fascism as something other than a mere homophobic construction. By this I mean that the kitsch of fascism potentially becomes a homosexual camp through the workings of a logic identified by Sedgwick as the logic of identification.[5] The identificatory logic of camp posits the possibility of a "What if . . . ?": What if the person who wrote this were homosexual too? Kitsch, meanwhile, operates along the lines of a logic of attribution: I recognize kitsch because I could never be guilty of it. In the one case recognition derives from identity, in the other from alterity. Now, if kitsch and camp both body themselves forth in an exaggerated representationalism (as Sedgwick argues, and as I shall go on to discuss), then it is always possible to (mis-)read kitsch in a camp manner. The logic of attribution whereby I identify fascist kitsch with the Other might be read as camp—and an identification with an aestheticized fascist mentality thereby established.

It is not simply, then, that a homophobic high modernist aesthetic chooses to conflate kitsch and camp—fascism and homosexuality—as fraternal modes of representationalism; the homosexual reader will surely also be able to make that connection too. If kitsch and camp can become identical at the level of the object, there is always the danger they will become identical in the subject. Rather than positing two forms of subject formation—identificatory camp and alienating kitsch—we need instead to examine their virtual convergence as an epistemological rather than straightforwardly aesthetic phenomenon: the surrender of the discourse of the Self to the dictates of the "Other."

Rather than taking this confusion of kitsch and camp as the basis for an identification of homosexuality and fascism as aesthetic constructs, I think we need to examine it as the basis of a homophobia, as the fundament of a renewed homosexual panic. Implicit in Sedgwick's etiology of homosexual panic in *Epistemology of the Closet* is its origination in that period of epistemological transition, wherein "homosexuality" develops out of a heterogeneity of actions into a fixable identity. In the prehomosexual (or "sodomitic") episteme, if no action can typify and fix an identity, I need not panic: I commit peccadilloes, but do not thereby become "a homosexual." Likewise, however, once homosexuality has been pathologized as an identity, I need not panic because the very pathology of that identity renders it other. I need panic only when I am caught between epistemic structures, when my high-spirited peccadillo risks branding me a homosexual under the newly emerging episteme. By rights, then, homosexual panic should diminish with the establishing of a clearly delineated homosexual identity in the twentieth century, but this has clearly not been the case; and the identification of homosexuality with fascism that we have just outlined helps explain the structure of a renewed homosexual panic.

If the homosexual can turn kitsch into camp—"mistake" kitsch for camp, in the example of fascist art—then he potentially sub-

verts the kitsch logic of attribution (what we might otherwise call
the logic of alienation) with the logic of identification. The meeting of kitsch and camp in the field of representation means that
the logic of attribution whereby "I" recognize the ideological moment in the Other is subverted by my potential—camp—recognition of myself in the Other. Alterity serves not merely as an imaginary prop for the establishment of identity, but is brought into
the very heart of the subject. The homosexual, in other words, acknowledges the "fascist within" in a way that the heterosexual liberal subject cannot (recognizes, in fact, that the "within" is a mere
function of the definitive "without"). It is not so much a question
of the homosexual "being" fascist, as it is of the homosexual acknowledging the supplemental inherence of the Other in the self—
the contingency of any being. What renders heterosexism homophobic—and what renders the modernist canon so totalitarian in
its dictates—is the invocation of a strict set of aesthetic and political binarisms even after the aesthetics of camp have deconstructed
them. Thus, rather than acknowledging the phobic moment in all
identity formation—the homology of Self and Other that must be
denied—we understand homosexuality as that libidinal structure
that delivers itself up (passive, feminine) to the Other. The homosexual deconstruction of the dialectic of identity (a kitsch logic
in its dependence on an attributive alterity of subject and object) is
recontained in pathology: the homosexual is someone who confuses Self and Other—either narcissistically or through a confusion of gender roles.

Having outlined the stakes of mimetology in the construction
of homo-fascism, I wish now to examine the ways in which the issue plays itself out both in theories of fascism and in queer theory.
Before so doing, however, I should explain my choice of texts in
this chapter. We have already seen—in that closing image from
Mackay, in which lovers lean over the spring of life to draw re-
freshment, with only the homosexual being denied the right to
drink—how Narcissus haunted the homosexual literary imaginary
of the early emancipationists in a curiously negative form. In this
chapter, I wish to examine the limits of narcissism both as an erotic

and as an aesthetic structure. Turning to a writer whose work could scarcely be more different from Mackay's late-nineteenth-century naturalism—turning, that is, to Jarry, a precursor of the antirepresentational avant-garde—I wish to demonstrate how the problem of Narcissus is one that in fact allows us to elaborate a representational taxonomy beyond—or across—the categories of realism and antirepresentationalism central to Sedgwick's vitally important work. For in Jarry's novel *Days and Nights* we encounter narcissism both as a thematic concern (as a virtual threat to the essentially paederastic and differentiated model of homosexual desire Jarry presents) and as an aesthetic determinant in the play of representation and antirepresentation—or of what Jarry will call *perception* and *hallucination*—in the novel.

It is my assertion that prevailing currents in queer theory have encouraged the conflation of sexual de-differentiation and an antirepresentational aesthetic. Based on the reasonable assumption that homosexual desire turns on similarity rather than difference, work on homosexuality and modernism has tended to see in this homosexual de-differentiation the closure of the differential space of representation. Without (sexual) difference, there can be no representation—or, rather, there can be only allegory. As I shall argue in the final chapter of this book, any celebration of an essentially antirepresentational sexuality (identifying homosexual writers with the extremes of abstract *écriture*) would feed into precisely those allegorical readings of homosexuality that will eventually link it with fascism.

We must insist, then—unflattering though it may be for queer critics schooled in the high modernist tradition—on the representational impulse within homosexual writing, on that stigmatized kitsch we fear may identify us with both aesthetic and political reaction. For while we might easily present homosexual writers such as Mackay and Jarry as polar opposites with regard to their respective (anti-)representational strategies, they nevertheless meet in various important ways. Most specifically, the traditionally mimetic realism of Mackay and the antirepresentational impulse in Jarry both play themselves out within a field of what I will call "diacritical sexuality"—the field, that is, of a differentiated paederasty. If I insist here on the persistence of a viable paederastic tradition within the mainstream of homosexual desire in this century, I do so neither to champion and recuperate that desire, nor specifically to challenge prevailing historical and sociological models of "the modern homosexual." My aim, instead, is to indicate the *aesthetic* importance of paederasty as a differentiated mode of desire that does not eschew the differential on which all representation must be based.[6] "Homosexual writing," I will argue, cannot be defined along the axis of representation and antirepresentation. It does, however, suggest alternative criteria of discernment, as we shall see.

By insisting on the continuum from Jarry to Mackay, I acknowledge not only the persistence of a form of masculinist homosexuality that has formed the backbone of this study, but also the diversity within that tradition: the diversity of political and philosophical positions we saw in Chapter 2 is matched by a diversity of aesthetic approaches. I wish to argue that the ambiguous relationship homosexual writers entertain to the trope of narcissistic mirroring—and to mimetology in the broader sense—is conditioned by the ambiguity of the mirror as a figure for self-grounding and for the impossibility of all such grounding. The mirror cannot reflect the as yet nonexistent homosexual—but can it bring the homosexual into being through the process of non-representability? Would this structure—a reflection on the unreflected, a conjuring up through mirrors of a nonexistent subject—replicate (from the perspective of theorists of homo-fascism) the process of fascist nation-building, whereby the *Volk* is established in its very absence as the collective of those who await its arrival? To the extent that Jarry too operates within the terms of a decidedly masculinist understanding of homoerotic relations, it is not inapposite to read his work alongside that of Mackay. Of course, the two could hardly be more technically dissimilar, but these dissimilarities arise, I think, from a common recognition of the performative function of the literary text. Where Mackay seeks to move toward the condition of subjectivity at the extradiegetic level—toward, that is, the condition of referentiality—Jarry takes the absence of origin (the absence of the referent) as structurally determinate: it is not the homosexual subject that is lacking, but subjectivity *tout court.*

In turning now to Jarry, then, I wish to examine what happens when textual performativity is embraced, when the text does not legitimate itself through its denotative function. I seek, in other words, to examine the possibility of a homosexual avant-garde, and to contextualize its political status in the light of my observations on fascist spectacle. Does the performativity of the avant-garde text have anything in common—as an organization of discourse—with a spectacular politics? In the avant-garde text of a Jarry, we confront narcissistic structures not as an alternative to referentiality, but as a limit case of reference; and performance not as the opposite of denotation, but as the "acting out" of the denotative function par excellence—the creation of the subject. Would an avant-garde constituted in these terms "embrace lack" in a way that threatens heterosexual faith in both subjects and objects, or is such an embrace itself just the foreplay to the romance of a performance, in which lack is overcome by its very avowal?[7] Is it possible for an avant-garde aesthetic to escape the paradox of identification with (and through) lack; to proclaim "I am lack" without falling into the hypostative logic of the great "I am"?[8]

Paederastic masculinism—Mackay's and Jarry's—works with two strategic deployments of the mirror trope. On the one hand, the imperfection of representation opens up an aesthetic space that the homosexual writer might inhabit: homotextuality, in other words, as the aporia of heterosexual self-grounding. Homosexuality, one might say, as the tectonic fault line of all representation. Or, on the other, is the mere figure of form—the nonessential form which the mirror offers as reflection—itself the model for a homosexual aesthetic?[9] Is there something in the perspectival flatness of mirroring, in the insistence on surface as a figure for depth, that leads to a homosexual aesthetic of surface—or elegance—as a travesty of Platonism? Somewhere between or within these possibilities, I feel, lies the possibility of a transition from an aestheticism to the avant-garde, from mirror as surface to mirror as abyss.

I choose *Days and Nights* from among Jarry's works for several reasons. First, it deals directly with the question of narcissism as a modality both of homosexual desire and of self-construction. Second, it inserts into the narcissistic scenario the diacritical difference of age by insisting on the paederastic nature of male-male attachments. Third, *Days and Nights* addresses Sedgwick's question of what happens to the body—the kitsch male body that is desired and represented—when representation itself loses its cohesive force as an aesthetic imperative. The body is now no longer an object of representation, but the very modality of representation, the obsessive central trope of the novel. Finally, in this work Jarry moves toward a model of homohistory—embedded in the structure of paederasty, "in the front to backwards sense"—that challenges any potentially homogenizing tendencies in Sedgwick's historical reconstructions.

It is time, though, to remind ourselves of Sedgwick's treatment of kitsch in *Epistemology of the Closet*, since it forms (along with theories of fascism) one of the subtexts of this chapter. If a confrontation with the question of narcissism seems inevitable in any treatment of developing notions of homosexual identity in the twentieth century, in this chapter it is not my aim to engage in the philosophical debate that the problem of Narcissus raises—a debate that, as Sedgwick acknowledges in *Epistemology*, all too often elides same-sex desire under the ubiquitous modernist trope of the "divided self." Instead, I wish to examine how a paederastic response to the problem of Narcissus led to the elaboration of new possibilities of cultural practice. By illustrating such possibilities, I aim to demonstrate how the political questions of the preceding chapters—and the problematic of homosexuality and fascism in general—have attained a new urgency and relevance in the emerging discourse of queer literary studies.

Fredric Jameson critiqued modernism's "repression of History" in the context of an analysis of spatialized form; and though Jameson himself does not explicitly do so, I think one might take Narcissus as emblematic of that spatialization, as the introverted self-absorption of the text in the moment of its own reflection.

Narcissus, then, is the repression of time by space: the "repression of History." But the implication of Narcissus in a psychoanalytic discourse of repression necessarily raises the possibility of other repressions—the set of repressions and interdictions within which the modern homosexual consciousness might, perhaps, be constructed as a peculiarly modern-*ist* construction.

It is this set of repressions that concerns Eve Sedgwick in her consideration of the narcissistic trope in modernism. She claims, in short, that the historical shift from differentiated (what I will call "diacritical") models of homosexual desire (such as paederasty) to de-differentiated models (such as narcissism) reconfigures the general cultural understanding of desire as predicated on a subject-object dichotomy.[10] Desire and identification threaten to merge. This paradigm shift involves, in turn, a self-reflexivity that modernist cultural practice embraces by emptying Narcissus of its male-male desiring dynamic. Narcissism acknowledges a shift in the understanding of desire, without coding it homosexually. For Sedgwick, modernism both depends on and "camouflages" a newly emergent structure of (homosexual) desire. Thus, she juxtaposes the "open secret" of homosexual identity with the "empty form" of modernist formalism in the following terms:

> This rhetoric of male modernism serves a purpose of universalizing, naturalizing, and thus substantively voiding—depriving of content— elements of a specifically and historically male homosexual rhetoric. But just as the gay male rhetoric is itself already marked and structured and indeed necessitated and propelled by the historical shapes of homophobia, for instance by the contingencies and geographies of the highly permeable closet, so it is also true that homophobic male modernism bears the structuring fossil-marks of and in fact spreads and reproduces the specificity of desire that it exists to deny. (165)

The structured forms of modernism—the clichés of the self-reflective text, the *mise en abyme*, and antirepresentational abstraction—serve, according to Sedgwick, to sublimate and decontextualize a specifically homoerotic narcissistic topos. Most notably, for example, the contemplation of the self—the act of self-mirroring—usurps any instance in the modernist text of a male-male relationship: it is not the other *man* that obsesses the male gaze, but the reflection he offers of the *Self.* Homosexual strategies of indirection—themselves dictated by a historically specific set of repressions—create the formal structure of the modernist "empty form" that will serve to repress homosexuality anew as the merely contingent content, as history.

Sedgwick is altogether more dialectical than Jameson in her presentation of the repressive forms of modernism. At once more Foucauldian in her recognition that the structures of homophobia are themselves productive in the construction of homosexual identity, and more Freudian in her insistence on the return of the repressed *as* the repressed, she demonstrates how the inevitable homosexual topos is itself similarly constitutive of the obsessive formalizing urge in modernism. Modernism constructs and represses the homosexual impulse that in turn determines its own construction. I would argue, however, that just as modernism constructs and represses homosexuality's "open secret," contemporary queer theory tendentially represses the historical avant-garde as a form of homosexual cultural practice, choosing, instead, to subsume it in a monolithically conceived modernism. Where Sedgwick will turn to kitsch and camp as aesthetic structures that refuse the antirepresentational thrust of modernism—refuse the abstraction of the masculine Other into a mere reflection of the degendered Self—I turn instead (or also) to the notion of an avant-garde whose practice consists not in the radicalization of an antirepresentational aesthetic, but in a movement beyond the ultimately representational terms that oppose realism and abstraction in the first place.

The tendential elision of the avant-garde can be demonstrated with reference to the role Wilde plays in Sedgwick's analysis. Although clearly a canonical figure in the reconstruction of a homosexual literary history, Wilde's position within the broader literary canon is rather less clear: the aesthetic of artifice he represents has been identified as both decadent and modern. It is only in recent years, in fact, that a theory of the avant-garde has been developed that can account for this apparently paradoxical position, and since the time of Bürger's critical reevaluation—in his *Theory of the Avant Garde*—of *l'art pour l'art* as a necessary stage in the development of the avant-garde, it is incumbent on us to see Wilde as, at the very least, a threshold figure in the development of the avant-garde. In terms of the two possibilities of mirroring outlined earlier—pure surface or infinite ungrounded regression—we can perhaps grasp most clearly the antipathy of modernism to figures such as Wilde. For it is precisely as a celebrant of artifice and surface that Wilde traditionally figures in literary history, as a figure separated by frivolity from the antithematics of modernism. And if Wilde is to be "rescued" it will be with recourse to the alternative model of mirroring—the *mise en abyme*—that camouflages homosexual specificity. In other words, these two possibilities of the mirror trope—surface and groundless depth—are what connect and separate the possibilities of modernist and "decadent" homosexual cultural practice.

To leapfrog, for a moment, Sedgwick's line of argument, we should take note of the position Wilde occupies in her literary historical model. Commenting on that elision of specifically homosexual desire in the problematic of narcissistic self-grounding, Sedgwick writes: "For Wilde, the progression from *homo* to same to self resulted at least briefly, as we shall see, in a newly articulated modernist 'self'-reflexiveness and antifigurality, antirepresentationalism, iconophobia that struggles in the antisentimental entanglement of *Dorian Gray* and collapses in the sentimental mobilizations of *Reading Gaol*" (161). Clearly, Wilde is being taken—"at least briefly"—as a practicant or precursor of literary abstraction, as an antifigural protomodernist. But the trajectory of his career is one that leads him back to the ultimately mimetic "sentimental mobilizations" of *Reading Gaol*. It is as if Wilde were being punished for sins against established norms of representation as well as for his crimes *contra naturam*. For Sedgwick, then, Wilde's role is ambiguous; he holds out the promise of a new, abstract aesthetic, but in so doing potentially effaces the specifically homosexual nature of his narcissism. Thus, the return to sentimentalism in *Reading Gaol* may be taken as both a regrettable lapsus (from the perspective of the logic of aesthetic modernism) and as the affirmation of a homosexual mode of sentimental creation, of homosexual "identity." Wilde squanders his position within the aesthetic canon of modernism, so to speak, only to secure his position within the pantheon of "modern" homosexuality.

To what extent, however, does Sedgwick's analysis extend to works that do not "deal with" post-representational aesthetic questions, but that *enact* them? As her students were quick to point out, *Dorian Gray* is *about* "The Problem of Mimesis—'Life and Art,'" and this very "about" reinstates representationalism through the back door: *Dorian Gray* is, after all, about a portrait.[11] Rather, the portrait itself figures the possibility of the text being "about" anything at all: it represents representation. Indeed, one might argue that *Dorian Gray* plays out a recurrent fantasy of radical representationalism—a fantasy that will come to haunt modernism as a cultural project—by positing the possibility of a representational work of art that continues to represent even in the face of temporal flux. In other words, then, the epistemic shift beyond representationalism—Wilde's "antifigurality, antirepresentationalism, iconophobia"—finds its paradoxically iconic, aesthetic form within a representational framework. Indeed, though Sedgwick wishes to articulate the relationship between the "open secret" of homosexuality and a modernism understood in terms of its orientation toward abstraction, the works she treats cannot be said to be truly abstract. The question she does not really tackle is that of the relation of homosexuality to the radical avant-garde.

What are we to make of passages such as the following, for example, from the perspective of an aesthetic epistemology that rejects the dichotomy of representation and antirepresentation: "And from the empty 'modernist' point of view, this full meaning . . . *this* insistence on narrative content, which means the insistence on *this* narrative content, comes to look like kitsch" (166)? Or "So as kitsch or sentimentality come to mean representation itself, what represented 'representation itself' came at the same time signally to be a very particular, masculine object and subject of erotic desire" (167)? For the traditional and de-differentiating valorization of an antirepresentational modernism is itself only possible within the field of representation, which Sedgwick's analysis never leaves. For the male body to represent representation—to be stigmatized, that is, by the ascetic antirepresentationalism of modernism as the prurient and obsessive object of textual desire, the desire, indeed, *for* representation—the structure of representation must be retained. Thus, Sedgwick's analysis of sentimentality as the modality of a desiring presence within a modernist aesthetic of structural evacuation can be tenable only if the epistemic shift she asserts has not, in fact, fully taken place. The argument is potentially self-defeating; for when the move to abstraction has been completed, what representation of representation is then possible? From what avant-garde (let us say, only provisionally, "antirepresentational") perspective can the desired male body be (represented as) stigmatized? The truly avant-garde text—transcending the trajectory traced by Sedgwick—also necessarily undoes the aesthetic judgment of kitsch.

The male body remains the trace of representation within an antirepresentational modernist aesthetic. The desired and desiring male body may indeed serve as kitsch object, stigmatized by the formalist abstractions of a modernist textuality that understands narcissism as a purely structural concept voided of all content. Nevertheless, within the logic of the antirepresentational, the male body clearly serves as trace; the (homosexual) body is that singular moment of representation that must be retained in order for the abstract to encode and represent its antirepresentationalism. It both makes possible and precludes the absolute of abstraction. If, as Sedgwick argues, the redefinition of homosexual desire through the prism of narcissism necessarily has broader implications for the cultural construction of all desire, then this supplementarity of the male body should not surprise us. The presence of such a body in the text is necessary to remind us—"modernists"—of what our narcissism shall not be.

I would argue that a conflation of avant-garde and modernism in Sedgwick's reading of Wilde tendentially forecloses the possibility of a non-Wildean model of homosexual identity by reifying a literary—and, ultimately, social and intellectual—history. Wilde's

fate in *Reading Gaol* is read as emblematic of the fate of homotextual practice post-Wilde: the return to representationalism in
this text marks the ambiguity of the early homosexual writer toward the project of literary experimentation.[12] What I would like to
suggest—and to demonstrate in my reading of Jarry—is the existence of an alternative literary and ideological homosexual tradition (likewise traceable back to the latter years of the nineteenth
century) that is antirepresentational to an extent that Wilde is not.
For antirepresentationalism in its most radical forms must reject
the very taxonomic force of the category of representation itself.
To Sedgwick's model of the "modern" homosexual—reified aesthetically, if not clinically, despite her protestations—I oppose the
historical possibility of a homosexual avant-garde.

Sedgwick links the emergence of a new mimetic constellation
to redefinitions of homosexuality away from those models that had
prevailed in the late nineteenth century. The two crucial distinctions I wish to work with here deal with, first, the movement beyond a paederastic ideal of same-sex love, and second, the movement beyond the assumption that attraction is predicated on difference. Of course, the two questions are linked: Sedgwick will see
in both developments a movement beyond diacritical models of
homosexual desire, and a process of what she terms de-differentiation. To reiterate the passage we dealt with earlier in the context
of the masculinist philosophical tradition, Sedgwick claims: "It is
with *homo*-style homosexuality, and *not* with inversion, pederasty,
or sodomy (least of all, of course, with cross-gender sexuality) that
an erotic language, an erotic discourse comes into existence that
makes available a continuing possibility for symbolizing slippages
between identification and desire" (159). In other words, the *homo*
in homosexual predicates the similarity of subject and object of desire: I desire what is like me. At the extreme, Sedgwick will isolate
a logic whereby desire itself is denied in its overdetermination by
the structures of identification: I do not desire him, I am he. In a
footnote to this page, Sedgwick develops the epistemological implications of this definitional shift:

The fact that "homosexuality," being—unlike its predecessor terms— posited on definitional similarity, was the first modern piece of sexual definition that simply took as nugatory the distinction between relations of identification and relations of desire, meant that it posed a radical question to cross-gender relations and, in turn, to gender definition itself. For the first time since at least the Renaissance, there existed the potential for a discourse in which a man's desire for a woman could not guarantee his difference from her—in which it might even, rather, suggest his likeness to her.   (159–60n)

Sedgwick's point is well taken, but at the same time an overstatement, for it tends to overlook the extent to which what appears to be an epistemic shift is nevertheless—like the shift "beyond" representation reflected in *Dorian Gray*—recontained within existing paradigms. Thus, the possibility of a homosexual identification predicated on similarity partakes of the logic of homosexual panic by erecting yet another homo-/hetero- distinction: the homosexual is now pathologized as a desiring subject incapable of distinguishing between identification and object choice. The "slippage between identification and desire" does open up a new paradigm of desire—one based on identity and similarity— but it is immediately pathologized as a specifically homosexual symptom. Moreover, the gender binarisms of earlier models are not overcome. The category of homosexuality is now to be constructed neither around the gendering of the subject, nor around the determinant of object choice, but rather as a modality of desire: homosexual desire is the desire that confuses identification and object choice.

In this context, Sedgwick's reading of *Dorian Gray* takes the text as an exemplar of the eclipse of paederasty as a sexual relation built on diacritical difference (in this case, of age, but also—in terms of its implications for all sexual relations—of gender). This de-differentiation of desire is further understood as having certain aesthetic implications: specifically, the collapse of diacritical difference in desire threatens a system of mimetic representation based on the differentiation of signifier and signified. Building from her reading of *Dorian Gray*, Sedgwick has the following to say:

> The suppression of the original *defining differences* between Dorian
> and his male admirers—differences of age and initiatedness, in the first
> place—in favor of the problematic of Dorian's *similarity* to the painted
> male image that is and isn't himself does several things. To begin with,
> the similarity trope does not, I believe, constitute itself strongly here
> as against an "inversion" model, in which Wilde seldom seemed par-
> ticularly interested and whose rhetoric is virtually absent from *Dorian
> Gray.* Rather, the plot of the novel seems to replicate the discursive
> eclipse in this period of the Classically based, *pederastic* assumption
> that male-male bonds of any duration must be structured around
> some diacritical difference—old/young, for example, or active/pas-
> sive—whose binarizing cultural power would be at least comparable to
> that of gender.   (160)

To simplify somewhat: in Sedgwick's reading—that fights hard to
avoid hypostatizing any simple historical break and concentrates
on Wilde precisely because he figures as a transition between alternative models of homosexual identity—paederasty is to mimetic
representation as de-differentiated (let us say, narcissistic) desire is
to abstraction. The relation of subject to object in traditional models of desire replicates the structure of signifier and signified that
grounds the possibility of mimesis. Desire based on similarity—on
de-differentiation—would threaten the very possibility of signification.

   I wish to unsettle this implicit parallel by arguing that the historical emergence of the avant-garde can, in fact, be accounted for
from within a homosexual tradition of specifically paederastic or
diacritical desire that goes beyond questions of representation. The
opposition of representation and abstraction is an entirely modernist opposition, itself caught within the episteme of representationalism: in the avant-garde, the abstract will be uncovered as a
condition of representation and vice versa. If the modernist canon
"camouflages" specifically homosexual content, Sedgwick—both
in her historical reconstructions and in the aesthetic conclusions
she draws from them—camouflages the persistence of paederastic
desire in the cultural activity of the twentieth century. On the basis of a reading of *Dorian Gray*—a text she takes as exemplary for
the concerns of cultural modernism—Sedgwick tends to overstate

the eclipse of the paederastic model. Wilde's presumed aesthetic centrality legitimates an insistence on the eclipse of paederasty that is extremely hard to justify empirically.[13] For example, the paederastic model retains a crucial importance as a diacritical moment within that otherwise "de-differentiated," resolutely male-male model of homosexual desire that she seeks to chart. As I hope to show, this coexistence of diacritical and de-differentiated desire within masculinism complicates the question of representation and reveals alternative avenues of cultural practice. Furthermore, the entire German tradition of those we have termed "masculinists" (Friedlaender, Blüher, Mackay, et al.) sought its legitimation in a reappropriation of the paederastic tradition. More than this, however—and here I touch on what might itself be the diacritical point of difference between Sedgwick's Wildean modernism and the nascent homosexual avant-garde of a Jarry—the paederastic model seems to open up the possibilities of an alternative aesthetic and an alternative literary exploration of the "homo-style," the possibility, in short, of a homosexual avant-garde.

I contend that the homotextual may be identified neither with representationalism, nor with its rejection, but with the inextricability of the abstract and the representational in what I will call— borrowing from Lyotard—the "figural."[14] Jarry's *Days and Nights* builds on this idea of a coexistence of aesthetic impulses (and models of desire) by implementing a play of what we might only by way of shorthand call the "representational" and the "antirepresentational." I propose Lyotard's notion of the figure here as a way of recasting the work of the mirror. Whereas, in the modernist tradition, the mirror serves to question the grounding of all identity by unsettling the possibility of any original term within the play of reflection, the figure allows us to rethink instead the possibilities of the mirror as pure surface. The figure does not enter into the game of "camouflage" and does not entail an interpretive search for the material: the work of the figure is at the surface. Lyotard cites Freud's use of hypograms from *Simplicissimus* to explain how the figure camouflages only by presenting. Like the pun that will say two things at once, it cannot be decided which "meaning" is masking which. Developing the Freudian hypogram into a model of inscription, Lyotard helps ground, I think, an avant-garde model of writing that would challenge prevailing modernist notions of *écriture*. The figure would render it impossible to determine whether the act of representation were itself oriented toward the representation, or whether representation were itself but a by-product of a textual play. Is the representation to be read literally or not? Lyotard would suggest—and the example from Freud would demonstrate this admirably—that it is precisely by a "literal" reading that we experience the work of the figure. By deciphering (in the radical sense, by stripping away the function of the cipher) the writing we arrive at the meaning that was never hidden at all.

The logic I seek to suggest by this use of the figure is the same logic that made it impossible to differentiate kitsch from camp precisely because each operates at the level of surface. Like the homosexual desire constructed in the theories of the Frankfurt School, the figure both is and is not what it is: it is itself by virtue of not being itself. This logic is one that is inscribed in Jarry's novel—in an exemplary "figural" manner, no less—through the foregrounding throughout the book of the face—the *figure*—of the hero's beloved. To figure the figural through the *figure* is itself a typically figural gesture, in which a representational displacement occurs and does not occur—in which the *figure* both *refers to* and *is* something else, something other. Indeed, *Days and Nights* concludes with a plaster cast—a representation—of the beloved's *figure* falling on the hero's head and rendering him unconscious: in a hallucinogenic text the figure will serve as both the beginning and the end of representation.

Like *Dorian Gray*, Jarry's *Days and Nights* both proposes and refutes a certain post-representational episteme. But if Wilde's position within the literary historical canon is of interest precisely because of its ambiguity (beginning or end?), Jarry seems to occupy a clearer position as a precursor of the twentieth-century avant-garde. Perhaps it is because he has been reclaimed as seminal, as a progenitor, by such as the Dadaists and the Surrealists that his heterosexual credentials have rarely been questioned. In a critical tradition that well exemplifies that camouflaging of which Sedgwick speaks, Jarry's specifically homosexual problematic has been consistently overlooked or sublated into the supposedly broader question of "the crisis of the subject," or the "problem of identity." His subversive textual strategies have rarely if ever been linked to a subversive sexual practice; Jarry is canonical in his anticanonical status, central in his very marginality. After my comments on the limits to Wilde's antifigurality or iconophobia, my choice of *Days and Nights*—one of Jarry's more "representational" works—is not motivated by a desire to establish the credentials of a homotextual avant-garde on the basis of a radicalized antirepresentationalism. Jarry is not avant-garde by dint of surpassing Wilde's merely modernist iconophobia, but rather in his articulation of the impossibility and paradoxicality of his own text where Wilde sought to thematize and recontain such paradoxes. The "representational" aspects of *Days and Nights* need to be read at the level of *figure*— as both representational and antirepresentational at one and the same time.

To offer a synopsis of Jarry's novel is, of course, to reinscribe it within a representational tradition—the tradition of the "about"— to which it will not conform. Subtitled *The Novel of a Deserter*, the text deals with the experiences of Sengle (who ironically takes his name from the medieval French for single, or individual) on his conscription for military service. Sengle seeks to have himself invalided out of the army and when his younger friend Valens is conscripted in turn, Sengle seeks to furnish him with the means of contracting a disease that will secure his release also. Clearly, the name *Valens* seeks to inscribe Sengle and Valens in an economy of *equivalence*—a narcissistic economy of self-grounding—that the very notion of the "sengle" seems to resist. Sengle's desertion is also effected in a series of drug-induced hallucinations, in which he fantasizes about mythical creatures that threaten to reengulf him in a regression to earlier phylogenetic stages. The novel ends in the disembodied voice of an official medical statement detailing Sengle's mental condition and accounting for the mania—

caused by a plaster-cast face mask of Valens (a revenge of the *figure* indeed!) falling from the wall of Sengle's study onto his head.

At the time of its publication—and in the limited critical treatment it has received since—*Days and Nights* was considered puzzling largely as a result of the interlacing of scenes of realistic depiction and scenes of extraordinary hallucinatory fancy. The experience of Sedgwick's students, for example, so quick to "identify" the thematic of *Dorian Gray* as the question of identity and division, is strangely distorted in the pedagogical experience of another professor, who is puzzled by "the inability of his pupils to identify with *Les jours et les nuits*, despite their expressed willingness to do so."[15] This "inability to identify" must, I think, be read at two levels. The novel does not allow itself to be reinscribed into the logic of an "about" as readily as Wilde's *Dorian Gray*: the students' "inability to identify" is perhaps itself indicative of the model of homosexuality outlined, for example, in the Frankfurt School rereading of Freud. What I am suggesting—as a definitive rupture between the fleetingly "iconophobic" modernism of Wilde and the more radically "figural" avant-garde of a Jarry—is that Jarry's text is not "about" homosexuality, it *is* a homosexual text. It is a homosexual text insofar as it homosexualizes the reader. This homosexualization takes place not by virtue of an identification, however, but through the withholding of any such identification. The novel is not "about" doubling, but rather doubles the reader between the "expressed willingness" to identify—that is, the desire for identity—and the inability to identify. In short, the logic of Wilde's text is still a logic of identity—this is no longer the case in Jarry.

One of the major obstacles to an appropriative reading—any "identification"—is the doubling in the text itself of descriptions of a perceived reality with an hallucinatory fantasy-text. This doubling is presented, moreover, as a split between the singular, ontogenetic narrative of Sengle and the phylogenetic desires that transgress the singularity of any individual narrative. This transgression, I contend, will form the field of homosexual representation. Toward the end of the novel the narrator comments on this

odd mixture of perception and hallucination, and—at the same
time—on the choice of title for this novel:

> Perfecting Leibniz' definition, that perception is a hallucination which
> is true, he saw no reason not to say: hallucination is a perception
> which is false, or more exactly: *faint*, or better still: *foreseen* (*remem-
> bered* sometimes, which is the same thing). And he believed also that
> above all there are only hallucinations, or perceptions, and that there
> are neither nights nor days (despite the book's title, which is why it
> has been chosen) and that life is continuous; yet that one would never
> be aware of its continuity, nor even that life exists without these pen-
> dulum movements; and life is primarily verified by the beating of the
> heart. (83)

What I wish to stress within this aesthetic is the deconstruction of
a traditional dichotomy of perception and hallucination—a dichotomy, that is, of representation and antirepresentationalism.
Days and Nights—for all that it intersperses hallucinatory and homoerotic passages with the representational narrative—nevertheless
motivates those passages within the logic of representation; usually by presenting them as drug-induced fantasies or as dreams.
The question I would seek to address is: Wherein lies the repression of the homoerotic and wherein the possibility of a homotextual practice in this novel? Is homotextuality the state of hallucination per se (i.e., antirepresentational), or the narrative motivation of such hallucinations within a representational narrative?

That Jarry renders such binary oppositions impossible should
be clear from the passage just cited: perception and hallucination
are of the same order. A deconstruction takes place, mirroring (in
the inverted form of the mirror, indeed) Leibniz's deconstruction
of that same binarism. Perception is no longer—as in Leibniz—
deemed to be of the order of hallucination; hallucination is now
of the order of a perception. Rather, hallucination becomes a
"foreseen" or "remembered" perception: Jarry's deconstruction
always involves introducing a temporal *différance* into the static
scenario of narcissistic reflection. This temporality will take two
forms in the novel's construction; first, there is a division of perception and hallucination along the lines of ontogenetic narrative
and phylogenetic or regressive sexual fantasy; and second, there is

a consideration of the temporal *différance* that inhabits the traditional differential—diacritical—relation of paederasty. By superimposing on each other the narcissistic and the paederastic paradigms of homoerotic attraction—in a construction he will call "adelphism"—Jarry simultaneously calls into question fundamental assumptions of mimesis by demonstrating the temporal *différance* at the heart of all desire for self-grounding. Paederasty functions as the reinscription of the temporal within the closed synchronicity of representation: its function is aesthetic as well as sexual.

The "hero" of *Days and Nights*, Sengle, is threatened in his role as subject both by the *abrutissement* of military life and by the regressive fantasies of his intoxicated imagination, inspired by the need to escape military regimentation. Although hallucination figures in the novel as a line of flight, a desertion, a point of escape from military regimentation, it nevertheless depends for many of its images on the military regimentation it flees, suffusing sexual fantasy with images of army life, and army life with an intrinsically erotic figurality. To return, for example, to that paradigmatic instance of what I have called the "figural" in *Days and Nights*, the *figure* of the beloved "brother," Valens is first evoked in detail in a description that cathects and reworks erotically a scene from the military lazaret: "The white countenance was absolutely that of a hospital ward. Embossed with candid beds, the nostrils seemed like the rising of a hundred hunched knees, and the forehead was drawn over the spirit like a white coverlet" (131). Of course, the invocation of the *figure* of Valens as figure is peculiarly apposite, for it implements, indeed, a typically figural mode of representation. For the *figure*—which, in the final chapter, we will see elaborated and vulgarized as a theory of allegory—both is and is not the thing it represents; it both does and does not displace the "real" object of representation. In other words, it is undecidable whether it is a "figure" at all. Like that homosexual desire reconstructed from the fragments of Frankfurt School theory, the figure is what it is only when it is being something else, enacts itself only where it already functions as a representation and displacement. Here—as in the *figure*—the erotic secret of homosexuality operates in and through the systems that seek to repress or displace it—the system of military regimentation, and the system of figural representation.

The hallucinatory scenes—in which denotative representation is displaced by imaginary monsters of sexuality from some phylogenetic past—typify the ambiguity of the novel. They are, in a sense, antirepresentational, but they are nonetheless narratively motivated as descriptions of drug-induced fantasies that push the characters beyond the limits of individual identity. The hallucinatory scenes can be read as the explicit enunciation of the homosexual attraction at the heart of an otherwise narcissistically homosocial and fraternal relationship, for they are obsessively concerned with the body as organism, rather than with the body as a figure for identity. Sengle's escape into hallucination is an escape into the erotic, but an escape that is frightening and threatening. Of particular note, though, is the aesthetic overcoding of what we can now see as a homosocial-homosexual dichotomy. Insofar as they can be distinguished, perception is on the side of realism in the novel—on the side of the strictly homosocial, exclusively male environment of the army—while hallucination is the modality of the homosexual; the modality, that is, of that which is not yet and, therefore, of that which can be perceived or described only fantastically, as the negation of all identity. At the same time, however, it is precisely the regimentation of the army that inspires (homoerotic) fantasies of a more fundamental—organic, or phylogenetic—loss of identity: the relationship of representation and antirepresentationalism is, ultimately, dialectical. In other words, Jarry develops the possibility of a specifically figural homotextuality from within the confines of the representational concerns of his novel. The figural would be the work of representation in the antirepresentational and vice versa—the work of desire in (rather than beneath) its repression. Jarry's novel seems to interlace even more inextricably Sedgwick's "open secret" and "empty form": the empty form is no longer that which neutralizes and sublates the specific homosexual content, but rather form awaiting content, mimesis in abeyance—the possibility of an as yet unrealized homosexual identity.

The relationship between Sengle and Valens could in many ways be read as a textbook case of Sedgwick's notion of narcissistic camouflage. The question of male-male desire is, indeed, sublated into the question of narcissistic self-constitution and homosexual desire thereby subjugated to the demands of a reflection on reflection itself. Clearly—as Sedgwick has demonstrated—the paradigm of narcissism serves as the meeting ground of a de-differentiated homosexuality and a modernist aesthetic project. For Jarry this contestation of the mimetic tradition leads also to a questioning of narrative temporality, a questioning that is itself rooted in a certain model of homosexual desire. Thus, in that passage on hallucination and perception quoted earlier, Jarry comments on the arbitrariness of the novel's title—"there are neither nights nor days"—and offers a typically modernist account of the novel's move beyond linear narrative. In the passage in question, Jarry describes an elaborate game in which the time of day is established according to the whim of the first and last female characters to find a place in the novel:

> There was an alarm-clock in the form of a skull scumbled with calcium phosphate, whose mandible muttered and clacked, and this was never allowed to wake anyone, its action necessitated too ugly a grimace. And there was a slate on which Ilane—for a bet which Sengle said was more childish than all the others—inscribed a number from time to time, wiping off its predecessor. And it was midnight only when the slate and clock agreed.   (21)

The question of temporality and its disruption is tied to the question of heterosexual relations. Although Ilane's game makes a mockery (in true "modernist" manner) of the temporal order, it nevertheless reasserts a counterorder of sorts, oriented around the moment of midnight as a moment of de-differentiation, a moment in which the actual time and the imagined time coincide. The disruption of narrative depends—no less than the disruption of representation—on a certain de-differentiation identified by Jarry, however, with *heterosexual* relations. Yet the first chapter closes with a reconfiguration of this heterosexual idyll of Sengle and his Ilane, Valens and his Margot; a break that also effects a rupture with this arbitrary heterosexually coded time: "Sengle proposing to efface it and begin all over again, the two couples set out on two tandems, since in the light of what follows Sengle required his tiredness to be marked, and his brother accompanied him everywhere because this dear head before him and not a yellow or white star was what distinguished day from night, so that he should not be too unhappy" (21–22).

The homosexual liaison is grounded here not in rupture with time and representation—the atemporal temporality of Ilane's game—but in the repotentialization of a narrative project. The possibility of narrative time—*Days and Nights*—is reestablished by the homoerotic attachment to Valens. It might not be fanciful, I think, to see in the sexually encoded rejection and subsequent reconstitution of sequential temporality in this chapter an example of what Sedgwick refers to in her discussion of kitsch: narrative representability is reestablished by the diacritical homosexual (or paederastic) relation. There is a recognition of the purely formal nature of narrative time at the very outset of the novel, but the novel then continues with the description of a bicycle ride in which that temporality is reconstituted by means of a homosexual attachment. In other words, the possibility of narrative representation—the stigmatic representationalism of which Sedgwick writes—is, indeed, anchored in a homotextuality.

If I have suggested that Sedgwick tends to fall into the binarisms she catalogs, we might, perhaps, counter her insightful characterization of the kitsch-logic of sentimentality with Jarry's countercategory of *nostalgie*, elaborated not as a longing for representation, but as the introduction of temporality into the narcissistic scenario. The chapter in Jarry's novel that deals with the question of narcissism in most detail should, by its very title, alert us to a (dia-)critical shift within the narcissistic paradigm: for the chapter is entitled "Adelphism and Nostalgia." What Jarry introduces into the solipsism of the mirror is a consideration of the temporal lapse operative within even narcissistic representation. Reflection has become *nostalgie*, a quite specifically temporal inflection of the sentimentality of kitsch outlined by Sedgwick. Furthermore, the homosexual form taken by this nostalgia is paederastic. As we shall see, the novel attempts to understand the constitutive role of a deferral in the construction of narrative temporality, but it is this same lapse that also opens up the space of an adelphic desire in which narcissism and paederastic models coexist.

This space of desire—the desire inherent in representation, the desire modernism supposedly stigmatizes as the desire *for* representation—Jarry designates as "adelphic" space, and the relationship of Sengle and Valens is consistently presented—in what might otherwise appear a textbook case of "camouflage"—as fraternal and adelphic. For Jarry, however, brotherhood operates within a differentiated system of hierarchies based on age rather than as a simple mirroring. It is this, I think, that Sedgwick fails to take account of, seeing in fraternalism the camouflage par excellence of homosexual desire in the modern novel. Even in *Tendencies*, where she modifies her readings of Wilde, Sedgwick still argues that "insofar as the name 'brother' functions as an alibi, as pure structure, it is homologous with a modern/deconstructive understanding of men's bonds with other men as 'homo,' as relations to an (always absent, lacking, elusive or eloping) Same in the homogenizing heterosexist scientism of homo/hetero" (67). Thereby she pushes the fraternal relation in the direction of identity, when for Jarry it marks, on the contrary, the irreducibly nonidentical (diacritical and representable) moment of desire. Indeed, as we shall see, the obsessive fear impelling this (dia-)critical paederastic difference—of adelphic brotherhood—in Jarry's writing is precisely the fear of this fraternal hierarchy becoming a relationship of the *jumeau* (twin), a relationship in which the temporal lag constitutive of differentiated affiliative relations is lost in a mere twinning or—to use Sedgwick's term—doubling.

Although we have characterized the relationship of Sengle and Valens as homoerotic, Jarry is at pains to desensualize that relationship in terms redolent of Sedgwick's camouflage: "Not sensual, Sengle was capable only of friendship. Yet to find himself

again in his Double predecessor, it was essential for him to recon-
noître, as a soul, a body beautiful enough to bear comparison to
his own" (48–49). Sengle's narcissism is certainly not of the kind
one might identify with nineteenth-century sexological notions of
sensualism, and is clearly motivated by a philosophical anxiety
about self-grounding. At the same time, however, aesthetic and
philosophical questions merge in Sengle's need to find his spiritual reflection in a beautiful body. In the strictest sense, though,
homoerotic desire faces here an existential question, such that, for
example, "Sengle was not sure whether his brother Valens had ever
existed" (47). Nevertheless, Jarry is also aware of the role of this
meditation on self-grounding within the more clearly defined parameters of a meditation on homosexuality. Thus, in the chapter
on adelphism, he quite explicitly privileges his own term "adelphism" over uranism (and is, therefore, aware of his own engagement in the polemic, from within which the homosexual eventually emerged in the late nineteenth century) because "the word
Adelphism would be more precise and look less medical than
Uranism" (48). In other words, Jarry does not simply sublate
questions of homosexual desire into the problematic of identity,
but engages in a direct polemic with an existing homosexual tradition from the perspective of an avant-garde artist. We must read
Days and Nights as a direct intervention in the construction of
male-male desire in the nineteenth century: and as such we must
read Jarry as offering an alternative both to the "Uranism" that
would eventually spawn "third-sex" theory and to the narcissistic
"doubling" that would eventually dominate psychoanalytic accounts of homosexuality. As a representative of the homosexual
avant-garde, Jarry offers not a third path, but a deconstructive
reading of these two—Uranian and narcissistic—forms of homosexual identity.

Of course, Jarry's introduction of the temporal topos into the
scenario of narcissism is not in itself anything new. Such, for example, is the very premise of *Dorian Gray*, and certain passages
from *Days and Nights* are reminiscent of Wilde. Thus, in front of
the photographs of Valens Sengle sees himself: "And then he saw

that he was perhaps mistaken and was looking at himself seven and a half years ago, and that he must have murmured the verses before a mirror which must have held his face without its ageing" (48). The difference, however, is that the nature of paederastic desire in Jarry—as opposed to the de-differentiating tendencies in Wilde's treatment of narcissism—dictate that the differential be affirmed. Unlike *Dorian Gray, Days and Nights* is not predicated on a desire to avert ageing, but rather on the desire that historical time itself be embodied and represented in the difference of lover and beloved. This embodiment, moreover, must assert the integrity of the *other* body, for—as we shall see—it is precisely when the body of the desiring subject narcissistically usurps the role of object of desire that Jarry's paederastic desire collapses into the de-differentiated effeminacy he fears.

Stated somewhat schematically: insofar as Jarry's novel charts the impossibility of a narcissistic fulfillment (a desire enclosed within itself), it problematizes also the aesthetic absolute of abstraction. More than this, the embracing of the impossibility inherent in desire serves to reconfigure narcissism and to champion an aesthetic that refuses to measure itself against binarisms of representation and abstraction. Such dichotomies are unacceptable from a "figural" avant-garde perspective, and yet undeniable from the perspective of the post-representational episteme. Thus, when, in his presentation of narcissism, Jarry observes how "Sengle was discovering the true metaphysical cause of the happiness of loving: not the communion of two beings become one, like the two halves of man's heart which, in the foetus is both double and separate; but more that enjoyment of anachronism and of communing with his own past" (48), he quite explicitly rejects a tradition of dichotomism, with the impossible hope of reconciliation it holds out. Instead, adelphism is understood as an experiment with history in which two historically diverse moments are lived as one eternal moment. The movement beyond an essentially dialectical model of historical *bonheur*—the movement, that is, beyond reconciliation—is figured as a movement into the realm of *jouissance*, an explicit eroticization of anachronism.

Jarry's presentation of paederasty, therefore, addresses questions of historical reconstruction as well as questions of desire. Indeed, Sengle's desire for Valens seems to address the fundamental impossibility of self-identity—and, moreover, to posit the paradox of homosexuality as the condition of that impossibility. The experience of anachronism is described in the following terms:

> The present, possessing its past in the heart of another, at the same time lives out its Self and its Self plus something. But if a moment of the past or present existed separately at one point in time, it would be unable to perceive this Plus something, which is quite simply the Act of Perception. This act is, for the creature that thinks, the most supreme enjoyment [*jouissance*] conceivable: there is a difference between that and the sexual act of brutes like you and me—Not me, Sengle corrected himself. (48)

This passage is remarkable for its eroticization of the philosophical questions of reflection and self-grounding. It reverses the logic of camouflage central to Sedgwick's observations on modernism. The ventriloquized voice of the narrative attempts precisely that form of camouflage Sedgwick writes of: *jouissance* is ascribed solely to the formal philosophical experience—the empty form—of a (narcissistic) reflection on reflection. Sengle, however, corrects himself, rejecting the reduction of *jouissance* to the abstract "perception of perception": for him, the sexual act is entirely commensurate with the *jouissance* of reflection, because it is itself caught within the diacritical reflection of paederasty. Sexuality is not sublated into philosophical reflections on reflection—quite the reverse. Whereas Sedgwick assumes that the camouflage of modernist formalism serves merely to elide the specificity of male-male desire, in this passage Jarry effects quite the opposite: questions of philosophical self-grounding are subverted into an elaboration of same-sex desire. Jarry quite specifically articulates the possibility of a (non-)identity grounded on a (homo-)erotic experience. Narcissus is the aporia of reflection: to posit narcissism as the condition of homosexual identity is to posit the homosexual as the impossibility of identity as such.

This insistence on the paederastic, diacritical difference also has clear aesthetic implications: indeed, the interplay of "perception" and "hallucination" in this novel might be taken as evidence of those effects. If Sengle insists on the erotic possibilities of philosophical reflection, he does so in the name of *perception*: *jouissance* ("this Plus something") is "quite simply the act of perception." Thus, the textual move from figural perception to a post-representational hallucination cannot seamlessly be mapped onto a putatively "avant-garde" erotics of pure *jouissance*. Sexual pleasure is not of the order of free textual play and antirepresentationalism. Jarry, in short, represents an avant-garde tradition that does not eschew representation—itself represented in the male body—as kitsch. *Days and Nights* is a threshold text precisely because it opens up the possibilities of an eroticized pleasure within representation itself, rather than positing *jouissance* as the condition of post-representational textual play. In other words, whereas Sedgwick seeks to portray a modernist tradition in which the specifically homoerotic referent is stigmatized as the residue of an anachronistic aesthetic of representation, Jarry offers an avant-garde alternative in which the homoerotic cannot so easily be mapped in terms of representation. (This is not, in other words, a Barthesian textual play in which homosexuality is effectively elided.) Homosexual desire is no longer that which defies representation—a love that dare not (or cannot) speak its name—but inscribed at the very heart of a system of representation dependent on diacritical difference. Paederastic homosexual desire eschews the repressive aesthetic of the sublime.[16]

Adelphism is presented as a response to the aporias of reflection, for the "Self plus something" that always escapes reflection is lived in the moment of the lover's loving his own past in the embodied present of the beloved. This supplementary "plus something"—in other words—is being identified not only with the "act of perception" (i.e., the perception of perception itself) central to reflection, but also with a specifically temporal lapse. The problem, of course, lies in assessing the extent to which this presentation of homosexual desire truly offers a viable alternative to the aporetic construction of narcissistic self-grounding. Jarry's adelphic model consistently faces the possibility of its own sublation into the de-differentiated structures outlined by Sedgwick. This possibility is figured within the text as the virtual conflation of signifier and signified, an elision of the diacritical difference that makes representation possible. For Sengle's desire to live at one and the same time his Self and the Self plus something could potentially lead to a form of narcissism, in which the self becomes both subject and object of desire. This is not what happens, however, despite Sengle's flirtation with such possibilities:

> He had attempted to create within himself this memory of Self by shaving his sparse moustache and inflicting upon his body a meticulous Greek depilation: but then he realized he was more in danger of looking like a fairy [*tapette*] than a little boy. And above all it was vital for him to remain what Valens was to become, until that ill-starred day when, their two and a half year age difference being no longer evident, they would be mistaken for one another, being too like twins. (49)

This passage is particularly important, for it demonstrates that paederastic desire—as envisaged by Jarry, at least—still seeks to represent, but reworks the erotic possibilities of representation itself. Sengle fears the day when the absolute conflation of signifier and signified—subject and object of desire—becomes possible in the similarities of the two bodies. The desire for self-grounding seems to consist in the desire for similarity, but the singularity of the self is actually established only by dissimilarity and difference. If Sengle fears the day when Valens becomes like him (the signified loses itself in the signifier), he also recognizes the futility of a total self-absorption in Valens (the signifier loses itself in the signified). The present of Valens is the past of Sengle—or, rather, the present of Valens is the possibility of the reliving, the re-presentation of the past of Sengle. In Valens, Sengle re-presents his past. Desire, meanwhile, is the living modality of remembrance, remembrance as present rather than past. Thus, Sengle cannot become the thing he loves because he would no longer be the thing loved by the beloved. The reciprocal imperative, then—the need for desire to complete itself—sets in motion a parallel historical imperative in which Sengle is equally obliged to represent—re-present—the future for Valens, the re-presentative of his own past. Thus, the structure of reflection is essentially temporal, and adelphic desire itself becomes the condition of representation for Jarry.

This passage is important, however, for other reasons: for what Sengle fears is not simply a collapse of the diacritical difference, but also a return to a model of effeminate homosexuality, to the condition of the fairy, the *tapette*. In Jarry's masculinism, Wilde's momentary iconophobia is seemingly replaced by a more straightforward homophobia. If masculinists invoke the Greek paederastic ideal as a countervalue to the dangers of effeminization and de-differentiation, those same effeminate models of homosexuality nevertheless reemerge precisely from within that Greek model of desire. It is precisely when—"inflicting upon his body a meticulous Greek depilation"—Sengle seeks to aestheticize the body (his own body) that he risks effeminacy. Indeed, in the danger of shaving off that "sparse moustache" we surely see replicated that moment from the Eldorado bar visited by Lewis. Just as it was the last remnant of chin stubble that there reinforced the perception that a representation (a *Täuschung*) was taking place, here it is once again to the pores of the body that the signifying differential retreats. The Greek paederastic ideal, as a vehicle of masculinist homosexuality, threatens—through an excess of representational zeal—to become precisely that form of de-differentiated effeminacy it seeks to resist. The Wildean aestheticized homosexual persona, then, is but one effect of the logic of de-differentiation of which Sedgwick writes. Representational difference will, ultimately, come to represent the more fundamental *différance* that makes possible the fiction of identity. It is quite precisely a splitting—an adelphic narcissism—that prevented the good professor's students from identifying "despite their expressed willingness to do so." That which resists a heterosexual identificatory reading sets up the possibility of homosexual nonidentity, an "identity" grounded in the traditional differentiation of signifier and signified reworked in terms of the *paederastic*—not strictly homosexual—body.

As *différance*, however, the effeminizing possibility of a twinning cannot be contained within the purely externalized differential figure of adelphic paederasty. The *tapette* emerges from an organic state of twinning inherent in the body—as a structure latent within the body itself. Thus, for example, when Sengle first dons his military uniform, he becomes physically aware of the process of de-differentiation he is about to undergo:

> And the jacket sleeves were long—regimental sizes envisaging a differentiation less distinct, with respect to the shorter arms, than that between anthropoids whose feet were hands, but whose hands were also feet, comparable to the jellyfish which has but one hole for anus and mouth. (27)

The return to an earlier state—effected by military regimentation—is figured as an organic conflation of the mouth and the anus. The (homo-)sexualization (and doubling) of the body takes place not at the level of individual bodily relations (as sexuality), but at a depersonalized and depersonalizing phylogenetic level. The experience of conscription brings latent organically "doubled" structures to the fore; de-differentiating military homosociality threatens to become explicitly homosexual and—in this case—explicitly anal. The army makes fairies of us all.

Suddenly—in this organic twinning—the problematic of language ("the mouth") is overcoded with the problematic of a sexuality figured in explicitly anal terms; and this development is enabled by the act of conscription. Sengle's desire to escape the heterosexual symbolic order—his desertion of language—is, as Sedgwick might conclude, motivated by a desire to silence the anus. The army—as a de-differentiating device—provokes phylogenetic hallucinations of an alternative de-differentiation, rendering explicit the question of homosexuality in terms antipathetic to Jarry's diacritical model. In other words, the army—as the regimen of language—both forms and deforms the question of male-male desire. Sedgwick's de-differentiation is identified here with homosocial repressive orders rather than with an erotic homosexuality, but beyond this the passage also casts an entirely new light on the question of de-differentiation and the status of language. For now we find that the mouth—the only uniquely individual part of the body, as Jarry contends—was itself always already doubled. If the mouth is what separates individuals, it is itself nevertheless inextricably linked—phylogenetically—to the anus. In other words, it would appear that the mouth is championed not only in resistance to the external regimentation of language, but also in order to suppress the anus. The resistance to language is at one and the same time the repression of a phylogenetic anality. It becomes impossible—within the structure of this characteristically ambiguous *figure*—to tell whether the desertion of language (of the mouth) is a rejection of heterosexual regimentation, or of homosexual anality.

The fear of an explicitly homosexualized homosociality is figured, then, as a fear of a conflation, the conflation of the mouth and the anus. Now, however, it is not simply homosexual fantasy, but homosocial structure—the military—that threatens to unleash the powers of de-differentiation linked to the *tapette*. Military service threatens to bring about the feared conflation both through the regimental de-differentiation of bodies and organs and through the hallucinations its provokes. What seems to be taking place is an organic twinning of the body with itself, rather than with its own narcissistic and paederastic reflection: the body is always already double. Sengle—despite deriving his name from the latinate *singulum*—is never singular, but always double. Moreover, desire consistently realizes itself in precisely those structures and figures that seek to thwart it. The army—as both figure and structure—would be paradigmatic here.

Of course, the conflation of mouth and anus forces us to reconsider the explicitly nonlinguistic, non-oracular—a-delphic—thematics of the novel. The adelphic rejection of the question of language becomes an avoidance of the question of anality. The physical "homosexual panic" bodies itself forth—as Sedgwick has argued—as a metaphysical anxiety. However, the play of perception and hallucination—of homosociality and homosexuality—is complicated by the fact that the realization of Sengle's desires releases precisely those forces that threaten his paederastic, diacritical model of desire. The oral-anal anthropoid of army life is at one and the same time that which Sengle seeks to "desert," and that which realizes his desire. Thus, the resurgence of the mouth at the end of the novel both sublates and articulates the question of an anal affection. Sengle kisses the plaster-cast of his brother's *figure*—"Sengle leaned toward his brother whom, by now, across the distance, he could tell was free, so as to give him back all the affection of the good kiss of a sonorous light. The plaster mouth became flesh and red to drink the libation of Sengle's soul. The lamp had turned red, then black, the metal died out in the eye and the air poised a mist of tears" (131–32)—and in so doing resensualizes what had been desensualized in their homosocial liaison. What Jarry leaves us with—in this closing argument for the always already self-twinning organic body—is the inescapability of the *tapette*. The desire to unify the body into one self-contained organ—the bodily figure for the desire for self-grounding identity—is what conjures up the *tapette*. In other words, it is the very logic of identity—the subject at the heart of heterosexual desire—that invokes the *tapette*. It is *heterosexuality*—as an identity-logic—that depends on an epistemology of the fairy.

I have argued that Jarry allows us to posit the possibility of an avant-garde, homotextual practice that cannot be subsumed under the rubric of that modernist "empty form" outlined by Sedgwick. But I have also argued that the distinction of the avant-garde from modernism cannot be effected purely in terms of strategies of (non-)representation; that Jarry finds in the *figure* of the beloved the abstraction at the heart of all representation. To flag my argument as a response to Sedgwick: Jarry does, indeed, confront the possibility of both a sexual and a representational de-differentiation that would potentially deny the specificity of homosexual desire. However, he does so through the paradigm of paederasty (a paradigm Sedgwick takes to be in eclipse) and in opposition to an effeminizing superimposition of categories of masculine and feminine on homosexual desire. I am arguing, then, that adelphic, diacritical desire—celebrating "anachronism" in a gesture that is itself anachronistic, if Sedgwick's model holds—far from being in eclipse, actually opens up the space of a homosexual avant-garde aesthetic in the twentieth century. Sedgwick's implicit distinction between kitsch and high modernism does not take into account the literary and cultural practice of an avant-garde of which Jarry himself was a precursor—an avant-garde that drew its shock value precisely from the admixture of kitsch and formal asceticism.

Jarry's reworking of the homoerotic as a distinct mode of the epistemological has direct philosophical as well as aesthetic implications. It is my contention that Jarry's *adelphic*—or fraternal— Eros is at the same time an "a-delphic" or non-oracular eros. I might best illustrate this contention—placing Jarry at the interstices of the philosophical questions of reflection raised repeatedly in this book—by means of a detour through the Narcissus myth itself. In Ovid's *Metamorphoses*, the story of Narcissus is prefaced by the prophecy of Tiresias, to whom Liriope (the boy's mother) turns for an augury of the child's future. She went

> And asked Tiresias if the boy would ever
> Live to a ripe old age. Tiresias answered:
> "Yes, if he never knows himself" (68)

At the root of Narcissus, then, is the problem of self-knowledge— or rather, the problem of pleasure and self-knowledge. The prophecy of Tiresias clearly parodies the injunction of the Delphic oracle, the famous "know thyself." His prophecy, one might say, is a-delphic. It contradicts the very cornerstone of the philosophical project, and the fate of Narcissus would seem—insofar as he attempts to know himself—to mirror the fate of speculative philosophy. Narcissus himself, then, is a threshold figure, whose homosexuality, as soon as it is recognized as such, inaugurates the double bind of the philosophical search for self-knowledge. What we must remember, however, is that Narcissus is precisely *not* an exemplar of the Tiresian injunction—Narcissus *does* seek to know himself, he *does* discard the a-delphic for the Delphic. He is precisely *not* the embodiment of an alternative "homosexual" epistemology in this myth. As a philosopher—reflecting on reflection, seeking to know what he should not know—he reenters the realm of heterosexuality.[17] The a-delphic—or, in Jarry's paederastic terms, adelphic—injunction of Tiresias offers the possibility of a non-philosophy, of an alternative, "non-oracular" relationship to desire, one that does not reduce experience to the ground of the cognitive self and the self-legitimating voice. In this sense Tiresias (himself a figure of indeterminate gender) posits the possibility (in ignorance) of an a-delphic, non-philosophical—in short, homosexual—epistemology.

This skeletal reading of Narcissus allows us to reframe the characteristic modernist—or post-Romantic—question of literature and its relation to philosophy in specifically sexualized terms. Far from embodying some sort of "homosexual" alternative, Narcissus brings to a head the contradictions of a heterosexual philosophical tradition that seeks to reconcile the potentially dichotomous categories of pleasure and knowledge. The homosexual response, then, must necessarily be *post*narcissistic in its observation of Tiresias's a-delphic injunction. By conflating the adelphic and the a-delphic, we arrive at a fraternal erotics that does not partake of the logic of camouflage, but that does not seek to sublate the desiring subject through knowledge of the self either.[18]

This observation is not without its dangers for queer theory. We have already seen how it was precisely a reading of the post-identitarian, postnarcissistic dilemma within an anachronistically narcissistic framework that led Adorno to see homosexualized fascism in the cathecting of the void that had been the Self. On the other hand, as Eve Sedgwick has pointed out, there is a danger in moving too abruptly from the homosexual syntagm to the putatively paradigmatic question of identity per se; for such a movement tends to despecify and dehistoricize the specifically—"indicatively"—male, homosexual scenario of self-reflection. Since mirroring figures the impossibility of self-knowledge as self-immanence, it is by its very nature a-delphic: for the delphic oracle is a command to self-knowledge enunciated by the self-present, self-legitimizing voice. In Jarry's representation, however, it is important to note that the erotic attachment between Sengle and Valens is quite explicitly non-oracular, non-oral. In the first tableau, for example, we encounter "Sengle and Valens, unresponsive

to the girls, but not talking to one another because by being together they understood each other well enough" (21). The bal-
ance to be drawn is between a nonlinguistic mutual understanding, and the danger of complete immersion (silencing) in the Other.
Linguistic difference—effecting and confirming the division of the
self and its interlocutor—is replaced by the space of a temporal *différance*, of past and present. The linguistic division of speakers is
replaced by the paederastic division of age in lover and beloved.

Consequently, Jarry reinscribes the problematic of language
within the parameters of a meditation on temporality. As in the
original Narcissus myth, the relationship of the adelphic lovers—
Sengle and Valens—is based on a failure of language, that is figured as an echo across that gulf distinguishing military from civil-
ian life: "Then he learned that Valens had left France and was veg-
etating in fever-ridden India, about the same time as Sengle was
cloistered inside the convict-hulk of the military snail. A letter took
two months to get there, and its echo slept a span of four months"
(47). As in the case of Narcissus's spurning of Echo, the failure of
a reiterative or purely tautological model of truth is here ascribed
not simply to the impossibility of absolute representation, but to
the temporal lag of the echo. Yet again, it is on the temporality of
representation that Jarry insists: the central dichotomy—the dichotomy around which sexuality is organized—is, then, for Jarry,
a temporal one (past-present) rather than one of gender. The a-
delphic structure of Sengle's relationship to Valens should be understood as an attack on the privileging of the oracular, of a principle of truth through revelation. In fact, one might best understand *Days and Nights*—as its subtitle suggests—as a desertion, as
a narrative oriented toward the effacement of discourse. Thus,
while at the beginning of the novel the most perfect communication is that which is possible between Valens and Sengle, requir-
ing no language, the very constraints of language will themselves
subsequently be troped in terms of a military regimentation. Thus,
for example, Sengle observes the alienation of language in its mim-
icking by deaf-mutes, whose very training foregrounds the systemic and systematizing function of all meaning: "It was mouths

militarily tamed for the convention of language that the little deaf-mute girls at Auray would watch closely before answering them with the geometry of a uniform gymnastics" (130).

Days and Nights: The Novel of a Deserter details the desertion of language. Indeed, as a conscious filter for the narrative voice, Sengle is, by the end, quite literally silenced, replaced by the disembodied authoritative voice of a medical report on his *manie fu-rieuse*. Language is itself that military service that Sengle seeks to escape, for the anus-mouth is unavoidably distended by the regimen of language. Language is presented—in this "uniform gymnastics"—as that which reduces the specific to the interchangeable, as that which, in other words, de-differentiates. Thus, the insistence on a diacritical paederasty—homosexuality as *différance*—is consistently threatened by the very regimen of language it sets up. Language—like the army—must be deserted: hence the silence between Valens and Sengle. Language as regimentation: such is the subtext of the entire novel, and the experience of con-scription should be read also as an experience of in-scription—the inscription of desire into an already existing symbolic regimen.

To return to the narcissistic scenario—to what Jarry refers to in a chapter heading as the reflective "silvering of the pond" (*Tain des mares*)—we can appreciate immediately how the paederastic Eros figures itself as a break with representationalism—as a break, that is, with the "binarisms" of representation and abstraction. For it is at the pond of narcissistic reflection that Sengle contemplates Valens in what is arguably the most openly homoerotic passage of the book: "His tawny-gold chest clicked gently against the flat water and for a brief glimpse his hips had a bronze tinge about them on the sides, like a faun not midway between man and beast, an athletic ephebe rather, worthy of casting in metal" (60). If Sedgwick argues in *Epistemology of the Closet* that the male body—as narrative content—"represented 'representation itself'" (166), Jarry obliges us to amend that observation and thereby escape the stigma of kitsch that Sedgwick sees applied to homosexual cultural production in the twentieth century. Now the male body represents not representation, but its impossibility—indeed, its irrelevance to the immanence of desire. The male body—in this alternative paederastic reinterpretation of Narcissus—does not represent representation, it figures figurality, breaking the mirror in which reflection is possible, yet effecting the impossible reunification of what lies above and what lies below the reflecting surface.[19] Whereas Mackay's homosexual was caught in the impasse of representation—obliged to drink, but doomed to die of thirst; bound to represent, but unrepresentable in the muddied waters—the most urgent image of desire in Jarry's novel pierces the "tain of the mirror," literally interposing the male body across the surface of reflection. Such desire ruptures the ultimately mimetological binarisms that frame even Sedgwick's analysis. As such, the practice of a homosexual avant-garde "figures" a break not only with an aesthetic of representationalism, but with the episteme of mimetology in general.

CHAPTER 7

Murder and Melancholy: Homosexual Allegory in the Postwar Novel

> Allegory goes away empty-handed. Evil as such, which it
> cherished as enduring profundity, exists only in allegory, is
> nothing other than allegory, and means something other
> from what it is. It means precisely the non-existence of
> what it presents. . . . By its allegorical form evil as such re-
> veals itself to be a subjective phenomenon.
>
> Walter Benjamin,
> *Origin of German Tragic Drama*

What does it mean to come to conclusions about fascism? Have we finished with that which is concluded—are we done with it? Does the very possibility of conclusion not itself acknowledge an internal logic by which any conclusion could be recognized as such? To draw conclusions about fascism, potentially, is to acquiesce to a self-serving fascist logic, in which fascism itself serves as conclusive proof.[1] I propose in this final chapter that the prevailing tactic of post–World War II culture has been to enclose fascism as the figure of an unclosable, irrational logic, and that it is through the trope of homosexuality that this enclosure takes place. What is at issue is not simply the alterity of fascism—that its homosexualization ensures from the perspective of a heterosexist critical theory—but the *nonproduc-tive* function of fascism that homosexuality is assumed to replicate. Homosexuality cannot (re-)produce a discourse of truth any more than fascism: yet as the negative representation (or allegory) of this radical negativity, the homosexual trope in fact opens up both it-self and fascism to the production of truth and meaning. As an al-legory of fascism, homosexuality re-presents an absence, and turns it into a loss. The structure of allegory (which—as we shall see—is itself used to figure the structure of a self-defeating homosexual desire) ascribes to fascism a meaning: meaninglessness.

If I focus on a novel—Moravia's *The Conformist*—in this in-conclusive chapter, I do so advisedly, for the novel itself has served—in this century—a particular function in the remembrance and forgetting of historical trauma. Benjamin, for example, has ar-gued—in his "Theories of German Fascism"—that the novel served a specific function in Germany's attempts to process the loss of World War I. After an initial stage of guilt—and prior to a final glorification of loss itself as the quintessentially German ex-perience—post–World War I Germans engaged in "the attempt to forget the lost war. The bourgeoisie turned to snore on its other side—and what pillow could have been softer than the novel?" (123). To what extent do novelistic remembrances of fascism serve likewise as a pillow, an attempt to forget? What is being forgotten in this process? These are the questions that frame this chapter.

I suggest that novelistic reappropriations of fascism serve for us today much the same purpose as World War I served for Ben-jamin's interwar bourgeoisie. Just as—in Benjamin's formulation—the fascists sought to ontologize loss (of the war) as the basis of a national identity, so we in turn see in fascism something that—in being lost to all adequate representation—defines the very condi-tion of our existence. Might a novel such as *The Conformist*—like those novels of the interwar years—mark no more than a midpoint wedged between guilt and the ontologization of loss? This is the broader question to be addressed here, in the context of a reflec-tion on postwar recuperations of fascism; but I hope also to dem-onstrate how Moravia's novel exemplifies a conflation of fascism and homosexuality that is far from arbitrary. If homosexuality is to be invoked as a vehicle for the representation of fascism, we need also to ask why fascism is invoked as the representation of an equally unrepresentable—"unspeakable"—homosexuality.

The form taken by novelistic "forgetting" is, as Benjamin suggests, the form of remembrance: what we forget in novelistic reconstructions of fascism is the incommensurability of novelistic form to authentic remembrance. We forget, in short, that we have forgotten. It is as if we had witnessed the passage of history into the modality of the sublime, in which we can talk only of its unrepresentability—even as history itself becomes unthinkable as anything other than a series of representations. We should notice a paradoxical conjunction here: the "crisis" of historical reflection is coextensive with the "reduction" of history to reflection and representation. History is at once pure representation and absolutely unrepresentable. Thus, if we can reflect on fascism—and if I, in turn, can reflect on the concerns of this book—we can do so only from the position of a certain revisionism that reinstates historical narrative as a discourse on the death (in fascism) of coherent narratives of history. If we can no longer represent a history that we in turn think of *as* a representation, are we ourselves potentially excluded from history? Is the task of the novel—in the terms of Lacoue-Labarthe and Nancy—an "appropriation of the means of identification" (299)? And, if so, must we acknowledge fascism as inaugurating an epistemological regime we still inhabit?

We might begin by returning to Benjamin's analysis of Germany's defeat in the Great War, where he asks, "What does it mean to win or lose a war? How striking the double-meaning is in both words! . . . To win or lose a war reaches so deeply, if we follow the language, into the fabric of our existence that our whole lives become that much richer or poorer in symbols, images and sources" (123). Losing the war means losing control of the means of representation. Whereas, however, this loss could still be recuperated in the interwar period as a *national* experience (and the nation thereby reconstituted as the collective of those experiencing a "loss" or lack) we now have lost even this radically negative discourse of nationalism. To acknowledge lack as the condition of (national) identity may threaten traditional philosophical discourses of the subject, but it also risks reenacting precisely those representational strategies we have come to identify with fascism. The first thing one loses in this loss of the "means of representation" (the echoes of Benjamin's "Work of Art" essay resonate here) is the very ability to represent that loss: Has a loss that cannot be represented actually taken place? Is it not, instead, an absence?

What, then, is to be gained by comparing that loss of World War I—analyzed by Benjamin as a constituent of protofascism— and the "loss" of Nazi crimes against humanity as the referent of either a juridical or an aesthetic representation? And what is the psychical structure underlying a novelistic forgetting that feeds into the celebration of loss as the ground of (national) identity? Given the rapidity with which the world found itself at war again after 1918, we might say that what ended definitively with that "war to end all wars" was a historical faith in definitive ends—a faith, that is, in a certain form of apocalyptic or even utopian history. The war to end all wars was, in fact, a war to end all ends. Meanwhile, what Lyotard has hypostatized in *The Differend* as "Auschwitz" seems to mark for contemporary theory both the totality of death (the genocidal idea of a death that will be complete and absolute, a "final solution") and the idea that death itself is not a totality; that there is something worse than death.

In novelistic forgetting, what is lost is loss itself. Rather, absence—that which undermines all attempts at constructing a self-present identity—is reconfigured in the novel as loss. Loss turns the original absence into a yet more fundamental presence that need only be regained. This presence, however, is not simply a fiction of plenitude: the protofascists in Benjamin's analysis do not ask themselves, "What if we had won the war?"—but inhabit absence as loss. It is the loss at the center of one's being that is "characteristically" German. One has "lost" the war precisely at that point where it becomes an absence, because the loss is unrepresentable.

The logic Benjamin suggests resembles the Lyotardian differend: one has no means of representing (juridically or, indeed, aesthetically) one's loss. Elsewhere, however (in the essay "The Sublime and the Avant-Garde"), Lyotard briefly suggests the distinction between a politics of the sublime, that—in Kaja Silverman's terms—"embraces lack," and a protofascist politics of the beautiful, in which ontological lack is relativized into a mere "loss" that will ultimately be made good. Benjamin seems to suggest an alternative political trajectory: for him fascism would consist in the ontologization of a (historical) loss (of the war), rather than in the historical relativization of an ontological lack. In his model, the Germans fall prey to fascism not in the denegation of their essential lack (as loss), but in their retooling of loss as essential lack. For Lyotard, protofascism seems to consist in the passage *into* a falsely redemptive history, whereas for Benjamin it consists precisely in the imaginary passage *out of* historical contingency.

This notion of a "loss of loss" is, in turn, fundamental to the structure of a melancholy described by Freud and invoked since World War II to define a putative historical condition. One theorist of Renaissance melancholy, Juliana Schiesari, has referred to a melancholic "suturing of lack and loss" clearly reminiscent of Benjamin's analysis, arguing that "The melancholic ego, in order to authenticate its conflicted relation between *innen* and *umwelt*, inner and outer world, is dependent on loss as a means through which it can represent itself. In so doing, however, it derealizes or devalues any *object* of loss for the sake of loss itself: a sort of suturing between lack and loss, an idealization of the loss that paradoxically empowers the ego" (42–43). This specifically literary and rhetorical analysis captures well, I think, the movement of Benjamin's analysis. In the reconstruction of a (national) identity, the very concept of "loss" is already recuperative: implying something that has been lost, it posits lack as the absence of a historical and ontological (or national) presence. More than this, however, the ontologization of loss ensures that loss can never be lost, since it becomes the very condition of national identity. If Benjamin has already identified this propensity in protofascist thought, the very same structure—this suturing of loss and lack—has also characterized post–World War II analyses of *responses* to fascism. I believe that the structure of melancholy marks not only the thematics of the particular novel in question here (as it clearly does), but the very relationship of the novelist to the project of representation in the wake of fascism.[2]

We need to be careful here. Clearly, any attempt to present melancholy as a historically conditioned psychical state partakes of the same idealist notion of history—the same subject-centered understanding of history—that has sought, elsewhere in this study, to cast homosexuality as a historically determined and determining pathology. I am proposing melancholy here not as a stage of history—as the psychical disturbance of a historical subject—but as the precondition of history, as that which renders any such historical subject inconceivable. Indeed, to hypostatize melancholy as a historical condition would be—in Benjamin's terms—to ontologize loss as the basis of an identity, to write a fascist history. I am no more suggesting, therefore, that fascism—or our own response to fascism—is somehow "melancholic" than I am suggesting that it is "homosexual." The structure of melancholy allows us to understand the process of (mis-)representation whereby we reconstruct fascism. I will deal with this question of melancholy in more detail in the reading of *The Conformist* to follow, but I would like at this point to insist on the ahistorical use that I make of the term here.

Freud distinguishes—in the essay "Mourning and Melancholia"—between a loss that is present to itself and a loss that has itself been lost; a loss, that is, in which we do not know what has been lost, or do not fully comprehend the significance of what has been lost. This second form of loss—the form I claim we encounter in representations of fascism—is the state of melancholy. Melancholia is clearly implicated in the phenomenon of "novelistic forgetting" posited by Benjamin. In Moravia's novel, for example, the homo-fascist protagonist Marcello will be possessed by a "melancholy that had pursued him from time immemorial" (220) as if it were the condition of melancholy that itself rendered time "immemorial." Moravia glosses Marcello's melancholy existentially as "a melancholy mixed with regret, such as is aroused by the thought of things that might have been, of things that the act of making a choice compels one to renounce" (220). In his presentation of melancholy, meanwhile, Freud foregrounds the question of loss, suggesting "that melancholia is in some way related to an object-loss which is withdrawn from consciousness" (*Standard Edition*, 14: 245). I would argue—on the basis of this definition—that the problematic of melancholy is clearly overdetermined with respect to fascism and its historical representation. For in this slippage from consciousness of loss—the slippage that turns mourning into melancholy—what is lost is not simply the object, but the experience of loss itself. Thus, we might reinterpret the process of adjustment analyzed by Benjamin in "Theories of German Fascism" as a therapeutic mourning: protofascism is "reactionary" precisely insofar as it regains its own loss and renders it the negative ground of an ideology of mourning.

At the same time, however, the historical inability to represent negatively suggests the sublimity of that which is to be represented. "Perhaps"—the protofascist logic of the interwar years would run—"I cannot represent myself because my Being is not of the nature of representation. The very inability to ground myself representationally establishes my groundedness in a historical real that is beyond or prior to representation." The loss of a symbolic structure facilitates the construction of an imaginary (or "imagined real") national identity. If one has lost loss, one perhaps never lost at all. Protofascist ideology, Benjamin contends, is the paradoxical "regaining" of loss: having lost the war both literally and as the ground of figuration, Germany regains that loss by reclaiming loss itself as the condition of the Germanic sensibility. In this sense, we might say that fascism both is and is not melancholic. For what the German has lost, he can name—that is, the war; and by turning this loss into an "inner victory," the protofascist German ontologizes loss.

This consideration of mourning and melancholy—the "suturing" of melancholic lack and the loss implicit in mourning—seems to have brought us some way from the question of sexuality. I would contend, however, that the question of mourning—a trope central to sociological analyses of the post–World War II sensibility—is intrinsically sexualized; that the desire for a restorative process of mourning will be figured repeatedly as a desired return to heterosexuality, as an antidote to a historically pathological melancholic homo-fascism. As we saw in Chapter 1, in *The Inability to Mourn* the Mitscherlichs quite explicitly identify mourning with a heterosexual loss of someone who "enriched me through his otherness, as man and woman can enrich each other" (27–28). The present political state (characterized here not as melancholy, but as the *resistance* to mass melancholia) results from a still unmastered, narcissistic (homosexual) attachment to the *Führer*. The Mitscherlichs at once repress homosexual melancholy, while paradoxically identifying the German problem as the repression of that melancholy. They posit a return to mourning—to heterosexuality—as a means of dealing with the fascist past.

It is not merely fascism, but the Germans' relation to it that is homosexual and narcissistic. The Mitscherlichs further note how "the German propensity for loving the unattainable so uncompromisingly that thereby the attainable is forfeited has been a recurrent theme of German history ever since the days of the Holy Roman Empire" (6). If *The Inability to Mourn* represents a political and historical desire for "working through"—for a restitution of the historical work of mourning—what I seek to stress in such thought is its complicity with that suturing of loss and lack found in fascist mentality. The Mitscherlichs once again ground the Germans' supposed love for the unattainable in the historical memory of the Holy Roman Empire: the lack at the heart of a political ideology becomes a mere (historical) loss on which national identity is grounded. This work of mourning, we might say, is the work of the novel as theorized by Benjamin: it is the forgetting of lack, the representation of lack as loss.[3]

This slippage of politics into a consideration of representation allows us, I think, to recast the homo-hetero / mourning-melancholia opposition in rhetorical terms. What we encounter in thinkers such as the Mitscherlichs is a desire for a political sym-

bolic that is itself intrinsically aestheticized—a "symbolics of loss,"
to use the problematic terms of that theorist of Renaissance melancholy quoted earlier. This symbolic rhetoric is invoked to
counter what we might, by way of contrast, call a politics of allegory. Take, for example, the following observation from *The Inability to Mourn*:

> After the enormity of the catastrophe that lay behind them, return to
> a traditional orientation was impossible for the German people. Tra-
> dition was the very thing the Nazi regime had most lastingly de-
> stroyed; and, in any case, it was a highly dubious tradition. What now
> survive are remnants of external habits, patterns of behavior and con-
> formisms that, like stage props, conceal a very inarticulated way of
> life. Moreover, these stage props are set up everywhere and give Ger-
> man political and everyday life a theatrical and unreal flavor.   (28)

On the surface, the Mitscherlichs are analyzing the rupture of a
political tradition—"a highly dubious tradition" for which they
have little sympathy. The analysis is itself couched in terms familiar from Benjamin's critique of the aestheticization of politics—a
critique that also opposed a certain notion of political theatrical-
ity. Nevertheless, I would contend that the Mitscherlichs typify another form of reaestheticization, the desire to return to a unified
political symbolic order. They mourn the loss of a coherent political subjectivity, the reduction of symbolic unity to "inarticulate"
"remnants" and "props," into a theatricalized and fragmented
public sphere. This state of political consciousness is what I will
later characterize as the politics of allegory, in which political syn-
tax becomes fragmented. Returning at the end of this chapter to
the question of allegory through the analyses of Benjamin, I will
show how the theatricalized allegorical function identified here
with both melancholy and homosexuality necessarily feeds into a
recuperative historiography, that—failing to see either in allegory
or in a narcissistic homosexuality a challenge to the rhetoric and
politics of identity—chooses instead, to *identify*, to identify, for
example, homosexuality with fascism.

   If the Mitscherlichs—in their own way—are concerned with
restoring a national identity, just as, in Benjamin's analysis, the

Germans of the interwar years were, Moravia clearly sees his novel *The Conformist* as caught within the self-same problematic. The writing of *The Conformist* seems to arise from precisely one of those reversals of defeat and victory that characterized Benjamin's analysis of protofascism. That the novel form makes certain assumptions about historical representability is a fact by no means lost on Moravia. In response to a question on just this topic, for example, he answers as follows:

> *Do you believe in the possibility of a historical and national novel? One, that is, which in some way represents the recent or not so recent achievements of Italy? In other words, do you consider it possible to reconstruct happenings and destinies that go beyond the individual, and are outside their historical time?*
>
>   I would like to answer this question by asking others. Is it still possible to believe in History? Can national histories still exist in Europe? And what *is* the history of Italy, teeming as it is with defeats that are victories, and victories that are defeats, with the Risorgimento turning into Fascism?[4]

Moravia's response is thematically rich. First, it acknowledges the political and national implications of novelistic discourse—implications made explicit in Benjamin's analysis of fascism. What Benjamin characterized as the protofascist distortion of national history seems—in the wake of fascism's defeat in Europe—to have become a definitive historical condition; or rather, a condition that forecloses the possibility of history. Moravia questions not only the possibility of history but, more specifically, the possibility of a *national* history. His comments nevertheless reinstate the possibility of a national representation at the same time as they seek to question it. He identifies *Italy* with the sense of crisis of representation: Italy is the place where victories become defeats and defeats victories. In other words, by the very same gesture that seems to question the integrity of history and the nation state, Moravia reinstates a concept of Italy as a mutation in historical consciousness. Crises of historical temporality—assumed at first to be synonymous with questions of geopolitical spatiality—actually displace themselves onto the quasi-spatial representation of nation.

   In light of our consideration of historical representability, it is important to stress this ideological move on Moravia's part: for if we have derived from Benjamin a model for understanding the novel as a reflection on history that serves to reinstate a potentially outmoded historical paradigm, Benjamin can also provide us with a model for understanding Moravia's pronouncements here. In their reflection on the Great War, Benjamin argues, the Germans "began with an effort to pervert the German defeat into an inner victory" and finally arrived at a mystic post-rationalization of defeat in "the novel assertion that it is precisely this loss of the war that is characteristically German" ("Theories of German Fascism," 123). Is it not a very similar illogic that Moravia seems to inhabit here? History—or at least *Italy's* history—consists of "defeats that are victories and victories that are defeats"; from the Risorgimento to Fascism, the geography and history of Italy are shaped by the ruse of History. In their loss of the war, the Italians in fact regain history—not the old teleological history, but the history of reversals. In other words, the Italians can now hypostatize the loss of the war—and the "loss" of history it entailed—as both a national reaffirmation and as a reconnection with history. At the moment it denies itself—at the moment it declares itself lost to history—Italy reaffirms itself, through a political inversion, as the locus of history's loss to itself.

Moravia's comments seem to imply that the possibility of nation and the possibility of narrative are so closely tied that the loss is, indeed, more radical; that it is more than a specific political loss (fascism's loss, democracy's gain). It is a loss to representation; the condition of unrepresentability. Whereas the Germans, according to Benjamin, ontologize the loss itself, Moravia embraces a notion of history—the history of Italy—in which it is not the loss, but the reversibility of loss and gain that forms the ontological and national ground. Italy, then, becomes the country that cannot posit itself as a historical subject in even the radically negated sense. The ontological ground of the nation is not a loss (as it is in Germany) on which a (negative) identity can be grounded; it is a certain position of historical irony (one is reminded of Marx's analysis of the Eighteenth Brumaire—Mussolini's reinvocation of ancient Rome as a repetition in comic form of a tragic historical origin). Or, one might say, the Italians have lost not only the war, but even the loss of the war: they have lost loss itself, and thereby find themselves within a certain historical melancholia. The reversibility that characterizes Italy's history negates even the radical negativity of the Nazi nation: one's negative origin might, after all, reverse itself into the partiality and contingency of history.

I seek here neither to conflate, nor to distinguish, Nazism and Italian fascism. Moravia is in no sense a protofascist, nor does he draw on the ideological stock of the interwar fascists, but his very attempt to represent (fascism) has involved him in that cyclical historical forgetting (of history) described by Benjamin. His presentation of the history of Italy as a history of reversals and inversions—of losses that prove themselves to be victories, and of victories that are subsequently lost—destabilizes for the postfascist novelist even that radically negative, loss-oriented ground of fascist representation. The model of history imposed in Moravia's presentation of postfascist Italy negates even the possibility of a radical negation. If my loss might subsequently prove itself a victory, I have lost even my loss as the starting point of a mimetic project. Thus, when Moravia speaks of the reversibility of Italy's history, there is no more absolute negativity than there is absolute positivity. It is loss (as a negative ground of identity) that has been lost—and it is within this melancholic situation that Moravia seeks to characterize the (im-)possibility of representing fascism. This historical loss of loss, I claim, marks a characteristically melancholy relation to history.

Even once we have isolated melancholy as a historical sensibility, however, we are faced with reconciling the structure of melancholy with the theme of homosexualized fascism. What is it about melancholy that seems to link the two structures? To what end is the homosexual instrumentalized in this melancholic relationship to history? Freud's essay certainly suggests a link by characterizing melancholy in a vocabulary that suggests the popular iconography of homosexuality. He notes, for example, that "in mourning it is the world which has become poor and empty; in melancholia it is the ego itself" (*Standard Edition*, 14: 246), and that, unlike the mourner, "one might emphasize the presence in [the melancholic] of an almost opposite trait of insistent communicativeness which finds satisfaction in self-exposure" (14: 247). Such feelings of diminished self-worth alongside a compulsive exhibitionism characterize not only the iconography of a popular homophobia but also, more subtly, the dialectical structure of homosexuality already encountered in Adorno and to be replicated in Moravia. We will recall from our consideration of Adorno: first, only repressed homosexuality is protofascist, but all homosexuality is self-repressing, and second, even in the act of self-repression the homosexual enacts his desire, which is a desire for repression and renunciation. Thus we have replicated in melancholia the essential structure of a fascisticized homosexuality that is insistently declarative even where it seeks (as it must) to renounce itself. Furthermore, Freud's conclusion "that the disposition to fall ill of melancholia (or some part of that disposition) lies in the predominance of the narcissistic type of object-choice" (14: 250) clearly reconnects melancholy to the homosexualized problematic of narcissism central to this book.

Critical theory—I would argue—has conflated a certain historical melancholy manifested in relation to the problematic of representation (of history) and a melancholic caricature of homosexuality, to the extent where homosexuality can stand in as a compromise formation for a historical condition of melancholy we can no longer escape. To put it bluntly: if we can represent the problematic of fascism through the psychology of the homosexual (the *only* way, it would seem, that Moravia feels such representation is possible, at least for him) then we have necessarily exempted ourselves from the all-embracing crisis of representation that we feared fascism had inaugurated. *The Conformist*—as a mimetic treatment of fascism—reassures on two levels. First, it reassures by homosexualizing fascism in the figure of its protagonist, Marcello, thereby opening up the possibility of a postfascist return to a political and (hetero-)sexual normalcy. It is as if the collapse of the progressive bourgeois public sphere were being identified with the emergence of homosexuality as a historically determinant character structure. Second, however—and more fundamentally—Moravia's project reassures by asserting the very possibility of *any* postfascist representation. By psychologizing fascism in individual terms, *The Conformist* retains categories of public and private that fascism itself has rendered anachronistic, and displaces the task of representation from the public to the private level. In other words, the novel does not merely promise a return to a representational system scrambled politically and sexually by fascism—it is itself the fulfillment of that promise. The novel forgets the very crisis of representation to which it supposedly attests.

If Moravia offers only further questions and inversions in response to that fundamental question regarding national representability, he elsewhere obliges with apparently straightforward answers. On certain questions, his position shows no sign of hesitation; as for example, when he is quizzed about the motivation behind *The Conformist*:

> *What are the historical facts behind* The Conformist?
> The Rosselli murders. Furthermore, I wanted to add to this what I myself had known of fascism. Everything depends upon the equation: the protagonist is a fascist because he is homosexual.
> This equation still seems true to me today: a fact that takes on a negative value on the individual level transforms itself (or thinks it does) into a positive value on the collective level. For example, d'Annunzio's decadentism is transformed into patriotism.[5]

In this form, Moravia's claim gathers together many of the themes that have run through this study, and I would like to isolate certain elements of his startling assertion (matched in its certainty, perhaps, only by Adorno's similar pronouncement in *Minima Moralia*) by way of résumé. We must note, for example, the structural analogy drawn to d'Annunzio (a rabidly *hetero*sexual protofascist, if ever there was one) as a way of identifying homosexuality with decadence. D'Annunzio's private vice (heterosexual decadence) becomes fascism, just as private homosexuality becomes public as fascism—therefore, we are to conclude that homosexuality is decadent too. Moreover, while it would be glib to accuse

Moravia of homophobia (and the trajectory of my argument here, indeed, would be to move beyond any such accusation and to examine the broader historical implications of his claims); it should also be noted that while the personal vice only thinks it is transformed into a public virtue, it does not only think it is a vice. Moravia's scrupulousness in disclaiming the public virtue of fascism serves to demonstrate the disingenuousness of an ideological ploy we have encountered several times: it is not simply unavowed homosexuality that is vicious and protofascistic. Homosexuality really *is* a "negative value."

It is also important to examine the context of the question and the structure of the response, which link—at least for Moravia— the question of homosexuality and the question of mimesis. The question has, in fact, been sparked by Moravia's description of the particular problem he posed himself in attempting to write *The Conformist*, when "once again I learned that it was impossible to write a novel on the basis of reality and historical fact."[6] Fascism endangers the mimetic project, but there is something in Moravia's passage from the aberrant "positive value" of fascism to the private vice, the "negative value" of homosexuality, that once again makes it possible to write a novel, and, more specifically, a novel about fascism. If fascism disfigures history and acquires an antirepresentational negativity, homosexuality—as the "negative value" on which it is supposedly based—serves as the negation of that negation, as the dialectical and determinate possibility of novelistic rerepresentation. It is this specifically dialectical process that we must note here: the negation of a negation that paradoxically identifies homosexuality and fascism. The homophobia of Moravia's novel is inextricably linked to a dialectical understanding of both history and narrative. It is the homophobia of the dialectic, at last, that we must confront in any examination of homosexuality and fascism.

For we begin to note a recurrent structure of inversion in Moravia's pronouncements. The Risorgimento becomes fascism, the private vice becomes a public "virtue," d'Annunzio's heterosexuality becomes protofascist homosexuality—and defeats become victories, victories defeats, in much the same way that they did for the interwar German protofascists. The logic of inversion employed by the critical novelist seems once again to parallel the logic of Benjamin's protofascists. Furthermore, we have already seen how Moravia's narrative fears are conditioned by a greater fear about the possibility of writing a history at all. Elsewhere in this interview, however, he offers a personal reason for the problems of representing fascism, accounting for the aesthetic limitations of *The Conformist* by referring to "my immaturity as a writer." Once again, the play of public and private reasserts itself—but this time in the novelist's reflection on reflection. Once again, a private weakness—the immaturity of Moravia—masquerades as public virtue. The private vice of his writerly immaturity in fact becomes the condition of possibility of a novelistic renaissance. *The Conformist* is not, then, a novel "about" homosexuality, nor, strictly speaking, a novel "about" fascism: homosexuality is only that "negative value" that makes possible the representation of the negative—fascism. In this double negation—the negative value that displays the negativity of the political—a newly positivized historical and political sensibility emerges in our confrontations with fascism.

I will later seek to explain this move both in terms of the representational episteme of melancholy and in terms of the dialectical negation of negation within which historical identities are narratively produced. Rhetorically, we confront the passage from allegory to symbol, from the recognition of a displacement (homosexuality for fascism, private for public, etc.) to the assertion of an identity (homosexuality *as* fascism). As the negation of that which negates representation, homosexuality gives the semblance of a presence, while avowing its imposture as a mere negation. Within the economy of representation, homosexuality pretends to be something it is not—pretends to be something that in turn pretends to be something it is not (i.e., fascism, a victory that is a defeat, or vice versa). In pretending to be a pretense, however, homosexuality actually replicates and reenacts—representationally—the original pretense it merely pretends to be. This identification of homosexuality and fascism—within the terms of a dialectical negation of negation, a double pretense reminiscent of those transvestites encountered by Lewis—lays bare the metaphysic of a representational system, lays bare, in other words, the very pretensions of representation. In its very *in*adequacy, homosexuality adequates representationally the "inadequate," negative historical nature of fascism. Something in the arbitrariness of the conjunction—homosexuality for fascism—replicates the perceived historical arbitrariness of fascism itself.

Of course, it might be objected that any representational conjunction could be invoked as equally arbitrary—as equally a negation of fascist negativity—and therefore we need to demonstrate how homosexuality comes to figure as *essentially* arbitrary. In our representations of fascism, homosexuality figures the accidental nature of a philosophy of essence. Through the prism of homosexuality, fascism appears as an inevitable accident. I will return to this logical paradigm when I examine the "primal scene" of *The Conformist*, in which the protagonist commits a murder. First, however, I wish to remain with those broader questions of nation and representation raised by the questions posed to Moravia and by the responses he gives. As a response to the question of whether it is possible to go "beyond the individual," *The Conformist* demonstrates the futility of any such movement "beyond." For in concentrating on the homosexuality of a single protagonist Moravia has rescued the project of mimesis only by means of reinstating the category of the private as the possibility of "public" representation. In other words, it is not simply a question of fascism being unrepresentable, but of homosexuality functioning as the medium of representation of the unrepresentable.

Homosexuality figures as an allegorical representation of the unrepresentable. Indeed, we might say that Moravia's diagnosis— "the protagonist is a fascist because he is homosexual"—not only serves to represent fascism, but also to undo its ideological pretensions. By presenting fascism in the private sphere as homosexuality, Moravia demonstrates the fact that fascism is, indeed, a "negative value" after all. Fascism is never as negative as when it is homosexual (because, of course, it is not homosexual). Thus, we can only conclude that within our entire problematic of homosexuality and fascism the relationship between the two will not have been one of historical causality, but rather of aesthetic recuperation. Fascism seeks not only its origin in homosexuality—but also its representation.

But why—in this distinction of public and private—should it be precisely homosexuality that provides the vehicle for the representation of fascism? In answering this question I think we can begin to address a recurrent theoretical ambiguity: whether it is repressed homosexuality or homosexuality per se that theory has understood to be protofascist. Again and again, where we have seen this distinction made, we have seen how homosexuality—despite the distinction—consistently reveals itself to have been always already repressed. For the writers in question the act of repression itself constitutes the structure of homosexual desire. In submitting (through repression) to the interdiction of his desire, the homosexual perversely enacts a desire to submit. In other words, homosexuality acts itself out in its nonfiguration; precisely when it denies itself, eschewing representation, homosexuality is present, enacts itself. Likewise, fascism seems to present itself only as a representational lacuna. The logic of this displacement is one that has already been intimated in Adorno's presentation of homosexual desire as a desire that enacts itself only in its very self-renunciation.

What does this structure mean for the relationship of figuration existing between homosexuality and fascism? It would seem that a desire that actualizes itself in its self-negation lends itself perfectly to a certain allegorical structure (homosexuality stands in for fascism) that then serves to establish a structure of identity (homosexuality stands for and as fascism). Precisely because the ruse of homosexuality is to enact itself even where it renounces itself, even when it is renounced in its specificity as a mere trope for the structure of fascist ideology, it remains homosexuality: it both "is" itself and that which it represents. Submission to the structure of the trope is but another example of the self-displacement and surreptitious self-fulfillment of homosexual desire. Homosexual desire "is," we might say, allegorical. Moravia will then use the differential structure of the trope to establish (through the double negation) a relationship not only of analogy, but of (motivated) identity. It is this second rhetorical gesture—the passage from the differential structure of the allegory to the identitarian logic of the symbol—that most clearly demonstrates the status of homo-fascism as the phantasm of a desire for presence. Homosexuality is the symbolic recuperation of an unrepresentable historical phenomenon, the (re-)presentation of absence.

But if there are structural and rhetorical reasons for the conflation of homosexuality and fascism, I wish to turn now to a consideration of the specific and substantive ways in which they are interwoven in Moravia's novel. What I propose here is a reading of *The Conformist* that examines its concern with the nature of historical ending—symbolized in the end of Mussolini's regime in Italy—through its interweaving of the discourses of sexuality and politics (or homosexuality and fascism). I aim to articulate in and through the psychoanalytic models of the authoritarian personality invoked by Moravia a necessary—and necessarily—historical mutation in our own understanding of history.

By using *The Conformist* as the point of departure for such a consideration, I seek to examine both the extent to which fascism ushers in a change in our historical sensibility, and the extent to which any such change is further attributable to a reconfiguration of the categories of sexuality. I wish to reflect on homosexuality as a compromise formation that enables the continuation of novelistic reflection. How does the homosexualization of fascism function in the recuperation of fascism for representability, in the recuperation, in fact, of the very possibility of historical representation *tout court*? Although I will contend that Moravia finally lends himself to precisely that logic of "novelistic forgetting" that Benjamin identifies with the historically somnolent bourgeoisie, my broader concern here will be with a theory of history centered around the crisis that is fascism and inflected by a theory of heterosexuality. Precisely because it questions notions of history traditionally troped heterosexually, fascism will be labeled homosexual.

The novel's "hero," Marcello Clerici, is first presented as a
sadomasochistic child from a disrupted family. He is isolated from
his friends both by an excess of masculine cruelty (significantly,
when Marcello seeks to involve his friend Roberto in a game of
killing lizards, "Roberto, in refusing his proposal, had invoked maternal authority in support of his own disgust") and by an excess of
physical femininity (he is teased and taunted as "Marcellina" by
his schoolmates). From the very outset, then, Marcello's pathology is presented in terms of a confusion of gender, a confusion in
which the extremity of one gender trait seems to have been exacerbated by traits of the opposite gender. There is something effeminate in his masculinity, something controlling and masculine
in his femininity. This confusion is elaborated—by a conflation of
effeminacy and homosexuality that is all too familiar—into a specifically sexual dilemma.

As a child, Marcello is "seduced" by Lino, the chauffeur from
a local villa—though both at the time and in later life he suspects
that he was more active than passive in this seduction. Lino lures
the child to his room, where he makes sexual advances to him,
only to recoil in shame, urging the none-too-reluctant child,
"Shoot, Marcello . . . kill me . . . yes, kill me like a dog" (64). Marcello complies, then steals away undetected. This encounter acquires all the importance of a primal scene in Marcello's subsequent development, as he seeks both to live up to the guilt he has
brought on himself and to make good the ostracization from bourgeois society that such guilt involves. Understandably, Marcello is
attracted by fascism, which responds to this double bind by rendering cruelty itself the norm: as a fascist he can both acknowledge and repudiate his guilt as a political and existential condition.
The body of the novel then concerns itself with Marcello's betrayal
of a former professor—an anti-fascist exile in Paris—and with his
compulsive linkage of the sexual and the political. (For example,
he combines his honeymoon with the assignment that will lead to
Professor Quadri's death. While he develops a passion for Quadri's
young wife, Lina, she in turn becomes enamored of Marcello's
own wife, Giulia.)

The historical backdrop of the novel's conclusion is the fall of Mussolini's government in Rome—a patriarchal fall that obviously also bears catastrophic implications for the fascist protagonist Clerici and his family. Marcello seems at once resigned and euphoric at the collapse of the regime, and—leaving his young daughter at home—takes his wife Giulia out into the streets of Rome to "witness . . . the fall of a dictatorship" (296). Fleeing Rome with his wife and young daughter, Marcello is waylaid by an Allied bomber, and the family is destroyed by this peculiarly twentieth-century deus ex machina.

We must first confront that scene of seduction, for it replicates in graphic fashion the same structure of homosexual desire that underpinned Adorno's analysis of the authoritarian personality. Although the child, Marcello, is clearly coquettish in his sophisticated response to the chauffeur's advances, it is in the shooting scene that we can discern once again the play of avowal and renunciation familiar from Adorno's analysis. Moravia describes the moment of the shooting thus: "In a manner that was both terrified and deliberate—just as though he felt he had to comply with the man's request—he pressed the trigger" (65). The shooting is profoundly ambiguous, functioning not only as the rejection of Lino's advances, but also as a compliance with the man's desire: Marcello does what is requested of him by shooting Lino. Thus the murderous act of denial (Marcello's denial of his own homosexual desire) is simultaneously an act of avowal, a profoundly sexual act. In its extreme form, the play of desire and renunciation supposedly at the heart of homosexual libido is a murderous desire—or, in Adorno's analysis, a desire that projects its own masochistic self-hate into a murderous sadism. Thus, for example, Marcello is active in the murder only insofar as he responds passively to Lino's desire. Where Adorno analyzes the interplay of renunciation and desire in homosexuality (in his desire to submit, the homosexual always enacts his desire in renouncing it) Moravia goes one step further, identifying this process with the act of murder. Sadomasochism thus fulfills an essentially homosexual and narcissistic function: the act that annihilates Lino as the embodied projection of Marcello's own desire is an act that acquiesces to the demands made by that desire—Lino's demand for death.

The relationship to Lino clearly dramatizes some of the aporias of homosexuality as envisaged by Moravia, and while that relationship seems caught in a structure of repression, we should remember that repression played no part in Moravia's initial dogmatic assertion: "the protagonist is a fascist because he is homosexual." Moravia assumes *all* homosexual desire is so structured. Lino is the figure who allows for at least the possibility of representing homosexual desire, as the alienated projection of the desire of Marcello himself. But the murderous rage toward Lino—a rage, remember, that actually replicates and is compliant with the structure of desire—is overdetermined. On the one hand there is the rage at the resurfacing—even in compromised and projected form—of the repressed desire; while on the other there is the rage at that which—through representation—has appropriated and displaced the subject's desire. The representation of (one's own) desire (in the other) threatens both to unmask the desires of the projecting subject and to deprive him of his desire. This, I think, is the sense in which what I will call the "allegorical" structure of homosexual desire operates. The desire of the other both "is" and "is not" mine ("is" mine, in fact, by not being mine, by repressing me as a desiring agent). On one level ("he represents my desire") there is a loss of desire; while on another level there is a loss of the (repressive) "loss" of desire, in the undoing of repression ("he represents my forbidden desire—and it is my desire"). In representing homosexual desire, then, the novelist is caught between a thematics of repression and loss and a further, double loss—that is, remembrance as a loss of that "loss" we call repression.

As must be apparent from the terms in which I frame my consideration of homo-fascist desire above, I feel that Moravia's novel articulates a notion of history—and of the function of desire in history—that is essentially melancholic, and that sees homosexuality as the allegorical vehicle for the representation of that melancholy. The "allegorical," self-displacing work of homosexual desire (as presented here) itself stands in an allegorical relation to a history thought in terms of reversals and displacements. Might, however, such melancholy—as a historical condition—itself be on-tologized as a national characteristic, or as a condition of Italian nationhood itself? In fact, Moravia's novel seems to suggest pre-cisely this, foregrounding as it does Marcello's relationship to his father and the possibility of a patrilineal historical narrative. In the reading that follows of Moravia's presentation of the Oedipal con-figuration, I wish to suggest that Moravia projects his own rela-tion to fascism into the phenomenon of fascism itself; the relations *to* the thing become the determining characteristics *of* the thing itself. In other words, the ideological working of an imaginary re-lation to real conditions allows us to rethink the very structure of reification as a mode of historical narrative construction. The re-lations that become things (reification) in our ideological recon-struction of fascism are our relations to the thing that those rela-tions have become. In other words, fascism becomes a privileged instance of historical projection in which we seek to represent and contain our own loss of historical experience.[7]

In *The Conformist* melancholia—as a loss of loss—is specifically thematized in terms of a possible rupture of the patrilineal inher-itance grounding the historical continuum. I wish, therefore, to spend some time now examining the scene in which Marcello—as a young adult—accompanies his mother on a visit to his father in an insane asylum; a scene in which the question of fascism and his-torical neurosis is posed most acutely. This episode "begins" with a curious *Nachträglichkeit*: we learn that Marcello's ghoulish and "cadaverous" (127) mother has a lover—her chauffeur, Alberi. Suddenly, the primal scene involving Marcello and Lino is dis-placed and reinterpreted by this "anterior"—though historically subsequent—relationship. The recurrent figure of the chauffeur clearly invites us to reinscribe the origin of Marcello's homosex-ual desire in terms of the Oedipal configuration: Alberi is / is not the father: the "murder" of that other chauffeur, Lino, is there-fore overdetermined. By "murdering" the chauffeur (Lino) Mar-cello both acts out and represses—through a logic that has become familiar—his own desire and reinscribes that desire in terms of a

traditional Oedipal (heterosexual) triangulation: he "kills" the
chauffeur who will have been the lover of the mother—that is, the
"father." Thus, the homo- and the heterosexual discourses of desire intersect: or rather, homosexual desire seems to figure as a misplaced libidinal reinvestment of the paternal relation. At the same
time, however, the fact that the connection Lino/Alberi/Father
is established only subsequent to the "murder" serves to question
the possibility of postulating any original desire, since the origin
will always already have been reconfigured from the perspective of
the mother's subsequent relationship. What would the mother's
desire for this chauffeur have told us about Marcello's (repressed)
desire for that other chauffeur? Are we to read Marcello's desire
as a desire for him who possesses the mother?

In fact, the figure of Lino anchors a whole sexual and symbolic
network that offers a glib libidinal framework for interpreting the
novel: Professor Quadri's wife, for example (desirous of Giulia and
desired by Marcello), is called Lina, as if she were a mere effeminization of the repressed first sexual partner. Again, Marcello's desire is for the desirer of the putative original object (the mother,
the wife). From our reading of Freud's "On Narcissism" in Chapter 2, we might say that Marcello's desire is the futile attempt of
the homosexual to place himself in the position of the subject of
desire: he desires to be the person who desires the proper object.
Thus, while the reconstructed triangle that passes through the
chauffeur Alberi might be reconciled with a traditional Oedipal
configuration, the desire for Lina—the desirer of his wife—cannot. In fact, the first Oedipalized configuration should be read in
the light of this second triangulation: Marcello "murders" the (homosexual) chauffeur/father, not because he desires the mother,
but because he does not. He seeks to inhabit the desire of the
chauffeur/father—as heterosexual desire—but cathects the position of desire homosexually (through Lino). In other words, homosexual desire reveals itself as the desire for (masculine) desire
and the recognition that the subject position of desire has been
evacuated. The homosexual is not a man because he *desires* (to be)
one.

Instead of entering into a consideration of the possibilities latent within the Oedipal structure with regard to its feminine object, however, it is important to concentrate on the functioning of the patrilineal and historical continuum within this "homosexualized" structure. I wish to demonstrate the way in which the Oedipal relation is deconstructed by this novel even where it seeks to maintain Oedipus as the interpretive touchstone for sexual normalcy. In a gesture that is not unfamiliar from other attempts to restabilize the political edifice after the collapse of fascism, Moravia seems to be offering the insanity of Marcello's father as a model for the political insanity of Italy under the fascists. Visited in the asylum, Marcello's father imagines himself to be minister of foreign affairs under the Duce (not, notably, the Duce himself—he has been displaced from the continuum of patriarchal representations). The father's delusion leads his doctor to comment:

> "But as far as the Duce goes, we're all just as mad as your husband, aren't we, Signora?—mad enough to need tying up, mad enough for treatment with the douche and the strait jacket . . . The whole of Italy is just one big lunatic asylum, ha, ha, ha."
>
> "In that way my son is certainly quite mad," said Marcello's mother, naively reinforcing the doctor's compliments; "in fact I was saying to Marcello, on our way here, that there were certain points of resemblance between him and his poor father." (144)

Of course the scene in the madhouse implies an apologetic assessment of fascism as madness—as historical aberration—but in Moravia's presentation this madness is not a momentary or passing historical neurosis, but involves a radical rethinking of history itself. The mother's unwitting confirmation of the doctor's psychopolitical diagnosis turns out to be all too glib, for in pointing out the similarities between Marcello and his father she asserts a continuity (a patriarchally inherited insanity) that insanity itself ruptures. This becomes clear when she goes on to explain the origins of the father's sickness:

> "The funny thing about it is," she went on, "that it was precisely with this idea of your being another man's son that your father's madness began . . . He had a fixed idea that you were not his son . . . And

> d'you know what he did one day? He took a photograph of me with
> you as a baby . . . " "And made holes through the eyes of both of us,"
> concluded Marcello.   (145)

The logic is confusing: Marcello's political "insanity" is predicated
on the fact that he *is* his father's son: whereas his father's insanity
originates in the idea that Marcello is *not* his son. Insanity is on
the one hand a patrilineal inheritance, and on the other the result
of a rupture in patrilineage. The one insanity, in other words, ob-
viates the cause of the other: if Marcello is insane because he is his
father's son, then his father's insanity is groundless.[8]

How are we to reconcile an interpretation of fascism that asserts a patrilineage ("I am insane politically because I am the son of
an insane father") with an interpretation that asserts the illegiti-
macy of such a lineage ("The father is insane because I am not his
son")? And where does this leave the "postfascist" novelist with
regard to a national or political patrimony? We might begin by
registering a displacement that has taken place in the father's identification with the mechanisms of fascist State power: he does not
imagine himself to be the Duce, but merely one of his minions.[9]
As minister of foreign affairs, indeed, the father has attempted to
place himself in the position of watchdog and supervisor of his
wife's "foreign affairs" and infidelities, regaining in insanity the
power he never held as a sane man. The delusion seeks to forestall
its own cause; by monitoring "foreign affairs" the father cuts at
the very root his own insanity. In this capacity, the minister of foreign affairs oversees his own displacement from the center of
power, from the patriarchal position. From the very "origin"
power is displaced—the father (even if he is the father) is not the
patriarch.

Insanity, then, results from the imagination of a break (in filiation), and perpetuates itself (in fascistic political form) in the acknowledgment of a continuity. The Oedipal configuration is at
once impossible and ineluctable in this novel. Impossible—as we
have already seen—because the father is always decentered: but ineluctable also—as I hope to show now—because it enacts itself
even in the act that marks that historical displacement. In *The Con-*

formist, the law of the father—enacted in castration—itself becomes profoundly ambiguous. We see this most clearly in the case
of the mutilated photograph. The mutilation of the photograph
demonstrates the ways in which the law enacts itself in the very
moment of its potentiary abdication. Even where the gesture of
violence seeks to express the breakdown of the patriarchal construct—a historical rupture—the aggression itself reconnects the
disaffiliated son with the structures of power. In mutilating the images of wife and "son," the father disowns both. The symbolic castration enacted in the piercing of the eyes takes place precisely because the father does not acknowledge the Oedipal filiation of this
non-son. The father "castrates" the son because he is not the son:
castration now denies rather than affirms the patrilineage. In this
sense, the mutilation is not a symbolic castration, but a castration
from castration.

Nevertheless, the violence done to the son in the photograph—
a gesture of *dis*inheritance—serves yet to reenlist the son into the
paternal symbolic order that castration inaugurates. In other
words, precisely by acknowledging the rupture of the patrilineage
(a purely imaginary rupture, since Marcello *is* his father's son) the
father paradoxically reinstates it. The act of mutilation that sought
to exclude Marcello from the symbolic continuum takes the form
of a castration—an induction into precisely that symbolic order.
Indeed, we should stress that the mutilation in this case is of a photograph—that is, of an iconic representation of the child—and is
therefore doubly ambiguous. This act of frustration at the collapse
of the patriarchal and symbolic continuum can only act itself out at
the level of the imaginary. Any rupture with the father, any rupture with fascism, any rupture with history becomes ideological in
its purely imaginary assault on the symbolic and social order. Might
we then conjecture that Moravia—the post- and anti-fascist—is
himself caught—as a producer of novelistic representations—in the
same ambiguous position to fascism as Marcello occupies with regard to his father? Is the disaffiliation that allows him (and us) a
critical, mimetic distance effected by a historical mutilation that
reenlists the novel into the episteme of its own representamen?

In fact, as we have seen, the Oedipal configuration no longer provides a framework for comprehension in *The Conformist* (as Moravia would like to pretend) but is itself subtly deconstructed, though not destroyed. Are we then to question the Oedipal meta-narrative of (dis-)affiliation that frames our own relation to fascism? Whereas Moravia consistently suggests that both homosexuality and fascism result from distortions in the functioning of Oedipus, *The Conformist* actually demonstrates the ineluctability of such malfunctionings as the condition of possibility of Oedipus itself. In other words, Oedipus is shown to function precisely by virtue of its breakdowns; and likewise, fascism (if it is, indeed, the effect of such breaks) proves itself latent within the supposedly stabilizing, normalizing—heterosexual—structures of Oedipus. Paradigmatically, the symbolic mutilation of the photograph that sought to represent the rupture of the patrilineage, itself acts as a symbolic castration, enacting the very patrilineage whose nullity it sought to represent. It is this passage into representation, specifically, that necessarily recuperates that which is beyond representation—fascism.

But what kind of representational system might we inherit from this insane (non-)father? In Marcello's case the very word of the father—the word of law, the word of the Duce—has been reduced to a schizophrenic logorrhea, to "an imaginary occasion of speech-making and ceremony" (140). It is as if Moravia were dramatizing—in the ranting of the father—the impossibility of representation: language loses its denotative function and becomes "occasional" performance or "speech-making." Clearly, this uncoupling of language from its denotative function problematizes our own relation to fascism: for if language is but a speech-making—a performance—our own attempt to recontain fascism at the level of the referent must fail. The inability to contain fascism or insanity as a referent within the denotative function leads us to question the status of the novel itself as just such a representation and containment. For even as speech becomes performance rather than denotation, it seems to lose its symbolic capacity for making sense (the father is, after all, insane) by becoming an "*imaginary* occasion"—an occasion, that is, *of* the imaginary. Might the novel itself become an enactment rather than a description of this imaginary? Might the very attempt to represent fascism implicate us in the same imaginary structures? Suddenly, the question of inheritance—am I the father's son or not?—becomes crucial. Just what would be the implications of this confrontation with the father for the project of "postfascist" representations of fascism? Does Moravia's own ideological projection in the reconstruction of fascism itself restate the centrality of fascism to our own imaginary repertoire? It is as if fascism refused to constrain itself at the level of topos and threatened constantly to structure the very modality of our representational thought. The problem will be: how to have done with fascism? And this will be a question of endings, a question raised in the motto of Marcello's father: "Murder and melancholy is his motto," said the doctor. "You'll find it written on all these sheets. . . . He has a fixation about these two words" (142).

If a reading of *The Conformist* encourages us to examine the (anti-)historical sensibility conditioning the emergence both of fascism and of a discourse on fascism through the tropology of melancholy, I should emphasize that we examine melancholy not as a way of psychologizing social and historical phenomena, but rather as a way of thinking their passage into (or out of) representation. Clearly, the melancholy inherited from Marcello's father is to be understood as a system of representation that challenges the symbolic order of a national culture, while performing the possibility of a new "imaginary" nation. If we seek—in psychoanalytic terms—to suggest here an opposition of "symbolic" and "imaginary," we should also invoke—at the level of a rhetoric—the parallel opposition of "symbolic" and "allegorical." For the trope of melancholy informing both Moravia's novel and sociological studies of post–World War II Germany also suggests its own representational system; a system identified—in Benjamin's work on melancholy in *The Origin of German Tragic Drama*—with allegory.

How, then, are we to sketch a relationship of allegory to the workings of a political imaginary? How would the figure of the homosexual facilitate the drawing of such parallels?[10]

Moving to conclude both this chapter and the broader project of this book, I wish to return to that "allegorical" structuring of homosexual desire outlined earlier in this chapter—whereby homosexual desire was supposed to submit itself happily to displacement, and even to its own displacement as mere tropological function. I wish to read homosexuality, in other words, not through the pathology of melancholy, but through the rhetoric of allegory. Could it be that there is in the allegorical instrumentalization of homo-fascism a moment of truth, a recognition of precisely that nonidentical Adorno sought in response to totalizing philosophical schemata? Might there not be in the structure of homosexuality a movement beyond the politics of identity (the politics, that is, of personal and national identities) that scandalizes a political and aesthetic order built on dialectical notions of sublation? In the face of such utopian possibilities, I wish to show instead how the putatively "allegorical" nature of homosexual desire—and the instrumentalization of homosexuality as allegory for fascism—have in fact served to reconstruct a failing symbolic order, in which the allegory necessitated by a collapse of the unified, embodied subject is necessarily resubsumed in a symbolic logic of identity. This recuperation, I will argue, is endemic to the structure of allegory.

Benjamin's consideration of melancholy and allegory in *The Origins of German Tragic Drama* suggests the allegorical instrumentalization of homosexual desire in representations of fascism, when he argues that "the allegorically significant is prevented by guilt from finding fulfilment of its meaning in itself. Guilt is not confined to the allegorical observer, who betrays the world for the sake of knowledge, but it also attaches to the object of his contemplation" (224). Benjamin's formulation of this "guilty" allegory is clearly reminiscent of that constellation of homosexual desire elaborated theoretically in Adorno and exemplified in Moravia's description of the homo-fascist seduction in *The Conformist*. Homosexual desire is "allegorical" precisely insofar as it "cannot find its fulfilment in itself" but only in the renunciation of itself. If homosexuality will serve as an allegory of fascism, this will be possible only because it is itself already predisposed to such allegorical displacements. Fulfillment for the homosexual consists in the very insignificance that allows him to be filled—passively—with meaning. His desire is to be so fulfilled, for he can find no *self*-fulfillment. Implicitly, we are asked not only to believe that fascism finds its "meaning" in homosexuality, but also that homosexuality somehow finds its meaning and fulfillment in fascism.

Elsewhere de Man has characterized the traditional function of allegory as the bearer of nonidentity in the following terms: "Whereas the symbol postulates the possibility of an identity or identification, allegory designates primarily a distance in relation to its own origin, and, renouncing the nostalgia and the desire to coincide, it establishes its language in the void of this temporal difference. In so doing, it prevents the self from an illusory identification with the non-self, which is now fully, though painfully recognized as a non-self" (207). De Man's observation that allegory renounces "the nostalgia and the desire to coincide" and "establishes its language in the void of this temporal difference" will surely remind us of Jarry, for whom nostalgia took the form of a paederastic celebration of embodied temporal difference. De Man "fleshes out"—literally perhaps—my assertion of a homosexual avant-garde tradition (of allegory) opposed to the symbolic identity logic of modernism. Indeed, Benjamin quotes Creuzer as a way of demonstrating the traditional valorization of the symbol at the expense of the allegory. Creuzer differentiates symbol from allegory by arguing that "the latter signifies merely a general concept or an idea which is different from itself; the former is the very incarnation and embodiment of the idea. In the former a process of substitution takes place. . . . In the latter the concept itself has descended into our physical world and we see it itself directly in the image" (de Man, 164–65).

The process of embodiment—the sensualization of the idea—has functioned as the privileged model of literary and cultural production since the end of the eighteenth century, notwithstanding the ambiguities in Romanticism outlined by de Man. If de Man's invocation of "nostalgia" throws us back on Jarry, Benjamin's citation of Creuzer surely returns us to the question of kitsch and representationalism foregrounded by Sedgwick. If, as Sedgwick claimed, the male body comes to stand for the representational object par excellence for a modernist aesthetic that eschews and stigmatizes all representation, then the modernist tradition will itself be obliged to revisit the traditional opposition of allegory and symbol. For the basis of the privileged symbol lies, in Creuzer's formulation, in its propensity to embodiment. If modernism rejects the (sensualized, homosexualized) male body, it does so because it senses that even bodies have now become mere allegory; the body is no longer capable of transcendent meaning. Antirepresentationalism, then, is not an attack on bodies per se, but an attempt to avoid recognizing the loss of meaning of bodies.

We, however, must face those problems inherent in the tradition of embodiment. For, as de Man points out, Coleridge's assertion that "the symbol is characterized by the translucence of the special in the individual" necessarily implies that "the material substantiality dissolves and becomes a mere reflection of a more original unity that does not exist in the material world" (192). The valorization of the symbol in terms of an "embodiment" always served, in fact, to *destroy* the body in its materiality, or, at least, to sublate it into a higher unity—the Idea, perhaps, of the body. Allegory, meanwhile—the modality of Jarry's nonidentical, paederastic desire—in its refusal to sublate the embodiment into that which it embodies respects the materiality of the bodily signifier, as Benjamin points out. Historically, this physicality has taken two forms. First, as exemplified—in Benjamin's presentation—by Winckelmann:

> Winckelmann still has this penetration of vision in the *Beschreibung des Torsos des Hercules im Belvedere zu Rom*: it is evident in the unclassical way he goes over it, part by part and limb by limb. It is no accident that the object is a body. In the field of allegorical intuition the image is a fragment, a rune. Its beauty as a symbol evaporates when the light of divine learning falls upon it. The false appearance

of totality is extinguished. For the *eidos* disappears, the simile ceases
to exist and the cosmos it contains shrivels up.   (176)

The physicality of the bodily signifier depends on its nonsub-
lation into the whole, even into that whole that is the body. Thus
Winckelmann—a figure whom Benjamin employs to display the
persistence of the allegorical even within the classical valorization
of symbol, but whom we are obliged, in this context, to read as a
cipher for the homosexual subversion of a national culture even at
the moment that culture is being established—is reduced to an
anatomical description of limbs. Again, this dismemberment (obviously a problem for any representational aesthetic that seeks to
re-member fascism) will be familiar to us. It was the very stuff of
Haug's critique—in our introductory chapter—of prurient homo-
fascist aesthetics. Such an aesthetic, we will recall, cannot represent whole bodies, but only members and limbs—*Glieder*—and
this inability clearly derived, for Haug, from the masculinist homosexual origins of that aesthetic, origins revealed in fascism's supposed fascination with *das Glied*—the phallus. Fascist aesthetics—
for Haug—were not phallic/symbolic, but rather phallic/allegor-
ical. That is to say, the phallus was always reduced to the level of
Glied and the totality based on it always a partial totality. This implicit distinction in Haug's argument is important, I think, because
it demonstrates the ways in which a phallogocentric heterosexual
homophobia has managed to reject homosexuality as masculinist
while itself retaining all the phallic privileges of representational
hegemony.

Benjamin will invoke the death's-head as a figure for allegory's
murderous assault on the unified symbolic body, but if allegory
serves to dismember the embodied subject, it serves also as the vehicle of its resurrection. The self-differentiating allegory offers as
the object of its allegorical representation an image of the self-identical subject. To revert to the parallel psychoanalytic terms we have
invoked in this chapter, the allegorical displacement of the "symbolic" serves to create an "imaginary" subject. The homosexual—
I would argue—is emblematic of such subjectivity in his guise as

homo-fascist. For the homosexual will be figured as a purely imaginary subject—a subject who merely imagines himself a subject, a subject lacking any object—and whereas allegory serves rhetorically by its very in-adequacy to the object it represents, it nevertheless serves as the adequate representation of the essentially inadequate homosexual.

In fact, the ultimate irony will lie in the fact that the homosexual comes to embody—in *The Conformist*, but also, I think, for almost any attempt to think fascism as a libidinal construct—precisely that regenerative and redemptive historical logic he supposedly undermines. The homosexual undermines the dialectical logic of an intrinsically heterosexual history, and yet it is he alone who will enable Moravia to undertake the writing of a novel about fascism. As allegory of an essentially "allegorical" attack on the symbolic logic of history, the homosexual necessarily posits—in this allegory of allegory, this negation of negation—the possibility of a dialectically regenerated symbolic logic.

If a symbolic recuperation of history is impossible, and if the homosexual (dis-)embodies that impossibility, the allegorical instrumentalization of homosexuality in the representation nevertheless necessarily creates the semblance of a symbolic order. As Benjamin points out: "And this is the essence of melancholy immersion: that its ultimate objects, in which it believes it can most fully secure for itself that which is vile, turn into allegories, and that these allegories fill and deny the void in which they are represented, just as, ultimately, the intention does not faithfully rest in the contemplation of the bones, but faithlessly leaps forward to the idea of resurrection" (232–33). Allegory always supposes a deferred realization, a resurrection and redemption of fallen reality. Yet in *The Conformist*—which I read now as paradigmatic of any attempt to represent fascism—any such regenerative or redemptive power has been lost to the heterosexual dialectic of history. In turning now to the two "conclusions" of *The Conformist*, I seek to show how the homosexual interference with novelistic closure will itself be reworked into a transcendence of closure. The homosexual Lino—*Pasqualino*, the child of Easter—serves both to interrupt a historical ending explicitly coded in (hetero-)sexual terms, and to transcend the historical apocalypse of fascism, resurrecting the possibility of novelistic representation.

Questions of fascism's unrepresentability have been well rehearsed, and we shall not return to them here. Rather than developing a general theory of posthistorical, postfascist sensibilities, let us return to the premise of this "concluding" chapter: namely, that it is the very possibility of conclusion and closure itself that is at stake in the historical representation of fascism. I would like to offer as a hypothesis that fascism marks the impossibility of historical conclusion and, consequently, of a "meaningful" history, and that novelistic "forgetting" would be the reinstatement of ending and closure, not simply in order to "have done with" fascism, but to resuscitate a myth of finite history. Further, it has been my contention throughout this book that the twinning of the political crisis of fascism and the sexual crisis of homosexuality responds to an anxiety about the precise nature of conclusion—or historical closure—itself. In short, the historical mutation that is/was fascism necessarily scandalizes a bourgeois historical consciousness invested either in (reproductive) notions of progress, or in eschatological notions of historical (and sexual) climax—a history structured, that is, around tropes of heterosexuality.

If these two historical tropes—reproduction and climax—suggest a particularly sexual historical itinerary, they allow us to think of historical representation as itself invested in the tropological structure of heterosexuality. In making this argument, I build on Jean-Joseph Goux's observation—in *Symbolic Economies*—that "there is a spectacular congruence—too close-fitting to be accidental—between the logic of the sexual itinerary *from a mother to a woman* and the course of social history according to Engels: from nature as mother to a different, transformed nature" (239). Even in its materialist form—comprising "a multiphased shift from inclusion in nature as mother, through a separation, and finally to an inclusive reciprocity with the *other* nature"—Goux argues that the prevalence of the dialectic ensures that "human history through the present has been limited to the history of *man*: history is masculine" (241). More fundamentally, however, Goux's thesis serves to demonstrate how this historical gendering is thinkable only within the technē of heterosexuality, for he questions the subject of history, but not the heterosexual compact within which that subject is created.

Tracing a phylo- and ontogenetic movement from the mother (*mater*, material, nature) through a cultural rupture and back to a recoupling with the feminine beyond the limitations of the maternal, Goux points out that the subject of history has always been thought—from a dialectical perspective—as masculine. But his own project of a move beyond phallic to genital sexuality does little to unsettle this masculine subject: he at no point addresses the heterosexism of the model he analyzes (and eventually buys into). While acknowledging that "each mode of exchange of vital activities, corresponding historically to a given mode of relations of material exchange, determines a dominant type of neurosis" (82), he never acknowledges the status of homosexuality as the sexual crisis of the general equivalent, as the resubjection of the phallus to the economy of pleasure. It is my contention that Moravia likewise needs heterosexuality not simply as *a* norm, but as the very condition of normativity. The desire to identify fascism—an unrepresentable historical catastrophe—with homosexuality is motivated by the threat that homosexuality also necessarily poses to structures of representation; structures dependent on the exclusion of the phallus from the symbolic economy.

The Conformist, a novel with two endings—or rather, a novel that articulates two senses of an ending, two senses (if this is possible) of "the end"—desires "heterosexual" historical closure as an intrinsic structural element of the dialectic. More than this, it demonstrates the frustration and impossibility of that desire—in the return of homosexuality. Of course, it would be foolish to propose some alternative idealist system—a homosexual alternative—to traditional notions of history, but it is nevertheless important in this last chapter finally to move beyond the culturally prevalent identification of homosexuality and fascism to a consideration of what it means to inhabit a world in which heterosexuality no longer makes sense of history. What does it mean to inhabit a world in which birth has been degraded to a eugenic exercise and death rationalized as an industrial process? With the death of what Lyotard calls "beautiful death"—in which I transcend my own death through subordination to a higher principle—what kind of life is left to us?[11]

Rather, what kind of life is left to the heterosexual family as the fundament of a historical and political dialectic perhaps most coherently expressed in Hegel's *Philosophy of Right* and most viciously realized in the homophobic genocidal project of Nazism? What is left for Marcello and Giulia? This is the question that resonates at the "conclusion" of *The Conformist*, as the former fascists confront the collapse of their world. Having left her home with Marcello to witness the fall of the dictator, Giulia seems oddly divorced from her fears for the future, and finally proposes:

> "Come and let's make love here . . . on the ground. . . . Everyone thinks about war, and politics, and air-raids—when they could really be so happy . . . Come on . . . Why, I'd do it right in the middle of one of their public squares," she added with sudden exasperation, "if only to show that I, at least, am capable of thinking about something else . . . Come on." She seemed now to be in a state of exaltation, and went in front of him into the thick darkness amongst the tree-trunks. "You see what a lovely bedroom," he heard her murmur, "Soon we shan't have a home at all . . . but this is a bedroom they can't ever take away from us . . . We can sleep and make love here as often as we like." (304)

The moment is one of sexual release, as well as of a release from the conjugal, socially reproductive, implications of the sexual act. Even as the enclosed space of the familial home is questioned—"soon we shan't have a home at all"—the sexual act itself effects a novelistic and libidinal closure. The heterosexual coupling in this "conclusion" is nothing more than that—a sexual rather than reproductive act. It is that practical coitus, no more no less, of the Hegelian dialectical imaginary.

The "second" ending of the novel is apocalyptic in a much

more obvious and traditional sense, articulating a model of historical finitude that is less provisional, less momentary: Marcello and his family are fleeing Rome when

> at that moment, from far away, the roar of the aeroplane as it turned became loudly audible again. He said to himself: "Oh God, let them not be hit—they are innocent"; and then he waited, resigned, face down in the grass, for the plane to come back. The car, with its open door, was silent, and he had time to realize, with a sharp pang of pain, that no one would now get out of it. Then at last the plane was right above him; and it drew after it, as it receded into the burning sky, a curtain of silence and darkness. (317)

In the shift from the first to the second ending, we have clearly moved to a more satisfactorily apocalyptic finale. Is this, perhaps, Lyotard's "beautiful death" in which the innocence of the victims paradoxically reasserts the unfathomable transcendence of the law and preserves the immortality of the victims who thereby enter the law?

Why the two endings? What is it that defers the completion of the orgasmic *petite morte* of a sexual coupling and necessitates the melodramatic finale of death and destruction? Why this move from the *petit récit*, in other words, to the grand narrative of unfathomable retribution and transcendence? I would argue that the relationship between these two endings depends on an ambiguity of difference and identity. The heterosexual coupling—devoid of any procreative function, any excess that might outlive and mark it—prefigures the apocalyptic death at the hands of the Allies. This "orgasmic logic," as one might call it, implies absolute closure and finitude: it will be public, but no one will witness it; there will be nothing beyond it to name it as closure. But of course there is something beyond it—that second, "apocalyptic" ending that, in reiterating and completing the orgasmic *petite morte* on a grand scale, undoes the work of the coupling—for the erotic figure of finitude is revealed as inadequate, as mere figure. Heterosexuality functions as a figure for historical closure, but loses its figurative power in the subsequent literalization of that which it figures. The novel's conclusions dramatize a crisis in the representational possibilities of heterosexual narrative: as a figure for historical closure, heterosexuality has become—literally—"inconclusive."

These two endings, then, rehearse the possibilities of historical ending already shown—through our consideration of Goux's work—to have been coded sexually: the practical coitus and apocalyptic destruction. Implicit in Giulia's sense of liberation, however, is an attempt to position the Hegelian imagination of an absolute, nonreproductive ending in opposition to a fascist ideology of totalitarian completion; to oppose, in other words, heterosexuality and fascism. This is a "practical" apocalypse, physical and partial rather than totalizing and transcendent, but it is—nevertheless—caught within the gendered heterosexual terms of the dialectic outlined by Goux.

I am omitting, however, perhaps the most crucial narrative moment in the transition from this first "death" to the second. The coupling of Giulia and Marcello, the simple coitus is, in fact, a *coitus interruptus*, for Marcello and Giulia are discovered by the park-keeper—Lino, who had not, in fact, died in the shooting incident. Moravia seems to acknowledge the impossibility of a return to any "beautiful death" (for is not the *petite morte* of orgasm the erotic expression of a beautiful death?) in the narration of a coitus interruptus. This time, it is Lino, the supposedly dead homosexual seducer from Marcello's past, who accidentally stumbles on the couple. The Hegelian idyll of a practical coitus is interrupted by the aberration of homosexuality no less than by the stifling conformity of fascist morality. Fascism seems, at the very least, to have foreclosed the possibility of a "reproductive" ending to the novel, a regeneration. Yet, as we have seen, the allegorical deployment of Lino, the homosexual seducer identified with Marcello's fascist sensibilities, serves the purpose of a narrative resurrection. As Moravia points out, it was only possible to write a novel about fascism from the perspective of the (homosexual) individual. What we might call the "reproductive" function of narrative—the function of representation—now falls not to the hetero- but to the homosexual.

We move in our conclusions only between the apocalyptic *pe-*

tite morte of coitus and its theatricalized realization in the form of a heavenly, yet nontranscendent retribution. But the conclusion of *The Conformist* is—as we have noted—about a resurrection, a rising from the dead. For it is Lino who returns from supposed death, and whose return allegorizes, in effect, his own allegorical function. His return is an allegory of the redemption from allegory.[12] Lino—*Pasqualino*—rises again; the death of Italy in one historical guise is redeemed in this imaginary Easter, this defeat that is a victory, this victory that is a defeat. This historical reversibility—this *inversion*—is a purely homosexual redemption from homosexuality.

Thus, the homophobia of the heterosexual political imaginary only *begins* with the identification of homosexuality with fascism as a historical rupture. It is completed with the recruitment of homosexuality to the task of historical and aesthetic recuperation, at the point where it is the homosexual alone who can generate narrative for a sterile hetero-logics of historical redemption. In other words, we might work with the fiction of homosexuality as allegory, but must resist the temptation of homophobic theory to subvert the nonidentical structure of allegory to the symbolic purposes of identification. If de Man's formulation brings us full circle to that structure of nonidentity suggested at the conclusion of our work on the Frankfurt School, the point is not to identify homosexuality with the nonidentical, but to engage in the *work* of nonidentification. For the logic of identification is precisely the logic that first conflated homosexuality and fascism. As Klaus Mann points out in the epigraph to this work: "we are not very far from *identifying* homosexuality with fascism" (my emphasis).

If we grant that heterosexuality serves to trope a certain dialectical notion of historicity (and this, of course, is Goux's problem; in retaining the dialectic, he fails to question heterosexuality), we must account for the historical crisis represented by a fascism—compulsively troped as homosexual—that seems to have ushered in, if not a homosexual, then at the very least a narcissistic episteme. Dialectically conceived, "heterosexual" history turns on two tropologically privileged moments: on the one hand, what we might call "reproductive history," the history, that is, of progress; and, on the other, what Goux sees in Hegel's imaginary construction of "a practical coitus, no more and no less, of masculine and feminine" (234). This latter we might call "orgasmic history." To think fascism within either of these paradigms would, of course, be highly problematic. Are we to "reproduce" and represent fascism? (raising questions of representability and the re-production of truth); or do we assign it to the realm of the orgasmic? (as a *jouissance* that constitutes the beyond of representation). It is this second option, of course, that constitutes precisely the temptation of a (sexual) aestheticization, a succumbing to the seductions of a "fascinating fascism." No, clearly the political challenge presented by fascism obliges us to think beyond the limits of a heterosexual history, to think—can one even say it?—"homosexually."

Reference Matter

Notes

Chapter 1

1. Reference to the historical works consulted as background to this book can be found in the bibliography. Of particular interest and importance, however, for my partial reconstruction of a historical milieu are the works of Stümke; Stümke and Finkler; Hohmann's *Der unterdrückte Sexus*; Lauritsen and Thorstad; Lautmann; Schilling; Sievert; and the collection *Eldorado*. Important original documents from the homosexual emancipation movement for the period in question can also be found in collections edited by Steakley and by Hohmann (*Der Eigene*). Further information on the persecution of homosexuals under Nazism can be obtained from Bleuel; Consoli; Heger; Herzer's essay on homosexual resistance fighters; Jellonek; Plant; and Rector. I draw heavily on the work of Stümke and of Stümke and Finkler in this chapter. Quotations from non-English sources throughout the book are in my translation unless otherwise indicated in the bibliography.

2. I deal with each of these particular instances in greater or lesser detail in this chapter or elsewhere in the book. Sedgwick's work will be particularly important in Chapter 6, but otherwise provides categories central to the book as a whole. Adorno will be considered in detail in Chapter 2. For a consideration of the problem of the "pinko," however—an issue not treated in this book, other than in the context of theories conflating homosexuality and all forms of totalitarianism—see the work of Hoch.

3. Nachman, "Genet: Dandy of the Lower Depths," 369.

4. The problem of "psychologizing" fascism has been commented on in widely differing studies. In *The Origins of Totalitarianism*, for example, Arendt complains that "we attempt to understand the behavior of concentration-camp inmates and SS-men psychologically, when the very thing that must be realized is that the psyche *can* be destroyed even without the destruction of the physical man; that, indeed, psyche, character, and individuality seem under certain circumstances to express themselves only through the rapidity or slowness with which they disintegrate. The

end result in any case is inanimate men, *i.e.*, men who can no longer be psychologically understood, whose return to the psychologically or otherwise intelligibly human world closely resembles the resurrection of Lazarus" (441).

This observation provides the starting point for what must be seen as the most adventurous and innovative approach to the question of "the fascist psyche" in recent years, Theweleit's *Male Fantasies*. While eschewing the terminology of a traditional Oedipalizing analysis, Theweleit works from the perspective of a pre-Oedipal understanding of his soldier males: "The 'ego,' in the Freudian sense of a mediator 'between the world and the id' exists only in a very fragmented form, or, indeed, hardly at all in soldier males. There is some question whether it has ever really been formed in them at all" (1: 204). If the notion of the "pre-Oedipal" tends to reassign Theweleit's analysis a place within Freudian paradigms, however, he will further insist that "it would also be wrong simply to define these men as 'psychotics.' They do not, in fact, seem to possess the Oedipal form of the 'ego,' and yet they are not, for that reason, in any way 'unadapted to reality,' nor do they have 'weak egos' or any other such disorder" (1: 209–10).

Theweleit will go on to draw from the work of Balint and of Deleuze and Guattari to offer an anti- rather then pre-Oedipal analysis of fascism. In essence, the resulting methodology examines "at face value" the fantasies of soldier males and resists (not always successfully) interpreting those fantasies with respect to their "real" meaning. When the soldier males rape, they are not "really" acting out some other impulse. To the extent that a work of literary and cultural analysis can resist "interpretation," I too seek to read "at the surface." As should become clear at the end of the book, where I recast the image of the mirror and further propose a Lyotardian theory of "figure," a resistant antihomophobic reading will necessarily privilege the surface of the mirror over the putative absence buried in its depths.

5. Of course, the analysis of the Mitscherlichs can be likened in this respect to that offered by Reich in *The Mass Psychology of Fascism*.

6. Commenting on the transportability of ideological material from one site of belief to another, de Certeau perhaps encapsulates my ambiguous relation to Adorno when he castigates "the unjustified assumption that the objects *believed* are the same as the act of *believing*, and that, as a corollary, there is something religious about every group in which elements that *have been* religious are still working" (184). If we substitute fascism for religion here, we have, I hope, clarified my position. The recurrence of homophobic commonplaces in Adorno's work does not render him fascist. However—and here I diverge slightly from de Certeau—

if we accept (as I shall argue later in this book, using the work of Lacoue-Labarthe and Nancy) that fascism might itself be defined as the reduction of the specific articles of political faith to mere rituals—if, in other words, belief is more important than what is believed—then even to assert the value neutrality of ideological material is to tread on extremely thin ice.

7. This point will be elaborated in some detail in the final chapter, in which the very structure of homosexual desire is shown—in a homophobic logic exemplified by Moravia's *The Conformist*—to be "allegorical" insofar as it realizes itself only in simultaneously realizing something else (i.e., its own self-negation).

8. The concept of a "homosexual panic" derives, of course, from Sedgwick's analysis—in *The Epistemology of the Closet*—of the "homosexual panic" defense commonly offered by the perpetrators of acts of violence predominantly against gay men. I use it to suggest a fear projected onto a conveniently externalized representation of a discourse's own internal instabilities.

9. That we should read fascism—or, at least, National Socialism—in this way is, of course, inevitable, and I certainly do not mean to suggest that "Auschwitz" can or should be disentangled from some "other" of and within fascism. This will be a constant problem: to resist a reading of the essence of fascism is to invite a dismantling of it to the extent where historical realities can be argued away as inessential and unimportant. If there is no essence of fascism, was Auschwitz merely accidental?

10. The locus classicus for the analysis of this "apocalyptic tone" is, of course, Derrida's "Of an Apocalyptic Tone Recently Adopted in Philosophy." The question also underpins the German *Historikerstreit*. For a consideration of the importance of "Auschwitz" to the postwar historical sensibility, see Friedländer's *Probing the Limits of Representation*; the work of Mayer, and the review of it by LaCapra; as well as the collection of documents from the *Historikerstreit* edited by Knowlton and Cates. The question of apocalypse is of crucial importance to queer theory through the heterosexual troping of history I confront in the final chapter of this book. Nowhere has the question of apocalypse with regard to queer theory been more lucidly elaborated than in Dellamora's *Apocalyptic Overtures*.

11. As Stümke notes in his *Homosexuelle in Deutschland* in reference to this article: "In segments of the communist press homosexuality had already been designated an 'unproletarian' phenomenon before 1933; and during the first Röhm affair it was even held to be the basis of the 'Hitler racket.' After the Reichstag fire the line holding that homosexuality was the characteristic sexual form of National Socialism consistently prevailed" (98–99). Stümke further cites anecdotal evidence from Gorky of the parallel drawn in the Soviet Union between fascism and homosexuality, as

well as the concrete historical evidence of the recriminalization of homosexuality under Stalin. In the Soviet Union homosexuality was routinely evoked as evidence of "the degeneration of the fascist bourgeoisie."

12. Hirschfeld's theories provide an important background to the presentation in Chapter 3 of a countertradition of masculinists. A complete reference of the works of Hirschfeld can be found in the bibliography edited by Steakley.

13. Benjamin's understanding of "aestheticization" as a specifically decadent and homosexual project is suggested by his argument in the essay on "The Work of Art in the Age of Mechanical Reproduction" that it constitutes "the consummation of *l'art pour l'art*" (242). This assertion is fleshed out in the "Pariser Brief" dealing with Gide, where the erotic credentials of aestheticization become all too clear.

14. Quoted in Stümke and Finkler, 150.

15. The idea of a politics of *Repräsentation* I draw from Habermas's analysis in *The Structural Transformation of the Public Sphere* of the prebourgeois public sphere, in which power needed always to be embodied—represented, that is, in a body. An ambiguous relation to "representation" as a political phenomenon can already be noted in Benjamin's "Work of Art in the Age of Mechanical Reproduction" in which the celebratory tone of the text with regard to mechanical reproduction and the proliferation of representations is undercut by the considerably more somber, less optimistic tone of the footnotes, in which representation seems to threaten political delegitimation. Sedgwick's work on the function of representations of the male body within (and against) a modernist tradition are clearly pertinent to this debate and will be considered in greater detail in Chapter 6.

16. The question of the "political coding" of sensual experience predates, of course, even the question of any libidinal politics. The preservation of subject-object dichotomies in the perspectival visual sense is commented on, for example, by Horkheimer and Adorno in *Dialectic of Enlightenment*, where such a logic is countered by smell "which is attracted without objectifying. . . . When we see we remain what we are; but when we smell we are taken over by otherness" (184). This alternative sensual epistemology is linked (in the fascist imaginary) with the Jew, whom the fascist envies for such sensuality. But it is also linked to the primitive instinct "which drew the male animal to the female in heat" (233)—i.e., to biologized heterosexuality. Both the Nazi and the homosexual, we might infer, insist on the boundaries of self established through perspective.

17. Lefort has noted how—for a bourgeoisie whose moment as the "subject of history" has passed—ideology will always consist in the production of a representation of that historical subjectivity; in the production of a "body." "What Marx is calling attention to," he claims, "with his em-

phasis on the constancy of what he calls the communal character, is *an image of the body* which eliminates the dimension of externality" (151). Analyzing a historical moment "when *representation* comes to mask the imperatives of the present" (174)—a moment Marx analyzes in the "Eighteenth Brumaire"—Lefort analyzes the function of the monarch as the personification of an otherwise disparate and historically reactionary non-subject. We might, I think, analyze the function of the monarch in the Hegelian *Philosophy of Right* in just these terms, and thereby implicate such a politics of representation—theorists of homo-fascism notwithstanding—in a peculiarly heterosexual historical dialectic.

18. That this armoring of the body is not a peculiarly fascist phenomenon is made clear in Foster's essay "Armor Fou," where the investment of the historical avant-garde in similar projects is examined.

Chapter 2

1. For a consideration of the various positions within the so-called Frankfurt School on the question of communism, see the survey offered in Jay.

2. Jean-Joseph Goux—whose work we will return to in the final chapter—perhaps develops in the most systematic way the notion of a historical neurosis when he argues that "the stages I have indicated (the major socioeconomic formations) produce a dominant symbolic coherence that corresponds to the neurotic syndromes analyzed by Freud" (79–80). The historical relation of economy to neurosis is not, however, causal: "If a neurosis does 'correspond' to a socioeconomic formation, a socioeconomic formation does not cause, in the pathogenic sense, a neurosis" (80). Although Laplanche and Pontalis make clear that nothing in Freud would allow us to characterize either homosexuality or narcissism per se as neuroses, Goux's definition of a historical neurosis—"*the symptom of a repressed historical period. . . .* The neurotic individual becomes the symptom of an era left behind" (83)—does allow us to glimpse, at least, a way in which homosexuality might figure in a historical analysis less resolutely heterosexist than Goux's.

3. Where Habermas will differ—at the very least, in emphasis—from the first generation of the Frankfurt School is in his assessment of the function of such pathologies in both fascism and capitalism. He argues that "deformations of the lifeworld take the form of a reification of communicative relations only in capitalist societies, that is, only where the private household is the point of incursion for the displacement of crises into the lifeworld. . . . Deformations of the lifeworld take a different form in societies in which the points of incursion for the penetration of crises into the lifeworld are politically relevant memberships" (87). In other words, Habermas argues that in a society in which socialization takes place by

way of a familial Oedipus (capitalism), the psychological pathologies made necessary by the need to legitimate an irrational system of material reproduction will necessarily differ from those produced by a society in which that familial structure has been by-passed or short-circuited by political structures (fascism).

We should also note the similarities between Habermas's definitions and Goux's assertion that "neurosis is the effect of a missing social enactment of a significant social conflict; the subject is obliged to act it out privately, thus deforming what used to be a collective task" (85). In both cases there is a passage from the public to the private that does violence to both spheres. In Chapter 6, I examine in the work of Jarry the way in which homosexuality is opened up precisely by the play of repressive "phylogenetic" forces that seek to foreclose it.

4. For a further consideration of the "postpatriarchal" society, see the essay "Authority and the Family Today" by Horkheimer, and the responses of Mitscherlich—in *Society Without the Father*—and Jessica Benjamin.

5. We can note a distinction between the Frankfurt School and Theweleit here. Whereas Theweleit takes seriously the narcissistic wound by invoking Balint's notion of a fundamental fault that predates the formation of the ego, for Horkheimer and Adorno the narcissistic is always just a regression from the perspective of an already established ego. Thus, precisely where they posit the collapse of the autonomous ego as the condition of postpatriarchal modernity, Horkheimer and Adorno nevertheless retain it as a yardstick to measure the regressive tendencies of the homosexual.

6. The question of an alternative homosexual epistemology figured anally is one developed by Hocquenghem, and one that I would strenuously reject. Bersani has elaborated on this question in the essay "Is the Rectum a Grave?"

7. In *Eros and Civilization*, Marcuse will specifically insist that "the function of sadism is not the same in a free libidinal relation and in the activities of SS troops" (203).

8. Adorno's disposition of homosexuality around a paradigm of sadomasochism bears consequences for the broader body of his work and might prompt us, for example, to reconsider the importance of the writings on Sade in *Dialectic of Enlightenment*.

9. Sedgwick's consideration of the process of "de-differentiation" in the emergence of the *homo*sexual is of importance throughout this book, and will be examined in its directly aesthetic context in Chapter 6. In Chapter 3, however, I seek to unsettle the hegemony of this model in our understanding of "modern" homosexuality.

10. As Sydney Pulver has pointed out in his essay on "Narcissism: The

Term and the Concept," the term itself has been used in a bewildering number of ways. He isolates four main usages:

1. Clinically, to denote a sexual perversion.
2. Genetically, to denote a stage of development.
3. In terms of object relationships, to denote two different phenomena:
   (a) a type of object choice,
   (b) a mode of relating to the environment.
4. To denote various aspects of the complex ego state of self-esteem.
   (109–10)

These four usages, in fact, are organized more or less chronologically in terms of their emergence. The first usage of the term by both Havelock-Ellis and Paul Näcke at the end of the nineteenth century was undoubtedly sexological: narcissism was a classifiable sexual perversion along with any number of clinically observable distortions of sensuality. By the time it comes to be used as a synonym for self-esteem the term has, as Pulver points out, lost any real diagnostic or even explicatory value. The more interesting field of possibilities—the field explored by Freud with specific reference to inversion—lies in that realm of either the developmental or object choice—in the tension, in other words, between genetic and structural (drive) models of personality.

    11. The reading I offer here is not dissimilar to the analysis of the soldier males offered by Theweleit in *Male Fantasies*, where it is the fear of—and attraction to—the possibility of feminine engulfment that characterizes the protofascist cruelty Theweleit calls "the white terror." However, Theweleit insists in his examination of "Homosexuality and the White Terror" that "it should be made clear from the beginning that the title of this section implies a connection that in fact does not exist" (2: 307). In other words, Theweleit examines as an ideological social fantasy what Adorno elaborates as social analysis. Adorno asserts the connection of homosexuality and fascism, whereas Theweleit asks, "Why then, under certain conditions does it seems possible to assert its existence?" (306). Resisting the ultimately homophobic conclusions of Dannecker and Reiche, Theweleit buys into the rather utopian alternative epistemology suggested by Hocquenghem's notion of anality.

    If Theweleit is adamant that "terror does not derive from homosexuality; instead, male bonding fosters a tendency toward the formation of aggressive 'homosexual' practices, which may spill over into any number of other forms of aggression" (2: 337n), he is not always convincing in his implicit differentiation of homosexuality and "homosexuality." Thus, for example, he will argue that "Hocquenghem defines the liberating quality of homosexuality as its capacity to decodify sexual codes; but in the fascist male this is precisely the element that is missing" (2: 325), and then argue that "what the soldier males seem to find enjoyable is the *representation* of sex-role inversion" (2: 330). Which of these "homosexualities" is more acutely aware of the presence of a code: homosexuality per se or that "homosexuality" so encoded it can only be invoked between quotation marks?

12. "Women, especially if they grow up with good looks, develop a certain self-contentment which compensates them for the social restrictions that are imposed upon them in their choice of object. Strictly speaking, it is only themselves that such women love with an intensity comparable to that of the man's love for them" ("On Narcissism," 88–89).

13. In the essay "On Narcissism" Freud envisages an alternative to sublimation—the process of idealization, in which "this ideal ego is now the target of the self-love which was enjoyed in childhood by the actual ego. The subject's narcissism makes its appearance displaced on to this new ideal ego, which, like the infantile ego, finds itself possessed of every perfection that is of value" (94). The process of idealization is identified with the construction of the ideal ego, which—in later writings—tends to function as a synonym for the superego. This essay is interesting, however, precisely because it does not simply conflate the ego ideal with what we will subsequently come to know as the superego. Instead, Freud points at the narcissistic and essentially internal provenance of this concept, pointing only at the end of the essay toward "a social side."

The danger in simply conflating the ego ideal and the superego lies, I think, in the parallel conflation of sublimation and idealization. Freud writes: "The formation of an ego ideal is often confused with the sublimation of instinct, to the detriment of our understanding of the facts. A man who has exchanged his narcissism for homage to a high ego ideal has not necessarily on that account succeeded in sublimating his libidinal instincts" (94). In other words, narcissistic (self-)idealization leaves libido intact by creating for it the object it might otherwise have been disappointed in. Sublimation, meanwhile, substitutes objects for other prohibited objects. Rather than the nonrepressive sublimation Marcuse speaks of we might, instead, speak of the function of Narcissus in facilitating an alternative to sublimation—idealization. Idealization, rather than mediating desire, insists on the immanence of desire by creating for itself the objects it desires. To this extent one might argue, then, that homosexual desire—as a form of narcissistic idealization—resists subsumption into the symbolic as dictated by the operation of outside forces and inhabits an immanently libidinal lifeworld. It is for this reason that Adorno waivers on the question of "submission": homosexual idealization does not "submit" to the dictates of reality and therefore remains dangerous.

14. Marcuse insists on the homosexual coding of both figures; thus,

Orpheus, for example, is extolled not as the lover of Eurydice, but as the
boy lover torn to pieces by the insulted Thracian women; the poet, whose

> love was given
> To young boys only, and [who] told the Thracians
> That was the better way: *enjoy the springtime,*
> *Take those first flowers!*   (236)

15. See the chapter on Mackay for an elaboration of this question in
the context of early homosexual agitation and literary practice. There I
examine the performative function of an ethical address to the Thou of a
homosexual readership and the implications of a paederasty that inflects
Freudian narcissism in a quite specific way—namely, as a desire for what he
himself *would have liked to have been.*

16. The line of argument I take issue with here is that represented by
the works of Gilman cited in the bibliography.

Chapter 3

1. For a consideration of the historical background to the homosex-
ual emancipation movement, consult the historical works in note 1 of
Chapter 1. Of particular interest are those original works by Iwan Bloch;
Brand; Braunschweig; Carpenter; Gerling; Grabowsky; Hoessli; Moll; and
Symonds. The question of the differences between "masculinists" and
"third-sexers" is the specific focus of the article by Oosterhuis.

2. Of course, one might wish to reflect further on the politics of the
aversion within queer theory to the treatment of a tradition so clearly
grounded in paederastic or even paedophile desire. Whereas the masculinists will be accused of *Tuntenhaß,* it must be acknowledged that opposition to their "masculinist" desire cannot be entirely abstracted from an
internecine political agenda.

3. See also Herzer's essay "Asexuality as an Element in the Self-Presentation of the Right Wing of the German Gay Movement Before 1933."

4. I use Stümke and Finkler here as emblematic of a broader trend
within continental queer historiography and sociology. The work of Dannecker and Reiche reflects a similar opposition to the masculinist position.

5. Indeed, as Silverman points out in her reading of Lacan in the introduction to *Male Subjectivity at the Margins,* such a model might be
taken as paradigmatic of all desire.

6. See the works of Lombroso and Nordau cited in the bibliography.
Although I have indicated my disagreements with the work of Gilman in
this area, it remains of historical importance. Perhaps the most interesting analysis of the question of degeneration in the context of a continental tradition of masculinism is Spackman's *Decadent Genealogies.*

7. Perhaps we need to make it clear here: what Friedlaender does not

accept is that a mode of desire determines a mode of identity. There can
be effeminate homosexuals, but they are not effeminate by virtue of their
desire. To this extent, then, there is the first move beyond biologism, in
which desire would be biologically (and, therefore, generically) determined.

8. We should also note the broader cultural impact of thinkers such as
Blüher on the German cultural mainstream. Thomas Mann's diaries demonstrate, for example, that it was in the form of Blüher's brand of masculinism rather than Hirschfeld's third-sexism that the problematic of homoeroticism found sympathetic expression in his work. Mann knew, met,
and approved of Blüher.

9. In general, Blüher's position vis-à-vis Freud is ambiguous: oppositional and yet cognizant of a debt owed to a thinker who has made an entire discourse possible. Thus, at one point he will argue in the following
terms: "If it is a question both now and later of combatting some of the
basic concepts of *Freud* and his students, it should be made clear in advance that Freud is not an arbitrary opponent. In opposing him one opposes psychiatry at its undeniably highest level. Any intellectual who has
not made that great leap inaugurated by Freud, and who still thinks in
pre-Freudian terms, remains of only historical interest" (1: 124).

Blüher's declaration of opposition to Freud should not blind us to the
centrality of what one might call the "Freudian problematic" to his work.
Freud may, in some sense, represent the enemy, but Blüher will concede
that he nevertheless defines the field of battle. Indeed, Freud's work is
presented quite explicitly in terms of an epistemological break: "The psychology that takes seriously everything that might occur in these imaginary constructs and seeks to trace them back to their original source is
called *analytical psychology* (psychoanalysis). It was discovered and developed by Freud's stroke of genius, that ranks in importance alongside those
of Copernicus, Newton, and Robert Mayer" (1: 46). For Blüher, Freud
represents a Copernican revolution, inaugurating a discourse that makes
it impossible to return to the simplistic equation of physiological and psychological fact in the analysis of either society or the individual human
psyche. For all that Freud inherits from the tradition of "inversion," "masculinism" would be unthinkable for Blüher without his uncoupling of psychical and purely biological phenomena.

10. Blüher is most concerned in his use of terminology to disentangle
the question of gender from the question of sexuality. In so doing, he offers a series of definitions that indicate the extent to which the German
language itself gets in the way of his argument. Let us begin with sexuality: "I hope I have made clear what I mean by *sexuality*: it is the original
root of all those concepts to be constructed in this book" (1: 36–37). Sexuality, then, is being accorded a certain primacy, a certain primitiveness,

a certain genealogical privilege—but this primacy, as we have seen, is a mere abstraction, since sexuality is never encountered outside of an erotic framework of meaning. Libido, meanwhile, functions more generically: "*Libido* is the Latin for *drive*—or, in Schopenhauer's terms, 'will' (stripped of its metaphysical connotations). This concept takes precedence over sexuality and is therefore the broadest" (1: 37). Libido, then, is a more generic term, but of interest here is the way in which Blüher conflates drive and will (*Trieb* and *Wille*), recalling the notion of the "objective will" he deems necessary to the human state. Clearly, the notion of the *Trieb* in no way designates the realm of an unconscious opposing the conscious calculations of the *Wille*.

11. Blüher's division of biology and psychology along the lines of a division of spatial and temporal discourses leads me to characterize his intervention in de Certeau's terms as a "tactic" rather than as a "strategy." De Certeau writes, "I call a 'strategy' the calculus of force-relationships which become possible when a subject of will and power . . . can be isolated from an 'environment.' A strategy assumes a place that can be circumscribed as *proper* (*propre*). . . . The 'proper' is a victory of space over time. On the contrary, because it does not have a place, a tactic depends on time" (xix). The distinction—carried over into Blüher's project—is important, I think, for it allows us to see that project as a tactical opposition to the attempts of a burgeoning discourse of psychoanalysis to control the realm of the homoerotic. Blüher attempts to ground not a "general theory" but rather a tactical theory of specific erotic attachments. As we shall see at the end of the chapter, from Blüher's perspective it is precisely Weininger's reduction of all desire to cognitive categories—to a "strategy"—that distorts his analysis.

12. When Blüher, then—in a move reminiscent of Friedlaender, but also to be found, for example, in Gide's *Corydon*—rejects the idea that homosexuality offends the laws of nature, we should take care to distinguish his argument from that of Friedlaender, or Gide. Blüher seeks not to redefine in an inclusive manner the idea of nature but to reveal as oxymoronic the very idea of the *Naturgesetz*—a concept that confuses nature and culture in an inadmissible fashion.

13. "The statehood of humankind," Blüher argues, "depends neither on his spirit nor on economics." Within the problematics of the State, argues Blüher, two basic positions are possible: the liberal ("One may think as little of the state as one wishes") and the conservative ("But one may also place the state as high as is possible") (1: 3). While presenting the two as possibilities, Blüher's insistence on the centrality of the fact of the State makes it extremely difficult for him to take seriously its liberal downplaying. In the search for a political ontology, Blüher does not analyze the "essence" of the human as something that might then be accommodated

or not, according to political concerns, but rather as the dictating element of any political configuration. Thus, if the State is the central fact of human existence, then the actual, political State must reflect this fact. This conservatism, then, is not so much a "political" conservatism, as it is a conservatism in the very understanding of the function of politics.

14. For a consideration of the ideological variety of the so-called conservative revolution see the somewhat apologetic work of Mohler and the critical study offered by Petzold. Blüher himself, like many who were in the early years not altogether unsympathetic to National Socialism, was subject to a *Schreibverbot*.

15. It should be noted here—though the question would merit much greater elaboration—that Blüher's critique is not in any sense necessarily right-wing. Indeed, it occasionally opens onto a strain of theory surprisingly reminiscent of Hannah Arendt in its insistence on the primacy of the political. For Arendt—as, indeed, for Friedlaender in the field of erotic relations—Plato can be taken as the originator of a debilitating political understanding. She argues in *The Human Condition* that with Plato begins a political tradition—exemplified in bourgeois social theory—of seeing politics as *poiesis*, as making, the creation of a thing: the State. For her this denigrates political action to the level of mere work or fabrication. Blüher I think, would concur. What is of interest in this context is the way in which Arendt actually provides us with an alternative way of conceptualizing fascist "aestheticization of politics." For, from her perspective— and, we might conjecture, from Blüher's—the bourgeois State is always already aestheticized, the product of an ideology of *poiesis* that remains subpolitical.

16. The focus on the autoerotic/alloerotic distinction is to be found also in Friedlaender and seems to derive from the work of Gustav Jäger, whom both Blüher and Friedlaender use as a source of physical theory. Thus, Friedlaender quotes Jaeger on this question: "The sexually normal individual *eo ipso*—but also the homosexual of every type—requires both a second person and a time and place to satisfy his lusts. The latter limitation keeps them from insatiability and temporal forcing. And the major limitation—the need for the second person—forces them to take an interest in others, prevents their egoism from taking control; and that is the powerful link that binds even homosexuals to human society" (203; quoted from Jäger, *Entdeckung der Seele*, 1: 263). Of course, this position is radicalized by the masculinists. Whereas Jäger writes of the alloerotic as an inclusive category—"*even* homosexuals"—the masculinists will take homosexuality as *the* paradigmatic alloerotic (and therefore social) form of sexuality.

17. It is worth noting that Blüher claims that such alloerotic masturbation is "not a problem," implying that autoerotic masturbation is. Fur-

thermore, though he will elsewhere offer a somewhat relativistic definition of perversion, he seems here to be laying the groundwork for a theory of perversion. The perverse is the autoerotic, that which resists the imaginary, that which remains in—and remains of—the real. (In a sense, then, it won't even be Eros, as he describes it elsewhere as the bearer of meaning.) What, then, is a perversion? "Theoretically speaking: let us assume that in the conscious will of the individual sexuality in its fully unfolded form takes on a *symphonic character*, in other words, that a series of partial stimulations serve to accompany and color a central motif, that has the orgasm at its heart. Let us call the path to orgasm the *central sexual motif*. A *perversion* would then be a partial stimulation that suddenly—and *against* the conscious will—drew all excitement to itself, destroying the symphonic nature of an unfolding sexuality. . . . It is not simply a question of the degree of pleasure and unpleasure, but also of its structure" (1: 106–7). Perversion, then, raises structural and hermeneutic questions rather than purely substantive questions. It results from an imbalance of part and whole. Of course, in order for a specific sexual pleasure to be characterized as a false insistence on the part as a whole, some external notion of "the whole" itself must be invoked. In the above passage, that "whole" is represented by the orgasm. We must therefore raise questions of the relationship of the orgasm to meaning, and of orgastic sexuality to social as well as sexual perversion.

18. Lyotard writes of the Jewish Oedipus: "Oedipus fulfills his fate of desire; the fate of Hamlet is the non-fulfillment of desire: this chiasmus is the one that extends between what is Greek and what is Jewish, between the tragic and the ethical" (401); he further cites "Hamlet's non-fulfillment of the paternal word as the modern's difference from the Greek" (398). This passage—in modernity—into the realm of the ethical is a passage into the realm of nonfulfillment as well as into the proscription of representation, since "the image-figure is rejected because of its fulfillment of desire and delusion; its function of truth is denied" (402). Thus, Hamlet—the Jewish Oedipus par excellence, for Lyotard—"un-fulfills his desire in representation" (in the play within the play) while "Oedipus fulfills his desire in non-recognition" (406). Desire and (re-)cognition seem to stand in an intractably antinomial relationship to each other—as, indeed, they do for Blüher.

The key question, then, in the structure of the Jewish Oedipus, concerns the (antinomial) relationship of Truth to representation. Truth becomes apparent not in its "own language," but as a process or work, within the language of representation of facts: "It is within the language of cognition itself that desire makes displacements" (395). The question, then, is one of the relationship of Eros to Logos, and it is precisely this question that forms the epistemological core of Blüher's work. For Lyotard, the tension between "the language of cognition" and the disruptive "truth-work" necessitates a deconstructive reading of Freud; for Blüher, it involves something very similar—a reading of Freud within a mistaken tradition of pathography.

19. In establishing the privileged societally constitutive role of the *Typus inversus*—and on the basis of the autoerotic/alloerotic division, Blüher offers a sexual typology consisting of (1) The "Mucker" or Faun, (2) The Pessimist, (3) Infantile Man, (4) The Pervert, and (5) The Typus Inversus. It is through the figure of the *Faun*—part of an elaborate sexual typology—that Blüher elaborates further on the relationship of Eros to Logos, arguing, Platonically, that in perceiving the Idea the subject posits and experiences itself: "For the first time one senses that one has a soul." This positing of a transcendental self does not take place in that perception of the specific that is the realm of Eros. However, Blüher goes on to insist, "There is an instinctual as well as a cognitive soul" (1: 90). The idealist dichotomy of body and spirit is rejected.

20. While I would stand by the designation of Weininger as an anti-Semite, it should be pointed out that he would reject the nomenclature, employing a logic that we find replicated again and again in the depiction of homosexuality. Anti-Semitism, he will argue, is itself Semitic, a harping on about irrelevant ideas of race, a purely Jewish concern: "The aggressive Antisemites . . . nearly always display certain Jewish characters, sometimes apparent in their faces." He will conclude that "the bitterest Antisemites are to be found amongst the Jews themselves" (304). Of course, he is, in a sense, proof of his own assertion, but it is interesting to note how he rejects biological racialism as itself a racial characteristic biologically (or physiognomically) traceable!

We should note, however, that Weininger's own indifference to physicality itself renders the figure of the Jew somewhat nebulous. In this regard, he specifies that "I do not refer to a nation or to a race, to a creed or to a scripture. When I speak of the Jew I mean neither an individual nor the whole body, but mankind in general, in so far as it has a share in the platonic idea of Judaism. My purpose is to analyse this idea. . . . But some reflection will lead to the surprising result that Judaism is saturated with femininity, with precisely those qualities the essence of which I have shown to be in the strongest opposition to the male nature" (304).

21. Weininger's asceticism is a rejection of orgasm as the giving of the self as property. Blüher, meanwhile, is specifically orgasmic in his rejection of the bourgeois property relations that constitute the Ego. Rather than consisting in the intellectual ability to perceive an idea beyond the specificity of the here and now—instead, that is, of being a Platonic subject—this subject exists precisely in the inability to perceive anything be-

yond the specificity of this impulse, in the refusal to acknowledge the transcendent. In becoming the horizon of its own impulsive needs, the subject constitutes itself for Blüher. Thus, this form of subjectivity consists not in the possibility of having, but in the impossibility of identifying a possessive subject. Being consists, here, not in the transcendence of beings, but in the identification (that is, in the construction of the possibility of identity) with beings. It is an ontico- rather than ontological philosophy of being. This onticological being is identified by Blüher with the moment of orgasm, with "kisses, tenderness, caresses, and the normal refinements of sexuality and the drives: those things one 'has' and yet does not 'have' once they happen. But in the spiritual man orgasm creates a great rush of the instinctual-ego, for which the only possible words would be: 'I *am* desire!' That complete surrender of all that one is to a massive desire is one of the most earth-shattering experiences of the high-minded" (1: 91). In other words, the moment of orgasm is figured not as an instance of loss or forgetting, but as an onticological moment of being that transcends not matter, but the bourgeois construction of (self-)possessive subjectivity. Orgasm is a moment of *Sein* rather than *Haben*.

22. Arendt has commented in *The Origins of Totalitarianism* on the importance of the new political phenomenon of statelessness to the emergence of fascism as a mass phenomenon. A reading of Weininger and Blüher on the diaspora further helps to explain the way in which the Jews had been politically prefigured as the "privileged" representatives of what was only to become a mass phenomenon in the twentieth century. Weininger argues that Zionism is specifically un-Jewish: "Zionism is the negation of Judaism, for the conception of Judaism involves a world-wide distribution of the Jews. Citizenship is an un-Jewish thing, and there has never been and never will be a truly Jewish State" (307). Blüher, meanwhile, will argue that "only the Zionists have the necessary active will for a people and creative spiritual values" (2: 171), but he too will see in this Jewish movement toward statehood a specifically non-Jewish phenomenon. Thus, Zionism threatens to fail, in his assessment, by becoming "Jewish"!: "Meanwhile the middle-men of Zionism have already set about cutting deals, politicking and speculating: in short, Zionism is well on the way to degenerating into Jewishness [*verjuden*]. This is a *very* sly people" (2: 171).

23. In other words, fantasized Jewish desires for Gentile women are ascribed to an over-cathexis of the real relation to the mother; a cathexis that seeks to cover its tracks in an extreme form of displacement that sees any sexual communion with one's own race as potentially incestuous. Judaism is therefore at once the height of a civilized social order based on the incest taboo and the movement of that order into the realm of the neurotic.

Chapter 4

1. Sedgwick in fact comments on how a faith in science proved to be the downfall of many otherwise liberating thinkers. Specifically, she comments in *Epistemology of the Closet* on Nietzsche's "one disastrously mistaken wager with his culture" (178), namely, the linkage of a moral discourse to the discourse of biology and the subsequent political mobilization of that hybrid discourse of eugenics.

2. Sedgwick argues in *Epistemology of the Closet* that "the 'Hellenic ideal' insofar as its regenerative power is supposed to involve a healing of the culturewide ruptures involved in male homosexual panic, necessarily has that panic so deeply at the heart of its occasions, frameworks, demands, and evocations that it becomes not only inextricable from but even a propellant of the cognitive and ethical compartmentalizations of homophobic prohibition" (138). If it is my contention that the paederastic model of Hellenic desire has been underplayed in the reconstruction of emergent homosexual identities in the twentieth century, I have myself, of course, underplayed certain elements of a debate that forms the very core of queer theory. For a consideration of the impact of the Hellenic in the emergence of "modern" homosexual identity, see Dellamora; and Halperin. For a consideration of Greek love in the light of a Foucauldian and post-Foucauldian methodology, see Halperin, Winkler, and Zeitlin; and Winkler.

3. We should note here a distinction within the paederastic tradition as represented in this book by Mackay and Jarry: it is a difference that may, indeed, correspond to key aesthetic differences. For Mackay, the photorealism of his represented desire fixes a differential, securing it from time. For Jarry, meanwhile, the very dynamic of paederastic desire will depend on the play of temporal differences, the acknowledgment of the implication of a "spatialized" difference in the temporal play of a *différance*. Both, in other words, insist on a differential in desire, but only Mackay sees that differential as an ontological guarantee of desire. For Jarry—as we shall see in Chapter 6—that differentiation always threatens to vanish with time, effacing desire.

4. We will be reminded, here, of the treatment of forgetting in the work of Blüher and Weininger. Whereas Weininger saw sexuality—at the moment of completion—as a "forgetting" in which the man forgets both his partner's and his own suprasensual reality, Blüher sees that forgetting as constitutive of an identity. Mackay—as we shall see from the presentation here—resembles Blüher, though his construction of identity is based on a radical loss, rather than the egotistical plenitude suggested by Blüher's all-embracing claim "I *am* desire."

5. In the context of the Hellenic tradition, Lacoue-Labarthe and Nancy perhaps help us understand the apparent (masochistic) cruelty at

the heart of Mackay's paederasty. Acknowledging a simplification that would tend to de-differentiate a set of otherwise radically different philosophical texts, they nevertheless claim that "it is known that the Germans discovered, at the dawn of speculative idealism and of romantic philology (in the last decade of the eighteenth century at Jena, among Schlegel, Hölderlin, Hegel and Schelling), that Greece, in reality, had been double: there had been a Greece of measure and of clarity, of theory and of art (in the proper sense of these terms), of 'beautiful form,' of virile, heroic rigor, of law, of the City, of the light of day; and a buried Greece, nocturnal, somber (or too blindingly bright), and the archaic, savage Greece of group rituals, of bloody sacrifices and collective intoxications, of the cult of the dead and of the Earth Mother—in short, a mystical Greece, on which the other, not without difficulty, was raised" (300–301).

Lacoue-Labarthe and Nancy do not claim that the "bad" Germany simply identified with the "mystical" Greece, but that the duality of any identity grounded on Greek precedent necessarily problematized the idea of any national self-identity. They point out how "the essence of the original Greek language, of *muthos*, is the capacity, shared by the German language, for *symbolization*, and therefore for the production or formation of the 'guiding myths' of a people" (301). We shall see in the final chapter—in the consideration of national symbols and "homosexual allegory"—how the homosexual seemed (and, indeed, seems) to threaten precisely this work of organic symbolization on which the nation is constructed. We shall return to Lacoue-Labarthe and Nancy in Chapter 6, where their analysis will help illuminate the relationship of an avant-garde homosexual aesthetic to an apparently "fascistic" political epistemology.

6. This formulation should already be familiar to us from the presentation of Adorno on the homosexual cathexis of the *Führer* in Chapter 2.

7. The grammatology of Mackay's paederastic formulations is important. This passage of desire into the realm of the subjunctive necessarily questions Sedgwick's invocation in *Epistemology of the Closet* of a set of terms she designates as "indicatively male." What I am suggesting, in fact, is that homosexual masculinism differs from straightforward homosociality in its purely subjunctive understanding of masculinity. This passage out of the indicative also grounds—as I shall claim in the chapter on Jarry—a poetics.

8. For a summary of Silverman's presentation of Lacan on the *objet a*, see Chapter 6, note 3.

Chapter 5

1. The redemptive and performative power of belief is a central question in the studies by Lacoue-Labarthe and Nancy, and by Lefort. I will deal with it in the final chapter, where I consider the function of the lit-

erary text in the formation of homosexual identity alongside the function of ritual in the fascist formulation of *Volk*. In essence, the structure of belief derives its legitimation not from the object of belief, but from the community of believers. To this extent, of course, it is charismatic. Thus, it is only when we attempt to translate the desire of the *Volk* for nationhood back into a model of individual desire that it ceases to "make sense" and must be stigmatized (as homosexual narcissism).

2. Lewis's notion of tolerance is, it should be pointed out, somewhat unusual. For example, he praises the Nazi's refusal to be misled into moralizing and presents the Nazi's indifference to these matters in the following terms: "And of course all these Bars and Dancings, with their Kaffir bands, are for him the squinting, misbegotten, paradise of the *Schiebertum*. 'Juda verrecke!' he would no doubt mutter, or shout, if he got into one. Sooner or later he would desire to be at the head, or in the midst, of his *Sturmabteilung*—to roll this nigger-dance luxury-spot up like a verminous carpet, and drop it into the Spree—with a heartfelt *Pfui!* at its big sodden splash" (*Hitler*, 28).

3. The terms isolated by Lewis are to be encountered most notably in the work of Reich.

Chapter 6

1. If, for Benjamin, fascism *à la Marinetti* is the "consummation of *l'art pour l'art*," for Bürger, aestheticism is the precondition for the avant-garde because "the self-criticism of the social subsystem that is art can become possible only when the contents also lose their political character, and art wants to be nothing other than art. This stage is reached at the end of the nineteenth century, in Aestheticism" (27).

2. Jarry's masculinist credentials would be attested to in works such as *The Supermale* in which the generation of texts is inextricably linked, however, to the (hetero-)sexual libido.

3. In her study *Male Subjectivity at the Margins*, Silverman stresses the importance of the *objet a* to any paradigmatic understanding of homosexual desire. Her encapsulation of Lacan is useful in this context: "Fantasy thus conjures forth a fictive object for a fundamentally a-objectal desire. It translates the desire for nothing into the desire for something. However, we must not forget that the *objet a* exists in a mirroring relation to the *moi*; it is 'one's own ego that one loves in love, one's own ego made real on the imaginary level.' It would thus seem crucial that we take into account not only how the object figures within fantasy, but how the ego comes into play. Part of what it means to pursue the relation of fantasy to the ego is to grasp that the subject's own bodily image is the first and the most important of all of the objects through which it attempts to compensate for symbolic castration—to understand that the *moi* is most

profoundly that through which it attempts to recover 'being.' The self, in other words, fills the void at the center of subjectivity with an imaginary plenitude" (4–5).

Lefort's work on capitalism's search for an embodiment of subjectivity might also be read through this lens. It is Lacoue-Labarthe and Nancy, however, who most succinctly demonstrate the importance of such formulations to the question of fascism at hand here. Describing "the emergence of German nationalism as the *appropriation of the means of identification*" (299) out of the hands of a Greek ideal it could only ever imitate from France, Lacoue-Labarthe and Nancy argue that "what Germany lacked, therefore, in practical terms, was its subject (and modern metaphysics, as the metaphysics of the Subject, did not complete itself there by any accident). Consequently, what Germany wanted to create was such a subject, its own subject" (299).

4. Again, I would return to de Certeau's distinction of spatial "strategy" and temporal "tactic" to suggest that Jarry's insistence on the temporal differentiation in desire (to be demonstrated later in the chapter) is what distinguishes the *practice* of homotextuality from the *space* of fascist representation.

5. Sedgwick makes these distinctions in *Epistemology of the Closet*, 156. Of course, any consideration of camp, kitsch, and fascism would also need to take as its reference point the essays of Sontag on "Fascinating Fascism" and "Camp." Saul Friedländer traces the emergence of a kitsch representation of fascism as a dangerous historical moment in our postwar attempt to deal with fascism.

6. Richard Dellamora has quite explicitly appropriated and redirected Sedgwick's trajectory in his formulation of an early-twentieth-century "Dorianism" that indeed draws an impetus from the model of *Dorian Gray*, but insists on the paederastic differential encoded in notions of Greek love. Dellamora's work is also important for its formulation of a notion of sexual "inversion" with respect to a trope of philosophical "inversion" derived from deconstruction. *Apocalyptic Overtures* is one of the few works that acknowledge the persistence of a paederastic model of desire in the homosexual "mainstream" of the twentieth century and use that model to problematize existing queer historiography.

7. The notion of "embracing lack" derives from Silverman's study of post–World War II films' attempts to shore up a depleted male subjectivity through the device of "female fetishism." A desire that embraced lack would reject such recuperative measures. I would only point out that the idea of an "em-bracing" itself potentially suggests a recuperation, a bracing of subjectivity. (Indeed, one of the characters in *The Best Years of Our Lives*, a film Silverman analyzes masterfully, might himself be said to exemplify such a "bracing." The amputee veteran, Homer, has braces in-

stead of arms. How is a homosexual [non-]identity to resist such a refig-uration of "embracing lack"?)

8. We should recall here the movement of identification in Blüher, where the immanence of a physical sensation—rather than causing us to "forget" our suprasensual ego, as it does for Weininger—actually leads to an expansion of the self, in which one declares "I *am* desire!" The very movement of dispossession and deappropriation itself spills over into a moment of identification. In other words, the very subjection of the self-identical to the play of textuality potentially expands rather than decon-structs identity.

9. Of the "surface function" of the mirror as a paradoxical realization of the platonic essence, Jean-Joseph Goux writes, "If the mirror and re-flection have gained such prevalence as metaphors in the 'theory' of knowledge, it is because of a remarkable technological property of the mirror, an instrument that, against all hope, has the marvelous power of *separating form from matter*. The mirror *re-presents* the visible 'form' of the object immediately and integrally, at a slight distance, as if recessed, in the background, but dispensing entirely with its matter. It is true that this form is not pure. It is not the structure, the essence, the concept of the thing, quite the contrary even. Instead of releasing the essential core, the mirror shows only the immediate appearance, the illusion being all the greater as the substance of the thing, what makes up its existence, is not given" (187).

10. Although Sedgwick seeks, in *Epistemology of the Closet*, to resist reifying assertions of radical epistemological shifts in favor of a consider-ation of the coexistence of alternative models, the hegemonic movement toward an identity based on de-differentiated desire does tend to estab-lish itself rather forcefully in that work. To this extent, *Tendencies* perhaps fits her intentions more closely. Setting out in *Epistemology* to problema-tize reified notions of "modern homosexuality" or "homosexuality as we know it today," Sedgwick (perhaps unavoidably) charts the "discursive eclipse in this period of the Classically based *pederastic* assumption" (160). I seek to modify this historical trajectory and to suggest that it can be challenged not only at the level of critical analysis, but empirically and his-torically—as well as aesthetically, in the practice of an avant-garde à la Jarry.

11. Sedgwick's analysis of modernism, based on a reading of *Dorian Gray*—leads her to comment parenthetically that "in a class I taught at Amherst College, fully half the students said they had studied *Dorian Gray* in previous classes, but not one had ever discussed the book in terms of any homosexual content: all of them knew it could be explained in terms of either the Theme of the Double—the 'Dividelf'—or else The Problem of Mimesis—'Life and Art'" (161). Of course, Sedgwick's own argu-

ment—following the "epistemology of the closet"—will show how those students were, in a sense, necessarily right. *Dorian Gray* can be explained (away) in these terms. Polemically, however, Sedgwick's reading tends to function as a restitution of lost content, even where she insists on the interplay of closeting and truth effects.

12. Of course, it would be necessary to question the implicit assertion of a "homosexual" aversion to aesthetic abstraction. As Sedgwick has pointed out, the abstractions at the heart of the modernist aesthetic often served to camouflage specific and substantive homosexual concerns. For this reason, it might be argued that a return to some modified form of "thematic" reading might be necessary to queer theory in the wake of a poststructuralist concentration on tropes that was itself informed by essentially modernist aesthetic presuppositions. Likewise, however, I would argue that it is precisely the emergence of cultural studies as a viable critical practice that necessitates a renewed attention—paradoxically—to *literary* texts. For the aesthetic and literary realms—the "traditional" realms of academic criticism—were at the same time privileged realms of cultural self-fashioning for emergent homosexual cultures. In other words, we must continue to read literary texts, but begin to read them differently— as cultural artifacts. There is a danger, I think, in a strain of queer theory that implicitly links cultural analysis to "low cultural" praxis (questions of kitsch and camp, etc.) not only because it overlooks the contribution of a queer problematic to the cultural "mainstream" (that one might rightly wish to dislodge), but also because it pushes a queer aesthetic tendentially into the realm of naive (or faux-naif) representation. We should—as Sedgwick has—insist on the tension of representational and antirepresentational affects.

13. Although Sedgwick tendentially replicates an Anglo-American critical conflation of modernism and the avant-garde, she does posit a "coexistence" of plural homosexualities that is extremely helpful. While her project potentially opens up a radically nonsynchronous—avant-garde— historical model, in which homosexual panic is produced by the coexistence of competing ("diacritically" paederastic, and de-differentiated narcissistic) models of homosexuality, the ultimately de-differentiating trajectory of the modern comes to establish itself rather solidly.

14. For an elaboration of Lyotard's *figure*, see *Discours, figure*, and the essays on "The Dream-Work" and "The Sublime and the Avant-Garde."

15. The professor in question is Henri Béhar, as quoted in Bridgman, 296.

16. In opposing the sublimation of homosexual desire into the *jouissance* of a Barthesian "pleasure of the text," I also part company with the analysis of the *figure* offered by Lyotard in "The Sublime and the Avant-Garde." For Lyotard, the deformation of the sublime at the hands of fas-

cist aestheticization lies in the deferral into a real future of that which must remain eternally and fundamentally absent in the aesthetics of the sublime. Essentially, the fascist reduces politics to an aesthetics of the beautiful. I hope to have shown how the collective of those in attendance of the (never to come) fulfillment necessarily constitutes a dialectical moment in the sublime—a moment of presence even in the acknowledgment of absence. Lacoue-Labarthe and Nancy also help us think this dialectic.

I should also point out here that my reading necessarily parts company with that which de Certeau somewhat surprisingly offers at the end of *The Practice of Everyday Life*. For all that de Certeau's categories have been helpful throughout the book for thinking the "tactical" nature of several of the texts discussed, the "hetero-centrism" of his analysis ultimately allows him to analyze Jarry only as an exemplar of the nonproductive (or simply self-productive) "bachelor machine." This "bachelor," I would suggest, acquires a problematic, euphemistic quality when applied to the homosexual text: it too becomes "camouflage."

17. Furthermore, Kenneth Knoespel, in a study of the development of the Narcissus story in the Middle Ages, reminds us with regard to this particular myth that "in antiquity the process of falling in love was conceived as an attraction to an image of the self seen in the retina of the beloved. In other words, falling in love with another was portrayed as falling in love with a reflection of oneself. Plato's *Phaedrus* offers a good account of this process" (11). Narcissism, which—we know—will serve as the recurrent topos of Freud's analysis of homosexuality, is, in fact, at the very root of classical sexuality per se. Thus, when Pausanias subsequently "heterosexualizes" the Narcissus myth in his reworking, he engages not in a piece of cultural reappropriation, but merely builds on possibilities already inherent in the story and serves as simply the first interpreter to return to the insistent question of narcissism and *hetero*sexuality.

18. This philosophical problem, however, is also clearly gendered, for it is around a confusion of gender and sexuality that the Narcissus myth plays itself out in Ovid. Tiresias's prophecy to Liriope parallels exactly his earlier intercession in a dispute between Jove and Juno. The earlier disagreement is described as follows:

> "I maintain," he told her,
> "You females get more pleasure out of loving
> Than we poor males do, ever." She denied it.
> So they decided to refer the question
> To wise Tiresias' judgment: he should know
> What love was like, from either point of view.   (67)

There is a familiar double bind here with respect to woman's pleasure: it is not a simple case of men barring woman the way to her own pleasure.

Quite the reverse: it is the men who assert the primacy of feminine pleasure. In so doing, of course—and by a characteristic analytic gesture—
men assume the power of knowledge over women's pleasure. Woman's
pleasure can be asserted only if she confesses her ignorance of that pleasure. Juno's pleasure can be asserted only in the mode of ignorance: she
cannot know her own pleasure. It is to this extent that her dilemma prefigures that of Narcissus: she will have pleasure—and he will enjoy a long
life—only *si non se noverit*. If Tiresias finds for Jove, his prophecy nevertheless replicates the double bind of Juno: life and pleasure will lie on the
side of ignorance. Sengle's refusal to distinguish between the brutish pleasure of sensuality and the pleasure of "the act of perception" seeks to deconstruct this tradition.

19. That this rupture of the mirror has aesthetic as well as epistemological consequences goes without saying. As Rodolphe Gasché points
out in a study whose title—*The Tain of the Mirror*—immediately suggests
Jarry's *tain des mares*. "It appears, then, that the disruptive and subversive
effects of 'literature' are directed not against logocentric philosophy alone
but against literature as well, to the extent that the latter submits to philosophy's demands. . . . 'Literature,' then, is scarcely of the order of being. It has as little being as, say, a between, a corner, an angle" (259–60).

Chapter 7

1. A consideration of this question of "making sense" can be found in
my presentation of the differing positions of Lyotard and Adorno in
Chapter 1.

2. Schiesari goes so far as to argue that "one could probably attempt to
multiply the analogies between Renaissance and post-modern melan-
cholies, but my suspicion is that we are dealing not with two different pe-
riods of dramatized loss but rather with the historical boundaries of a great
age of melancholia (in Foucauldian terms: an epistemic formation), whose
edges are co-terminous with the historic rise and demise of 'the subject' as
the organizing principle of knowledge and power" (2). While this assertion certainly allows for a constructive cross-pollination of various aspects
of Benjamin's work on baroque allegory to the analyses of fascism (a conjunction Benjamin certainly had in mind, prompted as he was by his exposure to Expressionism, and one I wish to take up at the end of the chapter), it is nevertheless guilty of two important errors. First, Schiesari's
framing of her assertion by a consideration of—to quote the title of the
book from which the quotation is taken—a "Symbolics of Loss" ignores
the impact of loss on the mode of its own representation. What is lost is,
in fact, the very possibility of a "symbolics." Any thematic reading of melancholy fails to problematize the radical representational disruption that
melancholy effects. For any such "symbolics," I wish to substitute—at the

end of this chapter—Benjamin's alternative structure of allegory. Second, to see in the twentieth century an ending of a melancholic episteme established in the Renaissance is to ontologize the question of loss in much the same way Benjamin claims the Germans ontologize the loss of the war. Something really is being lost—melancholy itself, as an epistemic structure.

3. It is by no means my intention—in denying a historical ground or origin to a political phenomenon—to thereby deny its specificity, conflating, for example, Italian Fascism and National Socialism. I should stress, however, that we are dealing here with ideological reconstructions of those political forms—reconstructions that do not always concern themselves with the niceties of political distinctions. Moreover, were I to utilize the question of homo-fascism as a way of distinguishing between German and Italian fascism, I would run the risk of taking seriously the critical conflation of homosexuality and fascism that I am seeking to oppose. A good example of the dangers of reinserting political distinctions into the ideological materials that efface such distinctions is provided by Pasolini's film *Salò: 120 Days of Sodom*, in which an underlying distinction is drawn between the Italian fascists' desire to "kill the same body a thousand times" and an alternative—presented in the form of a *German* quotation on the radio—which is to kill a thousand bodies only once. Implicit in this distinction is a division between two models of desire, one based on lack, the other on presence, and this distinction threatens—in turn—to aestheticize and valorize the impossible desire of Italian fascism. I wish to avoid such pitfalls.

4. Moravia, "Answers to Nine Questions," 190.

5. Siciliano, ed., *Alberto Moravia*, 72.

6. Ibid., 71–72.

7. The representation of fascism that emerges from *The Conformist*—in the figures both of Marcello and of his father—is an almost textbook case of ideological projection: a reified representation of the very work of remembrance and projection that has made the representation possible. Melancholy—the relation to the object as a relation of loss—is projected onto the object itself; fascism becomes a purely imaginary historical phenomenon in the strictest ideological sense. I am arguing that Moravia hypostatizes in the melancholy of his protagonist—that is, in the fascist psyche—the condition of his own relation to historical representation. This relation is then further hypostatized as the impossibility of a historical and national narrative—more specifically, as the impossibility and ineluctability of the post- or anti-fascist narrative imperative.

8. This madness of the father is clearly linked, I would argue, to the problematic of melancholy to be developed in this chapter. Taking Ham-

let—the archetypical, Oedipal melancholic—as a figure for the radical ambiguity of a melancholy caught between denotation and performance, for example, Juliana Schiesari writes, "Thus the melancholic subject, according to the scheme I am analyzing, is considered to be unaware of the origin of his illness but belies this unconscious aspect by the fact that he is speaking some kind of truth since he is aware of his self-exposure. The dilemma is not unlike the traditional problem Shakespeareans face in deciding whether Hamlet is 'feigning' his madness or whether he is mad *because* he pretends to be" (49). In many ways this observation takes us back to the structure of transvestism outlined in the chapter on Lewis. Is Hitler feigning homosexuality—as a "dreamy-eyed hairdresser"—or is he a homosexual *because* he feigns it? (As one of my students recently pointed out, moreover, the use of blinding as a trope of castration serves further to enlist Marcello's protofascism within a distorted Oedipal framework.)

9. The displacement of the father is replicated in Marcello's relation to his victim, Professor Quadri. Marcello is hired to facilitate the assassination of Quadri supposedly because Quadri is a former professor of his. In fact, Quadri never was his professor: we learn that Marcello met Quadri precisely on the day the latter left his position at the university to take up more practical anti-fascist activities. In other words, Marcello encounters in Quadri an abdication from the institutional framework of patriarchal power. Again, one suspects Moravia of a tendential Oedipalization of the conflict, but the analogies to the relationship to the father lie precisely in the ambiguity of the professor's patriarchal credentials. The "identity" of Quadri and Marcello's father is established precisely on the basis of the nonidentity of each with their own supposed power.

10. If I turn now to Benjamin for a way of examining melancholy as a relation to history and as a mode of representation, I do so by superimposing on his work Freudian distinctions of mourning and melancholy not explicitly elaborated by Benjamin himself. Although Benjamin can write of melancholy that "its dominant mood is that of mourning, which is at once the mother of the allegories and their content" (230), thereby blurring any semantic distinction of mourning and melancholy, I feel that the Freudian distinction functions implicitly in his work in the distinction of *Trauerspiel* and *Tragödie*, in which the former is melancholic (in the Freudian sense) and the latter a work of articulated cultural mourning.

11. The form of death that meets its own end in "Auschwitz" is what Lyotard, in *The Differend*, calls "beautiful death": "'Auschwitz' is the forbiddance of the beautiful death" (100). This beautiful death is an ethical construct in which the death that confronts us is transcended through our compliance to a collective imperative legitimating that death. Lyotard argues that in any death that can acquire an ethical dimension and itself

ground ethical actions "the 'reason to die' always forms the bond of a we" and that "by identifying oneself with the legislator who orders one's death, one nevertheless escapes the miserable fate of being the referent for every forthcoming phrase that may bear one's name: the scourge of the dead in Greek thought. One can only succeed in this by obeying the order, since by doing it, one decrees it anew as a norm. One thereby makes one's name enter into the collective name of the legislating authority, which is a constant addressor because it is a rigid designator. . . . Such is the Athenian 'beautiful death,' the exchange of the finite for the infinite, of the *eschaton* for the *télos*: the *Die in order not to die*" (100).

The "beautiful death" is at once an individual gesture and a collective project, assimilating the individual to the ethical collective at the moment of death. As a transcendent moment, then, the collective is predicated on such deaths. Auschwitz is the forbiddance of any such beautiful death because of its characteristic antiethical, nonreciprocal configuration in which "that which orders death is excepted from the obligation, and that which undergoes the obligation is excepted from the legitimation" (101). Lyotard insists that "the authority of the SS comes out of a we from which the deportee is excepted once and for all: the race. . . . But one cannot give a life that one doesn't have the right to have. Sacrifice is not available to the deportee, nor for that reason accession to an immortal, collective name. . . . This death must therefore be killed, and that is what is worse than death. For if death can be exterminated, it is because there is nothing to kill. Not even the name Jew" (101). The Jew is in no position to transcend his death by acquiescing to it in the name of the authority that demands it, since he does not inhabit a language game that allows him (or her) to occupy the ethical position of the command that demands death. The ethical division of interlocutors has been radicalized as a racial division, for in Nazi ideology the Jew is a Jew by virtue of this impotence. The Jew does not simply occupy a nonreciprocal position in language; "Jew" is the very name of that position (which is why not all Jews need to be Jews). The Jews are constituted as a race within genocidal logic because they are defined as the recipients of the command, as those incapable of inhabiting the command as an ethical imperative. To make sense of "Auschwitz" (as Adorno does in rendering it the moment of a historical imperative, the moment of an absolute death) is to traduce its senselessness, to coerce meaningless slaughter into an essentially ethical and apocalyptic construct (the Holocaust).

12. As Benjamin notes in the *Trauerspiel* book of the self-sublating allegory: "For it is to misunderstand the allegorical entirely if we make a distinction between the store of images, in which this about-turn into salvation and redemption takes place, and that grim store which signifies

death and damnation. For it is precisely visions of the frenzy of destruction, in which all earthly things collapse into a heap of ruins, which reveal the limits set on allegorical contemplation, rather than its ideal quality. . . . In it transitoriness is not signified or allegorically represented so much as, in its own significance displayed as allegory. As the allegory of resurrection" (232).

Bibliography

Adams, Barry. *The Rise of a Gay and Lesbian Movement*. Boston: Twayne, 1987.

Adorno, Theodor W., Else Frenkel-Brunswik, Daniel J. Levinson, and R. Nevitt Sanford. *The Authoritarian Personality*. New York: Harper, 1950.

———. "Freudian Theory and the Pattern of Fascist Propaganda." In Andrew Arato and Eike Gebhardt, eds., *The Essential Frankfurt School Reader*, 118–37. New York: Continuum, 1982.

———. *Minima Moralia: Reflections from Damaged Life*. Trans. E. F. N. Jephcott. London: New Left Books, 1974.

———. *Negative Dialectics*. Trans. E. B. Ashton. New York: Continuum, 1987.

Alford, C. Fred. *Socrates, the Frankfurt School and Psychoanalytic Theory*. New Haven, Conn.: Yale University Press, 1988.

Among Men, Among Women. Gay Studies and Women's Studies, University of Amsterdam Conference, June 22–26, 1983.

Angress, Ruth K. "Lanzmann's *Shoah* and Its Audience." *Simon Wiesenthal Center Annual* 3 (1986): 249–60.

Arendt, Hannah. *The Human Condition*. Chicago: University of Chicago Press, 1958.

———. *The Origins of Totalitarianism*. New York: Harcourt, Brace, 1951.

Bachelard, Gaston. *L'eau et les rêves: Essai sur l'imagination de la matière*. Paris: J. Corti, 1942.

Barbedette, Gilles, and Michel Carassou. *Paris Gay 1925*. Paris: Presses de la Renaissance, 1981.

Barthes, Roland. *The Pleasure of the Text*. Trans. Richard Miller. New York: Hill and Wang, 1975.

Barton, Richard W. "Education and the Politics of Desire: A Semiotic Analysis of the Discourse on Male Homosexualities." Ph.D. diss., University of Illinois, 1982.

Béhar, Henri. *Les cultures de Jarry*. Paris: Presses Universitaires de France, 1988.

Benjamin, Jessica. "Authority and the Family Revisited: Or, a World Without Fathers?" *New German Critique* 13 (Winter 1978): 35–57.

Benjamin, Walter. *The Origin of German Tragic Drama.* Trans. John Osborne. London: New Left Books, 1977.

———. "Pariser Brief <I> (msp. 496)." In *Gesammelte Schriften,* vol. 3, ed. Hella Tiedemann Bartels, 482–95. Frankfurt: Suhrkamp, 1972.

———. "Theories of German Fascism: On the Collection of Essays *War and Warrior* Edited by Ernst Jünger." Trans. Jerolf Wikoff. *New German Critique* 17 (Spring 1979): 120–28.

———. "The Work of Art in the Age of Mechanical Reproduction." In *Illuminations,* ed. Hannah Arendt; trans. Harry Zohn, 219–53. New York: Harcourt, Brace and World, 1968.

Berlin Museum. *Eldorado: Homosexuelle Frauen und Männer in Berlin, 1830–1950: Geschichte, Alltag und Kultur.* Berlin: Frölich und Kaufmann, 1984.

Berman, Russell A. "Aestheticization of Politics: Walter Benjamin on Fascism and the Avant-Garde." In *Modern German Culture and Critical Theory.* Madison: University of Wisconsin Press, 1989.

Bersani, Leo. "Is the Rectum a Grave?" In Douglas Crimp, ed., *AIDS: Cultural Analysis, Cultural Activism,* 197–222. Cambridge, Mass.: MIT Press, 1988.

Bleuel, Hans-Peter. *Strength Through Joy: Sex and Society in Nazi Germany.* Trans. J. Maxwell Brownjohn. London: Secker and Warburg, 1973.

Bloch, Ernst. "Der Nazi und das Unsägliche." *Das Wort* 3, no. 9 (Sept. 1938): 110–14.

Bloch, Iwan. *Das Sexualleben unserer Zeit in seinen Beziehungen zur modernen Kultur.* 7th–9th ed. Berlin: Louis Marcus, 1906.

Blüher, Hans. "Die drei Grundformen der Homosexualität." In *Jahrbuch,* ed. Wolfgang Johann Schmidt, 27–104.

———. *Die Rolle der Erotik in der männlichen Gesellschaft.* 2 vols. Jena: Eugen Diederichs Verlag, 1917.

Bohn, Rainer, Hans-Jörg Schimmel, and Eckhard Seidel. "Faschismus-Kunst-Homosexualität." In Uwe Naumann, ed., *Die Sammlung 5: Jahrbuch für antifaschistische Literatur und Kunst,* 146–47. Frankfurt: Röberberg, 1982.

Brand, Adolf. *Nachrichten und Werbeblatt der "Gemeinschaft der Eigenen."* Aug. 14, 1920.

———. *Paragraph 175.* Berlin: Der Eigene, 1914.

Braunschweig, M. *Das dritte Geschlecht (Gleichgeschlechtliche Liebe): Beiträge zum homosexuellen Problem.* Halle a.S.: Carl Marhold, 1902.

Brenkman, John. "Narcissus in the Text." *Georgia Review* 30 (1976): 293–327.

Bridgman, Theresa. "Innovation and Ambiguity: Sources of Confusion of Personal Identity in *Les jours et les nuits.*" *French Studies* 45, no. 3 (July 1991): 295–307.

Bullough, Vern L. *Sexual Variance in Society and History.* New York: John Wiley and Sons, 1976.

Bürger, Peter. *Theory of the Avant-Garde.* Trans. Michael Shaw. Minneapolis: University of Minnesota Press, 1984.

Carpenter, Edward. *The Intermediate Sex.* New York: AMS Press, 1983.

Consoli, Massimo. *Homocaust.* Milan: Kaos, 1991.

Dannecker, Martin, and Reimut Reiche. *Der gewöhnliche Homosexuelle.* Frankfurt: Fischer, 1974.

de Certeau, Michel. *The Practice of Everyday Life.* Trans. Steven Rendall. Berkeley: University of California Press, 1984.

de Felice, Renzo. *Introduction to Fascism.* Trans. Brenda Huff Everett. Cambridge, Mass.: Harvard University Press, 1977.

Dellamora, Richard. *Apocalyptic Overtures: Sexual Politics and the Sense of an Ending.* New Brunswick, N.J.: Rutgers University Press, 1994.

de Man, Paul. *Blindness and Insight: Essays in the Rhetoric of Contemporary Criticism.* 2d ed. Minneapolis: University of Minnesota Press, 1983.

Derrida, Jacques. "Of an Apocalyptic Tone Recently Adopted in Philosophy." Trans. John P. Leavey, Jr. *Seneia* 23 (1982): 63–97.

Dollimore, Jonathan. *Sexual Dissidence: Augustine to Wilde, Freud to Foucault.* Oxford: Clarendon, 1991.

Eissler, W. U. *Arbeiterparteien und Homosexuellenfrage: Zur Sexualpolitik von SPD und KPD in der Weimarer Republik.* Berlin: Verlag Rosa Winkel, 1980.

Foster, Hal. "Armor Fou." *October* 56 (Spring 1991): 65–98.

Freud, Sigmund. *The Standard Edition of the Complete Psychological Works of Sigmund Freud.* Translated from the German under the general editorship of James Strachey. 24 vols. London: Hogarth Press, 1953–74.

Friedlaender, Benedict. *Die Renaissance des Eros Uranios: Die physiologische Freundschaft, ein normaler Grundtrieb des Menschen und eine Frage der männlichen Gesellungsfreiheit.* Berlin: Verlag "Renaissance," 1904. Repr., New York: Arno Press, 1975.

Friedländer, Saul. "'The Final Solution': On the Unease in Historical Interpretation." *History and Memory* 1, no. 2 (1989): 61–73.

———. *Reflections of Nazism: An Essay on Kitsch and Death.* Trans. Thomas Weyr. New York: Harper and Row, 1984.

———, ed. *Probing the Limits of Representation: Nazism and the "Final Solution."* Cambridge, Mass.: Harvard University Press, 1992.

Gasché, Rodolphe. *The Tain of the Mirror: Derrida and the Philosophy of Reflection.* Cambridge, Mass.: Harvard University Press, 1986.

Gerling, Reinhold. *Das dritte Geschlecht und die Enterbten des Liebesglücks: Eine gemeinverständliche Darstellung der Liebe zum eigenen Geschlecht.* 3d ed. Oranienburg: Wilhelm Möller Verlag, 1919.

Gide, André. *Corydon.* Trans. Richard Howard. New York: Farrar, Straus and Giroux, 1983.

———. "Le traité du Narcisse (Théorie du symbole)." In *Oeuvres complètes,* vol. 1, 205–20. Paris: Gallimard, 1932.

Gilman, Sander. *Difference and Pathology: Stereotypes of Sexuality, Race and Madness.* Ithaca, N.Y.: Cornell University Press, 1985.

———. *Inscribing the Other.* Lincoln: University of Nebraska Press, 1991.

———. *The Jew's Body.* New York: Routledge, 1991.

Goux, Jean-Joseph. *Symbolic Economies: After Marx and Freud.* Trans. Jennifer Curtiss Gage. Ithaca, N.Y.: Cornell University Press, 1990.

Grabowsky, Norbert. *Die mannweibliche Natur des Menschen mit Berücksichtigung des psychosexuellen Hermaphroditismus.* Leipzig: Max Spohr, 1896.

Habermas, Jürgen. *The Structural Transformation of the Public Sphere: An In-quiry into a Category of Bourgeois Society.* Trans. Thomas Bürger with the assistance of Frederick Lawrence. Cambridge, Mass.: MIT Press, 1989.

———. "The Tasks of a Critical Theory of Society." In Steven Seidman, ed., *Jürgen Habermas on Society and Politics: A Reader,* 77–103. Boston: Beacon Press, 1989.

Halperin, David. *One Hundred Years of Homosexuality, and Other Essays on Greek Love.* New York: Routledge, 1990.

Halperin, David, John Winkler, and Froma Zeitlin, eds. *Before Sexuality: The Construction of Erotic Experience in the Ancient Greek World.* Princeton, N.J.: Princeton University Press, 1990.

Hamecher, Peter. "Die Tragik des Andersseins." Review of *Bücher der namenlosen Liebe. Die Aktion,* 4th ser. (May 16, 1914). Repr. in Sagitta, *Bücher,* 2: 387–88.

Haug, Wolfgang-Fritz. "Antworten auf die Kritiken an meinen Breker-Thesen." In Uwe Naumann, ed. *Die Sammlung 5: Jahrbuch für antifaschistische Literatur und Kunst,* 155–62. Frankfurt: Röderberg, 1982.

———. "Der Körper und die Macht im Faschismus: Zur Analyse einer Faszination am Beispiel Brekers." In *Die Sammlung 4: Jahrbuch für antifaschistische Literatur und Kunst,* 201–6. Frankfurt: Röderberg, 1981.

Hegel, Georg Wilhelm Friedrich. *Hegel's Philosophy of Right.* Trans. T. M. Knox. Oxford: Clarendon, 1942.

Heger, Heinz. *The Men with the Pink Triangle.* Trans. David Fernbach. Boston: Alyson Press, 1980.

Hermand, Jost. "Das Konzept 'Avantgarde.'" In Reinhold Grimm and Jost Hermand, eds., *Faschismus und Avantgarde,* 1–19. Königstein: Athenäum, 1980.

Herzer, Manfred. "Asexuality as an Element in the Self-Presentation of the Right Wing of the German Gay Movement Before 1933." In *Among Men, Among Women.*

———. *Bibliographie zur Homosexualität: Verzeichnis des deutschsprachigen nichtbelletristischen Schrifttums zur weiblichen und männlichen Homosexualität aus den Jahren 1466 bis 1975 in chronologischer Reihenfolge.* Berlin: Verlag Rosa Winkel, 1982.

———. "Schwule Widerstandkämpfer gegen die Nazis." In Schwulenreferat im AStA der FU Berlin, ed., *Dokumentation der Vortragsreihe "Homosexualität und Wissenschaft,"* 222–26. Berlin, 1985.

Hewitt, Andrew. *Fascist Modernism: Aesthetics, Politics and the Avant-Garde.* Stanford, Calif.: Stanford University Press, 1993.

Hinz, Berthold. *Art in the Third Reich.* Trans. Robert and Rita Kimber. New York: Pantheon, 1979.

Hirschfeld, Magnus. *Die Homosexualität des Mannes und des Weibes.* Berlin: Louis Marcus, 1914. Repr., Berlin: de Gruyter, 1984.

Hoch, Paul. *White Hero, Black Beast: Racism, Sexism and the Mask of Masculinity.* London: Pluto, 1979.

Hocquenghem, Guy. *Homosexual Desire.* Trans. Daniella Dangoor. London: Allison and Busby, 1978.

Hoessli, Heinrich. *Eros: Die Männerliebe der Griechen . . . Oder Forschungen über platonische Liebe.* 2 vols. Vol. 1, Glarus: Private publication, 1836; vol. 2, St. Gallen: Private publication, 1838.

Hohmann, Joachim S. *Der heimliche Sexus: Homosexuelle Belletristik im Deutschland der Jahre 1920–1970.* Frankfurt: Foerster, 1977.

———, ed. *Der Eigene, Ein Blatt für männliche Kultur: Ein Querschnitt durch die erste Homosexuellenzeitschrift der Welt.* Frankfurt: Foerster, 1981.

———, ed. *Der unterdückte Sexus. Historische Texte und Kommentare zur Homosexualität.* Lollar: Andreas Aschenbach, 1977.

Horkheimer, Max. "Authority and the Family Today." In Ruth N. Anshen, ed., *The Family: Its Function and Destiny,* 359–74. New York: Harper, 1949.

Horkheimer, Max, and Theodor W. Adorno. *Dialectic of Enlightenment.* Trans. John Cumming. New York: Continuum, 1987.

Hottentot, Wim. "Von Mann zu Mann: Die Varianten der Homosexualität in der Literatur." *Forum Homosexualität und Literatur* (1987, vol. 2): 93–108.

Hull, Isabel V. *The Entourage of Kaiser Wilhelm II, 1898–1918.* Cambridge: Cambridge University Press, 1982.

Jaeger, Gustav. *Entdeckung der Seele.* 3d ed. Leipzig: Ernst Günther, 1884.

Jameson, Fredric. *Fables of Aggression: Wyndham Lewis, the Modernist as Fascist.* Berkeley: University of California Press, 1981.

Jarry, Alfred. *Days and Nights: Novel of a Deserter.* Trans. Alexis Lykiard. London: Atlas, 1994.

———. *The Supermale: A Modern Novel.* Trans. Barbara Wright. London: Cape, 1968.

Jay, Martin. *The Dialectical Imagination: A History of the Frankfurt School and the Institute of Social Research, 1923–1950.* Boston: Little, Brown, 1973.

Jellonek, Burkhard. *Homosexuelle unter dem Hakenkreuz: Die Verfolgung von Homosexuellen im Dritten Reich.* Paderborn: Schöningh, 1990.

Jones, James W. "The 'Third Sex' in German Literature from the Turn of the Century to 1933." Diss., University of Wisconsin, 1986.

———. *"We of the Third Sex": Literary Representations of Homosexuality in Wilhelmine Germany.* New York: Peter Lang, 1990.

Kasher, Steven. "The Art of Hitler." *October* 59 (Winter 1992): 49–85.

Kennedy, Hubert. *Anarchist of Love: The Secret Life of John Henry Mackay.* New York: Mackay Society, 1983.

———. *Ulrichs: The Life and Works of Karl Heinrich Ulrichs, Pioneer of the Modern Gay Movement.* Boston: Alyson, 1988.

Kenner, Hugh. "The Making of the Modernist Canon." *Chicago Review* 34, no. 2 (1984): 49–61.

Knoespel, Kenneth J. *Narcissus and the Invention of Personal History.* New York: Garland, 1985.

Knowlton, James, and Truett Cates, eds. *Forever in the Shadow of Hitler? Original Documents from the Historikerstreit, the Controversy Concerning the Singularity of the Holocaust.* Atlantic Highlands, N.J.: Humanities Press, 1993.

LaBelle, Maurice Marc. *Alfred Jarry: Nihilism and the Theater of the Absurd.* New York: New York University Press, 1990.

Lacan, Jacques. *Ecrits: A Selection,* trans. Alan Sheridan. New York: Norton, 1977.

LaCapra, Dominick. Review of Arno J. Mayer, *Why Did the Heavens Not Darken? The 'Final Solution' in History. New German Critique* 53 (Spring/Summer 1991): 175–91.

Lacoue-Labarthe, Philippe, and Jean-Luc Nancy. "The Nazi Myth." Trans. Brian Holmes. *Critical Inquiry* 16 (Winter 1990): 291–312.

Laplanche, Jean, and J. B. Pontalis. *The Language of Psycho-Analysis.* Trans. Donald Nicholson-Smith. New York: Norton, 1974.

Laqueur, Walter. *Fascism: A Reader's Guide.* Berkeley: University of California Press, 1976.

Lasch, Scott. *The Culture of Narcissism: American Life in an Age of Diminishing Expectations.* New York: Norton, 1978.

Lauritsen, John, and David Thorstad. *The Early Homosexual Rights Movement (1864–1935).* New York: Times Change Press, 1974.

Lautmann, Rüdiger, et al. *Seminar Gesellschaft und Homosexualität.* Frankfurt: Suhrkamp, 1977.

Lefort, Claude. *The Political Forms of Modern Society: Bureaucracy, Democracy, Totalitarianism.* Cambridge, Mass.: MIT Press, 1986.

Lewis, Wyndham. *The Art of Being Ruled.* New York: 1972.

———. *Hitler.* London: Chatto and Windus, 1931.

———. *The Hitler Cult.* London: Dent, 1939.

Lieshout, Maurice van. "Homosexuelle zwischen Fiktion und Wirklichkeit: Grundüberlegungen zur literarhistorischen Beschäftigung mit Homosexualität." *Forum Homosexualität und Literatur* (1987, vol. 1): 73–86.

Lombroso, Cesare. *Crime: Its Causes and Remedies.* Trans. Henry P. Horton. Boston: Little, Brown, 1911.

Lyotard, Jean-François. *The Differend: Phrases in Dispute.* Trans. Georges van den Abbeele. Minneapolis: University of Minnesota Press, 1986.

———. *Discours, figure.* Paris: Klincksieck, 1978.

———. "The Dream-Work Does Not Think." In Andrew Benjamin, ed., *The Lyotard Reader.* Oxford: Blackwell, 1989.

———. "Jewish Oedipus." Trans. S. Hanson. *Genre* 10, no. 3 (1977): 395–411.

———. "The Sublime and the Avant-Garde." Trans. Lisa Liebmann, Geoff Bennington, and Marian Hobson. *Paragraph* 6 (October 1985): 1–18.

Mackay, John Henry. *The Hustler: The Story of a Nameless Love from Friedrich Street.* Trans. Hubert Kennedy. Boston: Alyson, 1985.

Mann, Klaus. "Homosexualität und Fascismus." In *Die neue Weltbühne,* Prag, 1934, 130–37. Repr. in Klaus Mann and Kurt Tucholsky, *Homosexualität und Faschismus,* 5–13. Kiel: Verlag Frühlings Erwachen, 1981.

Marcuse, Herbert. *Eros and Civilization: A Philosophical Inquiry into Freud.* 2d ed. Boston: Beacon, 1966.

Mayer, Arno J. *Why Did the Heavens Not Darken? The "Final Solution" in History.* New York: Pantheon, 1988.

Meve, Jörn. *"Homosexuelle Nazis": Ein Stereotyp in der Politik und Literatur des Exils.* Hamburg: Männerschwarmskript, 1990.

Meyers, Jeffrey. *Homosexuality and Literature, 1890–1930.* Montreal: McGill University Press, 1977.

Mills, Richard. "The German Youth Movement (Wandervögel)." In Winston Leyland, ed., *Gay Roots: Twenty Years of Gay Sunshine: An Anthology of Gay History, Sex, Politics and Culture,* 149–76. San Francisco: Gay Sunshine Press, 1991.

Mitscherlich, Alexander. *Society Without the Father: A Contribution to Social Psychology.* Trans. Erich Mosbacher. London: Tavistock, 1969.

Mitscherlich, Alexander, and Margarete Mitscherlich. *The Inability to Mourn: Principles of Collective Behavior.* Trans. Beverley R. Placzek. New York: Grove, 1975.

Mohler, Armin. *Die konservative Revolution in Deutschland, 1918–1932: Ein Handbuch.* 2d ed. Darmstadt: Wissenschaftliche Buchgesellschaft, 1972.

Moll, Albert. *Perversions of the Sex Instinct: A Study of Sexual Inversion Based on Clinical Data and Official Documents.* Trans. Maurice Popkin. New York: AMS Press, 1976.

Moravia, Alberto. "Answers to Nine Questions on the Novel." In *Man as an End: A Defense of Humanism: Literary, Social and Political Essays.* Trans. Bernard Wahl. New York: Farrar, Straus and Giroux, 1966.

———. *The Conformist.* Trans. Angus Davidson. London: Secker and Warburg, 1952.

Morrison, Andrew P., ed. *Essential Papers on Narcissism.* New York: New York University Press, 1986.

Mosse, George L. *Nationalism and Sexuality: Respectability and Abnormal Sexuality in Modern Europe.* New York: Fertig, 1985.

Nachman, Larry David. "Genet: Dandy of the Lower Depths." *Salmagundi* 58–59 (Fall 1982–Winter 1983): 358–72.

Nolte, Ernst. *Three Faces of Fascism: Action Française, Italian Fascism, National Socialism.* Trans. Leila Vennewitz. New York: Holt, Rinehart and Winston, 1966.

Nordau, Max Simon. *Entartung.* 2 vols. Berlin: C. Duncker, 1892–93.

Oosterhuis, Harry, and Hubert Kennedy, eds. *Homosexuality and Male Bonding in Pre-Nazi Germany: The Youth Movement, the Gay Movement and Male Bonding Before Hitler's Rise: Original Transcripts from "Der Eigene," the First Gay Journal in the World.* New York: Harrington, 1991.

———. "Homosocial Resistance to Hirschfeld's Homosexual Putsch: The Gemeinschaft der Eigenen, 1899–1914." In *Among Men, Among Women,* 305–14.

Ovid. *Metamorphoses.* Trans. Rolfe Humphries. Bloomington: Indiana University Press, 1955.

Petzold, Joachim. *Wegbereiter des deutschen Faschismus: Die Jung-Konservativen in der Weimarer Republik.* 2d ed. Hamburg: Pahl-Rugenstein, 1983.

Plant, Richard. *The Pink Triangle: The Nazi War Against Homosexuals.* New York: Henry Holt, 1986.

———. "The Swastika and the Pink Triangle: Nazis and Gay Men: An Interview with Richard Plant." In Lawrence D. Mass, ed., *Dialogues of the Sexual Revolution: Vol. 1, Homosexuality and Sexuality*, 189–99. New York: Haworth, 1990.

Pulver, Sydney. "Narcissism: The Term and the Concept." In *Essential Papers*, ed. Andrew P. Morrison, 91–111. New York: NYU Press, 1986.

Pynsent, Robert B., ed. *Decadence and Innovation: Austro-Hungarian Life and Art at the Turn of the Century*. London: Weidenfeld and Nicolson, 1989.

Rector, Frank. *The Nazi Extermination of Homosexuals*. New York: Stein and Day, 1981.

Reich, Wilhelm. *The Mass Psychology of Fascism*. 3d ed. Trans. Victor R. Carfagno. New York: Farrar, Straus and Giroux, 1970.

Riley, Thomas A. *Germany's Poet-Anarchist John Henry Mackay: A Contribution to the History of German Literature at the Turn of the Century, 1880–1920*. New York: Revisionist Press, 1972.

Sagitta [John Henry Mackay]. *Die Bücher der namenlosen Liebe*. 2 vols. 2d ed. Repr., Berlin: Verlag Rosa Winkel, 1979.

Schiesari, Juliana. *The Gendering of Melancholy: Feminism, Psychoanalysis and the Symbolics of Loss in Renaissance Literature*. Ithaca, N.Y.: Cornell University Press, 1992.

Schilling, Hans-Dieter, ed. *Schwule und Faschismus*. Berlin: Elefanten, 1983.

Schmidt, Wolfgang Johann, ed. *Jahrbuch für sexuelle Zwischenstufen: Herausgegeben im Namen des wissenschaftlich-humanitären Comités von Magnus Hirschfeld: Auswahl aus den Jahren 1899–1923*. 2 vols. Frankfurt: Qumran, 1984.

Sedgwick, Eve. *Between Men: English Literature and Male Homosexual Desire*. New York: Columbia University Press, 1985.

———. *Epistemology of the Closet*. Berkeley: University of California Press, 1990.

———. *Tendencies*. Durham, N.C.: Duke University Press, 1993.

Segal, Naomi. *Narcissus and Echo: Women in the French Récit*. Manchester: Manchester University Press, 1988.

Siciliano, Enzo, ed. *Albert Moravia: Vita, parole e idee di un romanziere*. Milan: Bompiani, 1982.

Sievert, Hermann. *Das anormale Bestreben: Homosexualität, Strafrecht und Schwulenbewegung im Kaiserreich und in der Weimarer Republik*. Special issue of *ergebnisse*, vol. 24 (April 1984).

Silverman, Kaja. *Male Subjectivity at the Margins*. New York: Routledge, 1992.

Sontag, Susan. "Fascinating Fascism." In *Under the Sign of Saturn*, 73–105. New York: Farrar, Straus and Giroux, 1980.

———. "Notes on 'Camp'." In *Against Interpretation and Other Essays*, 275–92. New York: Anchor, 1990.

Spackman, Barbara. *Decadent Genealogies: The Rhetoric of Sickness from Baudelaire to d'Annunzio*. Ithaca, N.Y.: Cornell University Press, 1989.

Staeck, Klaus, ed. *Nazi-Kunst ins Museum?* Göttingen: Steidl, 1988.

Steakley, James D. "Iconography of a Scandal: Political Cartoons and the Eulenberg Affair." *Studies in Visual Communication* 9, no. 2 (Spring 1983): 20–51.

———. *The Writings of Dr. Magnus Hirschfeld: A Bibliography.* Toronto: Canadian Gay Archives, 1985.

———, ed. *Documents of the Homosexual Rights Movement in Germany: 1836–1927.* New York: Arno Press, 1975.

Sternhell, Ze'ev. *Neither Left Nor Right: Fascist Ideology in France.* Trans. David Maisel. Berkeley: University of California Press, 1986.

Sternhell, Ze'ev, Mario Sznajder, and Maia Asheri. *The Birth of Fascist Ideology: From Cultural Rebellion to Political Revolution.* Trans. David Maisel. Princeton, N.J.: Princeton University Press, 1994.

Stümke, Hans-Georg. *Homosexuelle in Deutschland: Eine politische Geschichte.* Munich: Beck, 1989.

Stümke, Hans-Georg, and Rudi Finkler, eds. *Rosa Winkel, Rosa Listen: Homosexuelle und "gesundes Volksempfinden" von Auschwitz bis heute.* Reinbek: Rowohlt, 1981.

Symonds, John Addington. *Male Love: A Problem in Greek Ethics and Other Writings.* New York: Pagan, 1983.

Theweleit, Klaus. *Male Fantasies.* 2 vols. Trans. Stephen Conway (vol. 1), Erica Carter and Chris Turner (vol. 2). Minneapolis: University of Minnesota Press, 1987–89.

Ulrichs, Carl Heinrich. *Riddle of Man-manly Love: The Pioneering Work on Male Homosexuality.* Trans. Michael A. Lombardi. Buffalo, N.Y.: Prometheus, 1994.

Weininger, Otto. *Sex and Character.* Authorized translation of 6th ed. London: Heinemann, 1906.

Winkler, John. *The Constraints of Desire: The Anthropology of Sex and Gender in Ancient Greece.* New York: Routledge, 1990.

Wolbert, Klaus. *Die Nackten und die Toten des "Dritten Reiches": Folgen einer politischen Geschichte des Körpers in der Plastik des deutschen Faschismus.* Giessen: Anabas, 1982.

Wood, S. L. "Religion, Politics and Sexuality in Moravia's *Il conformista.*" *Italian Studies* 44 (1989): 86–101.

World Committee for the Victims of German Fascism. *Braunbuch über Reichstagsbrand und Hitlerterror.* 2d ed. Basel: Universum, 1933.

Index

In this index "f" after a number indicates a separate reference on the next page, and "ff" indicates separate references on the next two pages. A continuous discussion over two or more pages is indicated by a span of numbers. *Passim* is used for a cluster of references in close but not consecutive sequence.

Homo-style, 94–95, 151, 218, 221
Homotextuality, 209–11, 224–25,
    229, 233–34, 309–10
Hysteria, 23, 40, 196

Identification, 65–70 *passim*, 219;
    with mother, 49, 62, 167; with
    father, 68, 268; and idealization,
    68–70, 75; and myth, 180; as
    reading strategy, 224. *See also*
    Narcissism; Object choice
Identity, 18, 122, 207; decay of,
    43–44, 58, 67, 73–75 *passim*,
    289–90; and the nonidentical,
    73–78 *passim*, 92–93, 161–67
    passim, 176–77, 208, 233–38,
    274–75, 284. *See also* Identifica-
    tion; Repression
Ideoplasm, 92, 120
Imaginary, politics of the, 44,
    115–16, 127, 273
Incest, 107, 127–28
Infantilism, 117, 146
Inversion: as model of homosexual-
    ity, 93, 105–7 *passim*, 113–14,
    172, 178, 183–84, 189–90; as
    logical structure, 172f, 186–92
    passim, 254, 260
Irigaray, Luce, 2

Jäger, Gustav, 87
Jameson, Fredric, 173, 198f,
    212–14 *passim*
Jarry, Alfred, 32–36 *passim*, 138,
    199–202 *passim*, 209–12, 218,
    222–44, 275
Jews, 10, 74, 86, 102, 121–25 *pas-
    sim*, 315; and anti-Semitism, 89,
    110, 118–22 *passim*, 302; and
    Zionism, 303
Jones, James W., 23, 88
Jouissance, 232–34, 285, 309–10
Juridical discourse, 104, 132, 137,
    144–45

Kant, Immanuel, 122
Kitsch, 31, 178, 206–8, 212–16

passim, 222, 243, 276. *See also*
    Camp
Kommunistische Partei Deutsch-
    lands (KPD), 20–22
Krupps scandal, 20

Labor, division of, 100–102,
    113–14
Lacan, Jacques, 44, 201, 306–7. *See
    also* Desire
Lacoue-Labarthe, Philippe, 17–18
    180–81, 201, 247, 304–5, 310
Lasch, Christopher, 40
Lebensraum, 201–3 *passim*
Lefort, Claude, 124, 292–93, 307
Lewis, Wyndham, 2, 33–35 *passim*,
    171–98 *passim*
Logos, 119–20, 301. *See also* Eros
Lombroso, Cesare, 123
Love, 48–49. *See also* Unrepre-
    sentable, the
Lyotard, Jean-François, 8, 17; on
    "name," 9, 16; and "beautiful
    death," 13–14, 282–83, 314–15;
    on *differend*, 13–15, 248–49; on
    Jewish Oedipus, 117–18, 128,
    301; on *figure*, 221–22, 226–27,
    234, 239, 290, 309–10. *See also*
    "Auschwitz"

McDougall, William, 66
Mackay, John Henry, 2, 8, 23,
    32–36 *passim*, 80, 88, 103,
    130–70, 171f, 182, 203, 208–10
    passim
Mann, Klaus, 1–6 *passim*, 284
Marcuse, Herbert, 39, 52–55
    passim, 71–72
Marriage, 48–49; and miscegena-
    tion, 126
Masculinism, 10, 23, 79–82, 85–89,
    93, 99, 103, 119, 125, 135, 143,
    200, 210–11, 221; and hyper-
    masculinity, 55, 174, 183–90 *pas-
    sim*; defined, 81–82. *See also*
    Homosociality; Third sex
Mass psychology, 22, 66, 70, 73–74

Library of Congress Cataloging-in-Publication Data

Hewitt, Andrew
   Political inversions : homosexuality, fascism, and the modernist
imaginary / Andrew Hewitt.
      p.   cm.
Includes bibliographical references and index.
ISBN 0-8047-2639-6 (cloth : alk. paper). — ISBN 0-8047-2641-8
(pbk. : alk. paper)
1. Homosexuality and literature. 2. Fascism and literature. 3. Modernism
(Literature)   I. Title.
PN56.H57H49   1996
809'.93353—dc20
96-828   CIP

∞ This book is printed on acid-free, recycled paper.

Original printing 1996

Last figure below indicates year of this printing:

05 04 03 02 01 00 99 98 97 96